Intercultural Friendship

International Comparative Social Studies

Editor-in-Chief

Mehdi P. Amineh (*Amsterdam Institute for Social Science Research, University of Amsterdam*, and *International Institute for Asian Studies, Leiden University*)

Editorial Board

Shahrough Akhavi (*Columbia University*)
W.A. Arts (*University College Utrecht*)
Sjoerd Beugelsdijk (*Radboud University*)
Mark-Anthony Falzon (*University of Malta*)
Harald Fuhr (*University of Potsdam*)
Joyeeta Gupta (*University of Amsterdam*)
Xiaoming Huang (*Victoria University Wellington*)
Nilgün Önder (*University of Regina*)
Gerhard Preyer (*Goethe University Frankfurt am Main*)
Islam Qasem (*Webster University, Leiden*)
Kurt W. Radtke (*International Institute for Asian Studies, Leiden University*)
Mahmoud Sadri (*Texas Woman's University*)
Jeremy Smith (*University of Eastern Finland*)
Ngo Tak-Wing (*Leiden University*)
L.A. Visano (*York University*)

VOLUME 50

The titles published in this series are listed at *brill.com/icss*

Intercultural Friendship

*The Case of a Palestinian Bedouin
and a Dutch Israeli Jew*

By

Daniel J. N. Weishut

BRILL

LEIDEN | BOSTON

Cover illustration: White orchid tree blooming on Ahmad's land in front of the "apartheid road" and the Israeli–Palestinian separation wall, 'Anata, 2020.

Library of Congress Cataloging-in-Publication Data

Names: Weishut, Daniel J. N., author.
Title: Intercultural friendship : the case of a Palestinian Bedouin and a
  Dutch Israeli Jew / by Daniel J.N. Weishut.
Description: Leiden ; Boston : Brill, [2021] | Series: International
  comparative social studies, 1568-4474 ; volume 50 | Includes
  bibliographical references and index.
Identifiers: LCCN 2020041286 (print) | LCCN 2020041287 (ebook) | ISBN
  9789004372405 (hardback ; alk. paper) | ISBN 9789004444003 (ebook)
Subjects: LCSH: Interracial friendship--Palestine--Case studies. |
  Interracial friendship--Israel--Case studies. | Cultural
  pluralism--Palestine--Case studies. | Cultural pluralism--Israel--Case
  studies. | Intercultural communication--Palestine--Case studies. |
  Intercultural communication--Israel--Case studies. | Palestinian
  Arabs--Israel--Case studies. | Israelis--Palestine--Case studies.
Classification: LCC HN660.Z9 M8494 2021 (print) | LCC HN660.Z9 (ebook) |
  DDC 323.15694--dc23
LC record available at https://lccn.loc.gov/2020041286
LC ebook record available at https://lccn.loc.gov/2020041287

Typeface for the Latin, Greek, and Cyrillic scripts: "Brill". See and download: brill.com/brill-typeface.

ISSN 1568-4474
ISBN 978-90-04-37240-5 (hardback)
ISBN 978-90-04-44400-3 (e-book)

Copyright 2021 by Daniel J.N. Weishut. Published by Koninklijke Brill NV, Leiden, The Netherlands.
Koninklijke Brill NV incorporates the imprints Brill, Brill Hes & De Graaf, Brill Nijhoff, Brill Rodopi, Brill Sense, Hotei Publishing, mentis Verlag, Verlag Ferdinand Schöningh and Wilhelm Fink Verlag.
Koninklijke Brill NV reserves the right to protect this publication against unauthorized use. Requests for re-use and/or translations must be addressed to Koninklijke Brill NV via brill.com or copyright.com.

This book is printed on acid-free paper and produced in a sustainable manner.

For Ahmad and the Jahalin Bedouins

Contents

Acknowledgments XI
List of Illustrations XII

Prologue 1

PART 1
Autoethnography of an Intercultural Friendship

Introduction to Part 1 6

1 **Writing about Oneself** 7
  1 Relevance and Intent 8
  2 The Two Friends 11
    2.1 *Ahmad* 11
    2.2 *Daniel* 13
    2.3 *Our Friendship* 14
  3 A Case Study 16
    3.1 *Narrative Research* 16
    3.2 *Friendship Research* 18
    3.3 *Case Selection* 20
  4 Studying Stories 21
    4.1 *Observations as Data* 21
    4.2 *Methodological Concerns* 23
    4.3 *Cultural Relativism* 26

2 **When Cultures Meet** 28
  1 Identity and Value Orientations 30
    1.1 *Culture and Social Identity* 31
    1.2 *Value Orientations* 33
  2 The Intercultural Encounter 37
    2.1 *Intercultural Communication* 37
    2.2 *Intercultural Conflict* 39
  3 Honor and Aggression 42
    3.1 *Face and Honor* 42
    3.2 *Aggression* 44

3 The Worlds We Live In 48
1. My World 49
   - 1.1 *The Dutch* 49
   - 1.2 *The Israelis* 51
2. His World 54
   - 2.1 *The Palestinian Arabs* 54
   - 2.2 *The Bedouins* 58
3. Dealing with Conflict 63
   - 3.1 *The Israeli–Palestinian Conflict* 63
   - 3.2 *Bedouins, Law, and Conflict* 67
   - 3.3 *The "sulha"* 70

4 All about Friendship 72
1. Patterns of Friendship 73
   - 1.1 *Characteristics* 74
   - 1.2 *Gender and Culture* 76
2. Intercultural Friendship 78
   - 2.1 *Commonalities* 79
   - 2.2 *Opportunities for Interaction* 81
3. Friendship in the Realm of Conflict 83
   - 3.1 *Jewish–Arab Dialogue* 84
   - 3.2 *The Israeli Occupation* 87

PART 2
Four Cultural Dimensions

Introduction to Part 2 92

5 Individualism versus Collectivism 93
1. Perceptions of Friendship 94
   - 1.1 *Privacy and Togetherness* 97
   - 1.2 *Who Is a Friend?* 102
2. Getting Acquainted 103
   - 2.1 *Names* 104
   - 2.2 *Greeting Behavior* 105
3. Meals and Celebrations 107
   - 3.1 *Meals* 108
   - 3.2 *Celebrations* 110
4. Work Attitudes 114

CONTENTS

    4.1 *Labor and Leisure* 115
    4.2 *Child Labor* 118
  5 Friendship and Politics 120
    5.1 *The Wrong Side of Society* 121
    5.2 *Social Support* 123
  6 Conclusion: Individualism versus Collectivism 125

6 **Uncertainty Avoidance** 128
  1 Language and Communication 129
    1.1 *Verbal and Non-verbal Communication* 130
    1.2 *A Foreign Language* 134
  2 Mine and Yours 137
    2.1 *Finances and Favors* 138
    2.2 *Possessions* 140
  3 Time and Space 142
    3.1 *Flexibility of Time* 143
    3.2 *Flexibility of Space* 145
  4 Planning 147
    4.1 *Making a Plan* 148
    4.2 *Reaching Agreement* 150
  5 Taking Risks 152
    5.1 *Physical and Other Risks* 152
    5.2 *Giving Trust* 155
  6 Conclusion: Uncertainty Avoidance 158

7 **Masculinity and Femininity** 165
  1 Women and Men 166
    1.1 *Gender Roles* 167
    1.2 *Segregation* 169
  2 Being a Man 172
    2.1 *Emotional Expression* 173
    2.2 *Physical Appearance* 175
  3 Survival of the Fittest 177
    3.1 *Strength* 178
    3.2 *Violence* 179
  4 Conclusion: Masculinity and Femininity 181

8 **Power Distance** 185
  1 Honor and Dignity 186
    1.1 *Honor and the Family* 187
    1.2 *Dignity and Respect* 190

         2   Authority   192
              2.1   *Rules and Leadership*   193
              2.2   *The Oldest Son*   196
         3   The Occupation   198
              3.1   *Wealth and Poverty*   200
              3.2   *Freedom*   203
         4   Conclusion: Power Distance   207

9   **Challenges and Opportunities**   211
         1   Hofstede's Cultural Dimensions   211
              1.1   *The Use of Hofstede's Theory*   216
              1.2   *Four Dimensions*   218
         2   Studying My Friendship with Ahmad   221
              2.1   *Studying Our Friendship*   223
              2.2   *Representativeness*   225
         3   Personal Growth   228
              3.1   *Transformative Learning*   228
              3.2   *Value Change*   233
         4   Implications and Recommendations   237
              4.1   *Cultural Psychology*   238
              4.2   *Multicultural Personality*   239
              4.3   *Prejudice and Social Injustice*   241

Epilogue   243

Bibliography   247
Index   288

Acknowledgments

The completion of this book would not have been possible without the help of others. My deep appreciation goes to those Jahalin Bedouins and other Palestinians, who are too many to mention, for letting me into their lives. Specifically, I am indebted to Ahmad, who introduced me to his tribe, culture, and habitat, adopted me as part of his extended family, and provided invaluable info and support throughout the study of our friendship. For many years you have been the spice of my life and my heart is with you. May all your wishes come true.

This book started as a doctoral research study. I would like to acknowledge all those colleagues, friends, and family members who responded to requests for feedback and offered constructive input. I am most grateful to my three mentors: Jessica Muller, at the University of California (San Francisco), Haim Weinberg, then at the Professional School of Psychology (Sacramento, CA), and William Bergquist, President of the same school. In addition, my peers – Ronit Bisson, Motti Cohen, Racheli Lazar, Rivka Moshonov, Ronit Nesher, and Tal Schwartz – were like a bunch of cheerleaders, encouraging me toward the finish of this book. Moreover, there were Israeli friends who at times backed me but often made my life more difficult. I know there were occasions in which I made you freak out.

The stimulating questions and insightful remarks by my colleague Chen Bram, at the Hebrew University of Jerusalem and Hadassah Academic College, who encouraged me to expand on the socio-political context, anonymous reviewers, and both Ursula and David Blumenthal at Emory College, were indispensable. So were the latter's efforts and those of Benjamin Hary at New York University, in getting this book published. At Brill, things would not have worked out without the perseverance of acquisition editor Jason Prevost and series editor Mehdi Amineh, the meticulous language editing of Christine Retz, the esteemed assistance of Jennifer Obdam and especially, the ongoing support and enthusiasm of Debbie de Wit and Irene Jager.

Finally, I feel obliged to my parents who provided me with a stable socio-economic background and raised me in the light of a clear value system, without which I would not have accomplished the things I achieved in life, including this study.

Thank you all!

Illustrations

1. Ahmad and Daniel – Holding the world (June, 2009)   3
2. Radar diagram of scores for four cultural dimensions, based on Hofstede (IIIIII)   10
3. Greater Jerusalem (Ir Amim, 2019)   12
4. Alternative transportation routes and communities at risk of forcible transfer (UN OCHA, 2017)   61
5. Structure of the Jahalin Bedouin tribe   62
6. Individualism scores, based on Hofstede (2001)   94
7. Uncertainty Avoidance scores, based on Hofstede (2001)   129
8. Masculinity scores, based on Hofstede (2001)   166
9. Power Distance scores, based on Hofstede (2001)   186
10. Ahmad and Daniel – The world against us (November, 2011)   244

Prologue

A specific theme keeps recurring in my life: I sort out and tend to grow through encounters with unfamiliar cultures. I was born in a Jewish family in a small village in the Netherlands. After high school I migrated to Jerusalem (Israel), studied Psychology, joined the Israeli army, became a Human Rights activist, and studied Business Administration. These life changes involved becoming engulfed in various social and/or professional cultures. Each change came with major emotional, cognitive, and behavioral challenges, but simultaneously provided opportunity for personal growth.

Friendships have been a specific and important part of these intercultural encounters. In the last two decades, I have become friends with a Bedouin man who is a Muslim Palestinian. He lives a couple of minutes driving time from my home but on the other side of the separation wall between Israel and the Palestinian Authority and in a dissimilar environment. He too went through extensive transformation in his life, from a childhood in the desert to obtaining a university degree. The friendship has been for me a life-changing experience, and for Ahmad to some extent as well.

Though we have more than a few similarities, his worldview is in many ways opposite to mine, complementary and empowering. The fact that someone can perceive the world in such a different way than I used to do was for me an eye-opener, even though I was trained as a psychologist. Through him I learned tremendously about aspects of culture. But most significantly, being confronted over and over with his worldview, and grasping his perspective, changed me personally and professionally and enhanced a feeling of growth in both realms. Our friendship is a struggle against restrictions of various kinds: socio-political, geographical, cultural, and mental. It endures immense social pressures and has been extremely challenging for both of us. Realizing that the friendship is special, providing new insights and enriching our lives, I chose to study the opportunities and challenges involved at the time as part of my doctoral studies.

Studying a friendship is a demanding endeavor, which affects the friendship itself and raises ethical concerns, such as disclosure of personal information. Disclosure becomes even more delicate when there are major differences between the cultures re what is considered private. In addition, the socio-political context makes a close friendship across borders between an Israeli Jew and a Palestinian Arab risky in many respects and putting the friendship in the public sphere only adds to these risks.

Considering the friendship as an alternative form of social activism and despite the risks, we opted for publishing our 'stories of friendship', while relating to the personal as political, exposing the private and linking events, intimate thoughts, and feelings with broader trends and tendencies. We very much hope that our experience will be enlightening for others too.

FIGURE 1   Ahmad and Daniel – Holding the world (June 2009)

Stories of Friendship: About Friendship

Grasping the views of my friend Ahmad, an active partner in this study, was a major effort. Here is one of the very few times that I succeeded in obtaining from him a complete statement. I will present it here as a whole, since it exemplifies his way of thinking and communicating, which is circumstantial and makes ample use of metaphors.

Ramallah, September 2011. Once we were in the Palestinian capital Ramallah in a café, when Ahmad suddenly asked for pen and paper. He then wrote some points in Arabic and subsequently told me to note down the following text in English. We spoke in English for security reasons. Speaking Hebrew, as we usually do, would have disclosed my identity as Israeli or Jewish, which could have put both of us in danger.

"What means friendship for you? If you asked yourself who is my friend, is it a friend from your country or from another country? Did you speak another language? Somebody said: 'If you are looking for a friend who has no mistakes, you will not find him.' Do you think like that? Today it is a global world. Lots of people speak about how to turn the world into one village, an

open world. That means one language, open people, and more important – humanity. In this book I have just one message: 'Don't be afraid of another.' One needs more hope, love, and friendship. One needs to understand another. How can we live with the enemy? One needs to look at the half-full cup and not at the half-empty cup. This is a story between two friends; one of them coming from the desert, the other from a small country. The story speaks about two views, and how each one sees things through his eyes... Someday, when I sat with Daniel, he told me: 'Ahmad, we can change the world.' I told him: 'maybe.' And he sent to me an email with a picture of the world and two friends changing it (see Figure 1). I forgot this, but today when I write these words, I remember it. Now I have more hope than yesterday. There are a lot of names you can find in history books, important names, changing the world with war and blood, but we can find more names of those who change the world with peace and love. We are looking to see our names on a sign, and below will be written: 'This is a good way.' "

PART 1

Autoethnography of an Intercultural Friendship

Introduction to Part 1

Part 1 of this book presents the (mostly theoretical) background of this study on intercultural friendship, with Chapter 1 being an introduction to autoethnography (the study of oneself), the scope and relevance of the study and its methodology. Chapter 2 includes current knowledge regarding interculturality, the concept of cultural dimensions (or value orientations), and the complexity of the encounter between individuals of diverse cultures. This is followed by a section on honor and aggression, the knowledge of which is pivotal for fully grasping Bedouin or Palestinian culture. Chapter 3 provides the socio-political context of the friendship, with a description of my world, referring to Dutch and Israeli cultures, and my friend's world, referring to Palestinian and Bedouin cultures. Afterwards, there is a section on dealing with conflict. Part 1 ends with Chapter 4, including an overview of present findings on adult friendship, with special emphasis on intercultural friendship and friendship in the realm of conflict, as is the case in the friendship studied here.

Although there is some linkage, chapters stand on their own, each describing a distinct field of content. If you feel it is too much theory, skip Chapter 2, "When Cultures Meet". All chapters incorporate "stories of friendship" that give a taste of what the friendship is about and concern among others: our first acquaintance, settling a theft through the process of *sulha*; the 'Garage of Peace'; and what went wrong when lifting the washing machine... In contrast to the theoretically based Part 1 of the book, Part 2 contains a subjective description of reality as experienced within the realm of the friendship and presents an analysis of the four cultural dimensions studied, as well as the conclusions and implications of this study. This part includes many more stories.

CHAPTER 1

Writing about Oneself

In an era of globalization, in which the intermingling of cultures is on the rise, intercultural friendships are likely to occur more often. Bridging the challenges of intercultural friendship could be a small step toward social justice and a wonderful opportunity for personal growth. This chapter will describe the relevance and the intent of this study. Then I will provide a description of the friendship itself. Hereafter, I will explain the complexity of doing an autoethnographic case study, provide the research design and add a few notes of caution regarding the study of stories.

Stories of Friendship: The First Encounter

Jerusalem, Summer 2003. I was going home after a long day of work out of town. I descended from the intercity bus at the central bus station and halted a taxi with the purpose of getting home quicker. When I looked inside, I saw that another passenger was there already. I asked the driver about this person and he replied: "Do not bother; I will take you both." I thought "what the heck?" and entered. During the short drive, the three of us started talking. I enjoyed their company and at the end of our ride, I invited them in for coffee.

The passenger was Ahmad and since then we have been friends. The taxi driver was Jaffer, and he will play some part in my life as well. I was raised with notions of privacy and having distance from strangers. For me, it was unusual to join them in the taxi. In contrast, they were brought up with the idea of doing things collectively. Ahmad was not a paying passenger in the taxi, as I had interpreted at first; he simply had joined his friend Jaffer in his work. From a cultural point of view, inviting strangers in my flat was not at all in line with my Dutch background. In the Netherlands, invitations tend to be made much in advance, and there is little space for spontaneity, especially not with strangers. Nonetheless, enjoying their company and out of curiosity I trespassed cultural norms. For Ahmad and Jaffer the invitation was nothing out of the ordinary. Palestinians do not convey the impression of having this urge to plan. Israeli society has a mixture of cultures, but the dominant culture allows for some spontaneity. Still, in most Israeli Jewish circles it would be out of the question to invite two unknown Arabs for coffee at one's home.

1 Relevance and Intent

With heightened tension and polarization between Arab and Western cultures and ideologies, intercultural friendship takes on additional significance, but what can we learn from a study of a friendship between a Palestinian Bedouin and a Dutch Israeli Jew? Or why would such a study be of interest?

In previous centuries, the average person was inclined to stay within her or his own environment, surrounded by family, with little contact with people from other cultures. Nowadays, physical and mental borders disappear, and it becomes easier to communicate with people in other parts of the world via the Internet. Thus, there is an increase in intercultural contact, through both social media (Dekker, Belabas and Scholten 2015; Manago and Vaughn 2015; Shiau 2016) and virtual work teams including people with different nationalities (Gibson and Manuel 2003; Gillespie, DeJong, Williamson and Gill 2017; Hardin, Fuller and Davison 2007; Staples and Zhao 2006). Moreover, much more so than in the past, people tend to move around and intermingle with other cultures, either voluntarily or by force, temporarily or permanently, whether for vacation, jobs, marriage, as migrants, or otherwise (Lee 2008; Samovar, Porter and McDaniel 2009; van Tilburg and Vingerhoets 2006; Ward, Bochner and Furnham 2001). As a result, people are increasingly likely to encounter diverse ethnic cultures, and growing numbers of countries need to deal with issues related to multiculturalism.

Another development has taken place too. While the family and heterosexual marriage are losing their central place, especially in Western societies where people may move from one country to another on their own, friendships and alternative forms of intimacy and care are becoming progressively more important (Allan 2008; Budgeon 2006; Jamieson, Morgan, Crow and Allan 2006; Roseneil 2004; Roseneil and Budgeon 2004). And not just important; friendships were found to be essential to human development, and related to happiness (Demir, Ozdemir and Weitekamp 2007; Dunbar 2018; Garcia, Pereira and Corrêa de Macedo 2015).

But living together in a multicultural society is far from easy. Difficulties in multicultural co-existence appear within the context of migration and acculturation processes (e.g., Avila Tapies 2008; Chung, Bemak, Ortiz and Sandoval-Perez 2008; Hui, Chen, Leung and Berry 2015; Persky and Birman 2005; Roccas, Horenczyk and Schwartz 2000; Schwartz, Galliher and Domenech Rodríguez 2011), attitudes toward minority groups (e.g., Musso, Inguglia, Lo Coco, Albiero and Berry 2017; Urbiola, Willis, Ruiz-Romero, Moya and Esses 2017; Velasco Gonzalez, Weesie and Poppe 2008), in the workplace (e.g., Fitzsimmons 2013; Wilcox and McCray 2005) and in community services (e.g., Baum 2007a;

Howarth, Wagner, Magnusson and Sammut 2014). Therefore, there is increasing need for cultural competence, one's potential to function effectively in intercultural situations classified as intercultural traits, attitudes, and capabilities (Ang, Ng and Rockstuhl 2020). To fulfill this need and improve cultural competence, there now is an abundancy of programs; many of these for students of a variety of disciplines (e.g., Antal and Friedman 2008; Cheney 2001; Gilin and Young 2009; Maoz 2000a; Penbek, Yurdakul and Cerit 2009; Spajić-Vrkaš 2009; Tesoriero 2006; Zhang and Merolla 2007).

The difficulty in living together has to do with differences in value orientations. Our attitudes and behaviors are guided by values, and people are inclined to cluster together in groups, communities, and nations with similar value patterns (A. Berman, Berger and Gutmann 2000; Hofstede 2001; Ward et al. 2001). This grouping enforces stereotyping, while distancing between groups can reinforce prejudice (Cottam, Dietz-Uhler, Mastors and Preston 2004; Flache and Macy 2011; Samovar et al. 2009). Personal acquaintance with people from other cultures is one of the ways to reduce this prejudice. Therefore, friendships, as an intimate form of personal acquaintance, can be central in these intercultural encounters, providing the possibility of diminishing stigmatization, widening horizons, and enhancing mutual growth (Aberson, Shoemaker and Tomolillo 2004; Peterson 2007; Sonnenschein, Bekerman and Horenczyk 2010).

Studies on adult friendships, and intercultural friendship in specific, were rare until the last decade but are currently on the increase. Although there is now an abundance of studies on intercultural encounters, encounters between Westerners and Arabs or Muslims are much less studied. Furthermore, most of the studies on intercultural encounters either combine theoretical and quantitative knowledge or provide personal narratives, whereas integration of theory and a personal perspective seems rare.

This autoethnographic book refers to a friendship that crosses both cultural and national borders between Israel and the Palestinian Authority. The friendship thrives in the midst of the Israeli–Palestinian conflict, which is among the world's most prominent conflicts and in an environment that is not particularly conducive to the formation of friendships between Arabs and Jews. The ongoing political conflict with its many factors – historical, geopolitical, religious, and sociocultural – sets the stage for the present investigation. The study adds knowledge to the literature by investigating an exceptional friendship between two men of highly diverse cultures, filling part of the void concerning the interface between interculturality and friendship.

The question that was the focus of this research is as follows: What are the challenges and opportunities in an intercultural friendship between a Jewish

Israeli man of Western European origin (a so-called "Ashkenazi") and a Muslim Palestinian man of Bedouin descent? Bridging cultural differences involves emotional, cognitive, and behavioral challenges, which are often frustrating. However, these same cultural differences provide opportunities as well and may enhance personal growth. Challenges and opportunities are explained in detail, from the perspective of a Dutch Israeli psychologist, and illustrated expansively by stories of friendship.

The friendship has many aspects, but the study focuses on the cultural gap and the endeavors to bridge it through mutual understanding. It highlights certain characteristics of Bedouin and Palestinian cultures and to lesser extent those of Dutch and Israeli cultures. The book is relevant for anthropologists, sociologists, educationalists, and psychologists, interested in culture, values, and/or friendship. Furthermore, those who meet, deal with, or live in an Arab environment, and those involved or those who would like to be involved in intercultural friendships may find this book of interest as well.

I will analyze the friendship through the perspective of cultural dimensions or value orientations. The four cultural dimensions as suggested by Hofstede (2001) are most helpful in demonstrating the challenges and opportunities in the friendship, since he formulates his dimensions in concrete and practical terms, and specifically studied the cultures relevant for the present study. Hofstede's dimensions are individualism–collectivism, uncertainty avoidance, masculinity–femininity, and power distance. On all of the dimensions, he found large differences between Israel, the Netherlands and Arabic-speaking countries (see Figure 2).

In addition, he specifically stated that these dimensions could be used as a base for comparing cultures in the realm of qualitative research.

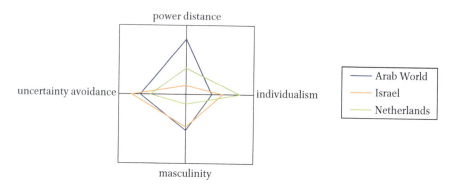

FIGURE 2 Radar diagram of scores for four cultural dimensions.
BASED ON HOFSTEDE (2001)

Getting ahead of myself, I will share that the findings fit well with Hofstede's dimensions of individualism–collectivism, masculinity–femininity, and power distance. Findings of this study do not fit well with the dimension of uncertainty avoidance and suggest an alternative way of relating to this dimension, as will be discussed later.

2 The Two Friends

Let us now introduce the two main subjects of this book, whom you have met already in the story above; one of them is my friend Ahmad, the other is me. Below I will share some factual details about each of us, emphasizing differences and similarities. This is followed by an outline of our friendship.

2.1 *Ahmad*

He stems from a family of Muslim Arabs and belongs to the Jahalin Bedouin tribe. His tribe was relocated from Beer Sheba (Israel) to the Judean desert (Palestinian Authority), by the Israeli authorities in the early 1950s. He is the youngest of ten children from his father's third – and last – wife. Though in Bedouin families it is customary to have more than one wife simultaneously, his father married his wives consecutively. Ahmad was born in 1975, while his mother was herding the goats. He lived in the desert, sometimes in a tent, and sometimes in a cave, until age 12. Then he moved with his family to a house in az-Za'ayyem, a Palestinian village adjacent to Jerusalem, under Israeli administration (see Figure 3, in the middle of the map). Some of his siblings live in neighboring houses, some in close-by villages, and a couple of them in Jerusalem.

As a child, Ahmad walked daily for hours to reach school. There, being a poverty-stricken Bedouin, he was initially looked down upon but – unlike other Bedouin children – he rapidly discovered that excellence brought him honor. He finished primary and secondary school while working after school hours. He sold pieces of aluminum he found so that he could buy storybooks to read while herding the family's goats. When he was out of money, he would look in the streets for old newspapers to read. During secondary school, he worked as shepherd, for which he was paid with a goat every three or four months. Later, he worked in and around Jerusalem in a variety of jobs such as guard, hairdresser, and gym instructor.

After secondary school, he went to prison for suspected anti-Israeli activities, where he continued studying. Being imprisoned for substantial periods of time is customary for many Palestinian youngsters. Though some may have

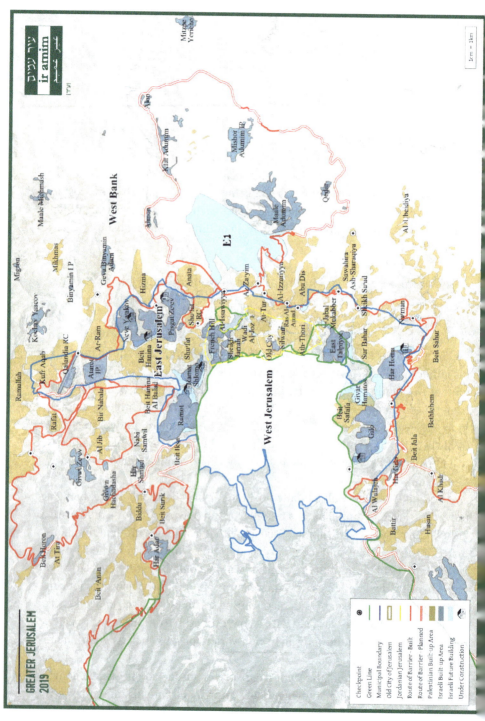

FIGURE 3   Greater Jerusalem
COURTESY OF IR AMIM, FOR AN EQUITABLE AND STABLE JERUSALEM WITH AN AGREED POLITICAL FUTURE, 2019

committed crimes, many are imprisoned on suspicion, or simply for entering Israel without a permit. Released from jail, he was strengthened in his wish to achieve higher education. His father pressed him to invest more time in work, build a home, and marry. However, he eventually agreed that Ahmad could enroll in al-Quds University (al-Quds is the Arabic name of Jerusalem), in Abu Dis, even before marriage, albeit after making some more money and buying a house. At university, he received a bachelor's degree in both Media Studies and Political Science. At the time of this study, he was working on a master's thesis in Political Science. He intends to continue studying for a doctoral degree. Together with one of his brothers, he has the highest academic education in his tribal clan.

Since the start of this century, it has become more and more complicated to enter Israel, until in the last couple of years it became too difficult because of the separation wall and the lack of opportunity to obtain an entry permit. Ahmad subsequently looked for jobs in the Palestinian Authority. At the start of this study he owned a garage and later also a tiny restaurant. Ahmad was elected sheikh of the Jahalin tribe, a volunteer leadership role in which he functioned as advisor for the members of his tribe, and as mediator in family disputes. Although he left this task, many still come to him for practical advice. He is married to a Palestinian-American woman. While this is uncommon among the Bedouins, there are some Palestinians who have U.S. citizenship and move between the two countries (Naylor 2013). Ahmad and his wife have four children.

Ahmad has Palestinian and Jordanian citizenship, but regards himself a global citizen, and after a legal battle of ten years, he managed to obtain a Green Card for entry into the United States, which was long after the events addressed in this book.

2.2   Daniel

Though in highly different circumstances, also my ancestors were forced to leave the place they were born. My parents, both Jewish, are Holocaust survivors. My father fled as a child with his family from Germany to the Netherlands before WW II, after which he assumed Dutch citizenship, while my mother is native Dutch. I was born in 1963 in a maternity clinic, which was the custom at the time in the Netherlands. This makes me 12 years older than Ahmad. I have four younger brothers, which is quite a lot for a Dutch family, but in a Bedouin family this number would be normal or even small. Like Ahmad, I lived most of my childhood in a small village but in the eastern part of the Netherlands. Unlike him, I had a Reform Jewish upbringing. I did not experience pressure from my family as regarding plans for life, but I was supposed to excel in whatever I chose. In my environment, it was expected to follow higher education and I did not consider otherwise. Unlike Bedouin families, my nuclear family dispersed; something nowadays common in Western Europe. My parents and siblings moved to various parts of the Netherlands, while some lived for substantial periods in other countries.

When I turned 17, my parents believed that as a Jew it would be good for me to study for a year in Israel. I enjoyed living there and stayed ever since. Unlike Ahmad, who had to support himself financially even as a child, I remained completely dependent on my parents until my first job, at age 20. As a research assistant, I still was not able to support myself, and I continued to receive financial assistance from my parents until the end of my studies. I studied for the first two degrees in Psychology at the Hebrew University in Jerusalem. This is close to Ahmad's university, but the two neighborhoods are separated by the wall between Israel and the Palestinian Authority, and worlds apart. Many years later, I obtained a Master's degree in Business Administration and a doctoral degree in Psychology, thus – like Ahmad – achieving the highest academic education in my extended family.

Israel has obligatory army service and so after my initial studies I was drafted into the Israel Defense Forces. I worked for several years in the army as a Mental Health Officer; a function in which I did reserve duty until a couple of years ago. I have worked in other mental health settings as well, among others as Professional Director of Elah, the center for people of Dutch origin and their families, in which position I made frequent use of taxis, as in the story above. I am presently self-employed as a psychotherapist, working with individuals and groups, and teach at Hadassah Academic College (Jerusalem) and virtually at the Professional School of Psychology (Sacramento). I live in French Hill, a neighborhood in Jerusalem (see Figure 3, in the middle of the map). As you can see, we live close to each other, but with a wall, *the* wall, in between.

The Netherlands does not recognize dual citizenship except in a few specific circumstances. I never applied for Israeli citizenship and stayed as a permanent resident, because I did not want to give up my Dutch nationality. The main practical consequence is that I am not allowed to vote for the Israeli Knesset (but can take part in local elections). Clearly, this state of dual cultural and national belonging affects my thinking and actions. Like Ahmad, I perceive of myself as a global citizen, which led me to volunteer in leadership roles in a range of nongovernmental organizations, concerned with human rights, social change, and/or group work.

2.3   *Our Friendship*

Let us now look at our longstanding friendship at a glance. As outlined above, we met in 2003, in a taxi. Initially, Ahmad and I were distant friends. Occasionally, he would visit me at home in Jerusalem and from time to time I visited him at the industrial area where he worked as overseer of the guards. I took pleasure in his warmth and spontaneity, his manhood, the – for me – exotic stories he told me about his life, his contrasting perspectives, and his intention of making the world a better place. I admired his success in finding a way to move beyond primitive desert life despite tremendous hardships and his excellent skills in contacting people of various backgrounds. He found me different from other Israelis he had met and appreciated my points of view. He also enjoyed my sensitivity, my interest in him, the way I plan life, and the fact that "I do what I say I'll do." Over the years we became closer, and we became motivating forces in each other's lives. Since 2008, when it became more difficult for him to cross the wall and enter Israel, my visits to his village and his family became more frequent, and through these visits I also became involved with other Palestinian Bedouins.

During the years when this study was conducted we met about twice a week, usually having Bedouin coffee or tea and frequently something to eat. We talk about the daily things of life, our work or studies, and our concerns. We mostly refrain from talking politics. We communicate in Hebrew, though we may use some Arabic or English. I tried to learn Arabic, but with only limited success, and he knows a few words of Dutch. He regularly seeks my instrumental support, such as finding or verifying information, or driving somewhere with my car. In contrast, I tend to call on him for emotional support when I am distressed about things. Before making decisions, I mostly gather information from the Internet and rarely ask friends for advice. However, when I get stuck in an interpersonal dilemma, such as whether or how to confront someone with whom I am not pleased, I will ask Ahmad for his perspective. During visits, I may join him on errands. For our enjoyment, we do not "go out" in Western terms (to a movie, live performance, museum, etc.), but we occasionally go to some place outdoors, such as a mountain or a desert and have a barbecue together with others. We infrequently dine in simple restaurants when we are hungry, and not as a pastime.

Together, we have taken small groups of people, both Israelis and foreigners, to visit and learn about the Jahalin Bedouins. I handle the organizational aspect of these tours and supply socio-political background information. He hosts the visitors, shares knowledge the life of the Bedouins, and makes sure that the guests receive abundant local food and beverages. I also became involved in several of Ahmad's projects, such as the garage, about which I will tell you further on, and later a small restaurant. We discussed his plans, and I invested some money. Now that the collection of stories for this study has been completed, I go to his place in the village three times a week, though he will not always be there or will be too busy to meet. These are my days of taking care of a variety of animals that we keep jointly. We have had cats, dogs, chickens, ducks, a couple of songbirds, and a rabbit. The animals provide food for many more intercultural stories that I hope to publish in the future.

Our environment was not conducive to our friendship, especially in its first period, but this has become better over the years. Both Ahmad and I have experienced substantial pressure to distance ourselves from one another. Despite the pressure, the friendship flourished. I met many of his male Palestinian friends and acquaintances, and he met some of my friends – mostly those who were born in other countries and less reluctant to meet Palestinians. It must be said that we are perceived as quite an extraordinary combination, not just because of all the differences mentioned above and the political tension but also physically. This is because we may look ordinary in our respective environments, but he is short and muscular with a dark complexion, while I am tall and lean with light skin; the contrast is striking.

We introduced each other to the traditions of our respective cultures, especially through our families, whose members eventually became used to our friendship. In the period of the stories in this book, I was in close contact with his nuclear family, and I also visited male members of his extended family. Despite the hardships in getting Ahmad a visa, we have traveled three times to Europe for holidays, where he met my family too. The trips themselves were a series of intercultural experiences, not simply because of the encounters with the cultures we visited but also between us. In fact, the same cultural disparities, which become clear when investigating the friendship in our regular environment (Israel/Palestine) and are the center of this work, were evident in other places as well. I will show this later through two stories from events in Amsterdam. Many of the aspects of our friendship mentioned here pertain to those activities common among intercultural friends (Lee 2006), and the friendship as a whole went through all stages that intercultural friendships tend to go through (Lee 2008). I will go into detail and share with you stories, from a two-and-a-half-year period within the friendship, in the succeeding chapters.

3 A Case Study

Jones called for diversifying research ideas in cultural psychology and suggested that researchers consider among others "the duality of 'belonging' (to groups, institutions, society, culture) and 'uniqueness' (individuality, difference, intersectionality) and [...] identify the ways positive psychological outcomes are achieved in complex multifaceted contexts and the mechanisms that produce them" (Jones 2010: 705). The present study is an attempt to do so, while describing the challenges and the opportunities encountered in a friendship of two unique individuals in the light of their belonging to distinct cultural groups.

3.1 Narrative Research

One of the clearest channels to explore and appreciate the inner world of individuals is through their verbal accounts and stories about their lives and reality. Narrative research starts out with a research question but usually not with a priori hypotheses, as is the case in the present study. It requires self-awareness and self-discipline in order to continue examining the narrative from various perspectives (Lieblich, Tuval-Mashiach and Zilber 1998). The analysis of relationships could be performed in a variety of creative ways but commonly begins with text that expresses aspects of the human relationship and afterwards initiates a conversation between the phenomenological account and a psychological understanding (Josselson, Lieblich and McAdams 2007).

Four approaches to narrative research have been delineated, differentiating between a holistic and a categorical approach, and between form and content (Lieblich et al. 1998). The first differentiation refers to the unit of analysis; whereas the holistic approach refers to the narrative as a whole, the categorical approach is more selective. The second differentiation refers to the reading (interpretation) of the text; whereas the content approach refers to the facts and their meaning, the form approach refers to the process and the way in which they are presented. The goal of this study was neither to describe Bedouin culture nor intercultural friendship as a whole but to investigate specifically the challenges and opportunities in the intercultural encounter. Therefore, the present study is limited to a categorical/content approach, referring specifically to the category of intercultural friendship, and focusing on the challenges and opportunities around certain topics that recur in friendship interactions. It relates to form and process aspects of the narrative mainly to highlight issues of content.

Life stories are told in a certain context. We can identify three separate but interrelated spheres: the broad cultural meaning systems or meta narratives that underlie and give sense to any particular life story; the collective social field in which one's life and story evolved; and the immediate intersubjective relationships in which a narrative is produced (Zilber, Tuval-Mashiach and Lieblich 2008). The first part of this book provides the broader cultural and socio-political context, whereas the second part focuses on both the immediate experience of the friendship and the collective in which it takes place.

The study follows in the steps of "critical autobiographies" (Church 1995; Tillmann-Healy 2003), using the author's life stories as base for social science.

The kind of autobiography used to understand a societal phenomenon was coined "autoethnography", an ethnography about oneself, a study in which the cultural experience of the researcher is central (Ellis and Bochner 2000; Humphreys 2005; Maydell 2010; Ohaeri and Awadalla 2009; Taylor 2008). "The intent of autoethnography is to acknowledge the inextricable link between the personal and the cultural and to make room for nontraditional forms of inquiry and expression" (Wall 2006: 146). In the autoethnography, the – detached – doing of the research and the – involved – being of the researcher intermingle (Mitra 2010). Moreover, autoethnography transgresses the boundaries between scientific and literary modes of truth telling and creates a discourse of ambiguity, contradiction, contingency, and chance (Bochner 2017). It is a relentless quest to find answers to questions about understanding and sharing our experience around the subject we study (cf. Ellis and Bochner 2000).

Although autoethnographies are becoming more common, autoethnographic methodology continues to encounter criticism in parts of the academic world. Critics of autoethnography relate among others to the absence of objectivity of the researcher, the problem of a single source of data, and issues of verification (Brigg and Bleiker 2010; Holt 2008; Wall 2006, 2008). Any autobiography – consciously or unconsciously – emphasizes a range of subjectively chosen elements, and thus distorts the picture, possibly making the study less scientifically grounded. As suggested by Howarth (1974), an autobiography is like a self-portrait. Baumeister and Newman described the process of creating an autobiography as follows:

> First, people interpret experiences relative to purposes, which may be either objective goals or subjective fulfillment states. Second, people seek value and justification by constructing stories that depict their actions and intentions as right and good. Third, people seek a sense of efficacy by making stories that contain information about how to exert control. Fourth, people seek a sense of self-worth by making stories that portray themselves as attractive and competent.
> BAUMEISTER AND NEWMAN 1994: 676

Therefore, autobiographies have been criticized as self-indulgent (Mykhalovskiy 1996). In response to the critique, guidelines for quality in autobiographical and narrative research were provided (Bullough and Pinnegar 2001; Josselson and Lieblich 2003), and these were followed in this study. In any case, we need to keep in mind that a life story is just one version of reality, as perceived by the individual at a certain time and in a certain context.

3.2 *Friendship Research*

Friendship research, after being for long a relatively neglected field, has attracted more interest only in the last decades, and stretches – primarily – over the fields of psychology, sociology, and education. The study of friendship is complex, especially because it cannot be studied apart from its social context, since the environment substantially influences the relationship (Adams and Allan 1998; Allan 1998; Roseneil and Budgeon 2004). In consequence, it was suggested that "different research methods in different environments are useful for exploring the complexity and multi-dimensionality of personal relationships and for understanding the interactive narrative processes through which such relationships are given meaning in situated contexts" (Davies and Heaphy 2011: 14).

Friendship research is performed through the practices of friendship, and in its natural context and pace, and studies based on specific friendships are gradually becoming more accepted as qualitative research (Al-Makhamreh and Lewando-Hundt 2008; Arnold 1995; Ellis 2007; Jackson 1990). We may look at the autobiography of a friendship as a form of "participatory research". Participatory research has been defined in various ways but generally refers to situations in which the researcher is an active participant in the community studied, in an attempt to understand the social forces in operation, and takes part in overcoming oppressive situations (Park 1993).

> The idea is that researchers, acting as facilitators and guarding against their own biases, seek to minimize any power differentials between them and the researched. The research design, therefore, is flexible, able to respond to changing contexts and emergent findings as they arise. [...] This means that those who participate have their knowledge respected, have control over the research process and influence over the way the results are used.
> LEDWITH AND SPRINGETT 2010: 93

Friendship research follows the ethics of friendship, a stance of hope, caring, justice, and even love (Tillmann-Healy 2001). This kind of research may take years, as is common practice in anthropological research, since understanding the development of cultural practices is a long-term endeavor (Rogoff 2003). In a friendship one cannot be solely involved with the research for one's own benefit. The research is secondary to the friendship and therefore often needs to make place for other friendship affairs. As much as possible, friendship research also entails using its process and outcomes for the benefit of the studied community.

People are apt to make friends in their own socio-cultural environment, though with globalization this is changing. Still, friendships across socio-cultural groups are exceptional.

> When friendships do develop across social groups, the bonds take on political dimensions. Opportunities exist for dual consciousness-raising and for members of dominant groups (e.g., men, Euro-Americans, Christians, and heterosexuals) to serve as advocates for friends in target groups. As a result, those who are "just friends" can become "just" friends, interpersonal and political allies who seek personal growth, meaningful relationships, and social justice.
> TILLMANN-HEALY 2003: 731

This is what this book is about. It is based on one single case of friendship – a friendship between Ahmad, a Muslim Palestinian man of Bedouin descent, and me, a Jewish Israeli man of Dutch origin – from which we may learn not only about cultural characteristics, but also about relationships, personal growth, and social (in)justice.

3.3 Case Selection

"Case study research excels at bringing us to an understanding of a complex issue or object and can extend experience or add strength to what is already known through previous research" (Soy 1997). Case studies have been especially helpful in creating high levels of conceptual validity, deriving new hypotheses, exploring causal mechanisms, and modeling and assessing complex causal relations (George and Bennett 2005). Even if this is an autobiographical study, it is important to identify the kind of case to be investigated. We may distinguish between several kinds of cases. Extreme or deviant cases are good for getting a point across. Critical cases permit logical deductions more than other cases, since if things are true for this case, it may well be the same for all other cases. Paradigmatic cases are exemplary in highlighting typical characteristics of a society. Some cases fall simultaneously into more than one category (Flyvbjerg 2004).

Let us look at the characteristics of the two parts of this friendship between Ahmad and myself from the perspective of case selection. Ahmad spent his youth in the most primitive environment. He struggled to get higher up, received higher education, and achieved a position of honor, power, and importance in his tribe. He also worked for many years in Israel, traveled abroad, and has had a lot of contact with the Western world compared with others in his environment. His life story is radical, and at the same time in many ways exemplifies Bedouin values and lifestyle. In addition, if things are true for him, they may also be true for many other Bedouins with less contact with Israeli or Western cultures. Therefore, Ahmad could be seen simultaneously as an extreme, a critical, and a paradigmatic case.

Living for over 30 years in Israel, I was widely exposed to a variety of value orientations, and during a long process of cultural adaptation, I had the chance of leaving behind, at least partly, those values originating in my Dutch upbringing. Therefore, challenges that I (still) endure in this friendship are likely to be similar to those experienced by many Westerners in their friendships with Bedouins or rural Palestinians. This makes me a critical case as regards Dutch or West European culture. In Israeli context, my position would not be perceived as deviant from a cultural perspective, but it would be regarded as extreme from a socio-political perspective since friendships between Palestinians and Jews are scarce in the present socio-political context. So, depending on one's perspective, one could look at the friendship as extreme, critical, or paradigmatic. Whatever perspective, the socio-cultural backgrounds, values, worldviews, and lifestyles of Ahmad and me are in many ways in sharp contrast. This dissimilarity is expected to be an asset in the exploration of the challenges and opportunities in intercultural friendship.

4 Studying Stories

Data for this study stemmed from participant observation and self-exploration. Like Tillmann-Healy, "our primary procedures are those we use to build and sustain friendship: conversation, everyday involvement, compassion, giving, and vulnerability" (Tillmann-Healy 2003: 734). I will proceed to present a summary of the ways in which the data were collected, analyzed, and presented. Afterward, I will share several of the methodological concerns and some thoughts about cultural relativism.

4.1 *Observations as Data*

Most ethnographic research has a distinct point at which the researcher enters the field and begins with the gathering of data, and a distinct ending when the researcher leaves the situation. By contrast, friendship is an ongoing venture, made up of innumerable events and circumstances. In auto-ethnographic friendship research, one gathers a great deal of knowledge in an unofficial way before the start of the research, and more knowledge is acquired after officially finishing the gathering of data. Thus, the number of our friendship stories continues to grow, while adding more understanding to the cultural differences. This incoming stream of knowledge is both an advantage and a challenge; an advantage because a mass of information attained over a prolonged period is available, and a challenge because somewhere one needs to put a limit on what information to use.

I dealt with this situation by making use of all *essential* information available to me. I started collecting and recording observations (field notes) in a systematic manner in June 2009 and finished in November 2011. I left out both recent developments pertaining to some of the stories that could have provided new insight, and poignant stories that appeared after early 2012. However, in a few instances, I added historical events that I had recorded in earlier years, and I also incorporated some information that I deemed essential but appeared after finishing writing field notes. Now and then, I added descriptions of later events concerning relationships with other Bedouins or Palestinians to provide more context and/or show universality of certain phenomena. One could criticize this approach since it does not stick to a clearly marked research period. My reasoning was that the selected period for gathering field notes was arbitrary and since the friendship is ongoing, the inclusion of any relevant knowledge acquired before or after this period is legitimate.

It was impossible to register all the events, even for a limited period, and I had to make a selection. I opted for choosing on the basis of striking cultural differences, whereas I often disregarded cultural similarities. In total, I registered over a hundred observations – the tip of the iceberg. Some of these notes were descriptions of a few lines only, whereas others were pages long. As much as possible, observations were documented soon after they occurred; sometimes first in a notebook. I wrote notes in a computer system, including information such as date, time of day, place, event description, people involved, quotes, and background information.

Subsequently, I created texts and stories of friendship based on my interpretation of recurrent and/or striking observations. In the next step, I read to Ahmad what I had written, so that he could tell me his perspective, add cultural information, or point out subtleties. For some of the stories I provided a detailed account, but often the events behind the stories were more complex than I could express. I presented the texts to him in bits and pieces since he was usually unable to spend much sustained time on them. After obtaining his ideas, I amended the texts and we often examined them again. Discussion and dialogue with Ahmad over the observations continued until April 2012.

In this book, I organized my observations around "stories of friendship" according to topics, representing each of the four cultural dimensions. The selection of topics was guided by the degree of dissimilarity between the cultures in this field, and not necessarily for their importance in the particular culture. Clearly, it is impossible to dissect a friendship into independent pieces; events do not occur according to chapters and cultural dimensions are interlinked.

Therefore, in any illustration it is possible to discern a variety of themes and topics. Many topics relate to more than one dimension. For instance, the topic "meals and table manners" is placed in Chapter 5, "Individualism versus Collectivism", though it is related to uncertainty avoidance as well. The opposite is true for the topic "mine and yours", which is placed in Chapter 6, "Uncertainty Avoidance", though from a content-analysis perspective it would belong in the field of individualism/collectivism. I could have used some of the stories of friendship as examples of other cultural dimensions. The choice concerning the placement of topics is based on the challenges and the opportunities as I – and not Ahmad – experienced them within the realm of the friendship, more than on their anthropological content. In addition, I could have made extensive use of linkage between the stories of friendship, the topical discussions, and the literature. In an attempt not to burden the reader, I refrained from doing so.

4.2 Methodological Concerns

In the process from collecting data to depicting the stories, there were two main methodological concerns, namely reliability and consent to disclosure.

One may question whether reliability is at all an issue in the present kind of research since we relate here to my own subjective experience. Undoubtedly, a researcher is embedded in his own cultural context and worldview (Hofstede 2001). Consequently, my worldview, shaped by the aforementioned environments, influences my perceptions and interpretations and my blind spots are likely to affect these observations, both introspective and external. Moreover, to what extent can we rely on our own memories? Even if written down as field notes, they are always selective (cf. Wall 2008). Having said that, we may consider that as an experienced clinical psychologist, I was trained in self-exploration and observation of others, and this – I hope – will enhance honest and accurate description. To augment reliability, I checked the accuracy of facts with Ahmad and/or others involved.

Research studies based on one sole case, like the present one, run the risk of indeterminacy because of more than one possible explanation, and of incorrect inferences. Multiple observations may reduce this risk substantially (George and Bennett 2005), but still it may be difficult to generalize from the findings. During the process of this study, I made an endless number of observations and could check their commonness. Even when I provide only one example for a certain theme, it is illustrative of many situations in which this same theme occurred.

Language, communication, and translation may also reduce reliability; this was of concern especially because of the complexity of incorporating and integrating Ahmad's voice in my writings. We not only communicate in distinctive styles but also in languages that for both of us are foreign. I wrote texts in English, my second language, whereas we reviewed them in Hebrew, which is Ahmad's second language and my third language. This procedure was chosen because Ahmad's knowledge of English is insufficient to read the texts, and because he has a clear – cultural – preference for oral over written communication. Furthermore, there were occasionally complications in cultural translation (cf. Bhabha 1994), which will be explained in Chapter 6, "Uncertainty Avoidance". To provide a taste of Ahmad's way of communication and use of language, I incorporated three stories of friendship (in the prologue, the chapter on interculturality, and in the epilogue), in which I left the text as close as possible to his style.

It was suggested that friendship with one's subject(s) of study "promotes better research ethics as it generates a form of mutuality based on partial relatedness, constructive dissent and playfulness, rather than hybridity, totalizing consensus and domination" (Ramírez-i-Ollé 2019: 299). Nonetheless, ethics committees have at times imposed rigid procedures that do not fit well with friendship research. One of the difficulties is that friendship research requires particular sensitivity to relational concerns, and among these are the ethical aspects of disclosing information (Ellis 2007; Tillmann-Healy 2003). The question of what information to embrace in the text on friendship and what information to discard was a delicate matter in this study, which required repeated conversation to achieve mutual understanding and agreement. Ellis (2007) wrote about the dilemma around disclosing sensitive detail, when publishing the story of caring for her elderly mother. She chose to be selective in sharing with her mother what she wrote. In contrast, I dealt with this issue by sharing all observations with Ahmad. Like Ellis and her mother, I found that while reading the observations to Ahmad, there were words or lines that I felt unable to share, since I was afraid that he would regard them as a blot on honor – either for himself personally or for his family – or otherwise inappropriate for publication. Unlike Ellis (2007), I opted for not publishing anything that I felt I could not share with him. The reason for doing so was that I considered it unethical to disclose and discuss with others information or ideas that I was unable to share with the person in question.

But there were more delicacies around the issue of disclosure. A friend is likely to anticipate that the study will portray a positive picture of her or his life and ways of thinking (cf. Baumeister and Newman 1994). As a researcher, the situation was a bit different. On the one hand, I wanted to make a good impression on the reader, like Ahmad, while on the other hand, I preferred to be as accurate as possible, while providing a balanced view and limiting distortions.

These two perspectives at times may be in conflict (cf. Wall 2008). In the end, we tried to be as open and truthful as possible and disclosed personal information that others could perceive negatively, or about which we felt uncomfortable. However, there were places in which Ahmad objected to disclosure. Hence, some texts and pieces of knowledge that I deemed important he vetoed, not only because of their irrelevance in his eyes but also because they could be harmful to his honor.

Blake (2007), in his review on ethics and participatory action research, refers to the idea of "negotiated consent", implying the discussion with the subject(s) under investigation about the information to be or not be disclosed. That is what we achieved in our case; there was extensive discussion between Ahmad and myself about what to include or not to include in my writings. I will come back to and exemplify sharing my observations with Ahmad in the last chapter of this book. The idea of negotiated consent involves the notion of power difference between researcher and participant. Though researchers often are perceived as those in power, participants essentially have substantial power as well, for example, through the selectivity of information they provide to the researcher (Dufty 2010). On more than a few occasions, I succeeded in fully grasping the complexity of situations only after examining them more than once, since often I would not receive all – to me – relevant information at the outset. Although some would regard both the selectivity in the information presented to me and my choice of topics as biases, bias in case studies does not have to be more than in other forms of research (Flyvbjerg 2004).

Ahmad was aware of the intent of this study and he wanted his story to be told. In contrast, his friends and family were mostly unaware of the research. This situation required a unique approach as regarding consent and confidentiality. Introducing this facet of my interest after – sometimes – years of acquaintance was uncomfortable. Sharing texts with Palestinians other than Ahmad and asking for written consent felt inappropriate, not only because we had no common written language but also from a socio-cultural perspective. I did ask several of these friends and family members for their – oral – consent to write about them but did not share with them what I wrote.

Throughout the process of writing, it became apparent that one might deem some of the actions described as prohibited, either culturally or legally. This situation required the utmost protection of confidentiality. I could have acquired this by drastically changing facts, which would have resulted in complete disguise. However, I recognized that radical concealment would harm both the authenticity and the possibility of verification of the research. I then decided to enhance the protection of confidentiality by using pseudonyms for all people affected, and masking most identifying information. This leaves the texts in line with reality, but only those featuring in the stories and their close relatives and friends are likely to recognize the situations. Furthermore, while taking into account that the friendship is an ongoing reality in a volatile and risky socio-cultural and political environment, some relevant pieces of information were omitted in order to safeguard the personal, social, and physical security of Ahmad, his family, and myself.

4.3 *Cultural Relativism*

Before sharing thoughts on interculturality in the next chapter, I want to make some separate but interrelated points regarding the relativity of culture. Several researchers have emphasized the difficulty of generalizing from cultural attributes and pointed at the considerable diversity also within both national cultures and perceived subcultures (e.g., Jones 2010; Matsumoto 2006; Schwartz 2014). However, with little knowledge of another cultural group, it is easy to stereotype. In fact, much has been written about the stereotyping of the Orient by Western powers (Said 1985; Varisco 2007). Further on, I will write about specific national societies and cultures, but one needs to realize that these are in flux, and whatever I will write it is my understanding at a specific point of time. Societies and cultures are co-created by the interactions of individuals and groups and are in constant change. The same is true for the intercultural encounter; it is the result of the specific dynamics created by the parties involved (e.g., Moon 2010; Pratt and Rosner 2012).

Having said this, the study required making certain cultural comparisons, which are based on generalizations deriving from the dominant cultures in which we grew up. This is a precarious endeavor. Throughout this book, I have drawn on the term "Western" cultures, though this is an oversimplification of the situation, because it does injustice to the large variety of cultures – both between and within nations – in Western Europe and the United States. Unless stated otherwise, I will use the term "Western" as referring to Caucasians with middle class status, Euro-American upbringing, and Judeo-Christian roots.

Moreover, Israeli and Dutch cultures (and to a lesser degree Palestinian and Bedouin cultures) consist of a variety of subcultures. For example, among Israeli Jews alone there are several distinct religious groups with divergent cultures and lifestyles. In addition, people may attribute to themselves characteristics of several cultural groups (Benish-Weisman and Horenczyk 2010). Accordingly, it is difficult to provide exact definitions of one's cultural identity, even though instruments for measuring this exist. As for the two of us, it is impossible to dissect the Bedouin, Palestinian, and Muslim cultures that are part of Ahmad's identity, as it is tricky to make a clear separation between Israeli and Jewish cultures that are both part of my cultural identity.

In addition, any friendship is affected by socio-economic factors (Allan 1998) and looking at the cultural influences of social class makes things even more complicated (Howard and Tappan 2009). I grew up on Western upper middle-class values, while Ahmad was raised on Middle Eastern lower middle-class values. My socio-economic status is lower than that of my parents, whereas his socio-economic status is higher than that of his parents. In this book one could learn from the stories about issues of class and social mobility, but in most cases I did not address them directly. Regarding the issue of power, oppression, and intersectionality, the situation is a bit different. In several stories I will discuss Ahmad's status as a Palestinian Bedouin male within his own society and vis-à-vis Israelis. Where relevant, I will attend to the power differential between the two of us.

Another point to be addressed is the relative viewpoint of the researcher. Studies on culture may be performed by an outsider to the culture (the "outsider" position) or from within the culture (the "insider" position). Both perspectives have their advantages and disadvantages, and it may be valuable or even essential to make use of both (Jones 2010; Maydell 2010). In this study, these perspectives intertwine. I did not come into the Bedouin community to perform research and disappear. My friend's friends became my friends and I spend a large part of my leisure time with them. I thus have had many opportunities to experience and observe a rich variety of intercultural encounters. Ahmad's feedback on the observations was a way to balance the findings with insider information. Even so, I did not grow up as a Bedouin and as much as I try, I will never be "one of them." They have some form of cultural solidarity that I cannot be part of and there will always be things that only those within their community will understand (cf. Hughes and Heuman 2006). Accordingly, it would be inappropriate to portray myself as either a complete "outsider" or an "insider"; I am somewhere in-between, a situation that is likely to affect my findings (Breen 2007; Rogoff 2003; Tillmann-Healy 2003).

Finally, cultures differ in what they deem morally good or bad, and it needs to be clear that there are no objectively good or bad values or practices (Rogoff 2003; Ward et al. 2001). What may be unacceptable in one culture could be the norm in another; e.g., child labor, or kissing between an unmarried woman and a man. Although I initially experienced as personally intolerable some of the cultural practices that I will describe subsequently, I tried to refrain from taking a judgmental stance.

CHAPTER 2

When Cultures Meet

Having set out the idea of autoethnography, let us now turn to the subject of interculturality, which we can define as "a set of multi-faceted processes of interaction through which relations between different cultures are constructed, aiming to enable groups and individuals to forge links between cultures based on equity and mutual respect" (Council of Europe 2019). The intercultural encounter is studied in parallel in a variety of disciplines, for example in management, international relations, communication, literature, education, psychology, sociology, and anthropology. There seems to be no coherent bulk of knowledge on interculturality and the various disciplines do not necessarily build on the same assumptions or use the same concepts (Ward et al. 2001). Taking a multi-disciplinary approach, as in the extensive work on culture's consequences (Hofstede 2001), the following overview will attempt to integrate information from divergent fields. After providing a description of an intercultural incident, I will address the ideas of culture, social identity, and value orientations. A discussion of the intercultural encounter will follow this. The chapter will finish with an expansion on the ideas of honor and aggression, both endemic in Bedouin culture and crucial for making sense of the friendship.

Stories of Friendship: 'Garage of Peace'

By the end of 2011, I had stopped collecting stories, but I decided to make an exception for the following story from within Ahmad's 'Garage of Peace', which provides more insight into Palestinian–Israeli relations (including ours), and in the way in which honor, power, and occupation intertwine. It shows the societal gap that needed to be bridged in order to maintain this intercultural friendship and shows our very distinct views on planning and priorities. Telling me this tale not only conveyed Ahmad's wish to be understood but also his aspiration to be a good friend and contribute meaningfully to my success in this research. The communication around this story turned out to be instrumental to the friendship. It was important to him that I use this story, and being a loyal friend, I will present it – almost as articulated, despite its wordiness.

Almog, January 2012. We met at a petrol station in the Judean desert, on the road between Jerusalem, Jericho, and the Dead Sea, and the outskirts of Almog, an Israeli kibbutz settlement. Although this was relatively far from where we live, it was a place with an Internet connection that we both could reach. We had planned to buy flight tickets online for our next trip to Europe. Despite the urgency of our travel plans, Ahmad insisted on clarifying to me – and through me – to the president of my university, whom he had met, what honor meant for him and for other Palestinian Bedouins. He dictated the following tale in Hebrew, which I instantly translated to English.

> Once upon a time I was standing next to the garage. Then came someone Jewish. I worked on his car and he still had NIS 200 [about €50] to pay. He did not have enough money with him, so I told him to come back the next day. The next day he came with his father. I had a good mood. His father was religious. I finished the work and he did not give me the money. His father told me and asked: "What is 'Garage of Peace'?" I said: "That is a garage in which Jews and Palestinians can meet together." He said: "The peace you speak about is that you will not be in this country." I replied: "You think I open a garage in your home?" He: "No, this is a place for Jews. God gave this land to the Jews. You will only leave by force."
>
> I was so angry and said: "Listen, if you want us to talk nonsense, that's what I will do but realize that this is the opposite of what I believe. According to religion, you and we are from the same father. Now you have power, and we do not have power. Consider that we are the children of Hagar, the daughter of the Pharaoh, which he gave as a present to Abraham and who gave birth to Ismail. The story of the Arabs started that way. Let us see what you did and what we did. We are by now 23 countries; the smallest is as least as big as Israel. We had the greatest emperor in the greatest time. We made a religion for more than a milliard of people. There are 56 Islamic countries. During the time we talk about, where were you? Now you have one country, Israel. Let us think of this country. Israel has 51% desert, 22.5% occupied territories. In Israel, there are 5.5 million Jews and 5.5 million Arabs. More than half of the country's money goes to the army. Think what would have happened without American money; what would the army do? You think that God made all people in his shape, so that they can help the Jews, while you think we are not people? Let us forget religion and talk about history. Everywhere you made problems. Everywhere they wanted to kill you; from Iran, to Nebuchadnezzar in Iraq, the Russians, the Germans and more. Did you not sit down once and think why this happens? There are now in the entire world 15 million Jews and the children of Hagar are 250 million.

As regarding the money, you think you have more money than the Arabs do. You forgot that the Arabs have below the desert money (petrol). There is enough to give all Arabs for 50 years $1000 or more, each month per person. You were strong when you stopped talking rubbish about religion. Therefore, you have a modern state. In the life of the modern people, there is something you have not heard about, which is peace. Without that, we are like animals; everyone eats the other. If you think you are better than I am, and I think I am better than you, there will be no peace. The 'Garage of Peace' is part of my modern thinking and I think this is right – and I am a Bedouin."
I then asked him to give me my money and not come back to the garage.

It was clear to me that in this rare incident, a Jewish Israeli client had touched Ahmad's honor and triggered a wave of anger, which he expressed in the form of a political monologue. However, I was not sure how Ahmad perceived his own attitude and asked for clarification. It turned out that Ahmad was aware of the one-sidedness of his words. He added:

For us, honor is so important that when someone touches your honor, you will go mad and you will talk nonsense like I did. That was the first and last time I spoke with someone Jewish like that, since I think it is not good what I did. I wanted to tell him: "Do not touch my honor even if I am not that strong. Our power stems from our honor."

In the meantime, someone called and wanted to meet Ahmad at the garage, so he had to leave. Booking of the flights had to wait until another occasion, even though it was clear that if postponed their cost would go up.

1 Identity and Value Orientations

One may perceive "culture" as a multitude of discourses within dynamic fields of interaction and conflict and define it in many ways (cf. Moon 1996, 2010). I opt here for the definition of "culture" as "the rich complex of meanings, beliefs, practices, symbols, norms, and values prevalent among people in a society" (Schwartz and Bardi 2001). Participation in culture is essential in creating social identities, while notions of identity are central in the process of adjustment in those places where cultures meet (cf. Curtin 2010). Differences in culture and thus different social identities are based on divergent value orientations, as I will explain below.

1.1 Culture and Social Identity

The effect of culture on our identity is mostly an unconscious process since culture tends to be taken for granted. We can relate to cultural groups as large groups, and large groups are driven by a social unconscious (Weinberg 2003). In the social unconscious of cultural entities, there are anxieties and defenses against these anxieties. In the interactions of large groups, the idea of "otherness" is powerful, both on the conscious and on the unconscious level, maintaining a division between "us" and "them" and creating social pressure to be "one of us", and not "one of them". Though the division is necessary to create a group identity, there are advantages in trying to overcome these forces. It was proposed that "we can enjoy human diversity when we are not preoccupied with the pressures and anxieties associated with the repair and maintenance of our large-group identity" (Volkan and Fowler 2009: 4). Becoming aware of these unconscious processes in the large group was suggested as enhancing the development of the individual on a personal as well as on interpersonal and social levels (Weinberg and Weishut 2011).

Our environment influences our personality in the way that ecologies shape cultures and cultures affect the development of personalities, so that there are both universal and culture-specific aspects in variation of personality (Triandis and Suh 2002). In fact, human development as a whole may be seen as a cultural process, and therefore humans could be defined in terms of their cultural participation (Rogoff 2003). Nevertheless, cultural participation is difficult to analyze. We are not necessarily part of just one culture. Instead, we may participate in a variety of cultures, in our own society or country, and even more if we travel abroad and immerse ourselves in other cultures. We also may incorporate in our identity aspects of one or more cultures or try to keep certain cultures as far away as possible. Moreover, we can both maintain and create new cultural ways (Rogoff 2003).

Nowadays, there are few countries with homogeneous cultures and most countries are culturally pluralistic, either unintentionally or by choice. Accordingly, cultural diversity is a "given", which, despite the difficulties in its management, was suggested as being highly desirable and a condition for the survival of humankind (Ward et al. 2001). Therefore, it would be more appropriate to refer to the "dominant" culture of a nation, rather than to the "national" culture. The dominant culture is most often, but not always, the culture of the majority of the population. Next to the dominant culture, countries may have a range of cultural influences brought in by minority groups. In the West, these minorities are generally immigrants, at least by origin, but this is not necessarily true in other parts of the world. An alternative way to looking at the dominant culture of a country as the national culture is relating to the average culture. Thus, empirical studies, in their attempt to identify national cultures, have made use of enormous samples and calculated means or other indicators on cultural variables (Fischer and Schwartz 2010; Hofstede 2001). We call this concept of majority and minority groups living together in a certain society "multiculturalism". In recent years though, there has been a tendency to leave behind the concept of multiculturalism and instead favor the term interculturalism, which acknowledges the possibility of identity flexibility and the growing presence of mixed identities (Verkuyten, Wiley, Deaux and Fleischmann 2019; Verkuyten, Yogeeswaran, Mepham and Sprong 2020).

Although we are all affected to some extent by the global developments that bring us together, for members of dominant cultures multiculturalism or interculturalism may not necessarily be a central part of life. Despite the notion that acquaintance with other cultures may be enriching, majorities are likely to turn a blind eye, ignoring or disempowering cultural minorities, to keep the status quo and their dominant position. Members of the majority are apt to expect minority group members to adapt to the norm (e.g., Schalk-Soekar, van de Vijver, et al. 2008). In contrast, people with a minority status usually continue to be confronted with their minority position through constant comparison. For them, the clash between their own status, attitudes, and behavior and those of the dominant culture is inevitable and can become a source of (di)stress. As a result, the intercultural encounter, which could be growth enhancing, may as well become traumatic (Anderson, McKenny, Mitchell, Koku and Stevenson 2017; Helms, Nicolas and Green 2012; Kabuiku 2017; Torres and Taknint 2015).

National governments, political parties, and organizations play a crucial role in this respect, since they can influence people's perception of intercultural differences in order to either foster intercultural integration or enhance xenophobia and exploit intercultural conflict (Boomkens 2010; Flache and Macy 2011; van de Vijver, Breugelmans and Schalk-Soekar 2008). Until now, and especially in Europe vis-à-vis waves of immigration, prejudice persists, and xenophobia is spreading, Reducing prejudice on the national level is not an easy task but putting the focus on why multiculturalism is important for society was found to be beneficial for attitudes toward immigrants when there was high cultural distance (Mahfud, Badea, Verkuyten and Reynolds 2018). The difficulty is not only at the side of the dominant cultures. Muslims in several countries in Western Europe were found to be less accepting of the European basic value of democracy (Eskelinen and Verkuyten 2018), and some Muslims of Turkish origin in both Germany and the Netherlands were found to disidentify with general society (Maliepaard and Verkuyten 2018). Both tendencies that are hampering social integration were related to religiosity. In contrast, intercultural friendship was found to counteract prejudice and xenophobia, and foster social cohesion (Bergamaschi and Santagati 2019).

1.2 Value Orientations

To appreciate the idea of culture, we must look at the values that are at its core. People build practices around these values, which manifest themselves in rituals, heroes, and symbols. Values are the most stable over time, while symbols are the most flexible. In our encounters with another culture, we are inclined to learn its practices, which can be observed rather easily, but typically do not gain knowledge of its underlying values (Hofstede 2001). The concept of "values" is most basic in the discussion of interculturality. There is an abundance of research on personal values. Values are universal (Schwartz n.d., 1992, 1994, 2006; Schwartz and Boehnke 2004; Weishut 1989), but different cultures are disposed to assigning more or less importance to distinct sets of values (Akiba and Klug 1999; Davidov, Schmidt and Schwartz 2008; Hofstede 2001; Laungani 2002; Musil, Rus and Musek 2009; Schwartz and Bardi 2001; Schwartz and Sagie 2000; Schwartz and Sagiv 1995). National dissimilarities in value orientations were related to a variety of matters, including happiness and well-being (Kasser 2011; Schwartz and Sortheix 2018; Vauclair, Hanke, Fischer and Fontaine 2011).

Though culture and values are intertwined, we need to be careful not to over-generalize the effect of culture on individual's values, since within cultures large variances were found between individuals on the basis of factors such as age (Roccas, Sagiv, Schwartz and Knafo 2002), personality (Bilsky and Schwartz 1994; Sawyerr, Strauss and Yan 2005), gender (Church 2010; Sawyerr, Strauss and Yan 2005; Schwartz and Rubel 2005; Struch, Schwartz and van der Kloot 2002), and socio-economic status (Vauclair et al. 2011). Despite a long history of the study of values among social scientists, we do not have a clear view of values (Bachika and Schulz 2011). Many aspects, especially the link between individual and national (country-level) values, requires more investigation (Knafo, Roccas and Sagiv 2011; Schwartz 2011).

Much of the behavior people find strange and hard to deal with when meeting those from a foreign culture may be accounted for by their divergent value orientations. There are several classifications of value orientations, so-called cultural dimensions, that can contribute to the understanding of the challenges and opportunities in intercultural encounters (Samovar et al. 2009). I will briefly touch on four of the most well-known classification systems, namely those by Kluckhohn and Strodtbeck, Hall and Hall, Inglehart, Schwartz, and refer to their relevance in the realm of the friendship portrayed here. Afterward, I expand on Hofstede's theory, which provides the theoretical frame of this study.

One of the earliest classifications of value orientations was developed in the 1950s by the American anthropologist Florence Kluckhohn and the social psychologist Fred Strodtbeck (Samovar et al. 2009). They saw cultures as situated on five cultural dimensions. (1) Human nature was considered to be basically evil, basically good, or a mixture of both. (2) The relationship between the person and nature was described as humans being subject to nature, in cooperation with nature or controlling nature. (3) Time orientation was seen as toward the past, toward the present, or toward the future. (4) Activity orientation was delineated as being, being-in-becoming, or doing. (5) Social relationships were depicted as authoritarian, group oriented, or individualistic. Later classifications incorporated parts of these dimensions. We can find dissimilarities on all these dimensions between Bedouin, Dutch, and Israeli cultures. Especially relevant for this study are the differences in social relationships, and orientation in time and activity. In line with the culture in which I grew up, my orientation is individualistic, directed to the future, and primarily toward doing. As I will explain later, my friend emphasizes collectivism, and focuses on the present, primarily on being.

The American anthropologist Edward Hall has proposed several cultural dimensions (Hall 1970). Two of these dimensions are most relevant in the studied friendship. The first is the differentiation between high-context and low-context cultures. In low-context cultures the meaning of provided information is in the information itself. In high-context cultures the meaning of the information is dependent on the context. Stated otherwise, in low context, the message is in the text; in high context, the message is between the lines. The second differentiation concerns monochronic and polychronic time. Briefly, in monochronic cultures people tend to value orderliness, do one thing at a time, and take commitments seriously; in polychronic cultures people tend to multitask, change plans easily, and put emphasis on relationships. Dominant Euro-American cultures (my background) are low-context cultures and follow monochronic time. In contrast, dominant Latin and Middle Eastern cultures (the latter being Ahmad's background) are high context and follow polychronic time.

The American political scientist Ronald Inglehart has studied cultures since the 1970s. He is director of the World Values Survey, a global network of social scientists who have carried out representative national surveys of the populations of over 80 societies. Inglehart (n.d., 2006) mapped countries on two main dimensions, traditional values versus secular/rational values, and survival values versus self-expression values. Inglehart (2006) found an increasing tendency in advanced societies toward values of self-expression because of their growing wealth. Along these two cultural dimensions, eight cultural groups of countries were identified: Confucian, Ex-Communist, Catholic Europe, Protestant Europe, English Speaking, Latin America, South-Asia, and Africa. He did not mention the Middle East, but according to the data, Egypt and Jordan were grouped together with Africa, while Israel was situated between the Ex-Communist countries and Catholic Europe. Looking at the discrepancy between us, clearly Ahmad is driven primarily by traditional values and survival, whereas I am driven mostly by secular/rational values and self-expression.

The Israeli social psychologist Shalom Schwartz has studied personal values since the 1980s in over 70 countries, and in the last decade his work was incorporated in the European Social Survey. He initially was concerned with values on the individual level and only later started to study the country level (Schwartz 2011). He put forward 10 types of universal values: achievement, benevolence, conformity, hedonism, power, security, self-direction, stimulation, tradition, and universalism (Schwartz 1992), which were subsequently refined into 19 basic human values (Schwartz 2017). He also provided a map of values on the country level (Schwartz 2006), which is more sophisticated than the one suggested by Inglehart. Measured with the widely used Schwartz Value Survey, value orientations showed substantial structural similarity across countries (Fischer, Vauclair, Fontaine and Schwartz 2010). Schwartz depicts 3 cultural dimensions in his map of value orientations. The first dimension, autonomy versus embeddedness, refers to the relationship between the person and the group. The second dimension, egalitarianism versus hierarchy, refers to how one guarantees that people behave in a responsible manner preserving the social fabric. The third dimension, harmony versus mastery, refers to how people relate to their environment. The three dimensions were replicated in a study that added a dimension of "self-fulfilled connectedness", referring to values that represent profound attachment to others as well as attributes of self-fulfillment (Vauclair et al. 2011). It needs to be noted that there is significant overlap between Inglehart's traditional/secular-rational dimension and Schwartz's autonomy/embeddedness dimension and between Inglehart's survival/self-expression dimension and both Schwartz's autonomy/embeddedness and egalitarianism/hierarchy dimensions (Schwartz 2006). When aligned on Schwartz's cultural dimensions, seven transnational cultural groupings can be identified: West Europe, English-speaking, Latin America, East Europe, South Asia, Confucian influenced, and Africa and Middle East (Schwartz 2006). Socio-economic, political, and demographic factors were suggested to give rise to national differences on these dimensions. These country groupings are highly – but not fully – similar to those found by Inglehart. The friendship, as will be addressed later, manifests the diversity as follows: Ahmad views himself as embedded in his community, while I see myself as primarily autonomous. He looks at society in a hierarchical way, while I am more inclined to see people as equal. He is mostly involved with survival, while I am more concerned with self-expression.

Last but not least, the Dutch social psychologist and anthropologist Geert Hofstede (Hofstede 2001) compared over 70 countries and regions in a continuing analysis of personal values. The research started in the 1970s and is based on surveys presented to IBM employees at all levels. In a later stage, he added data from people with other backgrounds. Using several measures, Hofstede found four dimensions that differentiate among cultures. He viewed these dimensions as independent, unlike the dimensions in the previously mentioned classifications. Hofstede ranked all investigated countries and regions for each of the dimensions and thus created four indices. He emphasized that generalization regarding these indices must be done with caution. The classification has received a good deal of criticism. Among other things, it was suggested that surveys may not be the best way to learn about values, that it is questionable to what extent one can learn from IBM's sales and engineering personnel about values of a nation, and that the study identified national cultures while disregarding subcultures. Also, some claim that his findings are outdated and that about four decades after the original study national differences on cultural dimensions may be less pronounced (Eringa, Caudron, Rieck, Xie and Gerhardt 2015). Moreover, it was proposed that Hofstede's classification may not be the most useful among the various theories, and that Schwartz's theory may be preferred, at least in some settings (Hsu, Woodside and Marshall 2013). Still, Hofstede's classification is the best known and most used of the cultural classification systems until today.

Hofstede's cultural dimensions are as follows: "Power distance" relates to the extent to which the less powerful members of organizations and institutions (like the family) accept and expect that power is distributed unequally. "Individualism" versus its opposite, collectivism, concerns the degree to which individuals are integrated into groups. "Masculinity" versus its opposite, femininity, refers to the distribution of roles between the genders. Finally, "uncertainty avoidance" deals with a society's tolerance for uncertainty and ambiguity. Later, he added two more dimensions: "long-term orientation", referring to values such as thrift and perseverance (Minkov and Hofstede 2011), and "indulgence versus restraint", referring to the allowance or suppression of needs like enjoyment of life and having fun (Hofstede n.d.-b). Since these additional dimensions were studied only in part of the world and not in all cultures relevant in the present study, I relate only to the original four dimensions.

Hofstede (2001) cited a host of research studies that used his indices and linked the dimensions to an immense number of variables. Among these variables are: attitudes toward a range of topics, satisfaction with personal or national issues, subjective well-being, emotional expression, conflict handling, and preference for certain pastimes. His findings were used in many academic fields, mostly in quantitative research, but he suggested that his work may be a base for qualitative research as well. His work is easily accessible (Hofstede n.d.-a) and was replicated in recent years (Beugelsdijk, Maseland and van Hoorn 2015; Minkov and Hofstede 2011, 2014a, 2014b) Though a huge comparison of values among consumers in 52 countries found an empirical base for the dimension of individualism, but not for masculinity–femininity (Minkov et al. 2019), several researchers have emphasized the continuing theoretic relevance of Hofstede's theory (Venkateswaran and Ojha 2019; Zainuddin, Yasin, Arif and Abdul Hamid 2018).

When we compare the cultural dimensions as suggested by Hofstede with those suggested by Schwartz (on the country level), we could postulate that Hofstede's dimension of individualism–collectivism is comparable with Schwartz's dimension of autonomy versus embeddedness. Hofstede's dimension of power distance is comparable with Schwartz's dimension of egalitarianism versus hierarchy. Furthermore, Hofstede's dimension of masculinity-femininity could be compared to Schwartz's dimension of harmony versus mastery (Hsu, Woodside and Marshall 2013). Hofstede's dimension of uncertainty avoidance compares less well with other theories. Part 2 of this book devotes a chapter to each of these value orientations, describing topic by topic how the cultural divergence between Ahmad and me affects the friendship.

2   The Intercultural Encounter

Until this point I have addressed aspects of cultures; now I will focus on situations in which cultures meet. People meet other cultures and value orientations when leaving one's country, as do tourists, immigrants, refugees, international students, and expatriates. People also may encounter divergent cultures within their own country (Ward et al. 2001). On top of this, there are increasingly more possibilities to virtual intercultural encounters both in work settings (Gibson and Manuel 2003; Hardin et al. 2007) and for leisure (Seder and Oishi 2009; Wimmer and Lewis 2010). The interaction between culturally diverse individuals is highly complex and the cultural discrepancy in the interaction asks for the creation of new forms of meaning and strategies of identification through processes of negotiation (Bhabha 1994). The intercultural encounter can be explored from different perspectives. Here I confine myself to the aspects of the encounter most relevant for this study, which are communication and conflict.

2.1   *Intercultural Communication*

A chief issue in the intercultural encounter is communication, since ways of communication are highly influenced by culture. Effective communication with people of other cultures requires "cultural intelligence", a combination of emotional/motivational aspects, culture- specific knowledge and other cognitive aspects, and cross-cultural behavioral skills, part of which can be learned (Earley and Ang 2003; Thomas et al. 2008). Language is the most clearly recognizable part of culture and most crucial in the intercultural encounter (Hofstede 2001). But people come to the intercultural encounter with divergent knowledge of one or more languages. Thus, command of language adds to the power differential that is present in the intercultural encounter (Thurlow 2010). Another issue that may hamper communication is anxiety, which is likely to be present in intercultural contact, especially when cultural communication skills are inadequate. Several studies referred to the need to reduce anxiety to achieve effective intercultural communication (Florack, Rohmann, Palcu and Mazziotta 2014; Khatimah and Kusuma 2019; Presbitero and Attar 2018). The importance of both language and communication skills in order to bridge cultural dissimilarities was documented widely (Samovar et al. 2009; Ward et al. 2001).

Cultures are divergent in their accepted ways of communication on (at least) two dimensions: directness and expression of emotions. Differences in directness refer to the idea of expressing verbally what one thinks in a direct and open way and/or expressing oneself in an indirect way, such as in one's posture or behavior. Dissimilarities in emotional expressiveness refer to the degree in which emotions are openly expressed (and perceived as relevant). A theoretical framework for understanding variation in conflict resolution styles was proposed based on high/low levels of directness and high/low levels of emotional expressiveness: (1) discussion style (direct and emotionally restrained), (2) engagement style (direct and emotionally expressive), (3) accommodation style (indirect and emotionally restrained), and (4) dynamic style (indirect and emotionally expressive)(Hammer 2005). Thus, in the Netherlands, politeness in conversation would include not interrupting the other speaker, while in Latin cultures digression from the main issue would be seen as a form of politeness (Ulijn 1995).

Communication styles in individualistic cultures and collectivistic cultures are dissimilar. A study on subjects from a variety of countries showed that low-context (mostly Western) cultures have a tendency to emphasize direct and explicit communication, while high-context (mostly Eastern) cultures have a preference for indirect and implicit communication (Adair and Brett 2005). Thus, nonverbal expression was found to be more common in collectivist cultures (van de Vijver 2017). Differently said, in individualistic cultures people tend to rely on the use of words to convey meaning, whereas in collectivistic cultures people do not rely on language alone for communication. Tone of voice, timing, facial expressions, and behaving in ways considered acceptable in the society are major means of expression (Anderson and Hiltz 2001). Hence, in Arabic (the language) and Arab cultures the way things are said, the emotional quality, and the created picture are more important than specific and exact information (Zaharna 1995).

Regarding emotional expression, universality of certain facial expressions of emotion shows that the emotional system is biologically based (Matsumoto and Hwang 2019). However, there also is a cultural aspect in the way we communicate emotions. It seems that cultural-value orientations exert a stronger influence on nonverbal as compared to verbal expressions of emotion (Wong, Bond and Rodriguez Mosquera 2008). Thus, individualism was positively associated with higher expressivity norms in general, in particular for positive emotions (Matsumoto et al. 2008). Furthermore, a study comparing Dutch individualists with Surinamese and Turkish collectivists found that emotions in collectivist cultures were more related to the assessment of one's social worth, to a large extent taken to reflect reality rather than the inner world of the individual, and more related to the relationship with the other rather than being confined to the self (Mesquita 2001).

There are more aspects of communication with a cultural base. Thus, the inclination to agree or disagree was found to be related to a difference in individualism–collectivism (Smith 2011).

This cultural divergence in communication may produce misunderstandings and sometimes hardships. For example, in a conflict-ridden Israeli–Palestinian encounter, in the Israeli group there was a predominance of an interruptive style of communication, while in the Palestinian group the communication style was non-interruptive. When Palestinians and Israelis met together, the Israeli interruptive style of communication dominated over the Palestinian non-interruptive style. Nevertheless, divergent communication styles underwent a process of change and Israelis became less interruptive and Palestinian interrupted more than when each group was by itself (Zupnik 2000). In any case, it is important to remember that some communication styles are more accepted in some cultures than in others and some communication styles may be more dominating than others.

I have already showed Ahmad's inclination to circumstantiality in the story "About Friendship" and it appears in the story at the beginning of this chapter as well. The different communication styles of Ahmad and me created complications both in the friendship and in the writing of this book and was something to get used to. These are things I will explain later.

2.2 *Intercultural Conflict*

It was put forward that we "are all inadvertently socialized to be racist, to take for granted the discriminatory practices of our society. Nevertheless, the individual, is not destined to be a prisoner of the language and concepts within which he or she is trained to think and to experience" (Altman 2000: 591). As mentioned before, it is in human nature to differentiate between "us" and "them", while defining "us" as a source of closeness and sharing, and "them" as different, negative, and a potential enemy (A. Berman et al. 2000; Volkan and Fowler 2009). People tend to stereotype other cultural groups, viewing their own ethnic group as superior to others, a phenomenon known as "ethnocentrism" (Cottam et al. 2004; Hofstede 2001; Rogoff 2003; Samovar et al. 2009).

Many research studies found that people react to other cultural groups more negatively and more intensely than to their own culture while creating mental images of these groups. These images of other groups have been recognized as pertaining to one of seven types: the ally, the diabolical enemy, the barbarian, the colonial, the imperial, the rogue, and the degenerate (Cottam et al. 2004), all having a rather negative connotation.

General group dynamics could explain this phenomenon of keeping away from and devaluing out-groups. Groups demand uniformity from their members and loyalty to group norms. It is expected that groups attempt to protect their integrity and effectiveness when confronted with deviant behavior (Festinger 1950). In case a group member becomes closely involved with people from another culture (an out-group), this may be viewed as out of the ordinary and threatening the group identity. Ways to restore the group equilibrium include putting pressure on the group member to restore conformity through persuasion or even punishment. Another option to reduce group dissonance would be rejection of the deviate, either through not inviting him back to the group or through psychological isolation. A tough reaction is more likely to happen when the deviant person is of high status in the group and/or the deviant behavior interferes with central group goals (Wiggins, Dill and Schwartz 1965). A third – and more hopeful – option would be that the deviant behavior influences and creates a change in the group. This is more likely to happen when the deviate is of high status in the group (Maoz 2000a).

When there are conflicts between social groups, this is likely to magnify the individual's awareness of the distinctive values of these groups. Consequently, in the case of a conflict between one's in-group and some out-group, as in the Israeli–Palestinian conflict, attachment with the in-group and hostility to the other group is likely to increase (Sagie, Kantor, Elizur and Barhoum 2005).

As a result of the ideas discussed above, intercultural encounters create certain recognizable dynamics. Several researchers have depicted the encounter with another culture as a process in stages (Bennett 1986, 2017; Deane 1991; Pedersen 1995), whereas later research related to the encounter as more complex (cf. Ward et al. 2001). The willingness to accommodate other cultures – whether in one's own society or abroad – was explained in terms of divergent approximation strategies. The literature relates to four distinct approximation strategies. Assimilation refers to the adoption of the other culture, while relinquishing the culture of origin. Integration refers to adoption of aspects of the other culture while keeping aspects of one's culture of origin. Separation (or segregation) refers to the rejection of the other culture, while remaining with one's original culture. Marginalization refers to the rejection of both cultures. Most research refers to the strategy of integration as generally most adaptive from a psychological perspective. However, each of these coping strategies has its advantages and may be appropriate in certain circumstances, depending on characteristics of both the original and the hosting culture and their interaction (Hofstede 2001; Ward et al. 2001). For example, in relatively wealthy European countries with a smaller gender gap, integration was favored, whereas in poor European countries with higher emphasis on masculinity, assimilation was preferred (Hofstede 2001).

Ward, Bochner and Furnham (Ward et al. 2001) view the encounter with a different culture as inherently stressful and describe the psychology of what was already termed "culture shock" in the 1950s (Oberg 1954). They explain that a large variety of individual, cultural, and situational factors influence the degree of experienced acculturation stress. Variables prior to acculturation affecting the amount of stress are, for instance, age, level of education, knowledge of language, and personality. Cultural distance is another variable linked to acculturation. A larger discrepancy on value orientations between two cultures is likely to create higher levels of acculturation stress. During the acculturation process itself we may add factors such as coping strategies, societal attitudes, and the availability of social support. Social support is of utmost importance for psychological well-being during acculturation and needed from members of the original culture as well as from members of the other culture. A bulk of research demonstrates that the acculturation process has affective, behavioral, and cognitive aspects. The affective aspects include those psychological processes involved in coping with cultural change, with the outcome of psychological adjustment. The behavioral aspects include processes involved in acquiring particular skills, with the outcome of socio-cultural adaptation. The cognitive aspects include the processes involved in developing, changing, and maintaining identity, with the outcome of cultural identity and intergroup perceptions (Ward et al. 2001).

Five practices were suggested to overcome intercultural conflict. At the behavioral level, they include listening and assertion. At the strategic level, they include negotiating and facilitating. At the level of ongoing learning, they include adapting (Glenn 2019).

In the 'Garage of Peace', as in the story above, the people involved are not simply a client with a broken car and a garage owner. They stand for two socio-cultural, political, entities in conflict. One can easily recognize the ongoing intercultural conflict in my friendship with Ahmad. Many of the topics raised above are relevant in the friendship. With time the shock effect decreased, but some degree of conflict and some level of stress as a result remained.

Although the intercultural encounter may be a major challenge, its outcome is not necessarily negative, since we know that personal growth can result from a variety of life crises and/or adverse situations (Schaefer and Moos 1992; Ward et al. 2001), from having a minority status (Ryff, Keyes and Hughes 2003), or from other forms of intercultural encounters (Linley and Joseph 2004; Montuori and Fahim 2004). I will relate to transformational learning and personal growth more in the last chapter on challenges and opportunities in the realm of the friendship.

3   Honor and Aggression

When referring to intercultural encounters in the Middle East, it is inevitable that issues of honor and aggression will be addressed. The concept of honor is central in Arab culture and not obeying the rules of honor may result in aggressive reactions. I will here expand on these subjects from a theoretical point of view to better understand in Part 2 of this book how honor and aggression play out within the friendship. In the next chapter I will go into detail about the violence and aggression that are a consequence of the Israeli–Palestinian conflict, which is the political context of the studied friendship.

3.1   *Face and Honor*

The literature refers not only to the concept of honor but also to the concept of face (in the sense of standing) and chooses the use of one or the other depending on the culture(s) in discussion, with the use of "face" usually preserved for cultures in the Far East. Although we may dispute this conception, face is regarded more inclusively than honor, while honor could be viewed as a special kind of face that is claimed by certain groups in society. It was suggested that face-related issues are an inevitable component in human conflict (Ho 1976). Since the two concepts are intricately linked and sometimes even indistinguishable, they will be discussed here together.

We may define face as "the respectability and/or deference which a person can claim for himself from others, by virtue of the relative position he occupies in his social network and the degree to which he is judged to have functioned adequately in that position as well as acceptably in his general conduct" (Ho 1976: 883). The concept of "face" has its origin in Asian cultures, but each person, culture, and society has its face-saving practices, which in many Western cultures may be named tact, diplomacy, or social skills. In cultures with high emphasis on face one can expect to be sustained in a particular face, and feel that it is morally proper that this be so (Goffman 1955). The importance of "face" was found to be related both to the individualism/collectivism distinction and to power distance. Communities with a higher level of collectivism and those higher on power distance tend to be more concerned with "face" (Oetzel et al. 2001).

People may want to save their own face but also that of others. The verbal and nonverbal actions taken by a person to make whatever he is doing consistent with face are named "facework" (Goffman 1955: 12). Facework is performed to protect one's own face or that of others from threat, possibly by avoidance or through corrective processes, and sometimes in aggressive ways (Goffman 1955). A study of four distinct cultures concluded that there is a remarkable deal of consistency across cultures regarding face and facework, though different cultures may tend to use diverse strategies to protect face (Oetzel, Garcia and Ting-Toomey 2008). Awareness of issues of face and facework were suggested as crucial in intercultural relations, and specifically in intercultural training (Imahori and Cupach 2005; Ting-Toomey and Kurogi 1998).

Individuals vary in the extent to which they endorse or reject a culture's ideals. As regarding face, honor, and dignity, only when we take into account both culture and individual factors we can meaningfully interpret people's behavior (Leung and Cohen 2011). Bearing this in mind, let us focus on cultural differences as regarding face and facework. Findings from one study, asking how students would act in certain imaginary situations, showed that U.S. Americans report on more direct, competitive, and hostile ways to protect their face than Syrians. Syrians were more inclined to cooperation and ritualistic actions to save face. The American facework strategies corresponded to individualistic, weak power distance, masculine and low uncertainty avoidance cultural dimensions, while the Syrian way corresponded to collectivistic, high-power distance, moderately masculine, and high uncertainty avoidance. As for communication with Arabs, it was suggested that the first rule is not to make them lose face, e.g., be less direct – and thus less offensive – in communication. In addition, one needs to be aware of the significance of social rituals and of nonverbal communication (Merkin and Ramadan 2010).

Now, let us turn to honor. Honor was defined in many ways, the simplest definition being "reputation". Cultures of honor are common in places where there is a lack of resources, where the benefit of crime outweighs the risks, and where law enforcement is missing. In cultures of honor, a man's reputation is key to his economic survival, and men want to be seen as strong and powerful. In these cultures, violence in response to an insult, in order to protect one's home and property, or to socialize children, is acceptable (Nisbett and Cohen 1996). Honor was also found to be related to risk taking, presumably because the latter provides social proof of strength and fearlessness (Barnes, Brown and Tamborski 2012). Notwithstanding, adherence to honor codes may as well result in acts of heroism and generosity. It was suggested that one cannot fully grasp these acts and the rituals that surround them without comprehension of the socio-cultural meaning systems that they spring from (Cohen, Vandello and Rantilla 1998).

A distinctive feature of honor cultures is the extent to which one's personal worth is determined interpersonally. A cross-cultural study on Spain and the Netherlands reported on a link between honor and individualism–collectivism. In Spain, with its emphasis on collectivism, honor was found to be closely related to family and social interdependence, whereas in the Netherlands, with its tendency to individualism, honor was associated with self-achievement and autonomy (Mosquera, Manstead and Fischer 2000, 2002a). In honor cultures, one's own honor and the honor of intimate others are interdependent. In honor cultures as compared to other cultures, not only is one's own honor more vulnerable to humiliations and insults by intimates than by non-intimates, but also being offended by others in front of intimates may lead to more negative feelings, especially of shame. It was proposed that if one's honor is diminished, the honor of one's intimates will be diminished as well (Mosquera et al. 2000). Thus, Spanish individuals responded especially intensely to insults – as compared to Dutch participants – when their family was involved (Mosquera, Manstead and Fischer 2002b).

3.2   *Aggression*

I will touch briefly on the subject of aggression. The concepts of culture, power, and aggression are interwoven. Issues of power are central in group relations, and will become evident in any large group (Cottam et al. 2004; Weinberg and Weishut 2011). Power may be used in positive ways enhancing society but may as well be used by the dominant group in coercive ways in order to subjugate other groups or individuals. Those in power regularly use a variety of measures to stay in power, aggression being one of them. In addition, aggression is often used to maintain pressure on people or subgroups to conform to the norms of the majority (Hopper 2003). It seems that every culture knows power struggles, which may become obvious by the following definition of culture as

> a set of affordances and constraints that channel the expression of coercive means of social control by self and others. All cultural systems represent solutions to the problems associated with distributing desired

material and social resources among its group members while maintaining social order and harmony. Norms are developed surrounding the exercise of mutual influence in the process of resource allocation, favoring some and marginalizing others. Violations of these norms by resource competitors are conceptualized as "aggressive" behaviors and stimulate a process of justified counterattack, escalating the violence.
BOND 2004: 62

Aggression is influenced by individual characteristic as well as by cultural factors (Cohen and Leung 2010; Leung and Cohen 2011). Moreover, aggression is valued differently in different cultures, and in some cultures it may be justified as a way to solve interpersonal conflict, in particular in cultures that emphasize honor (Anderson and Bushman 2002; Cohen et al. 1996).

It was argued that for a violent act to be considered aggression, there must be intent to harm:

Human aggression is any behavior directed toward another individual that is carried out with the proximate (immediate) intent to cause harm. In addition, the perpetrator must believe that the behavior will harm the target, and that the target is motivated to avoid the behavior.
ANDERSON AND BUSHMAN 2002: 28

Interestingly, when it comes to evaluating perpetrators' aggression, there are cultural variations pertaining to the relative importance of intent of harm. For instance, Israeli Jews of European origin put more emphasis on the intent of a perpetrator and Israeli Arabs and Oriental Jews more on the extent of created harm (Lubel, Wolf and Cohen-Raz 2001). Anderson and Bushman (2002) developed a General Aggression Model, in which they differentiated between two kinds of aggression: hostile and instrumental aggression. "Hostile aggression" refers to impulsive behavior intended to harm the other in response to a perceived provocation, whereas "instrumental aggression" is the planned behavior – not necessarily in reaction to a provocation – intended not just to harm the other but also to reach some other goal.

Justifying the use of power does not necessarily mean that people are themselves more aggressive. For example, an Israeli study claimed that Arab parents and teachers were more aggressive than their Jewish counterparts and Arab adolescents were more liable to justify aggression. Nonetheless, the Jewish adolescents were actually more aggressive and violent in their families, neighborhoods, and schools than the Arab adolescents (Sherer and Karnieli-Miller 2004). Cultural dissimilarities on the expression of aggression in the workplace were also found between Jewish and Arab Israeli employees. Jewish employees tended to express overt aggression toward their superiors, whereas Arab employees displayed a tendency to express covert aggression. This difference was linked to a divergence on individualism–collectivism collectivism (Galin and Avraham 2009).

There are studies about physical aggression by women (e.g., Weare 2018) and it was suggested that women may be as likely as men to aggress but cause less physical and/or psychological harm (Denson, O'Dean, Blake and Beames 2018). However, by and large, research shows that men are predisposed to being more physically aggressive than women. Fear of losing status and respect in the eyes of fellow men was perceived as the major concern that evokes aggression (Fischer and Mosquera 2002). Thus, peer norms tend to influence men's aggressiveness (Jacques-Tiura et al. 2015; Miller et al. 2016). Actually, it was proposed that "aggression is anchored in naturally-selected psychological adaptations – and, in the case of honor, importantly tied to cultural transmission – designed to solve the recurrent evolutionary problems of status and honor" (Klasios 2019: 29). Several studies refer to the relatively strong emotional reactions to insults by individuals from honor cultures and to their aggressive consequences. One study on men in the southern United States, where norms of honor are adhered to, showed that insulted men may react with aggressive or violent behavior (Cohen, Nisbett, Bowdle and Schwarz 1996). Another Dutch study found insulted men adhering to norms of honor to be more angry, less joyful, less fearful, and less resigned (IJzerman, van Dijk and Gallucci 2007).

Furthermore, acts of violence by men were linked to ideas about gender and masculinity (Nisbett and Cohen 1996). Much of men's aggression is directed against women, and frequent use of aggression can create situations of inequality and injustice, particularly for women and within the family (Haj-Yahia 2002; Herzog 2004; Malik and Lindahl 1998; Vandello and Cohen 2003). A study on Brazilians and United States Americans from diverse cultural backgrounds found that "(a) female infidelity damages a man's reputation, particularly in honor cultures; (b) this reputation can be partially restored through the use of violence; and (c) women in honor cultures are expected to remain loyal in the face of jealousy-related violence" (Vandello and Cohen 2003: 997). In the Arab world, where the family is the cornerstone of society, honor is central, and often perceived as being related to sexual purity (Dodd 1973). Issues of honor may turn into long-lasting family disputes, which through escalation may become violent. Thus, the urge to protect the family's honor can take severe forms and in extreme cases lead to blood vengeance (or "honor killing"), the obligation to kill in retribution for the death of a member of one's family or tribe, and a form of maintaining honor (Al-Krenawi and Graham 2000). And the threat to manhood was found to activate physically aggressive thoughts (Vandello, Bosson, Cohen, Burnaford and Weaver 2008). Therefore, heterosexual men were found prone to be more aggressive toward men perceived as feminine or gay (Ray and Parkhill 2019; Sloan, Berke and Zeichner 2015).

The environment in which I grew up valued unpretentiousness and shunned violence. In contrast, the friendship with Ahmad confronted me regularly with issues of face, honor, and aggression, which I found tough to grasp, as I will discuss later in several settings.

CHAPTER 3

The Worlds We Live In

In the previous chapter, I addressed issues of interculturality. In this chapter, I will present information about the specific cultures that will meet in the realm of the friendship and about the socio-political context. I will share just a few notes on each of these cultures, fully aware that this does injustice to the richness of each. I will begin with 'my world', describing the societies of both the Netherlands and Israel. This is followed by a description of Ahmad's world, as a Palestinian and a Bedouin. We may expect readers to be relatively acquainted with Euro-American cultures but much less with the Jahalin Bedouins, a specific group of Palestinian Arabs, living east of Jerusalem. Therefore, I expand more on central facets of Bedouin life and culture, referring specifically to issues such as democracy, leadership, and geography, which are tightly interwoven. But let us start with a story about a theft, which depicts how things are handled in alternative ways in Bedouin society. The story exemplifies several of the ideas that I will develop in the last section of this chapter.

Stories of Friendship: Settling a Theft

The Bedouin legal system is based on the concept of *sulha* (peacemaking). The following is an incident in which I had no part other than being a curious and attentive listener.

az-Za'ayyem, March 2009. I was supposed to visit Ahmad at his home, but during that day he repeatedly postponed our meeting. Afterward he explained and shared a – for me – thrilling experience. He had just finished a "sulha" over the theft of some bronze utensils, from the local church that was taken care of by a Palestinian Christian organization. The theft was committed by a member of one of the Bedouin families. This incident could have resulted in a longstanding dispute between the Bedouin community and the local Palestinians, but it was solved peacefully. The "sulha" was the end of a process of negotiation and attended by representatives from the organization and from the Bedouin families, including the whole council of families. Altogether, there were about 60 men. Ahmad functioned as mediator. To add force behind the need to solve the issue, he had brought along his heavy-built friend and helper, Dahud. The different parties sat together and finalized the agreement. The representatives of the organization had threatened to go to the police, something perceived as particularly shameful for the Bedouin community. Therefore, the family was eager to return the utensils. Eventually, an agreement was signed, which stated that a substantial sum of money would be given to the church in case a similar incident would repeat itself. They drank coffee and as part of the arrangement, and the guests were served a feast paid for by the alleged suspect.

1 My World

I was Sorn in the Netherlands, and the Dutch environment in which I was raised had vast impact on my development. When I migrated to Israel, life there added a new dimension to who I am. I will focus on Dutch and Israeli societies separately.

1.1 *The Dutch*

The Netherlands had 17.4 million inhabitants in 2020. In 2018, 53% of the population was non-religious, 37% was Christian (of various denominations), 5% was Muslim, and 5% adhered to another religion. In 2019, 24% of the population of the Netherlands was either a migrant or the child of a migrant, and this number is going up gradually (Nederlands Centraal Bureau voor de Statistiek 2020). As for Dutch society, Hofstede (n.d.-a) writes as follows:

> The Netherlands is indicative of a society with more individualistic attitudes and relatively loose bonds with others. The populace is more self-reliant and looks out for themselves and their close family members. [...] Privacy is considered the cultural norm and attempts at personal ingratiating may meet with rebuff. Due to the importance of the individual within the society, individual pride and respect are highly held values and degrading a person is not well received [...].

Hofstede's findings on the Netherlands indicate a low level of differentiation and discrimination between genders. The Global Gender Gap Index is an index introduced by the World Economic Forum, capturing the magnitude and scope of gender-based disparities (World Economic Forum 2020). It examines the gap between women and men in four categories: economic participation and opportunities, educational attainment, health and survival, and political empowerment. The gap in the Netherlands remained stable in recent years, though in comparison with other countries, the Netherlands did somewhat worse. In the index for 2017, the Netherlands appeared 32 out of 144 countries and in 2020, 38 out of 149 countries. This indicates that in the Netherlands there are relatively few gender-based disparities. Far from all people marry, but if they do so, this will often be relatively late and not necessarily with someone from the opposite gender. In 2018, the average marriage age for men was 38 and for women 35 (Nederlands Centraal Bureau voor de Statistiek 2020).

Hofstede's (2001) findings show a cultural tendency in the Netherlands to reduce the level of uncertainty by enacting rules to cover most settings. The notion that one needs to conform to written rules has become part of the Dutch social unconscious. For many a Dutch person, it is difficult to understand that life could be lived otherwise. The relative importance of rules is in conflict with the idea of tolerance of other cultural expressions.

> The Dutch are famous for being, as they call it, 'tolerant' and they are also firmly convinced of having this positive quality. However, an important element of Dutch culture is a strong desire for conformity: if you want to be one of 'the' Dutch, you will have to become exactly like them. Those who do not conform to the values that are commonly accepted by the Dutch are being socially excluded. This contradiction between tolerance and desire for conformity is mainly a problem because of the lack of awareness of people about this part of the Dutch culture. Social practice is much more influenced by the above-mentioned sense of conformity than by this so-called 'tolerance'.
> GORDIJN 2010: 217

The intercultural situation in the Netherlands is going through a process of rapid change.

> In the first decade of the twenty-first century, politics and everyday life in the Netherlands became polarized, under the influence of several conservative and populist movements that reflected a growing distrust of government and 'politics as usual', and a xenophobic and cultural conservative attitude towards migrants and migration, more specifically of Muslims and Islam.
> BOOMKENS 2010: 307

There are many studies on multiculturalism in the Netherlands, mostly on adolescents, investigating its complex relationship with variables like perceived threat and perceived social distance, knowledge and education, and contact with and prejudice toward immigrants. The Dutch were found to be slightly positive toward multiculturalism and this tendency remained stable in the first decade of this millennium, despite stricter regulations for immigration (Schalk-Soekar et al. 2008; van de Vijver et al. 2008). Taking a closer look, adolescents in the dominant culture expressed negative feelings toward Muslims, whereas stereotypes and symbolic, but not realistic, threats predicted their prejudice (Velasco Gonzalez et al. 2008). More contact with immigrants was related to less prejudice (Schalk-Soekar et al. 2008; Velasco Gonzalez et al. 2008). Regarding acculturation processes in the Netherlands, individuals from the dominant culture expected immigrants to adapt as much as possible, whereas immigrants favored maintaining their culture (Schalk-Soekar et al. 2008; Verkuyten and Thijs 2002). However, in a recent study it was both majority and minority group members who favored political assimilation over integration and separation of immigrants (Hindriks, Verkuyten and Coenders 2017).

1.2 The Israelis

The Israeli population, with 9.1 million citizens in 2019, is made up primarily of Jews (74%), of whom 56% are religious. A total of 21% of the population are Arab (mostly Muslim), and I will focus on them in the next section when referring to my friend's world. Overall, 5% of the population belong to other groups, such as the Druze and non-Arab Christians. A total of 69% of the Jewish population was born in Israel, whereas 55% have fathers who immigrated from other countries (Israel Central Bureau of Statistics 2020). The State of Israel has existed since 1948 and in its early years, Israel needed to absorb large waves of immigrants. These immigrants brought with them a variety of cultures. In an attempt to accommodate the multitude of cultural groups the idea of a social "melting pot" was created, in which "the interactions between the different groups yield a new essence, social and cultural, while the groups lose their original cultural attributes or have them considerably weakened" (Yuchtman-Yaar 2005: 93). As a result of the diversity of Israeli cultures, it became a blend of individualistic and collectivistic values, with Israeli Arabs tending more to collectivism than Jews, and with collectivism among both Jews and Arabs being related to the level of perceived intergroup threat (Oyserman 1993). In addition, Israeli Jews were found to be more individualistic than non-Israeli Palestinians (Sagie, Kantor, Elizur and Barhoum 2005).

Although Israel is often seen as a Western democracy, in spite of the above, it does not show a high commitment to the value of cultural pluralism, which is central in many Western democracies. Specifically, it was argued that the national agenda leaves no room for Israeli Palestinians, favors the culture and traditions of Jews of European and American origin, and is biased against the cultures and traditions of Jews of Asian and African origin (Yonah 1994). Around the turn of the century, the absorption of Ethiopian Jews and large numbers of immigrants from the former Soviet Union became a major sociocultural challenge. Moreover, the complex situation of second-generation immigrants called for dealing with issues such as transnationalism and inequalities based on race, nationality, religion, and citizenship (Elias and Kemp 2010).

Ethnic identification in Israel remains and is resistant to change (Lewin-Epstein and Cohen 2019), Jews of European origin ("Ashkenazim") constitute the political, social, and economic elite (Sasson-Levy 2013). Groups such as Ethiopians, Jews of Middle Eastern and African origin ("Mizrahim"), and Israeli Arabs cope with stigmatization (Mizrachi and Herzog 2012). And those from the former Soviet Union may perceive themselves as second-class citizens (Remennick and Prashizky 2019), whereas asylum seekers in Israel (Israel hardly recognizes refugee status) tend to be received with overwhelming negativity (Tartakovsky and Walsh 2019).

Regarding Israeli Arabs, a recent survey showed that about half of the Israeli Jews believe that Arabs should be expelled or transferred from Israel. At the same time, about three quarters of the Israeli Jews believe there is not much discrimination in Israel against Arabs, whereas – in contrast – about 8 out of 10 of the Arabs claim there is a lot of discrimination against Muslims (Sahgal and Cooperman 2016). This does not come as a surprise since Arabs are those who are subject of discrimination, and thus more aware of its existence. For example, Palestinian professionals in Israel were subject to forms of language expressing racism and micro-aggression (Shoshana 2016). Moreover, they found their interactions with Jews to be politicized and responded to this daily racism with silence (Mjdoob and Shoshana 2017). The situation is such that in hospitals, some Jews refuse to be treated by Arab medical staff, especially in periods of political tension (Popper-Giveon and Keshet 2018).

Hofstede (2001) regarded Israel a country with a diversity of cultural groups, and suggested that over the years there may have been value changes in this country, which are not necessarily reflected in his findings. He mentioned the value differences within Israel between Jews of Western ("Ashkenazi") origin, and those of North African ("Sephardi") origin and the Arab population, the latter groups being more inclined to collectivism. As regards the role of women he, among others, related to the pressure for dual careers, with masculine functions open to Israeli women, but noted at the same time Israeli women are supposed to become mothers and take care of the children. In Israel, disparities between women and men are larger than in the Netherlands. The gap in Israel between women and men is slightly increasing in recent years and compared to other countries Israel loses ground. The Global Gender Gap Report ranked Israel 44 out of 144 countries in 2017 (World Economic Forum 2017) and in 2020 64 out of 149 countries (World Economic Forum 2020). In 2015, the average wedding age was 28 for men, and 25 for women (26 for Jewish women) Israel Central Bureau of Statistics 2017). Officially, there is no same-sex marriage, but unofficial same-sex wedding ceremonies do take place.

Hofstede (2001) referred to the exceptionally low level of power distance in Israel, which is comparable to those of North European countries. Thus, the prime minister is referred to by his first name, and it is not rare for employees to challenge their superiors. Hofstede also suggested a link between Israel's intense national conflict and its high level of uncertainty avoidance combined with a tendency to collectivism. This combination of value dimensions is comparable to that of several other countries in which there is relatively a lot of internal conflict, as in Arab countries.

Within Israeli society there are several major conflicts:

> The conflict between religious and secular Jews, which originated in differing ideological standpoints, has spilled over to include territorial and resource issues. The conflict between the Western and Eastern ethnic groups, which originates in feelings of discrimination, has developed into cultural struggle. The conflict between Jews and Arabs, which originated in territorial struggle, has developed into a comprehensive struggle.
> SHIMONI AND SCHWARZWALD 2003: 549

From its independence until these days, Israel has been involved with numerous wars and large-scale military operations. Not surprisingly, trauma, and in particular the Holocaust, survival and glory, and especially the establishment of the State of Israel and its defense, are central in Israeli culture. It was suggested that despite major changes in Israeli Jewish society through the years, conflict-supporting beliefs and emotions of fear and hatred have remained dominant and continue to obstruct possible peaceful resolution of the Israeli–Palestinian conflict (Bar-Tal, Halperin and Oren 2010). Rightfully or not, the notion that the world is out to get the Jews seems to have become part of the Israeli social unconscious. I will write about the Israeli–Palestinian conflict later.

In 2020 the Israeli media, as well as the list of unsolicited incoming messages on my phone, show that there always is a common enemy. Benjamin Netanyahu, the Israeli Prime Minister for over a decade, makes clear who this is, while spreading fear among the masses. The enemy is mostly "the Arabs" (e.g., Fishman 2019) within Israel, in the Palestinian Authority, or in different countries. Other times, it is another country, "Iran" (e.g., David 2020), which is the enemy because of its nuclear threat. Sometimes it is the political "Leftists" (e.g., Shanes 2019), who are considered ant-Zionist, howling with the Arabs.

Note that both my Arab friend and I, a "leftist", are among the marginalized. Lately, the enemy is the pandemic "Coronavirus" (e.g., Wang, Horby, Hayden and Gao 2020), because at the time of this writing, my family, friends, and I are confined to our respective homes, though in various levels of lockdown.

2   His World

Ahmad's world is that of the Jahalin Bedouins, who live in cohabitation with rural Palestinian Arabs. I will first relate to Palestinian Arabs, then to the Bedouins, and finally to the Jahalin tribe specifically.

2.1   *The Palestinian Arabs*

Hofstede (2001) realized that there are dissimilarities among the nations within the Arab world but found cultural dimensions to be pretty similar. The Arab world, which is predominantly Muslim, is highly rule-oriented, while inequalities of power and wealth have been allowed to grow within the society. Leaders have virtually ultimate power and authority and there is an expectation and acceptance that leaders will separate themselves from the group. Arab societies do not readily accept change and are risk adverse. They are collectivistic, which is manifested in a close long-term commitment to the group, that being a family, extended family, clan, tribe, or extended relationships. Loyalty in a collectivist culture is paramount and overrides most other societal rules.

We may wonder though if the similarity of cultures in Arab countries is not partially based on Orientalism (Said 1985; Varisco 2007) – a form of ethnocentrism and lack of knowledge of the specific Arab cultures by Westerners. Hofstede (2001) actually acknowledged that the Arab world is not homogeneous and mentioned that the main reason for grouping the Arab countries as a region was the loss of country-specific data from his database. For example, if we were to investigate the issue of language, we would probably find that for many Europeans or Americans Arabic is perceived as just one language, despite the fact that there is enormous regional influence on word choice, syntax, and pronunciation. Thus, the Bedouins speak a very specific form of Arabic (Mares 2017). Variance between sedentary and nomadic Arabic is such that to an extent people from different Arab countries may not understand one another ('Varieties of Arabic' n.d.). What is more, one study showed that Arabs from the Gulf States were more collectivistic than those from Egypt, whereas both groups were more collectivistic than subjects from the United States (Buda and Elsayed-Elkhouly 1998).

If we compare the Arab world with other cultural regions, we find that throughout the Arab world power distance is valued higher than in Europe or in the United States, and so is collectivism. In the Arab world, there is more uncertainty avoidance than in the United States, or in Western Europe but less than within Mediterranean European countries (Hofstede n.d.-a). A different grouping of Hofstede's original ratings by Islamic countries, thus including not only the Arb world, but also specific countries from other continents, showed that they are all relatively low on individualism and relatively high on power distance, but rather diverse on both uncertainty avoidance and masculinity versus femininity (Pérez-Huertas and Barquín-Rotchford 2020). However, within the Arab world cultural dimensions may differ and/or change over time, which is at least partly the result of intercultural encounters. For example, one study found Syria to be more individualistic than as indicated in Hofstede's original rankings (Merkin and Ramadan 2010). Also, an Israeli study reported increasing emphasis on individualism among Arab high school girls living in ethnically diverse towns, as compared both to girls living in villages and to their mothers and grandmothers (Weinstock, Ganayiem, Igbaryia, Manago and Greenfield 2015).

One may observe issues of power distance among others in manners of communication. Arabs are often depicted as making use of expressive body language and being relatively loud in their speaking. In business, they may be inclined to a coercive style of interaction with subordinates. On a different note, Arabs allow for relatively much bodily contact between individuals of the same sex, whereas public contact between individuals of the opposite sex is not well accepted in many Arab societies (Samovar et al. 2009).

Throughout the Arab world there is a valuation of masculine traits over feminine traits (Al-Krenawi 1999). The emphasis on masculinity is more than in Western Europe, comparable to the situation in Eastern Europe, and less than in the United States (Hofstede n.d.-a). Moreover, although Arab gender roles are changing, men are generally viewed as superior, and women are in need of protection and guidance (Samovar et al. 2009). The Global Gender Gap Report does not mention the Palestinian Authority, but all countries in the Middle East (apart from Israel) and North Africa ranked 120 or lower in 2020 out of 149 countries (World Economic Forum 2020). This region has the highest gender gap of all regions. This gives some indication of the notable gender disparities to be anticipated in the Palestinian Authority. In 2016, the median marriage age for Palestinian men was 25, and for women 20 (Palestinian Central Bureau of Statistics 2017), around 14 years younger than in the Netherlands.

For the most part Palestinian Arabs live in the Palestinian Authority, Jordan, and Israel, though substantial numbers live in Syria, Lebanon, and other countries. In the context of the present study, I refer primarily to Arabs living in the Palestinian Authority, and specifically, those in a rural habitat called "fellahin". The latter, because of their way of living, are less influenced by contact with other value systems. This is in contrast with Palestinians in cities such as Ramallah who live a more modern life, which is increasingly affected by Western values.

The situation of the Palestinians living in this area is complex, with substantial socio-political and economic variance between three distinct groups. There are those Palestinians who are considered Israeli Arabs, i.e., who live in Israel, to whom I related in the previous section when describing the Israelis. Most of them are Muslim, but some are Christian. These Palestinians have full Israeli citizenship and are free to move around. There have been significant improvements in the educational levels of this group, but the gaps between Arabs and Jews are still large. The gaps in family size, education, employment, and wages and have led to major gaps in socio-economic status between Israeli Arabs and Jews (Myers-JDC-Brookdale Institute 2018).

Then there are the Palestinians who live in Israel, in East Jerusalem, who are residents of Israel and are free to move around. However, they do not have Israeli citizenship, and therefore have no voting rights. This group is either officially or unofficially denied access to the Israeli public sector because of ethnonational discrimination, inadequacy of Hebrew skills, Israeli education, or Israeli citizenship. Furthermore, their residency depends on their continuing presence in Israel. If they leave Israel, they lose their residential status (Shtern 2017).

A third group are Palestinians who come to work in Israel or Israeli settlements, in legal or illegal ways, but live in the Palestinian Authority. They are a significant factor in Israel's economy, but have no rights and can be fired at any moment by their employers, or if without a permit can be arrested by Israeli authorities (Awawda 2018; Busbridge 2017).

Then there are the Palestinians who live in the Palestinian Authority, under Israeli occupation, with all its consequences. Apart from severe restrictions in movement, thousands of them lost their homes or were displaced, and tens of thousands have been adversely affected by the destruction of their animal shelters, water cisterns and networks, agricultural roads, commercial structures, and other properties (United Nations OCHA 2019a).

In addition to the previously described groups of Arabs, there are the Bedouins, who live either in Israel, with full Israeli citizenship, or in the Palestinian Authority. The latter consider themselves Palestinian as well. I will discuss the life of the Bedouins in more detail in the next part. Having outlined the five distinct groups of Palestinians, I believe that most Israeli Jews would not know the difference between these groups and would relate to all as either "Arabs" or "Palestinians".

Let us now take a geopolitical perspective. The Palestinian Authority is geographically divided in the West Bank and Gaza. To make things more complex, in the 1990s Oslo Accords, the West Bank was divided into three administrative areas: Area A, with full civil and security control by the Palestinian Authority; Area B, with Palestinian civil control and joint Israeli–Palestinian security control; and Area C, with full Israeli civil and security control (State of Israel and Palestinian Liberation Organization 1995). Although this was the situation during the study and up to the present, recently both Israeli and Palestinian officials have called the administrative division into question. In 2019, Israel's Prime Minister declared his intention, if re-elected, to "apply Israeli sovereignty over the Jordan Valley and the northern Dead Sea" as a first step to the formal annexation of all Israeli settlements in Area C. Palestine's Prime Minister stated that the A, B and C division is no longer valid and issued a directive to expand Palestinian master planning in Area C (United Nations OCHA 2019b).

The population of the Palestinian Authority is about 5 million, not including Israeli settlements. It consists primarily of Muslims; Christians and others comprise about 1% of the total population (Palestinian Central Bureau of Statistics 2018). Palestinian culture is seen as an honor culture (Baxter 2007; Robinson 2008). The centrality of honor seems part of the Palestinian social unconscious. When honor is at stake, other options of experience, perceiving, or coping may be overlooked. This is something that affects our friendship.

There are several studies on Palestinian adolescents and students. Although some of these studies referred to Arab students in Israel and others to those in the Palestinian Authority, findings are similar. Family life is incredibly important for the Palestinians. A study in the mid-1990s demonstrated that Palestinian adolescents have expectations for traditional family roles, similar to those of their parents (Fronk, Huntington and Chadwick 1999). A couple of studies showed that Palestinian students evaluated collectivistic values higher than did Jewish students (Sagie et al. 2005; Sagy, Orr, Bar-On and Awwad 2001). Palestinian Arab students were found to have strong identities, as concerning both their Arab and their Palestinian identity (Diab and Mi'ari 2007). One study concluded that Palestinian students tend to distinguish between emotional and instrumental support and allocate sources of support accordingly; a tendency that is likely to have an impact on friendships. Emotional support was sought within the social network and instrumental support was sought within the family (Ben-Ari 2004). I will expand on the relationships between Palestinians and Jews in the next chapter.

Back to Hofstede, I found one work from the perspective of the Palestinian educational system specifically dealing with Hofstede's cultural dimensions. It refers to the Palestinians being oriented toward collectivism, with marriage being more a contract between two families than between two individuals and students showing a preference for working in groups. It positions them in the middle between low and high uncertainty avoidance, with fatalism being one of the pillars of faith and good and bad in the hands of God, while students are supposed to give the right answer without discussion. Palestinian culture is seen as a masculine culture, where husbands may get angry at their wives for giving birth to girls, where failing in school is seen as a disaster, and boys play tough games and are not supposed to cry. Power distance is seen as large, with the young expected to respect the elders, and teachers initiating all communication in class (Jaber 2015). These observations fit well with my findings.

2.2 The Bedouins

My friend Ahmad identifies as Palestinian Bedouin, an ethnic minority group among the Palestinian Arabs. The Bedouins are originally Arab tribal nomads, but the Bedouins from Algeria to Saudi Arabia go through socio-economic and socio-political change, which include colonial impacts, commercialization of pastoral production, occupational change, and settling down. So nowadays many Bedouins live sedentary lives and the term "Bedouin" is shifting from denoting a way of life to marking an identity (Cole 2003).

Seen through the perspective of Inglehart's (2006) value dimensions, the Bedouins live according to a traditional value pattern, with emphasis on survival. Through the perspective of Schwartz (2011), the Bedouins are embedded in collectivity, with responsible behavior being achieved through hierarchy (instead of egalitarianism), whereas in their relationship with the environment emphasis is on harmony (over mastery). In Bedouin life, honor is of utmost value and the honor code is central both in cultural ideology and for the individual (Abu-Lughod 1985). As a consequence, and comparable to other traditional cultures, besmirching honor may be taken to the extreme, and thus the practice of blood vengeance still exists despite the fact that it is illegal in most countries (Al-Krenawi and Graham 1997). Throughout the years, attitudes toward Bedouins have been ambivalent. With Arabic language and Arab identity having their roots in Bedouin life, the Bedouins were at times idealized. At other times, Bedouins were denigrated because of the arduousness of their life, simplicity, and roughness of character, and aspects of their religious and moral ideas (Leder 2005).

In many regions there have been clashes between the Bedouins and the local authorities over issues of land and resources, because of the former's nomadic lifestyle. It was suggested that "only seldom can pastoral nomads and state governments reach an agreement over land issues and resource utilization. While governments attempt to impose their control over nomads, the latter wish to avoid it by all means. The opposing forces stem from conflicting ideologies and opposing forms of space production" (Meir 1988: 251).

Some of the Bedouins arrived in the Negev desert (now southern Israel) before the expansion of Islam in the 7th century (Abu-Rabia 1994). Others arrived in the Galilee area in the north of Israel. In the late 1940s, there were about 100,000 Bedouins and 95 tribes in the Negev, but after the establishment of the State of Israel, Israeli authorities relocated the Negev Bedouins, leaving only about 13,000 by 1955. During the following years the Bedouins were forced to settle down in allocated towns and villages, which created major changes in lifestyle (Falah 1985). In spite of all of this, many Bedouin families have lived until now by raising flocks, a practice found to be a cohesive factor in the Bedouin family (Samovar et al. 2009). This seems to be relevant also for Bedouins in other places in Israel and in the Palestinian Authority. It is noteworthy that the tendency by the authorities to forcefully settle Bedouins is opposed to that taken vis-à-vis African pastoralists and European Roma, who have nomadic lifestyles as well (Mackay, Levin, De Carvalho, Cavoukian and Cuthbert 2014). Bedouins in the Negev have been referred to as having a nomadic state of mind, with its own characteristics of identity, time, and space, which is only gradually being transformed into a sedentary state of mind (Galilee 2019).

The Bedouins in Israel have Israeli citizenship, so legally they have the same rights as Israeli Jews. Some even join the Israeli army. In practice, their economic situation is much worse, and their social situation is rather different. For example, Bedouin society is a male-dominated society. Polygyny among Israeli Bedouins is common. Though there are no exact figures, estimates are that 20–36% of all Bedouin households consist of one husband with more than one wife, notwithstanding the fact that according to Israeli law polygamy is illegal (Abu Rabia 2017). Several researchers investigated the hardships of the Bedouins in Israel, especially from a gender perspective, in the fields of health care (Al-Krenawi 1996; Stavi, Kressel, Gutterman and Degen 2007), social work (Al-Krenawi and Graham 1997), and education (Abu-Rabia-Queder 2007; Lyons 2010; Pessate-Schubert 2003). Many pointed at the highly delicate position of Bedouin women, though some families seemingly cope better with their conflictual situation than others (Al-Krenawi and Slonim-Nevo 2008; Daoud, Shoham-Vardi, Urquia and O'Campo 2014; Slonim-Nevo and Al-Krenawi 2006). Though life among the Bedouins is based on tradition, with socio-demographic changes over the years, younger generations of Bedouins do not hold the same values regarding gender roles and relations between women and men as their grandparents (Abu Aleon, Weinstock, Manago and Greenfield 2019).

The struggle of the Israeli Bedouins has lasted until the current day. Bedouins in Israel continue to be marginalized by an inclination derived from nomadic social and political structure, by their positioning vis-à-vis the competing Jewish and Palestinian nationalities, and by their economic position (Jakubowska 2000). "Bedouin resistance to Israeli land and settlement policies began to mark the Bedouin increasingly as a 'dangerous population.' As a result, the interest in preserving the Bedouins' cultural specificity gave way to a new emphasis on the need to modernize the Bedouins" (Belge 2009: 82). "Bedouin identity" remains strong, but it is slowly making place for two different identities, that of the Arab/Palestinian/Muslim and that of the Bedouin/Israeli (Dinero 2004). Today, too, land disputes take violent turns. The case of the unrecognized villages of the Bedouins in the Negev desert in southern Israel has been in the news throughout the years because of forced eviction and recurring destruction of homes by Israeli authorities (Amnesty International 2010b, 2018; Plonski 2018). Related to these land claims, there is an ongoing discussion on the recognition of the Bedouins as an indigenous community (Margalit 2017; Yahel, Kark and Frantzman 2017).

Ahmad belongs to the Jahalin tribe of Bedouins, about whom I will elaborate as it provides a large part of the social and geographical setting of our friendship. For many years, the Jahalin tribe ("jahal" is the name in Arabic for a small child "who does not know yet") had their dwellings around Tel Arad, a place in the Negev desert in southern Israel. In the 1950s, the tribe was relocated to the West Bank, or more specifically, to the Judean desert, to the east of Jerusalem, which at the time belonged to Jordan. This area is now part of the Palestinian Authority, partially under Israeli control (Area A) and partially under joint Israeli–Palestinian control (Area B). Thus, members of the tribe do not have Israeli citizenship or residency unless they succeeded in obtaining this on the basis of either marriage or being the child of someone with this status in Israel. The Jahalin Bedouins originally lived by farming, and raising sheep and goats, but during the years, some switched to other kinds of work. They initially continued to live in tents and tin buildings, but with time, many integrated into Palestinian villages and towns (such as al-Eizariya). Therefore, it is possible to see villas and tents next to each other, often inhabited by the same families, who take honor in preserving their traditions. Around 7,000 Bedouins reside in 46 residential areas; approximately 90% of these depend on herding as their primary source of income. Over 85% of the homes lack connection to electricity and water networks (United Nations OCHA 2014). These residential areas may consist of just a few nuclear families, while the biggest have up to a

THE WORLDS WE LIVE IN

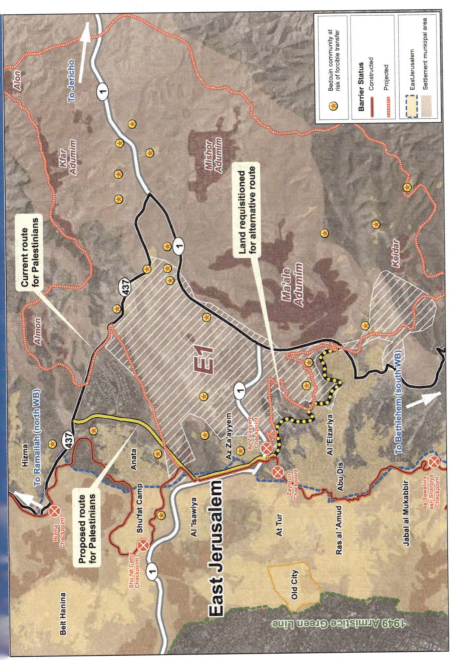

FIGURE 4   Alternative transportation routes and communities at risk of forcible transfer
COURTESY OF UN OFFICE FOR THE COORDINATION OF HUMANITARIAN AFFAIRS, 2017

few hundred inhabitants (see Figure 4). Though living conditions are often primitive, most adult men have cellular phones, many families have a television, and a few have a computer. Although some became affluent and own apartment buildings and shops, the Bedouins are considered the most deprived ethnic group in the Palestinian Authority (United Nations OHCHR 2011).

In the Arab world, there is strong loyalty to the family and to the tribe (cf. Obeidat, Shannak, Masa'deh and Jarrah 2012). In Bedouin society, the extended family is central and affects all aspects of life. Families decide for individuals on what to do next and disputes between individuals are resolved through their families. The elders of the extended family are highly honored and family stories pass from generation to generation. Families are organized in clans, clans in tribes, and tribes in confederations. The Jahalin Bedouin tribe is part of the tribal confederation Howeitat, and divided into three clans: Slamat, Abu Dahuk, and Sraea. Each clan consists of several descent groups (see Figure 5).

Pressure to marry is high and remaining single is unheard of. Many Bedouin men marry in their early 20s, with women marrying under the age of 20. Although they may marry up to 4 women, in the Jahalin tribe most men have either 1 wife or 2, as do some of Ahmad's brothers. According to Ahmad, the restriction of marrying not more than 4 women is one imposed by religion, whereas the dwindling practice of polygyny has to do with more democratization and limited financial resources. Jahalin Bedouin men do sometimes marry outside the Bedouin community, but it is rare for Bedouin women to marry a non-Bedouin. When a couple does not get along well, they may separate, but divorces are scarce and often the husband will continue to take care of his

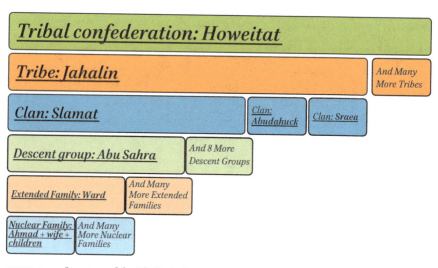

FIGURE 5   Structure of the Jahalin Bedouin tribe

estranged wife. References to family life will be made throughout the discussions of the friendship between Ahmad and me in Part 2. I will specify the difficulties of the Jahalin Bedouin in the realm of the Israeli–Palestinian conflict in the next section.

3 Dealing with Conflict

The Israeli–Palestinian conflict, and the Israeli occupation, is the décor of the friendship. As much was written about this conflict from many angles, I will touch on it briefly in an attempt to provide an overview of the complexity. The next part will relate to the situation of the Bedouins amid the Israeli–Palestinian conflict and the way they deal with law and order. The last part will relate to the *sulha*, a conflict resolution process, which is central in Bedouin life. Realizing the Bedouin perspective in this respect is essential for making sense of many of the stories to follow. Both topics – the Israeli–Palestinian conflict and the ways the Bedouins deal with conflict – may seem much apart but in real life they intertwine.

3.1 *The Israeli–Palestinian Conflict*

The Israeli–Palestinian conflict is originally a native versus settler conflict and was named as one of the most durable and intractable conflicts since World War II (Mi'ari 1999). The conflict is deeply embedded in the histories of both Muslims and Jews (Li 2019). Throughout the years, there have been various attempt to negotiate, but with little success. One major obstacle in the relationships between the two sides of this conflict is the mutual lack of trust. "Jewish Israelis tend to regard Palestinian Arabs, including those who are citizens of the state of Israel, as threatening and malicious" (Rabinowitz 1992: 517). This threat may be perceived as one or more of the following: a permanent existential threat, the realistic threat from Palestinians, the threat to Jewish hegemony in the State of Israel, and/or the threat to the moral worth of the Jews' national identity (Sonnenschein et al. 2010). Besides the realistic aspects of the conflict, unconscious processes resulting from socio-political trauma also seem to keep the different parties to the conflict apart (Brenner 2009; Shalit 1994; Weinberg and Weishut 2011). Actually, Palestinian and Israeli schoolbooks provide narratives portraying the other as the enemy and give little information on religion, culture, economic, and daily activities of the other group, or even of its existence on maps (Adwan, Bar-Tal and Wexler 2016).

Let me provide you with a few – tragic – facts. Most events described in this book happened between June 2009 and November 2011. This is in the years following operation "Cast Lead" by the Israeli military in Gaza. In this period, there were hundreds of attacks by Palestinians on Israeli citizens, including women and children. The attacks were mostly in the West Bank and Jerusalem, which is the geographical setting of the stories of friendship. The Gaza flotilla raid by Israeli forces took place in 2010, but there also were direct peace negotiations in that year. Near the end of 2012, after collection of the stories, Israel attacked Gaza in its operation "Pillar of Defense". Shortly after, the UN approved a non-member observer status for the now named "State of Palestine". In response, Israel approved expansion of housing in both Ma'ale Adumim and E-1, the area between Ma'ale Adumim and Jerusalem ('Timeline of the Israeli–Palestinian conflict' n.d.), where many of the Bedouins live.

During the period of the events portrayed, there were 235 Palestinian fatalities and 3,980 injuries, and there were 25 Israeli fatalities and 380 injuries. Still, this was a relatively calm period, seeing as how between 2008–2019 there were 5,560 deaths and 111,944 injuries in total on the Palestinian side, and 248 deaths and 5,578 injuries on the Israeli side. The numbers relate to those who died or were physically wounded as the result of direct confrontation. They do not include those who were affected by indirect results of the conflict, such as the lack of access to treatment and the collapse of tunnels, or who were psychologically injured. In addition, there are hundreds of Palestinian houses demolished annually in the West Bank (United Nations OCHA 2020). All this contributes to the tense background of the friendship.

Having provided numbers and chronology, let us look at some other aspects of the Israeli–Palestinian conflict, and the occupation specifically. Part of the conflict pertains to the establishment of Israeli settlements in the West Bank, for example the previously mentioned Ma'ale Adumim. The first settlement was built in 1976 and since then many followed; some are tiny, some are big towns. These settlements, which are illegal according to international law, are now scattered throughout the West Bank, hold a third of the land, and are still expanding. Palestinians are not allowed to enter the settlements, nor some of the roads connecting them. The policy of "apartheid", thus created, causes a large degree of suffering among Palestinians (Gelobter 2018). Through a process of social legitimation grounded in ideological and religious beliefs, settlements became so much integrated in Israeli life that most Jewish Israeli citizens seem no longer to consider Israeli presence in the West Bank as occupation. This constitutes a long-term strategy aimed at maintaining the occupation (Brockhill and Cordell 2019).

The separation wall (barrier or fence) between Israel and the West Bank, whose construction o began in 2002, is another aspect of the conflict with crucial influence on the friendship. This wall has emerged as one of the most prominent symbols of the Israeli occupation and the Israeli–Palestinian conflict as a whole and has been protested against as such (Dibiasi 2015). It can be perceived as a colonial border, deepening the subjugation of the Palestinian people. The building of the wall took many years, during which time it became increasingly more difficult for Palestinian workers to enter Israel, either legally or illegally (Busbridge 2017). The wall wends its way around Jerusalem and creates a large number of enclaves (see Figure 3). Things are so complicated geopolitically that in some places one may see a wall on both sides of the road. To pass the wall, one needs to go through a checkpoint. Depending on one's residency status, one is either allowed to move on or is obstructed. The existence of the wall by itself and the situation at the checkpoints, at which one regularly waits substantial amounts of time, in often unpleasant circumstances, and not receiving a respectful attitude by the guards burdens the lives of many Palestinians (cf. Bishara 2015; Rijke 2020).

With all of the above developments, it will be clear that for the Palestinian Arabs, enduring forms of violence, trauma, and resistance became central aspects of daily life and culture. Allen wrote as follows about life in the Palestinian Authority:

> The second Palestinian intifada against Israeli occupation, which began in September 2000, saw Palestinian areas repeatedly invaded and shelled by Israeli forces. [...] Commemorative cultural production and basic acts of physically getting around that became central to the spatial and social practices by which reorientation and adaptation to violence occurred in the occupied Palestinian territories. [...] Memorialization that occurs in storytelling, in visual culture, in the naming of places and moving through spaces is one way in which this happens. The concept of "getting by" captures the many spatial and commemorative forms by which Palestinians manage everyday survival.
> ALLEN 2008: 453

Hammack (2010) portrayed how contemporary Palestinian youth engage with a tragic narrative of loss supported by the social structure of ongoing intractable conflict and Israeli military occupation. He related as well to the current ideological divisions within Palestinian society between secular and religious nationalism. Some studies have tried to link the exposure of Palestinian youth to political violence with levels of aggression. While an earlier study did not find such a link (Barber 1999), a later study did (Qouta, Punamaki, Miller and El-Sarraj 2008). Note though that violence from the Palestinian side is not uniform. Mobilization of the people and protests that may lead to violence tend to spring from the middle class and/or students in many places in the world. Interestingly, in the West Bank there is a clear class differentiation in this respect, which is unlike anything elsewhere. It is those with lower income levels, living in rural areas and refugee camps (i.e., Ahmad's environment) who participate in often pre-organized mobilization (El Kurd 2019).

There are other voices too. Since the launching of the Oslo peace process in 1993, the term 'normalization' has been used to characterize policies that aim to recognize the state of Israel and to establish 'normal' relations between Israelis and Palestinians. A study of Palestinians found people to be more supportive of relations with Israelis within the political sphere than of interpersonal contact. Moreover, positive contact with Israelis was linked to a decrease in Palestinians' motivation for revolutionary resistance (Albzour, Penic, Nasser and Green 2019). This may come as a surprise, as in the West there may be an assumption that eventually Israelis and Palestinian would want to come closer. However, people at this end of the world have a different perspective.

When polled for the Israeli national elections in 2019, only 11% of Jews put the peace process on the list of five most prominent issues. Others, even if concerned about the Palestinians, simply did not prioritize a process leading to peace (Henning and Becker 2019). Unfortunately, exposure to political violence by both Israelis and Palestinians affects how they think, feel, and act to the extent that it has a public health impact. More than that, exposure to violence, through perceived psychological distress and perceived national threat, was shown to hinder support for compromise (Ayer et al. 2017; Canetti, Elad-Strenger, Lavi, Guy and Bar-Tal 2017). Those who exposed themselves to political violence, both on the Israeli and the Palestinian sides, were found to be less willing to support peace (Hirsch-Hoefler, Canetti, Rapaport and Hobfoll 2016).

Let us finish this section with a positive comment. Formed through the influence of historical experiences, common beliefs, religions, languages, and cultures, as in many other conflicts, identity perceptions are a root cause behind the Israeli–Palestinian conflict and national institutions play a major role in identity perceptions (Akkuş 2019). It was suggested that political action aimed at evoking empathy across the divide of identity could challenge narratives of victimization and strengthen identities committed to both commonalities and differences and thus contribute to resolving conflict (Franke 2018). The Qur'an was described as being encouraging of friendships between Muslims, Christians, and Jews (Zaidi, 2020). Furthermore, both Judaism and Islam encourage freedom of expression and being respectful of others, and both religions espouse the concepts of kindness, honesty, and cooperation. These commonalities could form a base for peace-building communication (Li 2019), in which Islam and Judaism can function to safeguard boundaries of a shared space (Mizrachi and Weiss 2020).

3.2   Bedouins, Law, and Conflict

In this part, I will address two separate facets of conflict in Bedouin society. First, I will relate to the place of the Jahalin Bedouins amid the Israeli–Palestinian conflict. Then, I will relate to the concepts of law and order among the Bedouins. In the next part, I will relate specifically to the Bedouin conflict resolution process called *sulha*.

The establishment of the Ma'ale Adumim settlement, which was founded in 1975 to the east of Jerusalem, and expanded vastly since 1982, had a major impact on the Bedouins (Shalev 2009). For the building of this large Israeli settlement, some Bedouins were once more evacuated (and compensated so they could build houses). Throughout the last decades, the Israeli authorities have created several building plans for the area between Jerusalem and Ma'ale Adumim (E-1). Therefore, most Bedouin dwellings have demolition orders against them and many of the Jahalin Bedouins remain in danger of being evacuated to make room for the realization of these plans. Also, movement of Bedouins and other Palestinians was limited as part of the plans for E-1 (Amnesty International 2012; Heneiti 2016; Shalev 2009; United Nations OCHA 2014, 2017) (see Figure 4).

There have been a number of court cases between the Jahalin Bedouins, supported by human rights organizations, and Israeli authorities to prevent evacuation and demolition of their property. A primary school was built in 2009 by an Italian NGO in Khan al-Ahmar, a place to which I will return subsequently. This village is located just to the east of E-1 but still is cumbersome for Israeli authorities as it is presumably too close to the highway. The school has drawn international attention as result of the threats to demolish it. The school was created from car tires so that it is not considered a permanent construction, making it legally more difficult for the authorities to obtain an order of destruction (Amnesty International 2010; Awad 2018; Greenberg 2010; Hass 2012; Panepinto 2017; Pely 2009). After many years, an Israeli High Court decision allowed the destruction of Khan al-Ahmar altogether and the transfer of its inhabitants elsewhere, but its demolishment was postponed repeatedly under international pressure (Navon and Diskin 2019). A pro-settlement organization then appealed to the High Court against postponing demolition of this village, which has only 180 residents (Freidson 2019). Moreover, Khan al-Ahmar became recently center of conflict, when a small right-wing political party made its evacuation a condition for dropping out of the national elections (Haaretz 2020), which would have been in favor of the right-wing Likud party.

Lately, the villagers of Khan al-Ahmar appealed to the International Criminal Court in The Hague with the help of a Dutch human rights attorney. At the time of this writing, the question remained whether this court has jurisdiction to hear war crimes cases in regard to human rights violations and alleged war crimes in East Jerusalem, the West Bank, and Gaza (Lazaroff 2020b). More on Khan al-Ahmar can be found in Chapter 8, "Power Distance".

Let us now make a swift change of focus. The Jahalin Bedouins are not used to going to national or international courts, as their way of dealing with conflict and their notions of law and order are distinct from Western ways of dealing with conflict and concepts like police and justice. The earlier story on settling a theft was an issue not just between individuals, but between the Jahalin Bedouins and the small Christian community of al-Eizariya, which comprises of a combination of local Palestinians and foreigners, and with whom the Bedouins usually get along well. This and many of the stories to follow show the dissimilarity in attitude toward law and order between the Bedouins and Western cultures. I will explain a bit more about this subject.

Having been in the last hundred years under continually changing national rule, specifically and respectively Turkish, British, Jordanian, Israeli, and Palestinian rule, the Jahalin Bedouins are not especially concerned with national laws. With little law enforcement, the various systems of law did not get a grip on much of the Palestinian population outside the major towns. The Palestinian legal system – the official legal environment of most of the Jahalin Bedouins – is relatively weak and centralized (Frisch and Hofnung 2007). It also is politically manipulated, leaving many Palestinians without adequate access to justice (Kelly 2005).

For an ignorant outsider, life among the Bedouins may seem to be without law and order, but this is not the case. The Bedouins have their own legal system, which dates to pre-modern times. Bedouin law is an institutional system, operating differently from legal systems common in the West. It emphasizes relationships highly, functions through the families, and receives its power from Bedouin tradition, as well as from the ineffectiveness of the national legal system. In Bedouin life there is heavy family pressure to behave according to accepted norms as prescribed by Bedouin law.

Consequently, Jahalin Bedouins will only rarely turn to the national authorities in cases of crime or conflict but will try to work things out through the (Bedouin) tribal system. Even after filing a complaint with the Palestinian police, the parties may opt to solve the issue according to Bedouin law. In rural places in the Palestinian Authority, non-Bedouins also follow Bedouin law, but because of weaker family ties, Bedouin law is less effective among non-Bedouins. In 2014, over 12,000 cases were submitted to tribal courts (Palestinian Central Bureau of Statistics 2015). The number of cases dealt with through

Bedouin law is presumably much higher, since in most cases no official complaint is filed. According to Bedouin law, one resolves disputes between individuals or families through a *sulha*, a process that will be explained in the next section. *Sulha* agreements are taken into account – at least to some extent – also in circumstances in which a case reaches an Israeli court (Tsafrir 2006). The result of all this is that now three legal systems operate side by side in the Palestinian Authority, which are tribal (Bedouin) law, Islamic law, and statutory law (Welchman 2009).

Central in Bedouin society are the sheiks. Sheikhs are the elderly, the wise men within the Bedouin tribes, and often the heads of the families. The sheikh takes a leadership role in the Jahalin community and his position is highly honored by Bedouins as well as other Palestinians. The sheikh functions as counselor and advisor for individuals, and as judge, mediator, and sometimes police officer in disputes between families and clans. Until recently, each clan could have several sheikhs and "sheikh" was not an official title.

From a governmental position, this situation was inefficient and created tension between the families. Therefore, the Palestinian Authority started a process of democratization. As my friend informed me, they created a position of "elected" sheikh. Apart from the above-mentioned functions, the elected sheikh became the contact person for the Palestinian Authority. In the present situation the former type of sheikh continues to exist next to the "new" sheikh. The sheikhs act in line with Bedouin law.

The Jahalin tribe in the Jerusalem area has circa 3,000 Bedouins with voting rights; these are the men from the age of 18 upwards. Women are not allowed to participate in voting, nor can they be elected. The members of each of the descent groups in the Jahalin tribe elect a representative for the council of families. The two descent groups that are least strong (as based on their property, wealth, level of education, size, and other aspects of status) do not have their own representative, whereas the two strongest descent groups have two representatives each. The council then chooses the next sheikh among themselves. The task of the council members is to support the sheikh and to solve issues that occur within their own family. The sheikh receives a modest salary from the Palestinian Authority, which is barely enough to cover the basic costs of living. In the first Jahalin council elections, in 2008, about 1.200 men participated, who elected a council of 11. The council nominated a woman to consult on women-related affairs; a matter perceived as a progressive step in the community. For the sake of family honor, this woman cannot participate in the council's gatherings.

Ahmad was one of the two representatives of the strongest descent groups, Abu Sahra, which is one of the nine descent groups in the Slamat clan. This put him in an advantageous position for the elections, after which he was appointed to lead the council. He was one of the few representatives on the council who has an academic degree, speaks both Hebrew and some English besides Arabic, and who is acquainted with the world of computers. Number two on the council was the other Abu Sahra representative, who took over from Ahmad as its head a few years later. Though this system is a political construct, the Jahalin Bedouins affiliate ideologically neither with a certain nation, nor with a certain political party. Nevertheless, they may support particular governments, parties, or political moves for pragmatic reasons, which is principally in order to receive backing for their nomadic lifestyle.

3.3 The "sulha"

One of the tasks of the sheikh is to conduct the *sulha*, a kind of ad hoc tribal court session, as in the story above. The *sulha* is a conflict resolution process between the respective families of a victim and a perpetrator, based on cooperation, negotiation, and compromise (Lang 2002). *Sulha* is the traditional inter- and intra-communal dispute management-resolution process, and the collective way of dealing with conflict, even if among individuals. The root of the name comes from "sulh", which means "peacemaking" in Arabic. The process predates Islam by about 400 years, and is practiced today, with variations, across the Middle East, in Lebanon, Syria, Jordan, Israel, the Occupied Territories, the Arabian Peninsula, and in many other Muslim countries (Sulha Research Center n.d.). The Palestinian *sulha* system is similar to the system in other countries in the region, but in the wake of the transformations in Palestinian reality, it developed some peculiarities (Fares, Milhem and Khalidi 2006).

The system works as follows. Either one or both parties in a case approach the sheikh. The sheikh who conducts the *sulha* needs to be from a family of standing, with a reputation as wise and respected, and someone who "has a say". A time is set for the parties to convene; gatherings could be only the few men directly involved or tens of people, including observers from families that are not directly involved in the case. At the *sulha*, each family has a representative (from the family or someone else) who speaks for the family. During the *sulha* process, there is utmost emphasis on social harmony, and central in the process is the concept of "honor" (Pely 2010). Fairness is fundamental in this respect, though what is regarded as fair may be different in Bedouin culture from what would be considered fair in many Western cultures.

The sheikh conducts a form of mediation, which may take hours, and finally issues a verdict. Bedouin law refers to the notion of "blood money", and most verdicts require one party to compensate the other in finances or assets. In conclusion of the *sulha*, if the parties accept the verdict, often the agreement is written on paper and there is a festive meal. If the parties do not agree, they may go to a second sheikh. As I was told, the ruling of the second sheikh can be turned down as well, but the verdict of the third sheikh is binding. In the formal process of the *sulha* only men participate, but women often have substantial informal influence behind the scenes (Pely 2011).

The cases dealt with in a *sulha* can be of any kind, but the rules are distinct from those in Western legal systems. For example, the whole family is responsible for the misdemeanors of any of its members, and male family members aged 16 and older – to a distance of first cousins once removed – can be held accountable and punished. Thus, if someone commits a felony, his or her whole family will be requested to pay the price, which is not just in honor but often also financially to the family of the victim. Not surprisingly, social scrutiny is enormous. The more severe the felony, the larger the family circle involved. Crimes weigh against each other and retaliation is accepted. So, when A steals a car from B and B then beats up A's brother, so that the latter is hospitalized, according to Bedouin law it is likely that no one will be punished. In most Western legal systems, both A and B could end up in jail.

It was suggested that we may learn to settle arguments through the *sulha* system not only in family conflict but also in other fields, including international negotiations (Gellman and Vuinovich 2008). I learned much about Bedouin law and the *sulha* process from Ahmad, who wrote his master's thesis on this subject. *Sulhas* are not necessarily large and official, as in the story above. One could deal with minor conflict according to the concept of *sulha* as well. For example, two people in dispute about some issue would come to Ahmad for mediation; or Ahmad, in conflict with someone else, would take his opponent to one of the elders of the tribe. Thus, *sulhas* became part of the friendship, both through listening to the stories about larger *sulhas* and through my presence in day-to-day situations that were handled *sulha*-like. I will come back to the ideas of law, order and the *sulha* in Part 2 of this book.

CHAPTER 4

All about Friendship

We all know what friendship is, and still it is difficult to define, since friendship refers to a variety of relationships, among these close intimate relations, kinship relations, and relations between nations or business partners (e.g., Desai and Killick 2013; Devere 2014). Even when relating only to friendships between individuals, they are harder to delineate than other social relationships, such as kinship or working alliances. We could define friendship by a relatively long definition, such as "voluntary interdependence between two persons over time, that is intended to facilitate socio-emotional goals of the participants, and may involve varying types and degrees of companionship, intimacy, affection and mutual assistance" (Hays 1988: 395). Yet, voluntariness may under some circumstances be more fictional than reality, for instance when the number of available people is limited or the social constraints governing the friendship pattern are rigid (Krappmann 1998). I suffice with a shorter definition of friendship as "a valuable, reciprocal, close relationship" (Devere 2010: 25).

Friendships exist in all societies and manifest themselves in a rich variety of culturally dependent ways. Apart from satisfying basic human needs, they fulfill an important social role. The expression of friendship varies as a function of value orientations and societal constraints, whereas overall almost no behavior can be excluded as an act of friendship (Krappmann 1998). Actually, it was suggested that "friendship is a multifaceted and complex phenomenon that must be studied in cultural and interdisciplinary context" (Keller 2004: 10). Focusing on interpersonal friendship in intercultural and interdisciplinary context is the objective of this book. I will now share an incident from the friendship and then present selected studies on patterns of friendship and intercultural friendship, with emphasis on men. Afterward, I will focus on the complication of friendship in the realm of high conflict, while referring specifically to the Israeli–Palestinian conflict.

Stories of Friendship: The Washing Machine

A simple incident depicts how culturally diverse the rural Palestinian or Bedouin way of dealing with life is from what would be customary in dominant cultures in Western Europe or North America, and how this affects the friendship.

Hizma, a Palestinian town, June 2011, at the 'Garage of Peace'. It was after midnight and for me late when I intended to go home. Ahmad and I had just finished going through what I had written on "uncertainty avoidance". Ahmad suddenly raised the idea that I help him with my car by taking a secondhand washing machine that he had appropriated to his home. This was a drive of a little over twenty minutes to another village. We received assistance from one of the workers in getting the machine in the car and I wondered aloud how we would manage to take it out of the car at his place. Ahmad did not seem concerned. He took the steering wheel. He is a good driver, but I found it frightening when on the hilly road his driving speed was far above the legal limit.

At his home, he asked me to help him with moving the new sofas inside. He had become owner of these sofas through some deal and they had been standing outside for several days. He said that the sofas were not heavy, but I warned that they still might be too heavy for me. There was hardly any light and my eyesight in the dark is not as developed as his. In the move, one of the sofas was damaged – a little – since I was not able to lift it high enough. After that, we transferred the washing machine. I saw that its handle was broken and asked how he will open it. He replied that he would find a way. Initially, Ahmad had said that he would stay at his home for the night, so I was surprised to see him locking the door after we finished the job. It turned out that in the meantime he had received a phone call that made him change his plans. (I had heard him talking on the phone but could not understand.) A family member was waiting for him in the garage and he wanted to go back. I brought him back to the garage, after which I went home.

Throughout this incident, Ahmad remained relatively calm. For him, this had been nothing out of the ordinary. In contrast, I had many reasons for being anxious and concerned, not the least of them about the damage to the sofa. This had been a heavy job for me; my muscles continued to hurt for days and my mind kept going back to this – for me – extraordinary incident.

1 Patterns of Friendship

Types of friendship were described in the literature millennia ago. Aristotle (350 BC) differentiated between three kinds of friendship: the friendship of goodness, the friendship of pleasure, and the friendship of utility. Friendships of goodness, based on the idea of loving each other unconditionally and doing good to one another, is seen mostly as an ideal. Since then, we have learned much more about friendship. I will outline common characteristics of friendship, which will be followed by research findings about how friendships are affected by gender and culture.

1.1 Characteristics

In the developed (Western) world one tends to associate friendship with pleasure, and the idea that people enjoy each other's company. But seeing friendship primarily as enjoying the other's company is not a universal phenomenon. Exploration of the experiences and interpretations of friendship outside the Western philosophical tradition demonstrates a shared understanding about many aspects of friendship, but also some subtle dissimilarities. Thus in some parts of the world friendship may be associated with more emphasis on instrumental or material aspects (Desai and Killick 2013; Devere 2010). The story above is a nice example of how Ahmad would rely on me instrumentally. Friendship of utility, dependent on what each side can do for the other, is more common in the Third Word. In the West this be viewed as exploitation and not as friendship (Joubran and Schwartz 2007).

Aristotle (350 BC) defined political friendship as a friendship of utility, comprising both legal friendship and moral friendship. According to Aristotle, political friendship creates concord in society and prevents violence and strife. It could thus "serve as model for contemporary communities, satisfying a growing need for social and global unity beyond liberty or justice" (Jang 2018: 417). Other philosophers, as Durkheim and Adam Scott, refer to the relationship among friends not just as a private personal bond between individuals but also as a public and political phenomenon (Mallory 2017; Mallory and Carlson 2014; Wilkinson 2019). More recent theorists have made diverse distinctions of friendships, like "instrumental and emotional" (Wolf 2004) or "inalienable, close, casual and expedient" (Paine 1970), depending on the functions they fulfill.

The kind of relations we have with family and friends are not necessarily very distinct. Thus, we may have similar relationships with good friends as with relatives. In addition, it may be hard to differentiate between functions associated with friendship and those associated with kinship, since this may vary between cultures (Krappmann 1998). With the years going by, the distinction between families and friends blurs, and people create personal communities that may include both family members and friends (Pahl and Spencer 2010). Having said this, in whatever way we differentiate friendships, they link people and communities together in some kind of reciprocally beneficial association that forms societies, as do families (Devere 2010).

Modern friendship studies mostly relate to friendships between people in North America and/or Europe, which is not necessarily the best reference point for this study, but I will refer to studies from other parts of the world where possible. Friendships are related to a diversity of variables. Among other things, it was reported that residential stability enhances local friendships (Sampson 1988), and that life transitions – in their various kinds – were found to lead to a lower number of friends, less contact with friends, and a lower likelihood of having a best friend (Flynn 2007).

Friendships vary in their degree of intimacy. "Subjects high in intimacy motivation reported (a) more dyadic friendship episodes, (b) more self-disclosure among friends, (c) more listening, and (d) more concern for the well-being of friends than did those low in intimacy motivation" (McAdams, Healy and Krause 1984: 828). Various studies related intimacy between same-sex friends to self-disclosure, and "capitalization" or the disclosure of positive events, was seen as promoting happiness, but only when the response is perceived as genuine (Bowman 2008; Demir, Doğan and Procsal 2013; Demir et al. 2018; Grabill and Kerns 2000; Shelton, Trail, West and Bergsieker 2010). A study on psychologists reported that intimate relationships, family, and friendships brought the most personal meaning to their lives (Kernes and Kinnier 2008).

Related, friendships require a certain degree of attachment. Attachment is a universal phenomenon (Sagi 1990), but there appears to be variance in attachment styles across cultures (Reebye, Ross and Jamieson n.d.; Schmitt 2003). Patterns of attachment were found to influence friendships. For instance, secure attachment was found to enhance more intimacy in friendships (Bender 1999; Grabill and Kerns 2000). Securely attached friends rated each other as less hostile and anxious, approached potential conflicts more directly, and felt closer to one another as a result of the conflict resolution process (Bender 1999). In contrast, "individuals with fearful attachment styles showed significantly less hope, self-disclosure, and relationship satisfaction than individuals with secure, dismissing, or preoccupied attachment styles" (Welch and Houser 2010: 351).

Difficulties in attachment and other factors may prevent friendships from developing smoothly. Therefore, friendships may be evaluated not just by their quality but also by their conflict (Demir et al. 2007). Thus, maintenance behaviors of positivity, supportiveness, openness, and interaction were identified as key factors in maintaining friendship (Oswald, Clark and Kelly 2004). Nevertheless, many people maintain not only supportive but also conflictual, ambivalent, or disappointing friendships. While supportive friendships are primarily maintained because of their positive aspects, less fulfilling relationships were found to be primarily compelled by one's own internal demands or ethical standards (Bushman and Holt-Lunstad 2009; Heaphy and Davies 2012; Smart, Davies, Heaphy and Mason 2012).

Seen from a health perspective, friendships may have both positive and negative effects on mental and physical health (Bushman and Holt-Lunstad 2009;

Furman, Collins, Garner, Montanaro and Weber 2009; Guroglu et al. 2008; Sias and Bartoo 2007), and are inversely related to the sense of loneliness (Akhtar 2009). They are considered essential to human development, and related to happiness (Demir et al. 2007; Demir, Tyra and Özen-Çıplak 2018; Garcia et al. 2015). In fact, friendships are perceived as the single most important factor influencing our health, well-being, and happiness (Dunbar 2018).

Clearly, individual characteristics also influence friendships. It was proposed that both social and psychological aspects of the individual affect one's choices regarding friendship patterns, both dyadic and networks, and that friendships affect one another (Adams and Blieszner 1994). Thus, people are different in the number of friends they have and in their patterns of friendships, with the choice of number and kinds of our friends based, among other things, on our personality. At the same time, it was found that our personality not only shapes the development of our friendships, but our friendships also shape our personality (Wrzus and Neyer 2016). This vicarious effect between personality and friendship is blatant in our friendship.

1.2 *Gender and Culture*

Different nations and different genders tend to enhance distinct forms of friendship; so, let us look at friendship from the angle of gender and culture, starting with gender and primarily relating to friendships by men. There are striking gender differences when it comes to friendship (Dunbar 2018). Research from several decades ago showed that women emphasize talking and emotional sharing in their friendships, while men emphasize activities and doing things together (Caldwell and Peplau 1982). The tendency of men to be more reluctant than women to engage in self-disclosure of personal information was documented widely. Consequently, men reported less intimacy in same-sex friendship than do women, whereas femininity (among men) was positively associated with intimate friendship (Williams 1985). Men who do disclose more personal information experience their relationships with other men as closer (Bowman 2008). Though gender expression has changed over the years, it is still common for men to be reluctant about self-disclosure. This phenomenon is related to sex-role expectations, which prohibit displays of emotional vulnerability among men. Thus, two masculine expectations: one behavioral (i.e., stoic), the other attitudinal (i.e., anti-feminine) make for variant forms of intimacy between male friends (either instrumental or expressive) (Migliaccio 2009).

Certainly patterns of friendship depend on personality. For example, men with high power motivation are inclined "to experience friendships in an agentic manner, understanding them in terms of opportunities to take on dominant, controlling, organizational roles" (McAdams et al. 1984: 835). Men of this kind were found to report more large-group interactions and less dyadic interactions than do men with low power motivation. Interestingly, power motivation among men correlated with feelings of guilt and frustration within friendships (McAdams et al.: 1984). One study pointed out that emotional restraint and homophobia toward gay men provided the most explanatory power for gender effects on both intimacy and support in men's best (heterosexual) friendships (Bank and Hansford 2000).

In an Israeli study, Kaplan (2006) described emotions between men in the light of the nationalism present in Israeli culture, and referred to the central role of the Israeli army when it comes to creating friendships between men. He depicted two models of friendship among men. The first model is the "cool" relationship, underscoring sociability and adventure seeking, involving nonverbal modes of communication and physical support. The other model is the "intellectual" relationship, stressing the exchange of ideas and soul talk (Kaplan 2007).

Furthermore, friendships periodically create interpersonal tension. Regarding tensions within same-sex friendships, it was suggested that tensions often associated with cross-sex friendships – such as jealousy, sexual attraction, variations in communication patterns, and attributions as to their "real" nature and purposes – occur in same-sex friendships as well (Arnold 1995). On the positive side, it was postulated that "strong emotional attachments between men could contribute not only to enriching men's emotional lives but also, and above all, to erasing sexism, racism, and homophobia from our societies" (Armengol-Carrera 2009: 335). Friendships among men could therefore play a role in promoting social equality.

Putting the focus on cultural dissimilarities in friendship, we see that there are differences between perceptions of friendship of those who tend to collectivism and those who tend to individualism. "Collectivists were more likely than individualists to report both attachment anxiety and avoidance, and anxiety and avoidance were both related to basing self-esteem on appearance and social support" (Cheng and Kwan 2008: 509). We also know that in individualistic countries' appreciation of friendships is more readily expressed verbally, whereas in collectivistic countries this happens primarily nonverbally (Bello, Brandau-Brown, Zhang and Ragsdale 2010). There is cultural diversity pertaining to intimacy in friendship as well (Glenn Adams, Anderson and Adonu 2004; Weinberg 2003). For example, findings from a study on Arab Israeli adolescents claimed that traditional societies foster specific characteristics of intimate friendship and found adolescents' intimacy to be related to their parents' parenting styles (Sharabany, Eshel and Hakim 2008).

It was proposed that social class has vast influence on our social behavior and friendship networks (Manstead 2018). Higher-class contexts tend to foster independent people, with large and loosely connected social networks, whereas lower-class contexts tend to foster interdependent people (Carey and Markus 2017). At the same time, people of higher social class were found to have fewer international friends than those of lower social class (Tearwood et al. 2015). It seems there could be a connection between social class and the cultural dimension of individualism versus collectivism. National cultures are comprised of the cultures of different sub-groups, and consequently comparing national cultures may do injustice to the variety of cultural differences we could find within each nation (cf. Moon 1996, 2010). Yet it is interesting to look at findings from cross-national studies, or studies comparing certain populations. One of these found that Jewish Israeli adolescents emphasized control of and conformity to friends less than Bedouin adolescents (Elbedour, Shulman and Kedem 1997). In Ghana, friendships were perceived to have a more practical base and friends were more interdependent than is common in the United States (Adams and Plaut 2003). An in-depth study on five German students in the United States reported that all struggled with difficulties in friendships with Americans. Hardships were named, especially in regard to the diverse interpretation of the word "friend" and divergent attitudes toward the public and private spheres (Gareis 2000). Another study showed that people in Poland experienced their friendships as less intimate and less intense than people in the United States (Rybak and McAndrew 2006). Generalizing in this respect across North America may be hazardous since there are variations in value orientations between parts of the country. For example, the inclination to collectivism was found to be stronger in the southern Unites States than in other parts (Vandello and Cohen 1999).

I never gave much thought to the idea of friendship and thought it was rather clear what one can expect from friends until I became involved in a friendship with someone from a different culture. The friendship with Ahmad made me reconsider the concept of friendship. I will expand on the different perceptions we have regarding friendship at the start of Part 2 of this book.

2   Intercultural Friendship

Friendship is seen as serving diverse individual and social purposes, and referred to as both an interpersonal and cultural enactment (Rawlins 1989). To fulfill these purposes, people are inclined to look for "their own kind". Thus, students in the United States were found to be racially homophilic and befriend people of the same race (Wimmer and Lewis 2010). Moreover, those with high ethnic identification tend to befriend same-ethnic peers who share their strong ethnic identification (Leszczensky and Pink 2019). This is not simply a social phenomenon. There is neurological support for the understanding that we look for similarity in our friends. A recent study based on brain scans showed evidence that friends are exceptionally similar in how they perceive and respond to the world (Parkinson, Kleinbaum and Wheatley 2018). Even the friends of our friends show similarity (Altenburger and Ugander 2018). Despite the general tendency to befriend those like us, some people opt for friends with unfamiliar cultural backgrounds. I will address the research regarding intercultural friendship, first in general, and then according to specific localities of interaction.

2.1 *Commonalities*

Dealing with friends from other cultures is complex and challenging on an emotional level, a cognitive level, and a behavioral level (Ward et al. 2001). Close intercultural relationships are often perceived negatively and receive significantly less social support from their surroundings (which also was the case for our friendship). They are filled with contradictions, and they require giving up on individuality to bond into an entity and participate as such in society. Moreover, they involve ongoing dialectics between the personal and the societal aspects of the relationship, regarding the degree of openness both within the relationship and with the environment, and concerning autonomy as opposed to interdependency (Chen 2002). Nonetheless, if successful, intercultural friendship can play a beneficial social role. Thus, intercultural friendships were found to improve interracial and intercultural attitudes (Aberson et al. 2004; Korol 2017). Relating to the mechanism of improving these attitudes, two studies found that multicultural experiences reduce prejudice by affecting part of one's personality, namely increasing openness to experience (Sparkman, Eidelman and Blanchar 2016). In fact, it was argued that "nothing can be more helpful in changing misunderstandings and prejudices than building friendships with those viewed as 'other'" (Peterson 2007: 81).

In the following section, I mention many research studies providing an abundance of information on friendship. One needs to keep in mind though that not a few of these relate to intercultural friendships of students, and generalization to national cultures must be done with caution. In addition, student friendships are often highly regulated through cultural exchange programs, which may over-determine cultural differences (Harris 2016). It is also important to be aware of a generational effect. Because of global tendencies of social media and migration, younger people are likely to have more interethnic friendships than older people (Muttarak 2014; Savelkoul et al. 2015).

Let us first look at what makes intercultural friendship start. Opportunity, preference, and introduction by third parties all led to more interethnic friendships (Savelkoul, Tolsma and Scheepers 2015). Students' greater endorsement of polyculturalism predicted increased intercultural contact and friendship (Rosenthal and Levy 2016). And valuing diversity was found to be a significant predictor of diverse friendships, increasing the likelihood that friends were diverse in race, religion, and sexual orientation (Bahns 2017). In general, intercultural friendships were found to be both motivated by and opportunities for self-expansion (Kristin Davies, Wright and Aron 2011; Paolini, Wright, Dys-Steenbergen and Favara 2016; Wright, Brody and Aron 2005). A few more characteristics were found to affect the start and development of intercultural friendships. A study on Japanese students in Australia named four factors with impact on their development: (1) frequent contact, (2) similarity of personal characteristics and age, (3) self-disclosure, and (4) receptivity of other nationals (Kudo and Simkin 2003). Partially complementary and partially overlapping with findings from this study, another series of studies found the following factors affecting the development of intercultural friendship: (1) targeted socializing, (2) cultural similarities, (3) cultural differences, and (4) prior intercultural experience (Sias et al. 2008).

Intercultural friendships tend to develop in stages. In a study of 15 intercultural dyads of friends (Lee 2008) three stages of intercultural friendship were found, with two transitional periods. In the first stage, the "encounter", the intercultural friends met for the first time, which was followed by a transitional period in which friends displayed various needs or interests motivating them to continue the friendship. In the second stage, friends tended to engage in frequent "interaction" that was followed by a transitional period in which there was a turning point. The turning point marked the start of a third stage, "involvement". In this stage the emerging rules (e.g., confidentiality, mutuality) and roles (e.g., the "peacemaker", the "lecturer") for both friends were better explained in terms or what is appropriate or inappropriate to do. These stages are similar to those found for friends of the same culture.

As for the contents of intercultural friendship, it is likely to involve certain types of activities. In an earlier study on the previously mentioned intercultural friendship dyads "seven types of activities were identified: (1) positivities/providing assistance; (2) rituals, activities, rules, and roles; (3) self-disclosure; (4) networking; (5) exploring cultures and languages; (6) emphasizing similarities and exploring differences; and (7) conflict/conflict management" (Lee 2006: 3). And regarding conflict in intercultural relationships, this was found to have negative effects on psychological adaptation and health (Shupe 2007).

Mutual trust is essential for establishing friendship and is culturally dependent. Within a given culture there may be agreement on what or whom to trust, but both the meaning of trust and what and whom to trust varies as a function of culture (Choi and Kim 2004; Houjeir and Brennan 2016), social group (Devos, Spini and Schwartz 2002), and between democracies and non-democracies (Jamal 2007). Diverging expectations concerning intentions and behaviors, which are apt to occur in intercultural relations, are likely to reduce trust (cf. Gibson and Manuel 2003). In the story of friendship above, having trust in Ahmad, I put my concerns aside and transgressed the cultural norms of the communities that shaped my identity, by doing something completely unplanned, including physical work for which in my surroundings I would have hired someone to do.

The issue of self-disclosure is also based on trust in friendship. Not surprisingly, in a study on Latinos, higher collectivism was related to more self-disclosure and self-disclosure was more profound toward those friends of the same culture (Schwartz et al. 2011). Albeit another study demonstrated that willingness to self-disclose among friends of dissimilar cultures varied according to the topic under discussion (Chen and Nakazawa 2012).

2.2 Opportunities for Interaction

But where do people make friends from other cultures? I already mentioned universities as places fostering intercultural friendship. Moreover, there is a growing number of studies promoting intercultural friendships among international students (Gareis, Goldman and Merkin 2019; e.g., Gareis and Jalayer 2018; Khatimah and Kusuma 2019). This is because with ongoing globalization, the ability to adapt and excel in an unfamiliar or diverse cultural setting (what we call "cultural intelligence") becomes increasingly important. Besides the formal projects, informal intercultural contact was found to have a profound effect on cultural intelligence (Lin and Shen 2019).

Students or not, younger generations are inclined to make their friends online. In the last decades, it has become easier to create intercultural friendships though social media. This has brought both opportunities and challenges. Among the opportunities for friendship through social media is enhanced access to social information and social capital, which lend themselves to forms of social support conducive to happiness. Challenges include the allure of instant gratification friendship, rising demands for promotional self-presentations, and the temptation to define self-worth and life satisfaction based on image, success, and popularity (Manago and Vaughn 2015). At the same time, there is an indication that intercultural friendship through social media may remain superficial. Thus, a social media study on Taiwanese students in the United States proposed that it may be easy to become connected but difficult to create intimate friendships (Shiau 2016). Moreover, in a Facebook-based study that examined the association between racial/ethnic homogeneity and subjective well-being among college students in the United States, researchers concluded that among those of European origin homogeneity of friendship networks on Facebook was related to subjective well-being, but this was not so for students of other origins (Seder and Oishi 2009).

One of those places that could provide the opportunity for intercultural friendship is the workplace. Though it is commonplace in the West to think that business and friendship do not mix well and that one had better keep the two separated, many people in different societies make friends at work, and in recent years, this axiom has been questioned. Several studies even point at the positive sides of business friendships (Ingram and Roberts 2000; Spence 2004). One study showed that workplaces had strong potential to create intercultural friendship and assist in the integration of immigrants (Kokkonen, Esaiasson and Gilljam 2015). Another study revealed that employees who experienced close intercultural friendships were more creative and innovative, and suggested that "going out with a close friend or romantic partner from a foreign culture can help employees to 'go out' of the box and into a creative frame of mind" (Lu et al. 2017: 1091).

This is not to say that cultural diversity at work always enhances performance. Individualists performed better when working individually, while collectivists performed better when in a group (Earley 1993). In collectivistic cultures, people anticipated more socio-emotionally oriented relationships at work than those in a Western culture (Sanchez-Burks, Nisbett and Ybarra 2000), and the importance of relationships and interdependence showed direct impact on work values (Hartung, Fouad, Leong and Hardin 2010). Cultural differences also created difficulties in communication in virtual work tasks (Fujimoto, Bahfen, Fermelis and Hartel 2007; Staples and Zhao 2006). One of these cultural differences pertains to the concept of time. Numerous studies on business negotiations relate to the difficulties in overcoming cultural variance in the perception of time (Adair and Brett 2005; Alon and Brett 2007; Brislin and Kim 2003; Macduff 2006).

From a geographic angle, it was postulated that friendship mediates structures of class and urban cognitive mapping, while creating the base for the formation of elites and the interchange of values with immigrants (Werbner 2018). Much of this has to do with residential intermingling of cultures.

Neighborhoods can be more or less diverse in ethnicity. Ethnically heterogeneous neighborhoods enhance intercultural friendship as compared with homogeneous neighborhoods, though living among many perceived ethnic minorities does not necessarily increase the probability of having friends of other ethnicities (Kouvo and Lockmer 2013). Especially for migrants, living in neighborhoods with natives enhances the possibility of close interethnic relationships (Pratsinakis, Hatziprokopiou, Labrianidis and Vogiatzis 2017). It was argued that for immigrants, intercultural friendships may actually become a bridge to acculturation (Akhtar 2009). Still, this doesn't mean that friends of other ethnicities are necessarily very different, since interethnic friendships tend to occur according to a "pan-ethnic" pattern, by which people with similar ethnic, racial, or national backgrounds befriend each other (Muttarak 2014).

In short, friendship "is about tolerance and putting up with the idiosyncrasies of your friends" (Devere 2014: 1). This requires overcoming anxiety and uncertainty. When the friendship is cross-cultural, it may have a broader influence than just between the friends involved and may function to diminish inter-group anxiety, as was found between Spanish-speaking immigrants and natives in Germany (Florack, Rohmann, Palcu and Mazziotta 2014), between Latinos and whites (Page-Gould, Mendoza-Denton and Tropp 2008), between Asians and Americans (Elisabeth Gareis and Jalayer 2018), and among Zimbabwean students in Indonesia (Khatimah and Kusuma 2019).

Bridging the cultural gap is essential for intercultural friendships to last and this is an ongoing process throughout the friendship, as is the case between Ahmad and me.

3   Friendship in the Realm of Conflict

Friendships are influenced by their political context, which in our case is the Israeli–Palestinian conflict. In Israel, Jews and Arabs (Palestinians) may meet on the street or for business, but their communities are separated. Most of the Israeli towns and villages are either Jewish or Arab, although there are some mixed towns. An older study in the mixed town of Acre found that Jews and Arabs living next door to each other had positive relationships but retained some social distance and no acculturation between the two groups took place (Deutsch 1985). This was in the early 1980s. Since then there have been several periods of war and other violent hostilities, and tension between Israeli Jews and Arabs rose substantially. Arabs and Jews within Israel are now deeply divided and live segregated lives. Relations between the two communities have worsened since 1995 and have become more violent (Smooha 2011). I will focus on research findings regarding dialogue meant to bring Israeli Jews and Palestinians closer. This will be followed by a more concrete portrayal of how the occupation plays out in real life and affects the friendship.

3.1 Jewish–Arab Dialogue

When discussing the topic of Jewish–Arab dialogue, the first thing that comes to mind is language. Hebrew is the dominant language in all domains of life in Israel. For Israeli Palestinians, Hebrew is a second language that is compulsory in the school curriculum, but lack of fluency in Hebrew makes it difficult for many Palestinians to function effectively outside Palestinian towns and villages (Amara 2007). By contrast, in the Palestinian Authority the dominant language is Arabic, and Hebrew is not a compulsory language. For Palestinians, whether living in Israel or in the Palestinian Authority, learning Hebrew may be a form of empowerment, whereas resistance to speaking Hebrew may be a form of resistance to Israeli oppression (cf. Rahman 2001). Some Jewish Israelis know Arabic from home or learned it at school, but most are not fluent in this language.

But language is not the main obstacle to dialogue between Israeli Jews and Palestinians; the main difficulty is in the socio-political field. Discrimination by Israeli authorities of Arabs is common within Israel, but Israeli oppression is blatant in the Palestinian Authority (Amnesty International 2018). Both resulting from and leading to this discriminatory and oppressive attitude explained above, stigmatization and racism became the normative attitude of Jews versus Palestinians in the public discourse in Israel (Falk and Tilley 2017; Herzog, Sharon and Leykin 2008; Mizrachi and Herzog 2012; Shalhoub-Kevorkian 2004; Shoshana 2016). These factors undoubtedly affect dialogue and created a social norm against deep connections between Israeli Jews and Arabs.

Honest and open dialogue requires a certain amount of self-disclosure, as was explained previously. However, as a result of the divide, the opposite – self-censorship – may plague Israeli–Palestinian dialogue. Self-censorship, the act of intentionally and voluntarily withholding information from others in the absence of formal obstacles, is salient in societies coping with threat and conflict. There are several motivations for people to opt for self-censorship. These are protecting the in-group, self-image, a belief, or a third party, avoiding external negative sanctions and gaining positive rewards (Bar-Tal 2017). Self-censorship seems to play a role on both sides of the dialogue and can make it difficult to become close.

In the last three decades, there have been a series of documented educational programs to improve relations between Jews and Arabs in Israel, based on the concept of coexistence and transformation through acquaintance with the narrative of the other (Hertz-Lazarowitz and Zelniker 2004; Kuriansky 2007; Maoz and Ron 2016). Studies of these groups describe opportunities but also hardships in dialogue between the two sides of the conflict, and I will mention just a few of these. One study of students argued that the readiness of Arab students for professional and social relations with Jewish students is greater than the other way round (Diab and Mi'ari 2007). Furthermore, despite motivation to participate in a Jewish Israeli–Palestinian coexistence program, narratives of Jewish youths reproduced conditions of conflict (Hammack 2009).

Several studies relate to contents and processes within these dialogue groups. In intergroup encounters Jews were usually perceived as dominant. Difficulties in solving conflict were related to a combination of unfavorable attitudes, oppressive behavior, and an institutional context that provides Israeli Jews with more rights than Israeli Arabs and Palestinians (Darweish 2010). Nevertheless, one study on power relations in educational encounter groups concluded that apart from the expected Jewish-majority dominance, Palestinians did assert minority influence on the dialogue (Maoz 2000b). Other dialogue groups achieved mutual understanding but showed difficulty in authentic discourse (Shamoa-Nir 2017) or decreased perceived equality between the groups (Shani and Boehnke 2017).

It was argued that many interventions to bring Jews and Arabs closer are fundamentally flawed since they do not deal with the actual political reality of young Israeli and Palestinian lives, which came with a call for action research emphasizing social transformation (Hammack 2011). Furthermore, others found that collective action was more effective in reducing prejudice and power differences between Israeli and Palestinian youths than dialogue based on co-existence (Hammack and Pilecki 2015). Israeli–Palestinian action research on an Israeli campus mobilized participants into changing their immediate environment and consequently their lives (Hager et al. 2011). A similar project in the United States showed strong emotions in the dialogue, and outcomes of critical self-reflection, development of friendships, and action for social change. However, the students continued to struggle with understanding each other and maintaining relationships (Dessel and Ali 2012).

It seems that the need for identifying with one's own group makes accepting the other more difficult, but this may depend on the kind of identification that exists in the group. Though ingroup *attachment* promoted desire for restorative justice and normative collective action among both Arab and Jewish Israelis, in-group *glorification* enhanced the wish for retributive justice and nonnormative action (Selvanathan and Leidner 2020). A recent study on dialogue groups found that among the Israeli Jewish students, the legitimacy of Palestinian narratives and trust toward Palestinians increased, while hatred, fear, and anger decreased. At the same time, it was asserted that – opposed to intuition – interpersonal contact can sometimes be a potential barrier for accepting the other (Zigenlaub and Sagy 2020).

Most of the above groups and projects were formed in the field of education. Moving to the field of mental health and social work, several studies were published on the difficult dialogue for Israeli therapists working with clients on the other side of the conflict; almost all refer to Jewish therapists treating Arab clients (Baum 2007b, 2011; Lichtenberg, Vass and Heresco-Levy 2003; Suleiman and Agat-Galili 2015), but one study focuses specifically on the Arab therapist–Jewish client dyad (Srour 2015). Although there are a few groups of mental health professionals involved with political and social issues within Israeli society in general and with the Israeli–Palestinian conflict in specific and socio-political involvement by therapists is growing, it was argued that Israeli psychologists at large have remained relatively silent and not taken an active stance. More than that, the Israeli mental health community's role in this conflict was disputed (Avissar 2007a, 2007b, 2009, 2017; Berman 2002, 2007; Dalal 2008; Strous 2007). A few studies assessed the almost impossible work of organizations that attempt to bridge the conflict (Cockburn 2014; Duek 2009).

Even if there is a willingness to communicate spontaneously, for example in large group encounters at conferences, it remains highly difficult for both sides to listen to and understand one another (Weinberg and Weishut 2011). One autobiographical study delineates the friendship between a Palestinian Muslim woman and an Israeli Jewish man, which started at such a conference. It successfully attempted to reconcile individual friendship with the Israeli–Palestinian conflict, and proposed that "friendships can have a practical application in changing social and political structures in an effort to resolve the underlying conflict" (Joubran and Schwartz 2007: 340).

There are only a few studies on dialogue in other geographic areas of high intercultural conflict that we can compare. Studies on friendships between Turks and Kurds found them to be positively influencing perceived threat and intergroup anxiety among both Turks and Kurds, whereas outgroup attitudes were affected only among the Turks (the majority group) and only when conflict was perceived to be lower (Bagci and Çelebi 2017; Bagci, Piyale and Ebcim 2018). A study on high-conflict groups in Iraq reported that "people who spend time within ethnically heterogeneous interaction spaces are considerably more likely to have friendship ties that cross ethnic group boundaries and, in turn, also to express general social trust, interethnic trust, and tolerance toward outgroups" (Rydgren, Sofi and Hällsten 2013: 1650). Indirectly related to cultural conflict, a study on political conflict in Spain found that only few WhatsApp groups managed to persist after someone raised the hot political topic of independence of Catalonia, and this was only because different political perspectives were respected (Garcia Yeste, Joanpere, Rios-Gonzalez and Morlà-Folch 2020). Respect for different political views seems uncommon in both Israel and the Palestinian Authority.

In conclusion, dialogue – let alone friendship – across the Israeli–Palestinian divide is extremely taxing. Then, let us now focus specifically on that part of the Israeli–Palestinian conflict that has enormous effect on the friendship, which is the Israeli occupation.

3.2 *The Israeli Occupation*

It is obvious that there is tension between the friendship and the political context and in the realm of the Israeli occupation, befriending Palestinians more than in a distant friendship is for many Israelis something unthinkable.

The occupation and the anti-Israeli sentiment create conditions in which the practical effects of the divide between Israelis and Palestinians remains almost unnoticed on the Israeli side and becomes shocking on the Palestinian side. For example, in the face of COVID-19, which reached most Israeli cities in March 2020, national authorities considered a lockdown – a measure with grave socio-economic consequences for those who lose mobility. The Israeli ultra-Orthodox city of Bnei Brak was locked down after 900 people were found to be infected (Jaffe-Hoffman, Ahronheim, Sharon and Halon 2020). However, the Palestinian city of Bethlehem was locked down by the Israeli army several weeks before, after only a couple of people were found to be infected with the virus (Jerusalem Post Staff 2020). I could share more information from a variety of reports and news items, but I believe that one obtains a better portrayal how friendship is affected by the occupation through a concrete example. It is not about a Bedouin, but Bedouins as well cope with financial hardships, live along the separation wall, suffer from closures, not just in times of COVID-19, and can be shot at. Mahmood, whom I have known for over two decades, is the only Palestinian friend I have who became acquainted with Ahmad through me.

Mahmood, in his 40s, grew up in a small Palestinian village. Many years ago he moved to the Dheisheh refugee camp, near Bethlehem. Though legally in Area A, under full Palestinian control, de facto Israeli army enters as much as in Area C. In practice, life in the camp is not much different than in other large Palestinian villages. Mahmood did not finish primary school and worked in Israel since he was a child; we became acquainted when he worked near where I lived. Since the separation wall has been completed, he cannot enter Israel and with little work in the camp, he and his family have a rough time making a living. In past years, Israeli soldiers shot both him and his oldest son (on separate occasions), from which they still suffer the physical consequences. His wife experiences health problems unrelated to the occupation. I had recently assisted him in opening a small rent-a-car business in the refugee camp, but as consequence of the lockdown because of COVID-19 people did not rent cars. This got him into severe financial hardship, even more than before. In contrast with the limited economic assistance Israelis received from the national authorities, he did not receive anything from either Israeli or Palestinian authorities. If he could not come to Jerusalem because of the wall before, now I also was prevented from coming to him because of the measures taken to prevent spread of the disease. We stayed connected by phone, and he shared information about his dire state. In the meantime, he works in a bakery, earning NIS 100 (about €25) for a 12-hour working day. A total of 14 people – he and his wife, children, and grandchildren – must live on this sum. He reported that he still is lucky, as others do not have work at all, and people come to the bakery begging for bread. He added that somehow the holes in the wall are lately unprotected by Israeli soldiers, so that Palestinian workers can again enter Israel (illegally), something that had not been possible for an extended period. I attempted to be sympathetic as far as I could, but although he and his family were among those suffering, I found it emotionally burdensome to know that they live on such a tight budget and are not able to cover costs for necessities such as medical care.

When it comes to friendship in the realm of conflict, the wall between Israel and the West Bank plays a crucial role. As I hold Israeli residency and Dutch citizenship, my freedom of movement across the area is much greater than that of Mahmood, Ahmad, and most of my Palestinian friends. As a result, the wall forced our friendships to unfold and develop in their habitat and not in mine. I believe that without the wall's existence, these friendships would have developed otherwise.

To clarify this point, I will explain a bit more about the location of the 'Garage of Peace', mentioned in the story at the start of this chapter. The garage where Ahmad and I spent quite some time over the years is in Hizma. This Palestinian village is adjacent to Jerusalem, i.e., in walking distance, situated mostly in Area C, i.e., under full Israeli control. However, the wall separated Hizma from Jerusalem, cutting off non-Israeli Palestinians from educational, health, social, and economic services. Access to Jerusalem is thus limited to those with Jerusalem residency who can enter the city only through the Hizma military checkpoint where they go through inspection. This generates difficulties in mobility and suffering. During the years, a little over 2,000 *dunums* of land (200 hectares or 500 acres) have been confiscated from the village by the Israeli authorities for various Israeli purposes, including the construction of urban settlements, bypass roads, and the wall. Furthermore, Israel undertakes actions against Palestinian homes and businesses under the pretext that they were built illegally. Israel argues that Palestinians living in this area must obtain permits from the Israeli Civil Administration for construction and for the reclamation of land. In practice, requests for these permits are often rejected under the claim that they do not fulfill the necessary requirements, forcing Palestinians to build without permits to keep up with population growth (The Applied Research Institute 2012). Not surprisingly, unrest in Hizma, with occasional stone throwing, has become common over the years, as are closures of the village by the Israeli army (B'Tselem – The Israeli Information Center for Human Rights in the Occupied Territories 2015).

In addition, there are big signs at the entrances of Palestinian villages around Jerusalem, like Hizma and Ahmad's home village az-Za'ayyem, requesting that Israeli cars not be taken for repairs to the – much cheaper – garages in those villages. As a result, the garage is often closed, or even if open, there are no cars to repair and the workers do not have money to bring to their families. Occasionally, it is impossible for me to reach the garage or Ahmad, as the roads are blocked. Moreover, I have been present at raids by Israeli authorities on the garage and other shops in Hizma. One can imagine that in Hizma sentiment toward Israelis is ambivalent, as they are perceived both as customers and occupiers.

In the year of the story about the 'Garage of Peace' at the start of this chapter and still for many years, we had to make an enormous detour to take Ahmad from Hizma to his home in az-Za'ayyem on the other side of Jerusalem, since without an Israeli entrance permit, he was not allowed to pass through Jerusalem. In 2019, a direct road between the villages was opened, which was dubbed the "apartheid road", as it has two parts, separated by a wall (Giovannetti 2019; Hasson 2019); one side for Palestinians, like Ahmad, and one side for Israelis, like me. This road shortens the way between the villages substantially, and this I believe is the only positive change in Palestinian mobility that has taken place in this area in the last decade. But still there is a problem for us to drive together. As he will be in danger of arrest taking the Israeli side, I join him and risk taking the Palestinian side, in the hope that in case of trouble my Dutch citizenship will rescue me. Lately, the Israeli government approved a continuation of this road to the mostly Bedouin town of al-Eizariya. This will improve mobility among Bedouins and other Palestinians even more, but the reason for the construction of the roads does not seem to be reduction of suffering, but so that Israeli (Jewish) housing plans for E-1 can start without hindrance from Palestinians (Lazaroff 2020a).

In reference to the story above, most of my Jewish Israeli friends would not dare going to Hizma or other Palestinian villages. My presence there makes many an Israeli Jew frown; let alone me taking the washing machine. While driving with Ahmad during the night from Hizma to his home in az-Zaʿayyem, I did something that in the present tense political atmosphere is considered by most Israelis to be out of the question. But for the friendship to thrive, I had to disregard what was expected of me by my Israeli friends, at least to some extent. Having said this, the main point in bringing this story here is that it exemplifies the divergence between my friend and me, on all four of the cultural dimensions to be addressed in Part 2 of this book: collectivism versus individualism, uncertainty avoidance, masculinity and femininity, and power distance.

PART 2

Four Cultural Dimensions

Introduction to Part 2

In Part 1, I explained the topical area, relevance, scope, and methodology of this book. I presented a literature study on intercultural issues and on friendship and provided background information on the various cultures involved, as well as on the Israeli–Palestinian conflict in which the friendship comes about. Part 2 continues with a subjective description of my experience of the friendship and the discussion of Hofstede's four cultural dimensions: individualism versus collectivism (Chapter 5), uncertainty avoidance (Chapter 6), masculinity versus femininity (Chapter 7), and power distance (Chapter 8).

Also in this part of the book, each chapter stands on its own. Furthermore, each chapter relates to several topics that portray cultural dissimilarities on this dimension. For example, work attitudes, taking risks, being a man, and honor and dignity. Each of the topics is exemplified by a story around two specific themes. The friendship is a process of continuous adjustment; affective, cognitive, and behavioral aspects of this adjustment are emphasized throughout.

Part 2 includes 21 more stories of friendship, in addition to numerous examples of events common or striking in the realm of the friendship. Among other things, I will relate to having a first birthday at 34, crossing the border between the Palestinian Authority and Israel, getting stuck in a traffic jam, the hardships of being a man, dancing with a drug dealer, and losing calmness over the sister of Mustafa's wife. Some of these stories are casual and relaxed, others are playful, and several are thrilling.

Note the place and date of each of the stories, as they are highly relevant. The situation is quite different when the event takes place in the Palestinian Authority, in Israel, or in the Netherlands. Also, as the stories are organized according to themes, they do not appear in chronological order, and events that appear later in the book may have happened earlier. This may require some mental juggling.

The last chapter (Chapter 9) starts with a summary of the challenges and opportunities stemming from the friendship. It continues with a portrayal of my experience in studying this friendship, which is followed by some ideas about personal growth as a result of the intercultural encounter. Part 2 ends with implications and recommendations of this study.

CHAPTER 5

Individualism versus Collectivism

The first dimension to address is individualism versus collectivism.

> The high side of this dimension, called Individualism, can be defined as a preference for a loosely knit social framework in which individuals are expected to take care of themselves and their immediate families only. Its opposite, Collectivism, represents a preference for a tightly knit framework in society in which individuals can expect their relatives or members of a particular in-group to look after them in exchange for unquestioning loyalty. A society's position on this dimension is reflected in whether people's self-image is defined in terms of "I" or "we".
> HOFSTEDE n.d.-b

On the scale for individualism, a higher score indicates a country more inclined to individualism and a lower score indicates a country more inclined to collectivism, as compared to other countries. The Netherlands ranked 4/5 on this scale out of 53 countries and regions; i.e., it is among those countries that value individualism most. Only the United States, Australia, and Great Britain ranked higher. Israel ranked 19, which is still above the world average. The Arab countries ranked 26/27, somewhat below the world average, and tending to collectivism (Hofstede 2001). Although the contrast on this scale between the Netherlands and the Arab countries is immense (see Figure 6), according to Hofstede the populations of many countries – especially Latin American, African, and Asian countries – are still more inclined to collectivism than measured in the Arab countries. We may postulate that the Bedouins, living a rural life, lean more toward collectivism than does the average person in the Arab world.

The differences in value orientation as regards individualism and collectivism may express themselves in many aspects of the friendship. I provide examples for four of these aspects, namely perceptions of the friendship itself, getting acquainted, meals and other celebrations, and work attitudes. Afterward, I will share some insights in the socio-political (collective) context of our friendship, as it comes about in the realm of the Israeli–Palestinian conflict.

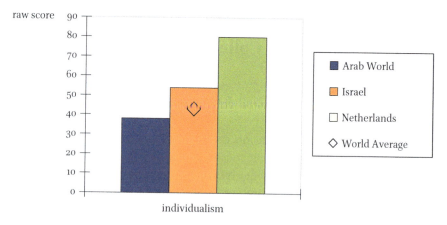

FIGURE 6   Individualism scores
BASED ON HOFSTEDE (2001)

1   Perceptions of Friendship

The story below demonstrates many of the intercultural differences that I will discuss later. Specifically, we can see here the various cultural dimensions: individualism/collectivism, uncertainty avoidance, power distance, and masculinity/femininity. However, at this point I will relate only to the themes of privacy and togetherness, and to the question "who is a friend?"

Stories of Friendship: The Netstick

Jerusalem, Friday night, December 2010. Ahmad and I are supposed to meet so that he can give me his netstick (a portable device that connects to the Internet and can be plugged into any personal computer or laptop). The next day my doctorate student cohort will have a workshop and the netstick will allow a student from Amsterdam to participate through Skype.

9.45 PM   *I just finished a Sabbath dinner with relatives, take off my yarmulke and call Ahmad from my car. I want to make sure that we will meet, since we have set neither time nor place. He tells me that he wants to come to Jerusalem. I am enthusiastic because this is the first time in about half a year that he will come to me. We have lots to talk about and are hardly ever in private; so this will be the opportunity. I am also highly fearful. I recall that he once visited me by surprise. When I opened the door, he was* standing there with his shirt torn and covered with blood. He got stuck in the barbed wire while crossing the separation wall between Israel and the Palestinian Authority. I also remember that about a month ago someone was shot dead by an Israeli soldier while traversing the wall near the place where he intends to cross. He wants to be sure that he can cross the wall tonight and will call me back in about a quarter of an hour.

10.30 PM   Ahmad calls and tells me that he and Akram, who works with him in the garage and who is a Palestinian Arab, have crossed the wall and are waiting for me to fetch them. They have some things to do. I am highly upset. I thought that he wanted to see me. Furthermore, I was already arrested for driving him in my car in Israel and take a huge risk, which I was willing to take in order to be with him but not necessarily for two people who want to do some errands. I wonder why he did not give me this information before, so that I could have made up my mind freely. However, there is a sense of urgency. It is only minutes driving from where I live. I feel that I cannot just leave them standing there and so they get in my car.

10.45 PM   In the car, Ahmad tells me that Suleiman got himself into trouble with Bedouins in the town of Lod. (Suleiman is the brother of Abdalla, a mutual friend, with whom we became acquainted the year before when he lived temporarily in Ahmad's village. Both Suleiman and Abdalla are asylum seekers and fled to Israel from Sudan.) The incident created tension between the local Bedouin and Sudanese communities. Ahmad is concerned and since he is both a good friend of Abdalla and a person of standing among the Bedouins, he wants to go there to try to settle the issue between the two communities. Jaffer, the taxi driver through whom Ahmad and I became acquainted, is supposed to come and fetch them from my place.

11.00 PM   Ahmad, Akram and I sit down in my living room and have something to drink. I make sure to obtain the netstick.

11.30 PM   After a few calls, it turns out that Jaffer did not know anything about the whole issue and is not available. Ahmad gets up and says: "Get ready, we're going." I realize that for him a communal issue has higher prioritization than personal issues. I also know that he does not differentiate between day and night in the same way I do. I realize that it is obvious to him that I will take them to the neighboring town. It is not that far; the drive will be no more than three-quarters of an hour. Again, there is the issue of risk. We could get arrested. Apart from that, this is usually not a time at which I go out; certainly not if I have a workshop on the morning of the next day. I say wait: "Let's discuss this." Nevertheless, it is obvious that I will take them.

00.10 AM During my years of acquaintance with Ahmad, I became accustomed to the idea that one can go to another town to meet someone without having an address. We ask around, and I eventually drop them at the central bus station. Our Sudanese friend Abdalla is supposed to live not far. They go and look for him by foot, with the help of a cellular phone. They apparently do not expect me to stay. I wonder if the reason is language, since they all speak Arabic, and my Arabic is not more than basic. Or am I not masculine enough? There could be fighting. Do they want to protect me, or would I be experienced as a burden? Or do they feel they are a burden on me? I say goodbye and beg them to be careful. They thank me for taking them to Lod.

After my workshop the next day, I go back to fetch them. From what I see, it looks as if Ahmad managed to resolve the dispute. I return the netstick, which had been very helpful, and take them home.

Postscript: Ahmad himself was upset with the way in which I drafted this story, leaving out many of the things that were important to him. Days later, he added the following information. He did not at all intend to bring Akram along. Akram was supposed to help him with getting over the wall but suddenly wanted to join. Ahmad did not feel comfortable saying no. He truly intended to see me, but on his way, he received a call about the incident in Lod, which forced him to change plans. He realized at the time that I would be upset over him having to go to Lod and therefore did not want to give me the new and disturbing information by phone, preferring to tell me face-to-face. He did not have the time to figure out how to reach Lod. Although telling people what to do is his general attitude, Ahmad thought it was self-evident that I could refuse to take them if I did not agree. He did not rely on me for driving them and if I had refused, he would have thought of another way. Nonetheless, knowing me, he anticipated that I would understand the situation and be willing to assist. Arriving in Lod, he did not want to involve me in the situation, considering it may become dangerous and that there may be fighting.

Only about a month later, Ahmad told me that the incident that created the upheaval was that Suleiman, the brother of our Sudanese friend Abdalla, had in his drunkenness approached a Bedouin girl and expressed obscenities. This was an issue of blood and honor for her family, and for Lod's Bedouin community as a whole. The Bedouins wanted revenge and Abdalla, being the brother, feared leaving his home, because they could take it out on him. The Bedouins already had beaten up Suleiman and injured him. Moreover, they kept him as hostage and threatened to kill him. Ahmad believed that they would fulfill their threat to restore their honor. As a sheikh himself, he went to the sheikh of the Bedouins in Lod in the hope he could make him change the minds of Suleiman's captors. The local sheikh had known Ahmad's father. They drank coffee and Ahmad asked him to intervene, to which he initially objected. Ahmad went back and forth between the different parties. In an attempt to get Suleiman out of the hands of his captors, he suggested that they hand over Suleiman to the Sudanese community and that his brother, Abdalla, would kill him himself, but this was refused. They were willing to put Suleiman on a plane back to Sudan. Abdalla had to make an extremely difficult and painful decision, whether to return Suleiman to Sudan. They had fled their home country almost a decade before because of the terrible situation there. Nonetheless, leaving Suleiman in the hands of his captors was a huge risk, so he had no real choice. The Bedouins bought a ticket and brought Suleiman to the airport, after which his whereabouts were lost.

Over a year later, I learned that Suleiman had opened a tire shop somewhere in Sudan.

1.1   Privacy and Togetherness

Until I met Ahmad, I had not given much attention to the concepts "personal" and "private", believing that these are self-evident. I found out that there is a large contrast between us on the question of whether or not something is a public or a private matter. For example, at some point, I told Ahmad I had received a letter for him from a company. With the absence of street names and addresses in Palestinian villages, it may take months, if at all, for mail to reach him at his home. Therefore, he usually asks letters to be sent to me. He asked me what is in the letter and was surprised that I did not know. If it was up to him, I could open his letters or check his emails without asking. For me, it was obvious that I would not do so without his consent. This is in contrast with the discussion of personal issues. Although there are personal matters that I would prefer not to disclose in public, I tend to be much less private than he is. He would not at all talk about personal issues in the presence of others. For him, especially the public disclosure of family-related issues is taboo. He sees keeping things private as a form of security, a way to prevent creating troubles within one's own family, between families, with friends, or with the State. He does not appreciate questions about personal issues and perceives talking about one's life as something for women. This is in sharp contrast with my attitude. I find it important to share emotions, events, and developments pertaining to the friendship with my friends, especially since the friendship with Ahmad is inviting and extraordinary in many ways. Ahmad did not understand my need to disclose personal information and recurrently felt uncomfortable or upset with the fact that I told others details about him or about our friendship. So even though he lives in a collectivistic community and I in an individualistic community, it was me favoring disclosure and him objecting.

The difference between us seems to be related to self-censorship. Stemming from a rather safe and protected environment self-censorship was new and bothersome to me, but it could be emphasized and possibly required for a Palestinian Bedouin living in a community exposed continually to a variety of threats. When I asked Ahmad about this emphasis on keeping things private, he shared that he learned to be private beginning in his earliest years. He recalled a story his mother told him in his childhood, in which an older man gave a boy from his family in Gaza a ride home on a donkey. The man tried to find out more about the boy, but throughout the ride the child kept silent and did not share a thing about himself or his family. The story was told as an example of not disclosing personal information even if under pressure.

At the same time, Ahmad considers fewer issues as personal than I do. For example, I would regard as personal my income or communications with others – for example, someone told me about her health problems – while he does not. However, if relevant, I would still consider talking about these personal issues. This of course would not include information about clients I have in psychotherapy, though occasionally I have shared with Ahmad things about clients without sharing identifying details. Having told something personal to someone else, I would imagine that this other person will respect my privacy and keep to him- or herself what I said. This may be a sensible expectation in an individualistic environment but not necessarily appropriate in Bedouin life, in which rumors spread easily and information that leaks out of the private sphere becomes public property and is likely to be shared. There is fierce social scrutiny, and people will talk. So, for Ahmad, what is personal needs to remain private. Thus, he would see a question about his wife's health as an infringement on his privacy. This – from my perspective, enhanced – emphasis on privacy may be a logical result of being continuously in groups. As a result of our acquaintance, Ahmad has become less private, realizing that people like me expect him to share more, but I still experience him as a relatively "closed" person. I have become more aware of the possibility that he may object to my sharing, which has in certain instances stopped me from telling things to others, but in other instances I have either forgotten or ignored his stance.

We may see the dissimilarities between us on the issue of privacy in our respective attitudes to the event described above. In Ahmad's understanding, the whole incident was something to be kept private. He did not share with me what actually had happened until weeks later, after I read to him an initial version of the story and he realized that essential parts were lacking. Although in general, men tend to share less than women, I was socialized in the Netherlands in which differences between men and women are relatively small. Moreover, among psychologists sharing is essential. From my point of view, it would be obvious to share immediately details of changes in plans, and certainly of an ongoing crisis. The story as a whole was so thrilling that it was highly tempting to share it with my friends and make it public. When I did so, Ahmad became angry. The diverse attitude between us regarding privacy continued to cause tension between us for many years but eventually we both adjusted to some extent and learned to live with our differences.

In Bedouin life, relationships are of the utmost importance. Ahmad experiences life in a group spirit, much enjoys the togetherness of his community, and is hardly ever alone. A large part of his life is outside and most of his friends are those who surround him physically, many of them being members of his extended family. Regarding the collectivity of family, whereas in my surroundings relatives further away than second cousins would hardly be considered family, his frame of family reference is the whole Jahalin tribe, many thousands of people. He will relate to those in his descent group as his cousins, even if he never met them. My experience is that when asked for one's family name, a Bedouin would usually mention the name of his descent group and not that of his specific family (see Figure 5).

Ahmad tends to meet friends on the street, at his brother's petrol station, or in his garage. He meets them unplanned, spontaneously, and often more than one person at a time – whoever happens to be there. He will spend an extensive amount of time if there is something to figure out together, for example a business deal or a matter requiring a solution. But he will usually not spend much time if the relationship goes smoothly, if there is no issue to work on, or with friends who are out of sight. He has no problem irritating others, as we saw in his relationship with me, but he will invest much time and energy – easily a couple of hours or more – if this caused trouble in the relationship. His investment in relationships is an issue to which I will return later since it affects many parts of life. Moreover, for him and many Bedouins, a community issue comes before anything else.

I am quite the opposite from Ahmad when it comes to togetherness in friendship. I consider myself a "not-that-social" person; though I have become more social during the years, I much enjoy being by myself. I have many friends but am more selective than Ahmad on whom to regard a friend. I usually meet friends in private, one-on-one, or with partners, at their homes or sometimes in a restaurant. My meetings with friends are planned and for limited periods, mostly not more than three hours. I invest in relationships with both close and distant friends on an ongoing base that is mostly virtual. More than Ahmad, I try to be considerate in relationships and – to prevent potential problems – I do not knowingly aggravate people. I expect that good friends will share with me important information about their lives, whether positive or negative.

There is also an enormous contrast between the two of us as far as it concerns the togetherness of our respective original families. Ahmad tries to keep his nine siblings at a "safe" distance, because he does not like their scrutiny and interference in his life. Nonetheless, several of them live in adjacent houses and are quite aware of his actions and engagement. Abu Omar, one of his brothers, is involved in his life more than the others are. They are in touch almost daily. His mother too lives next door and may bring food or help with cleaning. His father died many years ago. I find the way his family functions attractive because of its ongoing supportiveness, though I can see how this closeness could smother. I love visiting Ahmad's home and family and do so frequently. I feel connected to his family in such a way that it is noticeable. Actually, several members of Ahmad's family, and others as well, see me as part of this family.

By contrast, I meet my original family face-to-face once a year in the Netherlands. I speak with my four brothers on birthdays and once in a while in between. Like Ahmad, I have more contact with some brothers than with others. The conversations with my brothers are usually frank. The contact with my parents is more frequent, about once a month. Neither my parents nor my brothers have much influence on my life. Simultaneously, I do not think that there are things in my life that I feel I cannot tell them. In Jewish life, togetherness may be expressed in the traditional Friday night (Sabbath) supper, as in the story above. This was customary in my original family as well. Many Israeli Jewish families make an effort for family members to be together on Friday night. This is especially so for religious families, who will follow certain Jewish ceremonies during Sabbath dinner, but relevant for many secular families as well. As for Ahmad, he enjoys the openness of my family but finds the way the family functions cold and strange.

Whether it is friends or family, Ahmad has a lesser need to meet people alone than I have. Moreover, with his more collectivistic orientation he would not turn away someone who would like to join a social interaction. With some exceptions, he would not give in to pressure to be with him alone in case the arrival of others prevented that. This is also what happened in the tale above, in which his partner in the garage suddenly joined our meeting. By contrast, I would have no difficulty turning down someone interested in joining, by telling him or her that I would like to spend some time with someone else. Although Ahmad prefers group life, sometimes he feels that being continuously with people is too much for him as well. In this respect, we both accommodated each other. We mostly meet in the presence of others and sometimes he is available to be only with me.

When we look at the story above from the perspective of togetherness, it becomes clear that the togetherness as experienced by me at the traditional Sabbath dinner table is vastly different than the togetherness in the events to follow. I was affected heavily by the kinds of togetherness. It was as if having two separate personas, the nerd and the rebel, depending on the social environment. Moreover, there are several tightly knit social groups in this story, that are all considered marginal in Israeli context. The Bedouins in Lod are Israeli Arabs, as I have explained. Ahmad felt affiliated to them as Bedouins, even though they are of another tribe and – unlike him – have Israeli citizenship. The Sudanese asylum seekers remain in Israel conditionally. While some may have legal papers of residency, others do not. In this situation, Ahmad was the outsider (and I even more). Note the difference in social standing as I believe most Israeli Jews would perceive this, with the Israeli Bedouins being considered as second-class citizens, the Sudanese asylum seekers as infiltrators (cf. Orr and Ajzenstadt 2020), and the Palestinians (Ahmad) as the enemy. It was interesting to notice that there was interaction between the two communities at all, perhaps driven together by being seen as outcasts, and that there was an agreed way of solving the situation, by a form of *sulha* by the important people in the community. As both communities shun the police, involving Israeli authorities was not a desired option.

I wonder if a similar incident could have happened if one of the groups consisted of Jews and if so, how it would have developed. I believe that an insult by one person of the other group would not get the whole community involved. Therefore, I doubt that things would have escalated in this way. Furthermore, unless the story would have taken place in gangland, I reckon that police would have been called in by the Jewish side, where the police – though not universally, but still – are considered more than among Bedouins or asylum seekers as "one of us" and there to protect you.

1.2 Who Is a Friend?

I would regard a friend as the person who will lend a listening ear, is emotionally available for me, and with whom I enjoy spending free time. Having been raised in an individualistic environment, self-disclosure is for me an essential part of close relationships (cf. Chen 2002). I need people around me with whom I feel intimate and with whom I can share life experiences, both the pleasant and the unpleasant ones. Otherwise, I am rather self-sufficient. I do usually not expect friends to assist me in concrete ways or do me favors. For instance, if I needed money, I would go to the bank; if I needed to change apartments, I would rent a moving company. In Bedouin life, the friend is the person on whom you can count that he will be there to support you instrumentally, be it financially or otherwise. For example, Ahmad would become personally involved – possibly interfering in the situation – when someone had done an injustice to a friend of his, or he would send cash with a messenger to a friend in Jordan to help the latter pay for his wedding. For the Palestinian Bedouins instrumental assistance is often critical since life is a battle for resources and is full of dangers. The story above is another example of this, like the "Stories of Friendship: The Washing Machine", in the previous chapter. If you are a good friend, you will be there to assist, whether or not this is convenient for you.

The friendship with Ahmad is an asymmetric one. I see him as a significant other in the sense that he has remarkable importance in my life and well-being. I find it important to share with him things that affect me, to hear about his life and to assist where I can. Ahmad considers me an exceptionally good friend; he is concerned about me and involves me in his life more than he does any other friend. As he puts it, we are opposites: like black and white in the Chinese symbol – *taijitu* – of yin and yang. We see things in distinct ways and complement each other. In his words, he is "closer to nature and simple life", whereas I am more into the modern world. Ahmad rarely initiates talking about his life and hardly feels the need to share events. Regularly, I would find out about essential things in his life by incident or through my questions. He does rely on me for a range of instrumental issues, such as checking out or buying things through the Internet, doing errands in Israel, and reminding him of things to be done.

Ahmad assures me that he will be there for me in case of need, as he was for our friend Abdalla in the incident depicted above. On that day, he left what he was doing, defied the occupation by crossing the wall and entering Israel – something that could have put him in prison. He spent an entire day trying to solve the problem, knowing very well that there could be fighting, which would not just have endangered him physically, but also increased the risk of detention. Note that there was a large difference in risk taking between the various groups involved. The Bedouins in Lod have Israeli citizenship and were not at risk, whereas the Sudanese asylum seekers remained in Israel conditionally, if they had any legal papers of residency at all. Ahmad thus proved his friendship with Abdalla, something I believe few Euro-American men would be willing to do for their friends. Not just he, but also I put high emphasis on the value of loyalty altogether and specifically within the realm of friendship. Loyalty is a major reason for us to go along with the perceived "craziness" of the other and/or assist each other or those around us when needed.

It took me quite some time to adjust to this different idea of friendship, the expectations to help instrumentally, and the differences regarding self-disclosure, togetherness, and emotional support. In the beginning of our acquaintance things related to the dissimilar perception of friendship would surprise and often upset me. I would be frustrated when Ahmad was not there for me emotionally but also when he would not share with me important and/or emotional events in his life. Simultaneously, my instrumental support of him and his family were essential and a way for me to feel significant. Also, in later stages of the friendship, I would occasionally feel disappointed, for instance when I would visit him, anticipating to be with him alone but found him to be in the presence of others. For me, the feeling of "togetherness" in a friendship is at least partially based on being just with the particular friend. When I would confront Ahmad with my frustration, he freed time to talk with me personally. In these circumstances, he would usually be highly sensitive to my needs and say exactly the kind of things that I would like to hear at that specific moment. This ability I experienced as crucial in keeping us together as friends. Although I find being continuously in a group overwhelming, I came to enjoy the kind of togetherness felt in Bedouin life, which is so dissimilar from the individualism on which I was raised. I experienced it as heartwarming when people I hardly knew would come up to me and asked if there is something I need or that they can do for me, and/or invite me for coffee or tea. At some points, I even felt envy as an outsider and saddened for not being invited to certain social events.

2   Getting Acquainted

The process of becoming acquainted varies among cultures. I will relate here to the themes of "names" and "greeting behavior". First, let us visit the petrol station.

Stories of Friendship: Ahmad, Who?

az-Zaʿayyem, a Palestinian village just outside Jerusalem, December 2010. I passed by at Abu Omar's petrol station and asked one of the workers (in Arabic) about Ahmad. Most of the workers, several of them children between 12 and 15, belong to Ahmad's family. The response was "Ahmad? Which Ahmad? You mean Abu Omar's brother, Abu Ward? He is not around but come and have a seat."

2.1   Names

From names we can learn something about the importance of family life in both cultures. My full name is Daniel John Nicholas Weishut. Among Muslims, Christians, and Jews it is common to name children after figures from the holy scriptures. Daniel is the name of a prophet. In Hebrew it means "God is my judge" ('Daniel' n.d.). In most situations, Daniel is the name that identifies me. John is also my father's second name, and that of my parental grandfather. It was the first name of one of my ancestors. Nicholas was someone in my extended family who died at an early age not long before I was born. Naming someone after a deceased family member is common both in Jewish and in Dutch culture, and in Bedouin culture as well. Weishut, which means "white hat" in German, was probably the name given to my family at the time of Napoleon, referring to my family being involved in a profession in which a white hat was customary.

Ahmad's full name is something like Ahmad Mahmood Ward Abu Sahra. Ahmad was named after a prophet as well. Ahmad is one of the names of the prophet Muhammad, and means "a person in which praiseworthy traits are abundant, or one who deserves constant praise due to their good character" ('Ahmad' n.d.). Mahmood is the name of his grandfather from father's side. Among the Palestinians there are many recurrent names, such as Ahmad, Mohammad, and Mahmood, and therefore it is by and large not possible to identify someone by his first name only. Since in official Palestinian documents identification is often needed, one adds the grandfather's name as a second name to solve the issue. Ward (the Arabic word for flower) is the name of his extended family. Abu Sahra is the name of his descent group but is used in practice as the family name (see Figure 5). Commonly, Palestinian parents will be nicknamed after their first child. So, Ahmad, is infrequently called Abu Nimer ("abu" means "father of", and "Nimer" is the name of his eldest son). His wife is Um Nimer ("mother of Nimer"). Nonetheless, Ahmad goes mostly by the nickname of Abu Ward ("father of the Ward family"), a name given to him in his childhood. Ahmad explains that nicknaming a child "Abu 'something'" is an indication that from his behavior he is grown-up for his early age.

It took years (!) for my Bedouin friends to catch my private name, and they never learned my family name. While at first I thought that the lack of interest in my name was out of lack of interest in *me*, soon it became apparent that this was not the case. Your private name is simply not that important for Bedouins, let alone my family name. Among themselves, Bedouins are more interested in the name of one's extended family, as the significance is in the group one belongs to. The name of a foreigner is of less importance; he will be indicated in most cases in terms as "the friend of" or "the foreigner". The different attitude among the Bedouins toward names was not so much an obstacle as something to become accustomed to, and as a result, the challenge was mostly behavioral.

2.2 *Greeting Behavior*

On the first encounter, the cultural disparity is not just regarding names, it is greeting behavior altogether that is highly dependent on culture. For example, in close encounters in the Netherlands, one regularly greets complete strangers (Hofstede 2001), while in Israel and in the Palestinian Authority this seems to be uncommon. When meeting with Bedouins one needs to get into the habit of certain aspects of the encounter that may look strange to the Westerner. First, as a man, one only has access to Bedouin men and not to women. Later I will discuss issues related specifically to women and men and to the relations between them. Then, in Western Europe Caucasian male academics shake hands when they meet and say their name. Not presenting yourself with your name would be perceived as unmannered. When meeting a group of Bedouins, one usually greets those present with a "salaam aleikum", Arabic for "peace upon you", and shakes hands with all. Names are mostly left unmentioned.

In dominant cultures in the West, men may hug friends, with possibly some patting on the back. Kisses are mostly reserved for encounters with women or now and then with male family members. The number of expected kisses varies between countries; Israelis kiss twice and the Dutch give three kisses. For Bedouin men it is customary to kiss two to four times when meeting after a substantial separation. Kisses are mostly cheek-to-cheek, with alternating cheeks but could be twice on one cheek and then twice on the other. If the gap in the level of honor is large, as for a child and a respected older person, or an adult and a respected senior, the younger may kiss the older on the hand. Every now and then, children of my friends would kiss me in that way. No physical contact is allowed with Bedouin women, except for one's mother, wife, daughters, or nieces. Anyway, Ahmad is not so much into bodily contact; he kisses and touches his friends less than many other Bedouins or Palestinians I met. When we meet, we usually shake hands, as he does with many others. With other Bedouins or Palestinians, I shake hands or sometimes kiss (the Bedouin style).

In an encounter, a Westerner may immediately start with direct questions about the other's life. Two of the first questions are likely to be what the other person does in life, referring to either work or studies, and whether one is married and has children. For Bedouins both these questions are too direct. They will ask you to come and sit with them and have coffee or tea, as in the story above. Arabic coffee, which is very strong, will be offered in small cups. After some time, the host may ask where you come from; if this is from a town he knows, he will ask exactly from which part of the town. Questions about work will be asked at a later stage of the acquaintance, though possibly still in the first encounter. One assumes men over 25 years of age are married, though a question about one's family status may be raised in a subsequent meeting. Most often, there will be no more questions about one's nuclear family. Ahmad added that historically, Bedouins are not supposed to ask their guest for his name, where he came from, or where he goes, at least for three days. After that, they can ask. He sees this tradition as an issue of both privacy and security.

My experience is that in Palestinian villages one can encounter similar friendly behavior in shops. One often is offered coffee, and the shop employee is unlikely to ask for your name, but will show interest in you, whether you are local or from elsewhere, a first-time or a longstanding customer. This is very unlike groceries in my own neighborhood in Jerusalem, which I have frequented many times, and at which at best I receive a polite "shalom" (i.e., "hello", or "peace").

Apart from the issue of names, there were several other aspects of Bedouin-style introductions that required adjustment. Among the Bedouins and other rural Palestinians, I am almost always perceived as an outsider, a foreigner, by my distinct physique. Some consider me Israeli, and as a result are more reserved with me. In any case, I am in a position of getting a unique kind of attention; mostly this includes more looks, interest, or honor (for example, being served first or given more to eat or drink). But this could also take a different turn; infrequently, I am simply ignored. Occasionally, I am regarded "one of them", which I like most, though after a short introduction, I have to convey that I cannot follow the conversation in Arabic. Another point of adjustment has to do with starting a conversation. The questions one asks when meeting someone for the first time become an automatic part of getting acquainted. It was at times difficult to stop this automatism and stay aware that in this culture certain – to me standard – questions are not appreciated, at least not at an early stage of the acquaintance. As for kissing on encounters, until these days, I find it hard to figure out when it is appropriate to kiss a Bedouin and how many kisses I am supposed to give; this now and then creates awkward scenes.

3   Meals and Celebrations

Family and friends get together for meals and celebrations. These indicate what is important in life and are one of the entries to a different culture. I will first relate to meals, and afterward to birthdays and weddings. The following story takes place in the Netherlands. Going abroad together was quite an enterprise. It was highly difficult for Ahmad to obtain a visa for the European Union (Schengen visa), as it required getting hold of a series of documents to ascertain that he would return to the Palestinian Authority after his visit. Things were also complicated by the fact that as a Palestinian he is not allowed to fly from Tel Aviv (Israel). Consequently, I would fly to Amsterdam from Tel Aviv, while he would fly from Jordan.

Stories of Friendship: First Birthday at 34

At my parents' home, Amsterdam, August 2009. Before Ahmad woke up, I bought a lemon cake for his 34th birthday, put it on the table together with a present, and hung some garlands around the living room. Things looked very modest by Dutch measures. When Ahmad entered the room, he was surprised and said that this was the first time he had a birthday celebration.

That night, we went out for dinner to celebrate. I had made reservations in a fancy restaurant, knowing that on that particular day they had a relatively cheap offer. It turned out that they had one menu only, with several courses. It was French cuisine, with as first course a small but delicately prepared piece of food. We received a detailed explanation about its preparation, but Ahmad could hardly find it on his plate. The main course was a miniscule fish, which also came with an explanation. Seeing Ahmad's bewildered gaze, I felt highly embarrassed. It was not just its size, and the notion that explanations are inedible, but how could I give my "desert friend" for his birthday, of all things, a fish? We ordered bread, so he at least had something of substance. Afterwards, I took him to a snack bar and bought him a croquette from a machine; something I knew he liked.

3.1   *Meals*

Meals are a kind of daily celebrations. Ahmad had many meals with my family, and I had many more meals together with his family or with his friends. I like to eat with them. Since food, table manners, and general attitude are highly dissimilar in our cultures, we needed to learn how to eat in each other's cultures. We both tried foods that were new to us; some we found tasty and some we did not like at all. We had to adapt greatly regarding table manners. Clearly, part of the difference has to do with social class. My meals with Bedouins are often with manual workers, whereas my meals with people of Western origin are mostly with academics. Still, I believe that the dissimilarity in meals and table manners goes beyond the facet of social class. As for the general attitude around meals, I enormously enjoyed the Bedouin hospitality, while Ahmad less enjoyed the Dutch way of relating to meals.

Snack bars, from which both Ahmad and I liked to eat (as described above) were introduced in the Netherlands long before the concept of "fast food" infested the Western world. Many Dutch snack bars have walls of heated coin-operated hatches, with lots of goodies, croquettes being among the most popular items (White and Boucke 2006). There are no snack bars in Bedouin culture. Food is homemade and always excessive in quantity. One of my favorite dishes is *maqluba*, a Palestinian meat, rice, and eggplant casserole. The dish is cooked in a large pot, which is flipped over on a large platter, often in front of the diners, hence the name, which is literally translated as "upside down" ('Maqluba' n.d.). Where I visited, it was mostly made with chicken and fried cauliflower instead of eggplant. No meal is served without bread. Bread is so central that Ahmad, like many a Bedouin, would feel that in a meal without bread, something crucial is missing. This could be compared with the experience of people from other cultures as regarding the centrality of certain ingredients in a meal, such as salt, spices, or rice.

Among the Palestinian Bedouins, one eats hot meals between noon and midnight. Food is often served on an enormous platter. Everyone present is invited. This could also be the neighbor or the client in the garage, in case the workers happened to eat at that time. There are no fixed seats and anything that can function as a table or a chair will work out. For large groups, food platters may be placed on the floor. Food is usually superfluous – not like French cuisine as in the story – and served in one course. There usually is one big dish with several ingredients, and often some salads, olives, and yoghurt. Sometimes one gets soup together with the main course. Bedouins mostly start the meal together and Ahmad makes it a point that everyone is seated before starting to eat. That is, the men start the meal together, without the presence of women. The women will eat afterwards in the kitchen. (Young girls and boys are welcomed in both places.) I will expand about this separation later.

Jahalin Bedouins eat from the main platter and diners usually do not have their own plate. As for eating utensils, one mostly takes the food with one's hands, though there may be a fork or a spoon. They take pita bread and use pieces of it in a way Europeans or North Americans would use a fork. This may seem strange – at least I had to get used to this – but they may not start the meal before bread arrives, similar to how Europeans would not begin their meal without cutlery. Knives are used in the kitchen but mostly do not reach the diners. Bedouins do not necessarily finish the meal together; when one finished eating, one can move away from the table. At the end of a meal, there may be massive quantities of food left; if it is less, it is likely to be thrown out, so that the next meal will be fresh or newly cooked. Regarding drinks, it is customary to consume a sparkling soft drink with the meal. Alcohol is forbidden for Bedouins and other Muslims. After dinner, brewed Bedouin coffee and/or tea will be offered; often both, tea following the coffee. Commonly, no sweets are offered at the end of the meal.

Israel has many subcultures that may relate in varying ways to food and table manners, but generally, hot meals are eaten either midday or at night with a fork and knife. Everyone has an individual plate and serving pots or large dishes, from which the food is served, are usually put in the middle of the table. There typically is a surplus of food, whereas drinking customs vary. Guests are usually very welcome, but in an Israeli garage, if the workers had a lunch break they would not ask their clients to join them for a meal. Moreover, Israeli hosts – including good friends of mine – could be reluctant to have a Palestinian join a meal, which is the reason that I took along Ahmad only on a few dinner invitations in Israel. Dinner times are flexible, and coffee or tea are served afterwards, often with cake.

In comparison with Bedouin meals and to some degree with Israeli meals, in the dominant culture in the Netherlands meals are more regulated, and the difference is striking. In my family of origin, for example, tables are set in a strict way with specific spots for each of the eating utensils. In families, there are often predetermined seats for the various family members, and a guest too will be assigned a certain seat. Concerning guests, invitations are made long in advance and it is uncommon in this dominant culture in the Netherlands to invite someone spontaneously for dinner. During dinner, there is a strict behavioral code. For example, most people take the fork in the left hand and the knife in the right; one does not put one's hands or individual eating utensils into the main pot. The quantity of food is measured according to the number of invited diners, and with hot meals, unless in a restaurant, no bread is served. In most homes, hot meals are eaten only at night, traditionally (and in my home) at 6 PM, but with women being a large part of the workforce, nowadays this is closer to 7 PM. It is common for hot meals to have two or three courses, in which case soup would be the first – and not the second or last – course. With the meal one often will be offered an alcoholic beverage. Dutch people start and end their meal together, and commonly whole families sit together. One expects all food to be finished by the end of the meal. Leftovers will be preserved. At the end of the meal, something sweet and coffee – usually from a percolator – and/or tea will be offered, and one drinks either one of them but not both. Eating customs for those with immigrant backgrounds are significantly different.

In the Bedouin culture, hospitality is of the utmost value. A great deal of effort is made to make guests join the meal, and it is common to be asked repeatedly to join, even if at first one politely declined. Not joining could be perceived as an insult, so I learned to at least eat a little. This was not so much of a problem, since I very much appreciate Bedouin food, and I mostly loved to join. However, I needed to learn the custom of eating with one's hands, while using bread to "catch" other pieces of food. In the beginning this felt weird, and it took me years to learn how to do this efficiently. In the beginning of the friendship, when hosts saw how I struggled with getting the food to my mouth, they would offer me more utensils than the locals. With my Dutch background and used to the custom that one would keep also half a potato – if left over – for a later day, I grappled with the notion that food must be fresh and that leftovers are thrown away. This felt especially strange in a surrounding that is relatively poor. Regularly, I commented on the disposal of food, and eventually Ahmad adapted to my habit of returning leftovers to the refrigerator. Nonetheless, he continued to make fun of me, saying things such as: "You'll eat it even after twenty years." As for doing things the Western style, I was much aware of Ahmad's lack of ease with European conduct and etiquette around meals and celebrations. I felt the people in my surrounding more critical of his grappling with Dutch meals and manners, whereas his environment was more accepting of my unease with Bedouin meals and manners. Moreover, when other Europeans, Northern Americans, or Israelis were involved, for example, when we would take people around on a trip to show them about Bedouin life, I found myself in the middle, trying to solve discrepancies by making it clear to both sides what they could expect from the other.

3.2   *Celebrations*

Let us now turn to more official celebrations and focus on those two celebrations that are most relevant both in Bedouin life and in the friendship. The birth of a child is a major event in most cultures, and I had the opportunity to experience this in Jewish Israeli, Dutch, and Bedouin cultures. In the dominant culture in the Netherlands, it is customary to visit the parents and give presents when a child is born, but there usually is no big party. Among Dutch Jews, the party around the circumcision, which takes place eight days after birth, is usually private. Among Israeli Jews, when a boy is born there usually is a large ceremonial party, with possibly 100 or more attendees, at which the boy is circumcised, after which there is lunch and presents. Nowadays parties are sometimes held for Jewish baby girls as well. Among the Bedouins, when a boy is born, there is a festive meal served on huge platters for the extended family. The traditional dish is *mansaf*, made of lamb cooked in a sauce of fermented dried yoghurt and served with rice or groats ('Mansaf' n.d.). Afterwards there is Bedouin coffee. It is uncommon to bring presents. For girls, there may be a smaller event, or one will bring sweets to one's friends. I attended the party for the birth of Ahmad's youngest son, for which he himself had slaughtered the sheep. Circumcision of Bedouin boys takes place at an older age without any party.

In the Netherlands, it would be out of the ordinary to skip subsequent birthdays. In most families, one celebrates birthdays from the first until the last. Even without a party, presents and birthday cards are always there. It is customary to decorate the living room of the person with the birthday, even more than I did on the occasion described above. "Round" birthdays (20, 30, 40, etc.) receive more attention and often go with bigger parties. In the Netherlands, the individual is central. Quite the opposite for the Bedouins. The birth of a person is significant for society, but the individual is of less importance. For them, there is no incentive to celebrate birthdays, and they may not even remember their own. Regularly, I remind my friends of their birthdays. Nonetheless, times change for the Bedouins too. Nowadays children's birthday celebrations have become more common. I was present at the third birthday of Ahmad's eldest with his family and other children, cakes, small fireworks, and many presents.

My own birthday party some years ago with a small group of mostly Bedouin friends was one of the finest I had, somewhere on a hill in the Judean desert between Jerusalem and the Dead Sea. I did not know whether or not it would materialize until a few hours before the party. Ahmad took care that there would be two chickens; fortunately, I did not see the slaughtering. Then we went to have a haircut. Most Israeli friends would shudder at the idea of having a Palestinian put his knife on their neck – even if it were the hairdresser – but I felt comfortable. Fouad, a Bedouin hairdresser of Jordanian origin, became a good friend of mine over the years, and I invited him to join our party. We had a barbecue under the stars and my friends put a big cake on the bonnet of the car with a huge improvised candle. In striking contrast, I received tens of Facebook messages, numerous Skype notifications, emails and mobile text messages, and a series of old-fashioned calls and messages on my answering machine from non-Bedouin friends from all over the world, which was heartwarming as well.

Weddings are another story. I attended weddings in several cultures and in this respect too the disparity is blatant. Although from an anthropological point of view I could fill a chapter on weddings, I will relate to this point here only shortly, since their effect on our friendship was limited. In the Netherlands, two individuals who decide to marry usually had a long time – sometimes years – to get acquainted. Before the big step, they are likely to have lived together, learned to get along, were intimate, and probably love each other. Couples can be either of mixed gender or the same gender. Dutch weddings are usually planned many months ahead. Going by Dutch standards, my family has relatively big weddings, influenced by Jewish customs. Dutch weddings may go over several days, with a series of activities for various groups of invitees, including a reception, an official ceremony, a meal, and dancing in couples. If it is a Jewish wedding there is also a religious ceremony. Guests mostly bring presents. Weddings, like other Dutch celebrations, stand on ceremony and etiquette.

The situation in Israel as regarding the particulars of weddings rather depends on the specific socio-cultural environment. In most social circles in Israel, a marriage is something primarily between two individuals; though in the ultra-Orthodox community it is often arranged. Israeli weddings tend to have a few hundred guests, usually at one large happening. Families stemming from the Middle East, North Africa, and South Asia sometimes hold a henna celebration for the bride and her female friends and family in the days before the wedding. This tradition is practiced by Jews, Christians, and Muslims ('Henna' n.d.). It is customary for guests to write out checks for the newlyweds. Jewish Israeli weddings in almost all circles include a religious ceremony, an abundance of food, and dancing.

In Bedouin life, marriages are often arranged; they are a matter of the community as much as they are a choice between a man and a woman. One could compare this to weddings among ultra-Orthodox Jews, which are also mostly arranged and usually take place after just a few meetings between the presumptive bride and groom. Bedouin wedding ceremonies and festivities are usually planned not more than a month ahead and they will last for several days. Before the actual wedding, it is customary to have a henna celebration for the bride and in some families the groom will have a bachelor party as well. Unlike Israeli or Dutch wedding ceremonies, a party for the whole community is held in the open, often on a large field; more exactly, for the men in the community, since the women, including the bride, are not to be seen. Hundreds of men will come and go from midday until night. The richer guests will write out checks for the family of the groom; presents are uncommon. Around the field, there will be mattresses and cushions, on which men – especially the elderly – will sit or lay. *Mansaf*, sweets, and Bedouin coffee will be served to all. At night, men will dance the *Dahiyya*, a Bedouin form of *Dabke*, shoulder to shoulder, forming a large square around a singer. The women will have a separate party. An official ceremony at which a nuptial agreement is signed will take place within the close family circle.

Ibrahim is one of the sons of the second wife of Ahmad's brother, Abu Ya'akub. Unlike many of his cousins who grew up in the Palestinian Authority, Ibrahim was raised in Israel, in an Arab neighborhood of Jerusalem. He lives on the slope of the Mount of Olives, which is within walking distance from az-Za'ayyem, but now separated by the wall. Living in Israel is possible for him because his mother is among those Palestinians in East Jerusalem who have residency but no citizenship. Through his eyes, polygyny is recommended. He was 19 when I first had any significant interaction with him. I was giving him a ride when he told me that he was about to take his driving test and asked if I had a job for him. He was mostly concerned with marrying. He stated that he really wanted to marry soon but did not yet know whom to marry. I recognized that marriage is important in such a community-oriented environment, even if he himself lived in Israel and not with most of his extended family. This was not the only time that I had heard from Bedouin or Palestinian youngsters that they had set a time for a wedding, before having found a possible bride. This is counterintuitive to Western standards in which one first finds the most appropriate individual to partner with, and then the couple decides together on when to marry. I suggested to Ibrahim that he could wait some more and offered some reasons for postponing marriage. He asked about my marital status and mentioned that he believed that it was time for his uncle Ahmad to marry a second wife. As we discussed the idea of marrying, it became clear that Ibrahim was clearly aware of other options of relationships between men and women, but he preferred the traditional attitude.

I met Ibrahim again seven years later on one of my visits to az-Za'ayyem, and he asked why I had not come to his engagement party. I congratulated him and told him that I had not been aware of his engagement. He added that the wedding will be in four months and that he hopes to see me there. The encounter surprised me for several reasons: first, relative to Bedouin standards he waited many years before marrying; second, unlike the usual custom in Bedouin life, the marriage was scheduled far ahead – I later saw on Facebook an invitation with the specific date; and third, there was an engagement party, something which possibly had to do with the relatively large timeframe between the day the marriage was agreed between the families and the wedding. In his family, I was accustomed to a more traditional attitude to marriage.

Perhaps the difference could be explained by the fact that Ibrahim is of a younger cohort than those whose weddings I had attended previously. Another factor that is likely to have influenced his choices is that he lives and works in Israel, as opposed to his relatives in the Palestinian Authority, and is thus more aware of modern attitudes toward marriage. Several months later, Ahmad provided more context, informing me that Ibrahim's previous engagement had dissolved, and that the engagement party had been only for family, of which seemingly Ibrahim considered me to be a part; something that is more common. This incident thus turned into an example of a situation in which my interpretation lacks accuracy, because of limited access to information and my inability to see the whole picture. My observations were still relevant, but not exact.

Back to the idea of celebrations in general, I tremendously enjoy the Bedouin style of them. I look forward to attending the next festivity, and also participate a bit in Bedouin-style dancing, though I'm not good at it. At Jahalin Bedouin weddings, many people know me. I am mostly the only non-Palestinian, and often honored as such, which I very much appreciate. Concurrently, I feel now and then uncomfortable for standing out because of my height and skin color.

4 Work Attitudes

There is a major difference between Bedouin culture on one side, and North America and Western Europe on the other side, when it comes to work attitudes. I will address two aspects: the relationship between work, friendship, and leisure time, and the topic of child labor.

Stories of Friendship: At the Garage

Hizma, a Palestinian village just outside Jerusalem, January 2011. While Ahmad and I were in the garage office, Fawaz, one of the mechanics, came in with his about two-year-old son. He was angry. He wanted his salary. Ahmad explained to Fawaz (in Arabic) that he already received more money than he earned. Ahmad showed him from the notes he wrote in his diary how much Fawaz had brought in with his work, which was not a lot. The discussion took at least a quarter of an hour. Ahmad then became angry at Fawaz and raised his voice.

Shortly after, not having understood much from what was going on, I asked Ahmad what had happened. He informed me that two days before Palestinian police came to the garage with the intention of arresting Fawaz for some misdemeanor, and Ahmad had paid NIS 4000 (about €1000) to get him freed. The conversation continued as follows:
Daniel: [frowning] Did you take the money from the garage?
Ahmad: Did you think from my family? You really are a European! You would not have paid?!?
Daniel: You could have told me about this; I am your partner in the garage.
Ahmad: Do you not see how busy I am? If I tell you about everything that happens, it will take me an hour every day.
Daniel: So, tell me in five minutes.
Ahmad: [angry] Perhaps go home!
Daniel: [insulted] I intended to, but before, you told me to stay.
Ahmad: [changing to a soothing tone of voice] Do not take everything so exactly. Stay!
Things calmed down between us and ten minutes later I saw Ahmad and Fawaz talk in a friendly way, as if nothing had happened.

4.1 Labor and Leisure

I was raised in the Netherlands with the notion that friendship and business do not mix. In Bedouin life, as among rural Palestinians, the division between friends and customers is significantly less distinct than common in either the Netherlands or Israel. This is noticed in everyday life, an example of which is that Palestinian shop owners, unlike Jewish Israeli ones I encountered, are often remarkably friendly, shaking hands and offering me things for free, even without knowing me and having no idea if I will return. This could have to do with my being foreign, but my observations show that their behavior is similar with Palestinians. Customers easily become friends, and friends become customers or business partners.

Making a living in a Palestinian village, especially under occupation, with occasional military closures, is strenuous. I will say more about this aspect in Chapter 8, "Power Distance", and will limit the discussion here to work attitudes and the labor–leisure division. Overall, much business takes place with family and friends.

In line with this notion, Ahmad and I started Jahalin Tours, a small project to make people aware of Bedouin life. Although our perspectives and work attitudes are dissimilar, we managed to organize a series of tours, primarily for foreigners. I did the organizing, while he provided the content. We also assisted the Peace Center for Heritage in al-Eizariya with an online shop for "Palestinian Bedouin Clothing & Crafts", which sells handmade embroidery by Bedouin and other Palestinian women (Weishut n.d.-a, n.d.-b). Later, I became involved in Ahmad's garage, financially, organizationally, and emotionally. When we started the garage, I had known him for many years, and was aware of many of the differences in how we deal with life. I also had a background in Business Administration. I must say that for me the various projects were a mixture of labor and leisure; they were exciting, with a lot of work and little money.

The cultural differences were accentuated in our efforts concerning the garage. I was acquainted with a Euro-American way of doing business, emphasizing efficiency and organization. I invested many weeks in planning, preparing Excel sheets and trying to teach one of the workers how to fill them out. I was accustomed to the notion that time is money. Decisions in Dutch culture are typically made by consensus, which is based on values such as individual autonomy and cooperation (De Bony 2005). I had expected a similar way of decision making from Ahmad, but Arab businesses are run differently than in the West (cf. Houjeir and Brennan 2016; Najm 2015; Obeidat et al. 2012), and he preferred to manage things otherwise.

He once clarified that "relationships are more important than money" and that "the program of the garage is to take care of relationships." For him, the workers are like family and the clients like friends, in the light of which we can understand his angry reaction toward me in the story above. The garage thus functioned as a family business, with Ahmad as the authoritative head of the family, taking care of the workers' needs. He could spend hours in conversations with workers, suppliers, or clients; something he perceived as part of his job. People would come in to consult on all kinds of issues, not merely related to their car. It could be related to some business deal, or finding a suitable woman for marriage. He was very committed to his work and would invest enormous efforts to fix cars, even if it would cost more than he would earn. The question of who owes what was often more related to the type of relationship than to the exact costs or agreements.

Ahmad's way of dealing with things took much more time than I considered appropriate. In hindsight, I realize that it should have been obvious that running a business with emphasis on people takes more time than running it with an emphasis on money. Ahmad explained that apart from his general attitude of relating to the workers as some form of family, it is important for him to cherish relations with the villagers, as otherwise he as an outsider will not be able to keep the garage open. This would not have been an issue if the garage were in the village where he lives and where the Bedouins have much to say. It is in Hizma, which is run by non-Bedouin families. Note that in both villages, and despite the fact that there are village councils, at least according to Ahmad, it is the families that rule, whether officially or unofficially. Only years later I grasped the significance of having good relations with people, when in front of many of them my phone was stolen from my car in the garage. I will return to this event later.

Although I could appreciate Ahmad's investment in people, I found it hard to accept working without a budget, written plans, set opening times, and safety measures, to name a few things. The garage was in constant flux and there was too much uncertainty for me. He would make major decisions, such as hiring and firing people or about major expenses without consulting with me or even informing me (or anyone else). I experienced these surprises as disturbing. Within several months it became evident that the diversity between us is too large to bridge and that we would not be able to manage the business effectively together. Since then I have stopped my active involvement with the garage but continue to visit regularly. I did not withdraw my financial investment but gave up on the expectation of making money out of it. One thing that remained for some time after I was actively involved was the registration of the cars and the income from the business being recorded in a paper notebook despite the fact that they have a fully equipped computer. After a couple of months that disappeared as well.

In general, cultures have variant perspectives vis-à-vis the labor/leisure division (Manrai and Manrai 1995). In the West, for most people waking hours are divided in a somewhat rigid way between work (or studies) and leisure. (One may consider time for volunteering – which I do quite often – as a separate category or include it in either category.) In the Netherlands, most people work according to fixed hours and finish their job at a fixed time. The notion is that at work one works, and during leisure time one does not work. In my upbringing, this distinction was strict. For instance, I recall my father's reaction when I called him once from my office to get some piece of information from him. He said: "Aren't you at work?", implying that it is inappropriate to call him when I am supposed to work. Israelis are more flexible in this respect. Many Israelis will make private phone calls or errands during working hours. In the Arab world, there is no clear differentiation between work and leisure time (Samovar et al. 2009).

As compared to work attitudes common in the dominant North-Western European and American cultures, with the Bedouins the pace of labor seems slower and is interrupted with frequent breaks for a variety of reasons. Ahmad explained: "Work should not be too stressful." As a Bedouin one may take a break, sit with a visitor, do private errands, or sleep at any hour of the day, also during work. This flexibility of labor and leisure time has a direct impact on the friendship. I would enjoy the flexibility of coming to visit him at work, like many other friends of his. By contrast, he had difficulties with the notion that my working hours – which are mostly seeing clients – are inflexible and that I cannot leave work in the middle of it, as he sometimes would do. It took him years to realize that it is improper in my culture to cancel an appointment with a client at the last minute. I had similar, unpleasant, experiences with several other Bedouins who wanted to meet spontaneously, for example when they somehow had obtained an entrance permit to Israel. They were taken aback when I told them I cannot meet in the coming hours, something in their culture perceived as an inappropriate response.

The garage functioned seven days a week and Ahmad spent most of his spare time – including nights and weekends – at the garage with the laborers. Any social activity could be interrupted for work-related issues and he would get out of bed in the middle of the night to accommodate people's work-related expectations. Ahmad views himself in this respect as more drastic than other Bedouins; he believes that other Bedouins would take more time off than he does. Still, my impression was that in general many Bedouins stay more hours at their place of work than would be common in either Israel or the Netherlands but at the same take the notion of work much more leisurely.

I found it demanding to accommodate myself to the idea of flexibility of work and leisure time and to the idea that many social circumstances – private visits, outside barbecue, or other pastimes – ended abruptly, long before what I had anticipated, because work had to be done. Eventually, I accustomed myself to the idea that Ahmad never is completely free. Moreover, the idea that relations between people are more important than the financial benefit of the garage was hard to absorb. Though it was annoying to see how all my work for the garage was lost, I could grasp the advantages of this style of living. The most striking thing for me was that many things that I had considered as self-evident and not worthy discussing, such as that there will be clear planning, consultation between us, and that any repair must make a profit, Ahmad perceived as either problematic or unacceptable.

4.2 Child Labor

Although this topic does not connect directly to the story above, I cannot ignore the fact that among the Bedouins children work. In the dominant culture of the Netherlands, there is an unambiguous division between what children are supposed to do and what is done by adults. Children are excluded from many social and work-related activities. To put it simply, perhaps overly so: children go to school and afterwards are free to play. Children may be asked to set the table, throw out the garbage, or – when they are older – look after younger children when parents have an evening out, but requests from children to contribute to family life are limited. In Israel, the distinction between the lives of children and adults is comparable to the Netherlands in most conditions but less strict when it comes to social events. In Israel, children can participate in many social activities – such as social visits or dinner parties – from which they would be excluded in the Netherlands.

Bedouin children are socialized in playing a part in family and community life as much as they are able. They have many more responsibilities than would be common in the West and are gradually socialized into adult life. Springing from this attitude, Bedouin children are present in many adult activities. Ahmad would occasionally take his oldest son, Nimer, to the garage beginning age of 2. The mechanics too would now and then bring their small boys. The children observe and later imitate the adults. Ahmad said: "This creates a feeling of togetherness of the family. They are not requested to behave like that. They do it voluntarily because they enjoy it. We want our boys to become men, and this is how they learn it. It gives honor to the family to see your son behave like a man." As for responsibilities, small girls and boys are supposed to help in the house. They may look after their younger siblings, take part in the daily care of the house, and serve the men. At a later age, girls will remain at home to assist their mothers, while boys will go out to work at a youthful age.

A few examples: Ahmad took care of the goats from age five. His son Nimer would, on request, bring things from another room at age 2 and started looking after his baby brother at age 3. I was there one night when Ahmad's wife, Um Nimer, became upset with Nimer since she had sent him to the shop – in the center of the village – to buy a light bulb and he had come back without it. Nimer then was just over 4 years old. His cousin Amir has been working at his father's petrol station – the one I mentioned before – since he was 8. Amir fills the cars with petrol and takes care of payments. At age 10 Amir learned to drive a car. The phenomenon of working children can also be seen among non-Bedouin rural Palestinians. For example, next to the garage, a Palestinian child of about 12 years old ran a small grocery.

In contrast, I could not imagine my Dutch nephews – who are of similar age – or other Dutch or Israeli children taking so much responsibility. I had associated child labor with child abuse and children working for long hours in terrible conditions. This may be true in some societies, but I never encountered Bedouin children forced into work. My observations indicated that most Bedouins are fond of and protective of their children. At the same time, child labor – after school hours – is common and accepted, and as far as I could see, the children are happy to participate in the lives of the grown-ups. It is easy to discern the communal facets of the attitude to children at work. Children are part of the group and are requested to support the family and the community from a noticeably early age. It is common to ask Bedouin children to make coffee or tea, bring this or do that. When boys are big enough (and this could be at the age of 8 or 10), they become part of the workforce and assist in generating income.

Child labor conflicted with my Western value system according to which children are not supposed to work, and I experienced it initially as strange and confusing. Amnesty International, the human rights organization in which I have been active for many years, subscribes to the International Labour Organization Conventions of Child Labour (International Labour Organization 1973) and the Rights of the Child (United Nations OHCHR 1989), which put strict limits on the economic exploitation of children. My encounter with seemingly happy Bedouin children at work did not coincide with what I had believed. Child labor is an example of how the intercultural encounter "threatened" my value system and made me feel less certain about what is "right" and what is "wrong". It also made me more aware that even (my) basic assumptions about society are truths that can be challenged.

5 Friendship and Politics

One of the major difficulties in our friendship is without doubt its political context, which burdens the friendship in many ways. For an Israeli, the social toll of friendship with a Palestinian can be extremely high. For a Palestinian Bedouin to befriend an Israeli is exceedingly complicated as well. Politics affect us both, but I will share here my side only. It took me many months to recuperate from the following incident, which for many Palestinians would not be anything out of the ordinary. The incident occurred before the official start of collecting stories, but I have included it because it was crucial and affected the development of the friendship. After that I will expand on how the friendship put a strain on my relations with other friends, and on the paucity of social support.

Stories of Friendship: Crossing the Border

az-Za'ayyem checkpoint, October 2008. I gave Ahmad a ride, so that he would arrive in time for his taxi-driving test in al-Eizariya, a neighboring Palestinian town. Since he had forgotten his identity card, we intended to stop at his home to get the card. At the checkpoint between one Arab village, on the Israeli side of the wall, and another (his) village, on the Palestinian side, Israeli soldiers halted the car. Both of us were detained, Ahmad for being in Israel without a valid permit and me for giving a ride to someone without a permit. We were taken to a nearby military police camp and put behind bars.

Thoughts were rushing through my mind. I found it hard to believe that this was real and not a movie. I recognized myself as a law-abiding citizen and it thus was a shock to be suddenly considered a criminal. What had happened to me?

Ahmad was interrogated first, and after about half an hour I was interrogated as well. Ahmad was released without condition, since he was regarded as "clean" by the security forces. My fingerprints were taken, and the car was confiscated for a month. I was released on bail and informed that I will be charged in court.

5.1   *The Wrong Side of Society*

I believe that most friends in Western Europe or North America do not consider the relationship between their friendship and politics, even if such a relationship may exist. In Israel, national politics are more in the foreground and may create heated discussions on divergent points of view, over which friendships could fall apart. Politics are inescapable when the friendship concerns an Israeli and a Palestinian, even if the national politics are not discussed within the friendship, as in our case. This could already be learned from "Stories of Friendship: The Netstick" but it never became as clear as in the story I just described.

In Israel, the extent to which one is confronted in one's daily life with the Israeli–Palestinian conflict depends on the geographical location. In the center of the country, one may succeed in going through the day without conscious disturbance of the national struggle, whereas in the south, near Israel's border with Gaza, there have been periods of ongoing confrontations, in the last year through attacks with balloon bombs coming from Gaza. In Jerusalem the conflict cannot be ignored and is for many an integral part of daily life. There were years that I feared driving behind buses, wary that they could explode by means of a suicide bomber. Once on my way to university, I had the scary experience of arriving at a bus stop at which a bomb had exploded a few hours earlier. If that was not enough, I had friends and clients killed in terrorist attacks.

The French Hill neighborhood where I live was built in 1971 as one of the first settlements in East Jerusalem. Despite my liberal views, I chose to live in an urban settlement around the time I started collecting the stories in this book. The apartment had many of the qualities I wanted, but still its location bothered me. I then consulted with a couple of friends (both left-wing Jews and Arabs) and did not encounter fierce objection. Eventually, I justified my decision by telling myself that unlike settlements in the midst of the West Bank that are open to Jews only, in French Hill Palestinians can move freely and rent or own apartments. When I came to live there, the neighborhood was primarily populated by upper-middle class secular Jews (like me). This group has been steadily diminishing as two new groups moved into the neighborhood: ultra-Orthodox Jews and Palestinians (Israeli Arabs). This social mix has caused inter-ethnic as well as intra-ethnic collisions (Shtern and Yacobi 2019). In my building we find a mixture of these three groups. Tension is tangible, partly based on stereotypes, but partly very practical. For example, attitudes vary toward smoking or turning on electricity on the Shabbat. Being on the house committee, I attempt to navigate between the expectations of the various neighbors as much as I can.

In French Hill, there was a series of attacks by Palestinians in the period between 1992–2004 ('French Hill attacks' n.d.). In addition, I live within walking distance of East Jerusalem. The Issawiya neighborhood of Jerusalem is adjacent to French Hill. In recent years, Issawiya has known a sharp increase in violent clashes between Palestinian youths and Israeli forces (United Nations OCHA 2019a). From home I can hear loud noises from the nearby Palestinian neighborhoods at night, but I cannot always identify whether these are from fireworks at weddings or from shooting by soldiers to disperse a riot. To keep one's peace of mind, one must repress this kind of thing. Things are calmer since the building of the separation wall, but even today the threat of death is always there.

The separation wall plays a vital role in our friendship; it is both a physical and symbolic way of separation between us. There are checkpoints on the roads to and from the Palestinian Authority and throughout its territory. Since I go regularly to the Palestinian Authority, this was not the first time I was stopped at a checkpoint. However, it was the first time I was detained. In fact, it was the first time in my life that I felt threatened by the law. From my naïve point of view, the notion that giving a friend a ride brought me to the "wrong side of society" was difficult to digest. The shock came in waves. First, there was the arrest, which by itself was humiliating. Then there was the painful understanding that I am paying a high price for this friendship, now that I have a criminal record and am facing trial. In subsequent months, dynamics of cognitive dissonance created substantial psychological discomfort (cf. Festinger 1957) and required that I revise my self-image, the image of my friends, and the image of the country I had been living in for almost 30 years. The ideas I had of myself as an appreciated member of society, and of my nation's authorities as relatively fair and supportive, just did not fit together with what I experienced around the incident.

There was another side to this story. From time to time, I had faced reluctance by Palestinians to become closer out of fear that I was an Israeli infiltrator. I experienced the arrest as a kind of initiation ceremony, providing me better access to Palestinians and Palestinian life. "Being arrested" felt as being more like a Palestinian. It gave me a feeling of entitlement to be accepted, with thoughts like "see what I am willing to do in order to be friends with a Palestinian." Nonetheless, this notion of an initiation ceremony was more in my mind than in reality, and not experienced by Ahmad as such.

5.2   *Social Support*

It was not just the incident, but also the reactions in my social environment that took me by surprise. I did not receive much support around this from either Palestinian or most Jewish friends, but for distinct reasons. I shared the story about the incident with circles of closer friends and found that it united opinions and affected my relationships. Reactions were dependent on the attribution of the cause of the event as either internal (dispositional) or external (situational) (cf. Heider 1958). In other words, locus of control over the event played an important role in the evaluation of the situation (cf. Rotter 1975). My Palestinian friends perceived the situation as something beyond my control (external locus of control) and did not regard the event something exceptional. Arrests are part of life for Palestinian Bedouin men, and I got the impression that few were never arrested. In contrast, most Israeli friends perceived the situation as one that I had invited (internal locus of control). In their eyes, I had broken the rules.

The tense situation between Israelis and Palestinians creates a notable deal of mistrust. More than a few of my acquaintances would adhere to the notion that Arabs are not to be trusted. I will return to the issue of trust in the next chapter but will here refer to how distrust of Arabs played out in my friendship with Israelis. Many Jewish friends were concerned about my actions and about me. Some of these friends condemned my behavior and some even considered the incident a rightful punishment. They hoped it taught me a lesson of being more careful and choosing friends only among Jews. More than before, I realized the collectivistic views of my Israeli friends, which became stringent opposite the "Arab enemy". They pointed at the complex Israeli–Palestinian conflict and could not appreciate my friendship with a Palestinian, which in their view was too dangerous. Some suggested that I am being (ab)used by Ahmad. My continuing involvement in the friendship with Ahmad even after this incident put a strain on and changed the relationships with some of my best Jewish Israeli friends. Ahmad as well experienced pressure for befriending me, a Jewish Israeli, but to a lesser degree. He explained this by the fact that Bedouins, being originally a nomadic people, do not identify nationally as much as Israeli Jews or Palestinian Arabs do. He and those around him, some of them themselves Israeli residents, identify with the Jahalin tribe, or with Bedouins in general, a collective that goes beyond borders.

Social support in intercultural encounters is of the utmost importance (Ward et al. 2001) and luckily, not all of my Israeli friends reacted in the same negative manner. Some Jewish friends did support me during this period. Particularly striking was the fact that Israeli friends who originally came from the former Soviet Union were more supportive than other friends. This compares with the finding from a study that showed that as compared to veteran Israelis, Arabs and immigrants from the former Soviet Union felt less obliged to comply with the law, believed more strongly in the supremacy of other laws over state laws, and were more willing to take the law into their own hands when their interests seemed threatened (Yagil and Rattner 2005).

For Ahmad it was difficult to understand why I made such a fuss about the event and why I felt the need to share the story with others. This was not only because he related to the event as something ordinary but also because it involved an issue of privacy and public image. He believes that one should not share bad things about oneself, not even when one was the victim of something bad. As in the story about the netstick and our trip to Lod, in his view the incident was something to be kept private since one's name being associated with something bad could harm one's public image. In my world, social scrutiny is lower than in his, and until this incident I was less aware of social scrutiny in my personal life. I was used to sharing, while taking in account only marginally the effect of such a disclosure on my social image. This incident made a change.

The incident and its consequences were a confrontation with how divergent perceptions can be. In the legal process, in which the prosecutor requested a prison term, I felt quite deserted by several friends and realized how much I was risking in this friendship – not only my social status but also my freedom. I found out that my perception was quite divergent from that of my friends. The separation wall and the many checkpoints often gave me "recollections" of the Holocaust, in which Jews – like my parents and grandparents – were stigmatized and had to hide, while others took part in the resistance. Despite the highly different circumstances, I experienced situations within the realm of the friendship as if I am taking part in the resistance, assisting Bedouins and other Palestinians in need. In fact, it was a form of resistance, just not against the Nazis and their collaborators, but against the occupation by the State of Israel.

The case was eventually dismissed on grounds of a technicality: the arrest took place on Palestinian territory and there was no witness to claim that (s)he saw Ahmad and me in the car in Israel (just a couple of meters away). Still, the incident caused major tension between Ahmad and me, chiefly because I experienced him too as providing little support, for reasons explained before. With such a pressure on the friendship to dissolve, I had to fight with myself and with my social environment to keep us together. As a result, this event became a turning point in our relationship and – paradoxically – brought us closer. Not long after, we decided to travel abroad together for the first time. Organizing this trip was a difficult endeavor for many reasons as I explained previously, but still more feasible than meeting in Israel. More on the impact of the Israeli–Palestinian conflict on the friendship will be discussed in Chapter 8, "Power Distance".

6   Conclusion: Individualism versus Collectivism

Differences in the friendship between Ahmad and me on the dimension of individualism/collectivism displayed a similar pattern to Hofstede's findings on Dutch, Israeli, and Arab cultures. In line with the cultures in which we grew up, in most circumstances I opted for an individualistic stance, while Ahmad chose a collective stance. For a Dutch person, the centrality in society of the individual is so obvious that it is hard to imagine anything else. For the Palestinian Bedouin the situation is the reverse; the community is central, life is lived with group spirit, and the individual is of lesser significance. Simultaneously, there is a prominent level of loyalty. I found that Bedouins will go out of their way to assist tribe members or related others who are in need. Although traditions and expressions are rather different, the collectiveness among the Bedouins compares with that among the ultra-Orthodox Jews, another tightly knit society, which puts enormous emphasis on community values.

The relative importance between the individual and the community is primarily an issue of priorities, as individualism and collectivism are not mutually exclusive. My experience was that is possible to integrate the individualistic and the collectivistic points of view and alternate between the two distinct and complementary perspectives, even though at times they may be in conflict. I found that cultures may tend to either perspective, but still as an individual, one may be able to provide attention to both the individual and the community aspects.

The challenges in my cultural learning were most of all in the cognitive realm. Understanding the social dynamics helped me in attuning my expectations. It took me years to fully appreciate a collectivistic attitude to life, but eventually I was able to adapt and see its many positive sides. The immersion in Bedouin community life felt as a fantastic opportunity for me and learning new customs was more an intriguing task than a hardship. Many of the collective events in which I participated were like adventures.

Then, one somehow needs to cope with one's disturbing emotions. It can be upsetting when events do not unfold according to one's expectations. Participating in "Ahmad's culture", he demanded that I do most of the accommodation, which at times felt unfair. Nevertheless, he also adjusted, for example, to the notion that I want and need personal attention. The dissimilarities on this value orientation created mutual frustration and negotiation in many situations and over an extended period. My understanding would help me to cope emotionally. Eventually, through Ahmad I widened my circle of friends enormously, which gave me much pleasure, and I started to enjoy community life. Still, I do not live in a group as he does, and sometimes I feel jealous of his being engulfed by friends and family, while he envies my privacy. This was lately accentuated through the COVID-19 pandemic. I stay in touch with many Israeli and international friends through various virtual media, as I do in other times. In contrast, much of the friendship with Bedouins is based on physically being together, which was prohibited by Israeli authorities. The atmosphere of togetherness was something I missed.

There was a need to adjust my behavior, especially in the beginning of our friendship. I felt uncertain about how to behave, something to which I will return extensively in the next chapter. On many occasions, I arrived unprepared. I then would observe the people around, look for cues, and try to adapt. This worked out mostly in a good enough way. Once in a while, I asked what to do. The required behavioral changes in the field of individualism/collectivism were of less difficulty than the cognitive and emotional challenges.

Initially, without being much aware of this process, I began to change my own attitudes and behavior in contexts that were unrelated to my Bedouin friends. In dealings with Westerners, I found myself doing – or proposing to do – things in a more collectivistic manner, though not necessarily in a Bedouin way. For instance, in a team within the human rights organization in which I volunteered with members from other continents I realized that email communication had created Western dominance within our international team. I then introduced the notion of cultural aspects of communication and proposed to share more of our thoughts in conversation, which is a more collectivistic way of communication. Having created a video meeting, I tried to listen carefully not just to the outspoken members of the team, but also to the members who were relatively silent.

I will finish this chapter with one more comment on the issue of in- and out-groups. It seems that the occupation and its socio-political and economic consequences strengthens the tendency to collectivism among Bedouins and rural Palestinians. Confronted with ongoing oppression, there is a need to stick together. A similar development takes place on the Israeli side of the conflict, where it results in a closing of ranks when confronted with political digression. My friendship with Palestinian Bedouins accentuated my deviation from the accepted social norms in my Israeli groups of friends. What I had seen as an individual choice, unrelated to my belonging to other social groups became a collective issue. Although I was never told so by close friends, the attitude I got by some acquaintances was as if I were a betrayer. This is a sign that even in individualistic cultures a collective spirit is aroused when there is a threat of severe deviance to norms. I found it something to be aware of in intercultural friendships.

Not everyone in one's social surroundings will be content when one befriends people from a culture that is significantly different, and negative reactions to such a friendship are to be expected. I believe the level of encountered antagonism is contingent on a variety of factors, but in particular, the general attitude and openness toward the specific social group to which one's friend belongs.

CHAPTER 6

Uncertainty Avoidance

The next dimension to address is uncertainty avoidance.

> The uncertainty avoidance dimension expresses the degree to which the members of a society feel uncomfortable with uncertainty and ambiguity. The fundamental issue here is how a society deals with the fact that the future can never be known: should we try to control the future or just let it happen? Countries exhibiting strong UAI [Uncertainty Avoidance Index] maintain rigid codes of belief and behavior and are intolerant of unorthodox behavior and ideas. Weak UAI societies maintain a more relaxed attitude in which practice counts more than principles.
> HOFSTEDE n.d.-b

On the Uncertainty Avoidance Index, a higher score indicates more avoidance of uncertainty. So, let us not get confused; a high score on the Uncertainty Avoidance Index means that people request certainty and are wary of uncertainty. On this scale, Israel ranked 19 out of 53 countries and regions, indicating a tendency to avoid uncertainty, which is higher than the world average. The Arab countries ranked 27, which is about average. We may postulate that the Bedouins, because of their less stable way of life, are less avoidant of uncertainty than the general attitude in the Arab world. The Netherlands ranked 35, which is below the world average. Thus, people in the Netherlands were inclined less to avoid uncertainty (Hofstede 2001); otherwise stated, the Dutch felt less of a need for certainty. It needs to be noted that the gap on this scale between Israel and the Netherlands is large (see Figure 7). Still, populations of many countries are more inclined toward certainty than measured in Israel, and the populations of many countries are less inclined to certainty than measured in the Netherlands.

Variations in our ways of dealing with uncertainty can be seen in many aspects of the friendship, as could be learned through the stories of friendship above and specifically through our trip to Lod, to assist our Sudanese friend (see "Stories of Friendship: The Netstick"). Below, I will give examples and outline five aspects of this dimension, namely the use of language and communication, concerns about finances, favors, and other possessions, the flexibility of

UNCERTAINTY AVOIDANCE

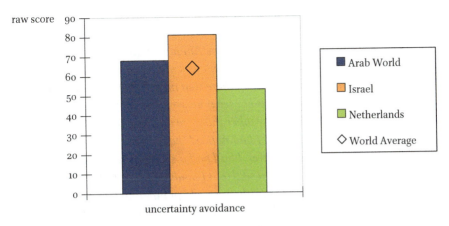

FIGURE 7   Uncertainty avoidance scores
BASED ON HOFSTEDE (2001)

time and space, the notion of planning and agreeing, and the extent to which people take risks and give trust. Although Israel appears higher on "uncertainty avoidance" than both the Netherlands and the Arab world, my experience is that on this dimension there are significant differences within Israeli society because of various cultural backgrounds. Therefore, in most of the discussions in this chapter, I will limit myself to the comparison of Bedouin and Dutch cultures and to how this difference affects the relationship.

Note that many of the following descriptions do not fit well with Hofstede's dimension of uncertainty avoidance, in the sense that it is me (the Dutch) and not my friend (the Bedouin), who is reluctant about uncertainty and expects things to be clearer, more organized, and more secure.

1   Language and Communication

Part of the problem in intercultural communication is the difference in national languages. Not less challenging is that the meaning of words – even if we understand them literally – is culturally dependent. I will expand on cultural variance regarding written, spoken, and non-verbal communication. Afterwards, I will address the difficulties in functioning in a foreign language. There are also cultural variations concerning the communication of emotions; I will refer to this topic in the next chapter, when focusing on manhood.

Stories of Friendship: Just Words

az-Zaʿayyem, June 2009. I went over to see Ahmad at his brother's petrol station about 11 PM. When I arrived, Ahmad was not there, even though he had told me that he would be working there that night. Instead, I found his brother, Abu Omar. I called Ahmad to see if he would be coming, but he replied that he is sorry but has some other things to do. I tried to hide my disappointment. A few days earlier, I had noticed that on the newly acquired pump there was no sign whatsoever. I had had a short conversation about this with Abu Omar, in which I had said that I would print the words "petrol" and "diesel", so that he could stick them on the pump. I now took the opportunity to show Abu Omar the signs I had made. I had worked on them quite a lot, to make them in the right size and in three languages (Arabic, Hebrew, and English). He thanked me but had already bought some signs from a shop.

1.1 Verbal and Non-verbal Communication

There are enormous cultural variations between the Dutch and the Bedouins on written, spoken, and non-verbal communication. For many people in North America or Western Europe, and certainly academics as both Ahmad and I are, writing is central in communication. We use writing for agreements, notes, invitations, reminders, messages of friendship, etc. We used to send our writings by letter or fax, then by text message (SMS) and email, and now often by chat. In contrast, there is hardly any writing in Bedouin life. Among the Bedouins, there is a clear preference to meet and see the other person's face and if this is not possible, they will communicate through their cellular phones. Although there are exceptions, many of the matters a Westerner would write down are remembered by Bedouins, and dealt with orally; agreements, calculations, and history in general. Even the sheikh's office, which I visited, does not have written documents.

When Ahmad does need to write something, like an email, he will invest much more time and effort than I would do in a comparable situation. This is not simply because of his limited knowledge of English but primarily because he will contemplate every line, trying – in his words – "to reach the other's heart". Therefore, he will be more concerned about the style of his writing and the impression his email will make on the receiver than about the facts. Originality is of less significance. We could compare this with the preference of many Palestinians on social networks, like Facebook, including my friends, for copying and forwarding eloquent quotes over writing original text. It seems that – at least in this respect – many Palestinians prefer not to deal with the uncertainty of originality. This preference by Palestinians for quoting over creating could be explained as well by their lower emphasis on individualism than on collectivism.

In Dutch culture, communication is open and direct; it is commonplace to tell the person exactly what you think. Dutch people are likely to say "yes" or "no" on questions that could be responded to with such an answer. Since honesty is valued highly in Dutch culture, Dutch people may express their honest thoughts in a direct way and also in circumstances which in other cultures this would be perceived as rude. They will say if they appreciate something but also if they dislike things, whether it is a meal or one's haircut, e.g. This is sometimes done in a harsh manner, which brought about the expression of "Dutch uncle, a person who issues frank, harsh, and severe comments and criticism to educate, encourage, or admonish someone" ('Dutch uncle' n.d.). Moreover, I, like many Westerners, anticipate factual information in response to my questions, and in interactions with others I want to be told whether or not my presence or something I did is appreciated.

In contrast, Ahmad and many Bedouins I met have a tendency for indirect communication. They are expressive and pleasantly warm in their communications; they may make use of a lot of figurative speech, and possibly exaggerations to establish a point. However, in their response to a straightforward question, they may be vague, offer a long and tangential response, or no response at all. Attempting to keep social harmony, they will leave many things unsaid and circumvent unpleasant answers. Therefore, they will not say "no" since this is neither polite, nor respectful, and may choose to say what you would like to hear. For example, when I left the car in the garage and would call later to ask if it was fixed, I either would receive no answer on the phone – which would be most common – or would be told that it is ready. Time after time, when I went to the garage I found that the car was not yet repaired. I regularly had to wait for hours or was asked to come back the next day.

There are more reasons for Bedouins to keep things vague, apart from not wanting to give unpleasant answers. My Bedouin friends do not feel comfortable in making commitments; things will happen when they will happen, God willing. In addition, Ahmad considers the concealment of his whereabouts as a form of protection. It is not that he has something to hide, but he does not want to be followed. I experienced this form of social scrutiny myself. On those occasions that I would move alone in the village, I would often receive a phone call from Ahmad asking what I was doing. Clearly, he had been informed of my whereabouts, whether at the hairdresser or at the bakery. Occasionally, it felt as if there was a secret service working behind my back. Sometimes, I circumvented circumstances like these by telling him ahead of time that I am entering the village (and asking if he needs something).

As much as I could appreciate Ahmad's intention of not hurting my feelings, I usually became irritated for not being plainly told "no" when appropriate (in my culture), because it put me unnecessarily in the – for me – unpleasant position of anticipating something. Ahmad realized how hard it was for me to cope with the lack of clarity. He learned to be more direct and overtly refuse me every so often. Even if this was disappointing at times, it was much less disturbing than not knowing where I stand as the result of an evasive or ambiguous answer.

Even if being told something clearly, I found it important to verify whether information provided was based on facts, and double-check later if the information remained the same. I encountered this need to verify information before building on it not only in my interactions with Bedouins, but also with other rural Palestinians. Until fairly recently I have found it burdensome not to be sure if I was told objective facts, or an idea that not necessarily will develop, or a personal impression, or "fake news".

One is supposed to understand what is meant from the context in which it is said (cf. Hall 1970). I once asked Ahmad about money he was supposed to return to me. He became annoyed. He had expected me to recognize that he is bothered by something else, and that this is not the moment to talk about money. He added that I also had raised the issue in a too direct way. He said that in case he wanted to speak with someone about money, he would say: "Perhaps we have coffee together." In the incident described above, I had turned the ambiguous situation into something unequivocal. I had interpreted Abu Omar's reaction to the suggestion to create signs for the pump as positive, assuming that he would have told me if he had had any objection or other ideas. I had related to our little conversation about this issue as a promise from my side and a kind of agreement. From his response, it is obvious that Abu Omar had interpreted my words otherwise. More about agreements will follow in the section on planning.

For the Dutch, words are almost holy. They are like facts. Not being exact is being untruthful. For instance, I recall my Dutch client, who corrected me when I greeted him with "good morning". The time was just after noon. How could I be so inaccurate? In contrast, for the Palestinian, words are ideas that need not be taken literally. When Ahmad told me that he would like to meet me on a certain night, it meant nothing more than that at that moment he had the thought of saying this to me, either since he really thought he would enjoy meeting me that night or in order to please me.

This difference between us in the use of words created substantial tensions. As much as I was aware of his use of communication, I would remain frustrated when he did not appear on the night specified. In addition, Ahmad would tend *not* to share information that he considered negative. He wouldn't tell me even important pieces of unpleasant information. This is related to matters being regarded as private, his public image, and his wish not to confront the other with bothersome information. The result of this kind of behavior from his side may be contrary to the intent, since I would interpret it as deceptive. As a result, I often had the feeling that I cannot count on him, that I am being told stories, and that he is not genuine. Once, in an effort to make Ahmad understand how I see the use of words, I told him that in *my* culture we have respect for words; we take words seriously. I asked him to be more attentive to this idea so that I will not become disturbed. He responded that he is aware of this contrast between us and does his best to provide me with clear information when he has it. Only after realizing the different use of words on a cognitive level, was I able to interpret better what was said (or not said).

Sometimes, there actually is an issue of conscious deception. As Ahmad explained to me, according to Arab culture lying is not seen as positive, but there are three exceptional situations in which Arab men are allowed (and recommended) to lie: (a) when your wife is asking too many questions; (b) to make or keep peace between friends; (c) to one's enemy. Whether true or not, this was more than merely a saying. On several occasions, I was requested to participate in lying for one of the aforementioned reasons. With these three exceptions in mind, lying was made easier. Thus, I lied to prevent upheaval on several occasions; examples of which are respectively: (a) to Ahmad's wife, about his whereabouts; (b) to Ahmad and one of his friends, about what negative things they had said about each other; (c) while in the Palestinian Authority, to Israeli soldiers, about my Jewish/Israeli identity. Though these first two examples are straightforward, one may question why, as an Israeli army officer myself, I considered Israeli soldiers as the "enemy". The reason was that, similar to the experience of many Palestinians at checkpoints in the West Bank, these soldiers could prevent the continuation of our journey or complicate my life if they knew that I'm Israeli (and not a foreigner). Even when they let me through, there were numerous occasions on which soldiers were unpleasant to me.

Although this concerned minor and non-harmful ("white") lies, with my Dutch upbringing and conception of the value of honesty, I found it incredibly hard to lie. At some point, I decided to speak with Ahmad about the issue and in particular about lying to his wife. Initially, Ahmad stopped the conversation because he felt that I insinuated that he is a liar. Only when I made clear that this was neither my intention, nor the reason for raising the point, could we continue. When he conceived of my difficulty in blurring the facts, he suggested as a compromise that I would tell his wife that he had asked me to refrain from always telling her where he is.

Ahmad is much more attuned than I to intonation and non-verbal messages. Thus, he repeatedly would be aware of my non-verbal communication before I was aware myself. He would notice and interpret my sleepy red eyes, disappointed gaze, or touch of my ear, which he interpreted as indicating some discomfort with the conversation. This for me was often a positive revelation and gave me the feeling of being understood without saying a word. Likewise, Ahmad expected me to understand him without clarifying matters verbally. Unfortunately, I am not that skilled in the comprehension of non-verbal communication, though I am getting better in it. I found it disheartening to interpret his ambiguous responses, and often erred in reading the context. Many times, I failed to make sense of the situation without explanation. Sometimes these situations substantially increased my anxiety. For example, I would make some kind of effort and did not know whether he appreciated it or was annoyed. Over the years, I improved communications with my Bedouin friends, but even now it can remain a challenge. I sometimes feel uncertain that I understand rightly or am unsure that I am interpreted in the way I want to be understood.

1.2   *A Foreign Language*

Arabic is the native language of the Bedouins. Older Bedouins, in particular those who in former years were more oriented toward Israel and worked there, speak some Hebrew. Most of the younger Bedouins around Jerusalem did not experience life before the wall, and do not speak Hebrew. In any case, in the present political context it is delicate to speak Hebrew in an Arab environment. The more educated Bedouins may know basic English, but this is the exception. For most there is little need to learn another language. Few Bedouins travel internationally, and if they do, this will be usually to Jordan or Saudi Arabia (Mecca), where one speaks Arabic as well. A couple of Ahmad's relatives went abroad for years, to live and/or study, and learned fluent Russian or English. Ahmad speaks several forms – or in his words "several languages" – of Arabic, the Bedouin style, the local style, and the city style. He speaks basic Hebrew and English as well.

I had to learn Arabic to communicate effectively but despite fervent attempts to grasp the language – through both a university course and some private lessons – my comprehension and speaking of Arabic remained at a low level.

When I do speak Arabic, it is slow and with major mistakes, and Ahmad does not have the patience to listen to it. Therefore, we usually speak Hebrew, except in those circumstances where we don't feel comfortable using this language in places in Ramallah, the capital of the Palestinian Authority, where it is safer for both of us to speak English (see "Stories of Friendship: About Friendship").

Since Ahmad's command of Hebrew and English is not as advanced as mine, I needed to simplify my use of language; something which over time became automatic. Interestingly, I started saying things his way, even though this was incorrect Hebrew. For instance, he would refer (in Hebrew) to a meal as "a meal of food", thus adding the – in Hebrew, as in English, unnecessary – words "of food". While talking with him, I would often use this same expression. This is a concrete example of "co-culturation", the reciprocal interaction between both our cultures (cf. Curtin 2010). But even when I try to speak basic Hebrew, Ahmad and I have frequent misunderstandings. These misunderstandings are partly based on the use of the language itself and partly based on Ahmad's (cultural) tendency to give the impression that he understood or agreed, because it is important to him to save face. As in the story above, the interpretation of what is said is culturally dependent, and we may use the same words but still interpret things differently. On many occasions, either of us said "but I told you," but evidently the message had not been understood.

Through the years, expectations about my level of Arabic rose and people increasingly tried to converse with me in Arabic, expecting me to understand more than I did. Now and then it happened that people would give me a speech about something, and I felt uncomfortable conveying that I do not comprehend. As I by now can make the culturally appropriate vocals and facial expressions, it was often assumed that I grasped the whole story, and more than once that was enough. Thus, I would be able to provide support to Bedouin friends who were upset about something, while grasping little from what they said. I felt ambivalent about this success, but at least it strengthened my belief as a therapist that more than learning the details of a bad story and responding with the exact encouraging words, it is the supportive attitude that is healing. When one-on-one with a Bedouin, the use of Hebrew would be possible from time to time, but encounters are rarely one-on-one. When in groups, Ahmad or others would sometimes try to give me an idea of the subject of conversation or of what is happening, but this was more the exception than the rule. As a result, I felt at a loss in many situations in which Arabic was the language of conversation. Often Ahmad would forget that I could not follow what was going on and would be surprised that I missed important pieces of information. My poor command of Arabic remains one of the things that keeps me an outsider.

A similar condition with foreigners could happen in the Netherlands as well, since not that many people speak Dutch. My experience indicates that in the Netherlands the tendency would be to turn to English (or sometimes German or French) if a foreigner was present. Alternatively, translation would be provided. My experience is that for Israelis, when there are foreigners among them the situation would be comparable to the situation among the Bedouins but not as extreme. Israelis would occasionally translate for the foreigners but would continue their conversation in Hebrew. Several of my Israeli friends expressed surprise about my attitude, which regularly leaves me in situations in which I hardly understand a word. They conveyed that they would have felt too uncomfortable to stay in such a situation. But I found several reasons to remain in these situations. I did not want to be a burden by continually asking for translation and I did not want to leave and by doing so insult those involved. So things were dynamic. Depending on a variety of factors – such as my mood, the reason for my presence there, and my available time – I was sometimes annoyed in those situations in which I didn't understand, while on other occasions I simply enjoyed the company and the atmosphere and deemed the content of the conversation of less importance.

Differences in command of foreign languages contribute to these diverse attitudes. In the Netherlands, the knowledge of foreign languages, English in particular, is of a higher level than the knowledge of English among many of the Israelis, whereas most Palestinian Bedouins do not speak English at all. We may postulate that the reason for Bedouins to speak Arabic has an ideological base as well, as speaking Hebrew has for many Israelis. In addition, both Bedouins and Israelis may find it difficult to grasp that someone cannot follow a conversation and how that makes this person feel. Nevertheless, a major cause of the cultural variance in this respect is the contrariness in value orientations. First, there is a different emphasis on individualism/collectivism. The Dutch are focused on the individual, whereas the Bedouins are focused on the group. Second, there is a different attitude toward uncertainty. The Dutch will find it important that each person present will be able to understand. For the Bedouins, the "being" is more important than the exact text of what is spoken. They will take care that you – as foreigner often before others – receive coffee or tea, and perhaps something to eat. The Dutch may be less concerned with the atmosphere or food but – more than the Bedouins – need to feel in control. Assisting you with the language would be part of helping you to be in control.

Culturally ingrained variations in the use of language are sometimes subtle and may go almost unnoticed. For example, it took me years until I became aware that the understanding of what is called "working" is different for Ahmad than for me. Ahmad would equate "work" with "making money", whereas

I would refer to "work" as something requiring a certain amount of effort. When I would be busy with volunteer work or reading a professional article, I would consider this "work"; Ahmad would not regard it as such. If he invested money in something, he would relate to it as if he or his money is "working". In contrast, I would neither consider an ongoing investment as work nor consider that my money could be "working". Until I realized the difference between us in the use of the term "work", this discrepant attitude to the concept of work caused confusion. The variation in the use of this term could be based on the characteristics of the specific languages, Arabic and English and Hebrew, but I deem it to be related to a difference in cultural approach to the term, something that would transcend a certain language.

I needed to learn a new language, not only the words but also their cultural interpretation. I succeeded in doing so to some degree. I can create a simple conversation in Arabic and can shop without using other languages. Despite my feeble command of the language, my involvement in Arab culture made me now and then think in Arabic. Some words became more readily available to me in Arabic than in other languages, and would come out unintended, like *mabruk* (= blessed, congratulations). This was fine in the realm of the friendship, but in my work with clients, I had to be careful not to turn accidentally to Arabic, which was likely to make them raise their eyebrows. My experience is that acquiring a new language comes with the development of a new part in my identity. It is as if I am a little different when I think in different languages.

2   Mine and Yours

The distinction between "mine" and "yours" may be self-evident for the Westerner. For the Bedouin, most things are "ours"; at least among friends. Although this topic is related conceptually to the dimension of individualism/collectivism, its challenge was in the field of uncertainty. I will explain here the themes of finances, favors, and possessions.

Stories of Friendship: Who Pays the Bill?

Jerusalem, October 2000. Our first intercultural difficulty happened a few months after we got acquainted, on my 40th birthday. I had invited a large number of friends to a party at a local bar. I had also invited a performer and some light snacks were offered. We had an enjoyable time. At the end of the evening, the owner of the bar informed me that there is one unpaid bill.

Later, I realized that the bill was that of Jaffer, the taxi driver, and Ahmad. I felt highly uncomfortable about the situation but eventually decided to confront them. As it had not occurred to me that guests would order from the menu and then not pay their bills, it had not occurred to them that they were expected to pay for themselves.

2.1   Finances and Favors

I do not recall how we settled this incident, but the situation clearly revealed a difference between Dutch, Israeli, and Palestinian norms. A humoristic guidebook on Dutch culture (White and Boucke 2006) relates to the Dutch as the stingiest people in Europe, having a hard time parting with their money. The book explains that this has several origins, including their Calvinistic history and their desire to not waste anything. Thus, when people go out to a restaurant in the Netherlands people "go Dutch": everyone pays his or her share. If one's expenses are paid for, one returns the favor as soon as possible. Similarly, presents in the Netherlands tend to be significantly smaller than is common in Israel, thus reducing feelings of obligation or debt toward others. For the Dutch, the notion is "I will not burden you and you will not burden me." In this sense, I admit that I am rather Dutch, though under the influence of the friendship nowadays less than in previous times.

In Israel, it is common for friends to bring food and drink to private parties, and costly presents are common. There would be no clear guidelines concerning events like the one described above. In an attempt to verify my intuition, I asked both Israelis and Dutch people (all Jewish), including some who were present at the party, how they would have acted. Almost all replied that they would have verified in advance who will pay before ordering from the menu. They would have wanted things to be clear from the start. With the Jahalin Bedouins, if you hold a party, friends will usually come empty-handed and all costs are yours.

For the Palestinian Bedouin, it is a fact that material things, including money, come and go. Therefore, if someone owes you money and you found out he earned money on a certain day, you better get your money on that same day, because otherwise you missed your chance. Thus, one day my friend could have a pile of banknotes in his pocket, and the next day he could be without money to buy food. In any case, one pays when one has the money, and not necessarily on the day one was supposed to pay. Delayed payment is considered acceptable. Having credits or debts in relation to friends and family members is part of the Palestinian Bedouin social system. In line with this understanding, Ahmad would go out of his way to assist someone financially, as he did when he helped finance the wedding of a friend. Of course, this has its limits, though sometimes one will be excused for not paying at all for the sake of keeping up good relations. For example, if a man is without money, either because he had been in prison (Palestinian or Israeli), or because he could not open his shop as a result of an Israeli closure, or most recently because of COVID-19, he may be exempt from paying rent.

There is flexibility in the workplace too as regarding finances. This is noticeable in various ways. First, the costs of a repair are likely to be higher than initially stated. Whereas in the West, one could be told in a garage about how much something is going to cost, in these surroundings one is told an attractive price, and in the process of repair other costs will be added. Several times I tried to explain – to no avail – that for someone like me it is better to give a higher cost estimate in advance, and then give a reduction if the costs were lower, than giving a lower estimate in advance, and raising it later. Even if in both cases I would pay the same, with the latter manner of presenting the price I would experience the deal as more expensive and possibly feel swindled, whereas in the former manner of presentation I would be pleased that it turned out less.

Second, payments to the garage are often dependent on the financial possibilities or relationship with the client, and not necessarily based on the time the mechanic spent fixing the vehicle. Third, in an environment where one hardly makes use of bank accounts, credit cards, or virtual methods of payments, one most commonly pays in cash. If there is a need to buy parts, cash is often given in advance, so that these parts can be bought. If not, payment is preferably made immediately after the car is fixed, but occasionally clients may pay later. I had to get used to the fact that payments are not always in money. Sometimes clients pay for the repair of their car in goods, such as a cellular phone or a watch. This way of dealing is uncommon in the modern Western world, where one almost always pays by some form of monetary transaction.

Last, with the same notion of responsibility regarding workers and flexibility in finances, salaries may fluctuate depending on the income of the garage, while at the same time expenses of workers that are not directly related to the garage could be paid for. Thus, Ahmad paid for the police fine of Fawaz, the mechanic in "Stories of Friendship: At the Garage".

It is a question of doing favors. For the rural Palestinian or Bedouin, the idea around sharing of finances is something like "I will do you a favor, and when the time comes, you'll return it," which is in sharp contrast to the situation in the Netherlands. This way of looking at things is so much a part of the culture that Bedouins may take affront when you do not allow them to go through great pains for you. Comparable to the Western notion of favors, among the

Bedouins favors tend to come with strings attached, which is the main reason I dislike favors being done for me.

Furthermore, favors are viewed as transferable between people, at least in the Bedouin and rural Palestinian collective world. For instance, in the garage Ahmad (or one of his workers) could make enormous efforts to assist a friend of mine. Such an effort then would be regarded as a personal favor to *me*. Raised on individualism, this notion of transferability of favors was new to me and it took me time to grasp it. Favors Ahmad did for friends of mine at times put me in an uncomfortable position and/or created tension between us, since I would not necessarily have done the same for a friend of either of us. More than that, I would not expect a friend of mine to do the same for me or to do anything at all in return for something I did, or someone else did on my behalf.

What makes the issue of financing even more complicated in a friendship is the difference in resources. Among the Bedouins, the richer person is often supposed to pay for the poorer person. A foreigner is by definition perceived as affluent, and the expectations were likewise so that people asked me to either pay for them or lend them money. I believe I actually was the richer individual in many social situations. Nevertheless, there were more than a few occasions when well-to-do Palestinians attended the event who were probably wealthier than me. In these cases, I needed to decide how much money to give, if at all, while it was often unclear to me whether or not I would get the money back.

For me, the issue of money was fraught with anxiety. The problem was not so much the amount of money that I was about to lose, which usually was not large, but the feeling of uncertainty. This is comparable to the difference between the Western concept of fixed prices and the idea that prices are negotiable, which is a common concept in other parts of the world. I never know whether I am expected to pay or not; if I am okay, stingy, or being used. Do I pay too much or too little? Do I give the money as a gift or as a loan? Even today I do not feel comfortable with these situations, which could occur in Israel as well. I prefer being told how much I am supposed to pay rather than having to suggest a price myself, as there is the possibility of either insulting the other person or paying more than needed. Similarly, I learned to prefer giving money as a present versus not knowing whether or when it will be returned.

2.2 *Possessions*

Greatly related to finances and favors is the matter of possessions. There is remarkable dissimilarity in how cultures relate to them. For the Dutch, there is a clear distinction between what is yours and what is mine. I previously discussed the cultural aspect of the concept of personal belongings when discussing my opening a letter addressed to Ahmad. I now will develop this a bit further.

According to Dutch concepts, a loss is a loss, whether it is money, time, or something material, and if you caused the loss, you are the one to blame. Therefore, you will be cautious about losing or damaging anything. In addition, you will take care that you have enough reserves, pay on time, and do your utmost to not borrow from others. Moreover, either you have or do not have something. One does not leave things up in the air. So, despite my affluent childhood environment, I learned to cherish possessions and to not throw away anything unless it cannot be used anymore. This also concerns trousers that are too small but still in decent shape, and leftovers from a meal, even if it is only half a potato. Everything will be used or re-used. One keeps things because you never know when they will be needed. Not surprisingly, with such a culture, flea markets are common in the Netherlands and considered mainstream. So are repair shops for anything. With this in mind, I will buy something new only if I really need it. Perhaps I overdo this, as I have clothing in my closet that I haven't worn for 30 years. The same goes for being heedless about expiration dates on food or medicine. But that is the way I am, and it certainly is a product of my Dutch culture, at least to some degree.

In Bedouin life, at one point you have something, at another point it will be gone. Whether he has or hasn't something, Ahmad easily throws out what he does not need anymore. Like other Bedouins I met, he is always willing to share with others. He and his friends borrow freely and commonly from each other, not necessarily returning things to their original owner. There is no use being upset for a loss and there is no need to blame someone for causing it. On many occasions, I found it more painful when something was lost or ruined than Ahmad, even if it belonged to him – money, a shirt, a new cup. He would move on, whereas I sometimes continued to sulk. I often found this strange, as I had imagined that in a relatively poor environment one would be more careful in handling objects and more upset with losses. But this was not the case. It seems there is a different kind of attachment, or at least an easier manner of letting go. This can be seen with pets too. Together, Ahmad and I cared for all kind of pets. I would be upset for weeks after a pet died. In contrast, he would move on immediately, stating "that's the nature of things," even though he too had been attached to the creature.

Another difference was related to more flexibility regarding ownership of possessions. Ahmad would expect that at his friend's home he could behave as in his own home – as long as no women are present – and vice versa. He therefore would see it as self-evident that he could fetch whatever he fancied from my refrigerator, use my towel, or take compact discs from my car. He did not imagine this to be different at my party so he ordered what he fancied. On our visit to the Netherlands, he could appear wearing my father's sweater. Not that I (or my father) would have objected, but in my culture this kind of thing is not done without asking permission, even among friends or family. One respects the fact that the item belongs to the other. Here again, the difficulty I had had to do with uncertainty. In cases where he took something, my thoughts would be like this: What happened to [the specific object]? Did he borrow it? Will he give it back? Not necessarily, but if he will, when? This was especially bothersome when it involved objects that I cared about, or those belonging to a Western friend who might be less appreciative of Bedouin customs.

I adjusted, but even after many years the issue of "borrowing" makes me feel uncomfortable. Sometimes I share my feelings, but more often I keep silent. My reasoning is that Ahmad does not see the importance of talking about emotions, which is an issue to be illuminated in the next chapter. Furthermore, if he would have asked me for the object in advance, I probably would have given it readily. Ahmad realizes the dissimilarity between us in this respect. He will be supportive when there is a loss. Instead of me taking things from him – as he does with my things – from time to time he simply insists that I take things from him, like clothes or food.

3   Time and Space

There is also a huge discrepancy between the Dutch and the Bedouin attitude toward time and space, as the following incident shows. Below, I will explain both themes.

Stories of Friendship: An Urban Desert

Trip with Ahmad to my family, Amsterdam, July 2010. I joined my father on a visit to my 101-year-old grandmother. When I returned to my parents' home in the late afternoon, my mother told me that Ahmad had gone out for a walk. At 6 PM the table was set, but Ahmad had not yet returned. We waited for some time and then had dinner. My parents were getting worried and at 8 PM they suggested that we call the police, believing that something could have happened to him. I realized that Ahmad was not aware of the strict Dutch dinnertime and that in his own environment he may return in the middle of the night without prior notice. I also knew that he had left without his phone and that he was not familiar with either the name of the street or the house number. While coping with my own worry and anger, I attempted to calm my parents, telling them that – knowing Ahmad – he will be fine. At night I tried to sleep.

At 6 AM, Ahmad entered, soaking wet from the rain and dead tired. He had gone downtown, where he made some new acquaintances. He stayed with them for a few hours and had enjoyed himself. He knows extremely well how to navigate in the desert but trying to find his way back in the similar streets along the canals of Amsterdam, he lost his way. He then walked for hours to find the house. In the meantime, rain had started. He then encountered a gypsy woman, who had given him a sweater to wear. Upon his return, he simply went to sleep. He was not aware of any upheaval he had caused, and I – happy that he was okay – could not be angry anymore.

3.1   Flexibility of Time

Cultures are diverse in their attitude to punctuality, with Latin American, Middle Eastern, and African cultures being much more lenient in time than European and North American cultures (Samovar et al. 2009). The Dutch will be precise and strict. Monday is Monday and 8.00 PM is not the same as 8.30 PM; in fact, in the Netherlands, one would distinguish between 8 PM and 8.05 PM. Arriving late by more than a quarter of an hour is out of the question. Meetings have not only a time to start but usually also a fixed time to end.

In Israel, there is great variety in relationship to time management, to such an extent that in planning I habitually ask whether the time reference is strict (Western) or flexible (Eastern). Both social and work-related situations can have a very tight time schedule or be very lenient, depending on the culture of the host. I recall that in my first years in Israel I was invited for dinner and arrived at the agreed time, only to find that my friend, of Eastern origin, was in the shower. But if I arrive ten minutes late to dinner at the home of a friend of mine of Western origin, I will be asked what happened. The same can be true for business meetings.

In substantial parts of the Arab world, time is more flexible and used as if it is endless (cf. Obeidat et al. 2012). For the rural Palestinian, 8 PM means sometime at night. Monday is around Monday, God willing, if things work out. Arriving at the exact hour is out of the question. Meetings usually do not have an ending time and may continue for many hours. My experience showed that if a rural Palestinian says that he will be with you "in a moment", this does not necessarily mean that he is already on his way to you; it may still take an hour or more until arrival. Occasionally, such a delay could be caused by an unexpected event, like a flat tire, a temporary Israeli checkpoint, or someone they met on the way, but the main explanation is the cultural difference in attitude.

The Bedouins are even more flexible with time. This may seem a grave generalization based on orientalism, but it really felt as if they only differentiate between past, present, and future; as if they are "time blind", hardly distinguishing between various points in either the past or the future. It is of utmost importance to consider this flexibility in the use of time, as well as their flexibility in the use of words (as was explained previously) and the flexibility regarding location (which will be explained subsequently). Taking this into account, one understands that "I'll be with you in a moment" from the mouth of a Bedouin is not even a promise that eventually he will appear. Many things may interfere.

One therefore may wonder how Ahmad or other Bedouins cope in their encounters with institutions. Actually, these encounters can be problematic. Ahmad found it strenuous to adapt to the relatively strict office hours or even the hours of his university classes, and as a result, he would find himself repeatedly in front of closed doors. He had been wearing a watch irregularly and it did not necessarily show the right time. Several weeks after the start of Daylight Saving Time, I pointed out to him that he had not yet changed the hour. I was not surprised to find out that he did not care to adjust it. He would not bother about an hour earlier or later, as in the story above; an hour for him one way or another is all about the same.

The metaphor "time is money" is – like other metaphors – a cultural construct according to which we live in the West (Lakoff and Johnson 2003). I take care of time, spend it carefully, and plan it. It seems that time is like money for Ahmad as well; it comes and goes, and he spends it when he has it. (This is my perspective; when asking Ahmad about it, I realized that he does not see much of a relationship between the two concepts.) The disparity between Ahmad and me in the notion of time – as one can learn from both our work in the garage and our visit to Amsterdam – was a burden on the friendship in its first phase. Every so often I found myself waiting for him, and – from my perspective – losing hours without good reason. This was even more annoying when it forced me to reschedule or give up other plans. I recall a situation in which he told me that he would be back in a minute. I hung around his brother's petrol station and called him several times to ask what happened but got evasive answers. Only after an hour, did I discover that he was far away and that it would take him much longer since he had something to deal with. These situations could outrage me.

Over the years, Ahmad adjusted somewhat on the issue of time management. He now may tell me in advance if something will take a lot of time. But the more pronounced change was in me. I became accustomed to the idea of flexibility of time and adjusted my expectations. I realize that in encounters with him – or with other Bedouins – anything could take much longer than I find reasonable – hours, days, or weeks. Also, when estimating the time span of *his* actions, I mostly rely more on my own than on his calculations. Most important, I no longer anticipate that he will be there at the time he said he would be. I wait for him as long as I want to wait, and I know that I will meet him only when I see him.

Coping differently with time around the Bedouins somewhat affected how I related to time in my relation to Jewish friends. I am a punctual person, and in the past, I would become upset if I or someone else was late. Nowadays, I feel more comfortable occasionally arriving a bit late (not too much and not too often), and I will not make a fuss if someone else is late. Furthermore, it is common for psychodynamic therapists to interpret clients' late arrivals. Recognizing that people may have a different perception of time or simply did not plan too well, I now rarely make this kind of interpretation unless it is a recurring issue.

3.2 *Flexibility of Space*

Hospitality is interpreted differently in Dutch and Bedouin cultures. Although I did prepare both Ahmad and my parents for the encounter, I should have done a better job in clarifying cultural diversity and expectations. The dissimilar expectations about hospitality as they come about in the incident depicted above are striking. In the dominant Dutch culture, visits are planned – often long in advance – and the guest adapts to the plans of the host. One does not simply appear at a friend's door, or – if invited – one is not supposed to stay overnight unplanned. When being a guest at someone's place for several days, one is supposed to say "goodbye" upon going out and to make known in advance roughly what time one will return. In contrast, visits among the Bedouins are unplanned and Bedouin hosts will adapt their own plans to accommodate visitors.

As for separating, most Bedouins and Palestinians I met say "goodbye" and shake hands when leaving, in a similar way to what is customary in North America and Europe, but it is also common to leave without any sign. More than once I was in situations in which Bedouins would simply disappear from the scene, sometimes returning later. Ahmad and I usually shake hands when we separate, but he could disappear as well. Sometimes he would return after hours, or after a day, not informing anyone where he was. This did not seem to bother others, but at times it did bother me. Being aware that I would react badly if he disappeared, he mostly gave me some minimal information concerning his departure or whereabouts. I will return to this point in the last part of this book, when I will share some thoughts about the process of the creation of the book.

The dissimilarity between us regarding the flexibility of space is much less obvious than that regarding flexibility of time. I relate to objects as each having its own place and people having their own space. I am used to houses and offices having an address and a phone number. For example, in my perception a person lives in building number X on street Y and has phone number Z. In Dutch dominant culture, a person who wants to go somewhere will probably ask for the address; meaning, for the name of the street, the number of the building, and the number of the apartment. In the past, one would have located the place on the map, but now most people use navigation applications such as Google or Waze. To make sure that nothing will go wrong, people make note of the phone number of the place they are going. I believe that is true in Israel too.

As we have seen in the story about our trip to the town of Lod (see "Stories of Friendship: The Netstick"), but also in the story above (see "Stories of Friendship: An Urban Desert"), this is different for Ahmad. He would neither know nor care about names of streets. Moreover, movement is central in his life, as it is central in Bedouin nomad life, and directions are not so much planned in advance as they are adjusted on the way. He would drive to another city without the address of the place to go and ask complete strangers on the way "Where is the garage of Abu Laban?" or "Where lives Mr. such and such?" Once we were in a suburb of the Palestinian town Ramallah, and Ahmad decided to pay a visit to one of his university teachers. He knew in which neighborhood his teacher lived, but nothing more. We went to the specific neighborhood and he asked the owner of a kiosk about the address, mentioning only the name of his teacher and describing his appearance. Then a small boy came out and took us to the right address. The teacher – who had not expected us – was happy to invite us in.

On numerous occasions when we intended to meet or when he wanted me to go somewhere, the directions I received were – from my perspective – awfully vague. They were something like "I will be in neighborhood X," or "I will be on the main road," or "in the street of the Post Office near the hotel with the steep stairs inside." Locating him was a challenge at which I mostly succeeded. This required substantial adjustment to recognizing that I will not obtain an address before I go somewhere. I learned to check in advance of a meeting with Ahmad whether he is in the place I think he will be or perhaps in a different location.

Unlike me, for Ahmad objects do not have a specific space; they can be either here or there. So, there is neither a specific place for the car, nor for the keys. When tired, he will rest his head wherever he is; not necessarily at his place or on his bed. This is different for spaces related to modesty, like a shower or women's quarters, which will have strict borders that must be respected, as I will explain in Chapter 7, "Masculinity and Femininity".

4   Planning

Although the topic of "planning" is intrinsically related to the topic of "time and space", it is such an important issue that I decided to put it in a separate section, in which I will review cultural divergence in making plans and reaching agreements. The following is the story of a small incident related to separations, leading to intercultural difficulties around the issue of planning.

Stories of Friendship: Goodbyes

Jerusalem/az-Za'ayyem, Wednesday morning, November 2010. When Ahmad married his American wife, Um Nimer, their intent was to live together in the United States. However, they encountered great difficulty in getting him a visa. It was important for them that their children be born in the U.S. and acquire U.S. citizenship, and as a consequence, Um Nimer and the children moved back and forth between the Palestinian village and the U.S. Throughout the past year, they lived with Ahmad, but in a few days, they will go back to the U.S., where they will remain for about half a year, during which time Um Nimer will give birth. This departure – on which they decided months ago – is a difficult event in the life of the family. They cannot fly from the relatively nearby airport in Tel Aviv, because – like many Palestinians – they cannot enter Israel freely. Therefore, they will need to travel half a day, via the Allenby Bridge, to reach Amman (Jordan) and fly from there. I wanted to come and say "goodbye". Um Nimer and the children are usually at home and awake until midnight, but this kind of a visit needs to be planned, since – for cultural reasons – she cannot receive male guests without the presence of a male family member. I called Ahmad on the phone and the following is an excerpt of our conversation.
Daniel: When can I come and say "goodbye" to your family?
Ahmad: Come on Friday or Saturday.
Daniel: But isn't the flight on Friday night?!?!
Ahmad: My wife knows that kind of things. So, perhaps come today or tomorrow, and take them to the Allenby Bridge on Friday.

Daniel: That is fine, but if you want me to help, we need to plan that, so that I will be free. Especially, since you said before that the bridge closes at 10.00 in the morning.

Ahmad: Yes, so perhaps I will go there tomorrow to get them a number, because in the morning it will be terribly busy.

Daniel: I did not know one needs a number. By the way, didn't you say that you want to join them into Jordan?

Ahmad: Yes, I will.

Daniel: You realize that they will have lots of luggage and that I cannot take all. My car is small. Perhaps there need to be two cars.

Ahmad: Yes, you are right.

Daniel: About meeting… I can make it later this morning, or tonight or tomorrow night but in both cases only late at night.

Ahmad: Ok, so let us talk later.

Daniel: Ok

4.1 Making a Plan

Cultures vary widely in time orientation, the respective values they place on the past, the present, and the future (Samovar et al. 2009). My personal experience is that Bedouins give importance to "being in the moment". They are mostly oriented toward the present, while taking the past heavily into account. Israelis as well tend to emphasize the present, but for them both past and future are relevant. Western Europeans and North Americans tend to relate much less to the past. They will consider the present but will be oriented toward the future and will try to forecast and control it. This orientation toward the future requires planning. For Westerners, the idea of planning is an obvious part of life. The Dutch like to leave little uncertainty about what is to come. One tends to control details of events. Among the Bedouins, planning happens in other ways. I have touched on this topic in the section on "work attitudes" in the previous chapter but I will expand on it here.

Ahmad explained Bedouin planning as follows: "There are differences among the Bedouins, with some being more organized than others. However, if a Dutch person would like to plan 90% of life, the Bedouin would plan for about 20%. We may plan to pray or to eat; we also may have plans for the future. I have plans for each of the workers in the garage and for the future of my family and myself. I have no written plans, but I have plans in my head. Because they are in my head, plans are not so exact, and sometimes I forget things, or I may change them. I do not stick to what is written. We are not like the Europeans, who have had generations of planning. We dwelled in the desert and were subject to a hot and dry climate; this much influenced our ways of planning." On another occasion he explained how nature can guide planning: "We moved around according to the availability of food for the goats, and the sun guided us in when to get up or go to sleep. This changed only when we started to settle down."

In these words, Ahmad referred to the history of the Bedouins, but remember that his first years of life were in this semi-nomadic lifestyle, living in a tent or cave. In later years his family moved to permanent housing, but he retained a nomadic state of mind (cf. Galilee 2019). His attitude regarding planning is in line with findings from a recent study on Israeli Bedouin women in the Israeli Negev, the place where the Jahalin Bedouins lived before their transfer in the early 1950s. This study relates to the fact that planning has traditionally not been highly valued in the Bedouin context but found that the younger generation is more aware of its importance. The older generation sees less of a need to plan, as eventually things happen according to God's will, and they rely on faith (Braun-Lewensohn et al. 2019).

In Western style, travel arrangements and goodbyes – such as those in the story above – would be organized long before. People involved would know – at least more or less – what, when, and where something is going to happen. For the Bedouins, there is much more space for spontaneity. Things will remain open until they happen. In some respect, one can compare it with a pendulum, which sways back and forth until it stops. Circular or contradicting movement can be observed, seemingly without purposeful direction. Thus, on many occasions, while seeing Ahmad move in a certain direction, I would join him and continue on that path in a direct line. This could be related to a program of work for the garage, ideas for a house renovation, or the planning of the departure of his family. When moments or days later he changed directions, I still would be in the previous course of action, not realizing that he turned. Likewise, he would not understand why I continued building on a previous thought. This often led to clashes between us. In other conditions, not a lot seemed to take place until some factors converged and tipped the balance toward action; then action could be immediate and without much additional consideration. In this way, weeks could go by in which I would wait for him to deal with something, and then suddenly it had to be done instantly, without much talking. For the outsider this may appear an impulsive manner of dealing with things, which is unlikely to be successful. Regularly, I would stop him and suggest that we first talk things over, to which his amazed response would be something like "so what did we do until now?" My paucity of Arabic adds to my inability to grasp plans, but my understanding is that the essence is a cultural difference regarding planning.

As for the "Goodbye" story above, I believe that for many a Westerner it is hard to remain calm in an interaction like that, even though things will mostly work out fine if done in the Bedouin style. In this case, everything was arranged only on the morning of departure. Ahmad took the luggage to the border before dawn, and I came to say "goodbye" a little later and then took the whole family to the bridge in my car.

Another short dialogue with Ahmad will better clarify how he relates to planning: Ahmad called me at half past eleven at night, while I was already in bed. We did not manage to meet that day. I asked if he would possibly have some free time during the following morning. He replied in surprise: "You ask me about tomorrow? You think I know what I will do in the next hour?"

I found it extremely challenging not to take it personally and not to feel insulted when a friend did not appear for an appointment or told me that he will do something (like calling back or taking care of something) and simply did not do it. It was just slightly easier to realize in advance that it is likely he will *not* do what he said he would do. In addition, I struggled with the understanding that for many Bedouins decisions on courses of action are neither a linear consequence of planning, nor necessarily based on facts. I had to remind myself repeatedly that this way of perceiving the notion of a plan is different from mine. Still, I found it incredibly difficult not to be judgmental about these situations and relate to them merely as cultural differences. Had he been a Westerner, I would have asked myself what kind of friend makes a promise and then does not keep it. In the dominant culture in Western Europe and North America, at some point one probably would confront the friend. What if the person is a Bedouin? This is his style of living, his culture. If one confronts him, he will lose face, something that is likely to increase the difficulties and not solve them.

4.2   *Reaching Agreement*

There also is a clear dissimilarity between how both cultures relate to agreements. As mentioned before, many Bedouins tend to refrain from refusals. If they are in disagreement, they will respond in an evasive manner or simply agree in the understanding – for them – that the context will explain that it actually is a "no". I will return to this idea when I discuss the issue of "honor". By contrast, many a Westerner, accustomed to straightforward talk if one does not agree, may find this confusing, if not highly frustrating. For a Dutch person, a non-response is often assumed to be an expression of agreement, and a "let's talk about this later" is assumed to be a concrete suggestion, while for many a Bedouin both are polite ways of turning someone down. For instance, on several occasions I expected something from Ahmad, while he actually did not have the opportunity to fulfill my expectation. In other instances, the intention to fulfill the expectation was there, but the absence of planned action prevented fulfillment. In both types of situations, Ahmad would feel uncomfortable telling me to my face that he could not do it and I would feel uncomfortable asking him. Consequently, an unpleasant tension around certain open issues could stay for weeks or months.

Even if both sides agreed on some idea, there still may be confusion. On many occasions, I thought that Ahmad and I had agreed on something, which turned out not to be the case. In Dutch dominant culture, when you talk with someone about what you are going to do, you expect exactly that to happen, or otherwise you will notify each other as if there were an official agreement. One may agree on an appointment at a fixed day and time many months in advance, and if needed, one changes the appointment in a timely manner. For the rural Palestinian, plans are intentions. Intentions may change according to the circumstances and actions can turn out hugely different from stated intentions. There is no need to notify people about changes in action, since what was said in advance was never meant to be a fact. You plan for not more than a few days ahead, at best, and you better check before your appointment whether it is still standing, even if you agreed on meeting that same day.

In many Western cultures, one expects to be told facts unless some degree of uncertainty will be stated. Take the following situation. The price is X. Tomorrow, I will fetch you Y. Let us do Z later. If you responded "ok", we may expect in the West that this is going to happen. The price will not change, I will fetch the item tomorrow, and I expect us to do what we agreed on. If one is not completely sure, one will mention that by adding "perhaps", "possibly", or "let me check this," etc. In regards to the signs I prepared for the petrol station (see "Stories of Friendship: Just Words"), unless stated differently, I would believe there is an agreement. Also, in the story above, I would have anticipated prior agreement to a plan regarding the "goodbye". Not so for the Bedouins. Uncertainty is part of the initial statement, without being mentioned, and agreements can always change.

Sometimes though there are clear disagreements. In the West, in case of disagreement, one figures out who is right and who is wrong by checking the facts. For the Bedouins, other things besides facts will be taken into account. In case of disagreement, the eventual decision is to a considerable extent based on questions such as how to keep the relationship and what is the power differential between the parties involved. It is customary to involve more people in the disagreement, each of whom will come with their own weight in the discussion. The disagreement will possibly be reconciled through a *sulha*. Issues of power differential will be addressed in Chapter 8, "Power Distance".

5 Taking Risks

Hofstede (2001) warned against confusing uncertainty avoidance with risk avoidance. Nevertheless, the two concepts are related and variance in attitude toward risk taking is relevant when it comes to intercultural friendship. Dutch life can be regarded as rather calm. Israeli life is often more challenging. Life for the Bedouins is full of physical and other risks; without taking risks – sometimes big risks – one cannot live.

> ### Stories of Friendship: The Traffic Jam
>
> *al-Eizariya, November 2009, early night. Bill, the President of my university, came from the U.S.A. for a visit. Bill, Ahmad and I got stuck in a traffic jam somewhere in this small Palestinian town, probably because of a car accident. Palestinian traffic laws exist, but al-Eizariya is in Area B, i.e., jointly controlled by Israel and the Palestinian Authority, and paradoxically, it has neither Israeli nor Palestinian police. Thus, for about two decades no governmental authority has enforced the law. No one around seemed to care that cars were all over, and people were driving in whatever direction they thought appropriate, irrespective of the lane they were in. In my perception we were stuck, but Ahmad saw this otherwise. He was not interested in having us wait until the traffic jam dissolved and decided to make the car jump the barrier between both lanes. Although in my eyes it was obvious that it was impossible to do so without severely damaging the car, he succeeded. The car only made a strange squeak. Then, he took us – in the dark – downhill, through an unpaved bypass with huge gaps in the road. I was overly concerned, not just because of the situation but also because of Bill's possible discomfort and negative impressions. This could easily go wrong, but it did not. We did leave the car a few times to lower its weight and get over the bumps, but eventually we managed to return to the main road and made it home safely.*

5.1 *Physical and Other Risks*

We can relate to risk taking in terms of comfort zones: "A comfort zone is a psychological state in which things feel familiar to a person and they are at ease and in control of their environment, experiencing low levels of anxiety and stress" (White 2009). It seems that when it comes to physical danger, the comfort zone for many rural Palestinians is larger than for many Westerners. They would feel fine in a variety of circumstances in which those used to living comfortably in the West may feel insecure. In general, it seems that most Westerners are less willing to give up physical security, and the Dutch, specifically, experience even a little physical insecurity as dangerous.

The incident above provides some indication that Palestinian Bedouins may take more risks and cope more easily with certain kinds of physical danger than Westerners. Moreover, my impression is that for many a Westerner physical integrity and life itself are of utmost value, while among the Bedouins they may be risked more easily for ulterior values, such as honor. It is beyond doubt that many Westerners would have perceived the situation in this story as too risky and would have refrained from getting involved. In the present political atmosphere, many Westerners (and Israelis even more) would perceive merely being at the place we were – an alley of a Palestinian town – as too risky. In contrast, in al-Eizariya it was a normal part of life. On our way, we met many people and they all looked friendly and calm. That is, they were calm relative to what is common in Middle Eastern or Mediterranean cultures, in which people tend to be emotionally less inhibited than in the global North and West, especially when it comes to the expression of frustration and anger. People were accustomed to cars driving against the supposed direction of the traffic and no one looked surprised by our small group going down such a bad road. Even the truck in front of us that tilted to such a point that it was about to hit the truck coming from the opposite direction did not cause any upheaval. The calmness around us had a reassuring effect on us.

Ahmad is in the habit of saying that he does not know fear, which therefore makes him extreme in his risk taking. His risk taking was noted by others in his environment but did not bother them even when his behavior could affect them. But for me this was different, and repeatedly, I found myself the only person questioning his actions. Sometimes with Ahmad and his family, I struggled to keep my calm, because I felt that the physical risks were too great. In contrast, he more than once became upset with my – in his view – overreaction to small events, such as his wife using a huge knife to open a can, or his not yet two-year-old son climbing over the wall of the veranda.

Risks were evident in many situations. I previously mentioned time-related risks including such things as not checking deadlines and arriving for a flight at the last minute. Examples of other risks are speeding with his car, driving on the last drops of petrol, going somewhere without any money, or crawling over the separation wall between Israel and the Palestinian Authority. Perhaps

I would not have mentioned these examples were it not for the fact that I saw those around him do the same. The way of thinking must have be something like this: If there are no police, why stick to a speed limit or use a seat belt? If one does not have money, why would this stop someone from trying to go somewhere? If one cannot enter Israel in the legally sanctioned way, how does one enter Israel? So, regarding the issue of taking risks, apart from the cultural aspects, socio-political and economic factors were at stake.

The downside of comfortably taking risks is that things go wrong more often. Seen from my perspective, this makes one vulnerable, but from his perspective it is nothing out of the ordinary. Accordingly, I would often be more concerned than he was, even though if things went wrong, they would affect him more than me. Thus, he would get stuck on his way, sometimes during the night, and walk a long distance to find petrol. Likewise, every time he entered Israel, he knew he could get arrested, and this happened, but it seemed that it worried him less than it worried me. In both kinds of situations, I would sometimes be able to help, but still the risk was his.

Something about the Dutch and their need for assurance that everything will be safe and certain is evident in the fact that in 2016 the Dutch spent the highest percentage of their income on insurance, as compared to other European countries (Verbond van Verzekeraars 2017). I personally am insured for my health, my profession as a psychologist, my pension, my apartment, and my car. The insurance expenses are quite high. The idea of insurance via an insurance company is not part of Bedouin life. Ahmad does not have the burden of insurance expenses. On several occasions, he lost substantial amounts of money and assets because something went wrong at the garage or with his car. There was no insurance to cover the costs, but as he once commented, "my family is my insurance," and on another occasion, "for your brother you'll forget the world." He would rely on his family in case of need. This kind of reliance on family support would be extraordinary in Western individualistic countries, where people may prefer trusting banks and authorities rather than relying on their family.

With some kinds of risks, I became more like Ahmad and distinct from members of my family; for example, regarding health-related issues. I will clarify this through two situations that occurred on the same visit to my family in the Netherlands. On one occasion, Ahmad was bitten by a horse. My father wanted to take him to a doctor to make sure that he was okay. On the other occasion, Ahmad found a hedgehog in the garden and wanted to show it to my nieces. My sisters-in-law stopped him out of worry that it would transmit diseases. In both cases, neither Ahmad nor I saw a reason for concern.

But there was also concrete physical danger for me. Palestinian existence is not that safe, and with Ahmad, life is even more hazardous. I obviously would have enjoyed more objective safeguards, but if I wanted to be more than a distant friend, I had to give up part of my security. Ahmad was often unaware how exceptional his actions were for me, and how much I experienced them as risky. An example of this is the trip in the mountains, during which he asked me to jump off a four-meter-high cliff, something I had never done before. His presence gave me – rightfully or not – some sense of security. I somehow dared to make the jump and landed safely, which boosted my self-confidence.

5.2 Giving Trust

I experienced the friendship, in total, and its consequences as both an emotional and a physical risk, which required an enormous amount of trust in Ahmad and those around him. The event outlined above – our trip in al-Eizariya – (see "Stories of Friendship: The Traffic Jam") is one of many examples. The uncertainty involved in the friendship occasionally gave me elevated levels of anxiety, excessive worry and fear, and immense stress. In addition, the more I became involved with the Palestinians, the more I distanced myself from Jewish Israeli friends, who did not appreciate my involvement with Palestinians. All of this took a heavy emotional toll.

Several Jewish friends warned me that I endanger my life and perceived me as naïve. Although from the outside things may look more dangerous than from the inside, in some ways they are right. Ahmad lives in a violent, anti-Israeli atmosphere and was not always around to protect me in case of need. The villages I frequented were not strongholds of Hamas, the Palestinian organization responsible for most attacks on Israelis in these years. However, it happened that a Palestinian friend would tell me about someone passing that he is Hamas-related, adding something like "don't worry, as a friend, no one will dare to harm you." Once I had some terrifying moments when driving through Issawiya, an Arab village in Israel, which I mentioned previously. I was on my way back from a visit to az-Zaʿayyem and close to home when I found myself in my car in the midst of a demonstration of hooded Palestinian youngsters armed with clubs. They did not pay attention to me, and I assume they had not realized that I was Israeli. Of course, if I had known about this event ahead of time, I would have taken another route, but Palestinian demonstrations in small villages are not published in advance in the Israeli national media.

I had to rely on Palestinian friends to a considerable extent, and sometimes they did warn me about imminent danger. At one stage, Ahmad advised me not to come to az-Zaʿayyem for a month or so, as there had been negative rumors about me and he was concerned that I could be attacked. Likewise, Mahmood, my other long-standing Palestinian but non-Bedouin friend, whom I had visited in previous decades in Dheisheh, the refugee camp near Bethlehem, preferred that I not come to his home anymore. He believed that a visit by me, a Jewish Israeli, could endanger both of us.

There were more sources of concern than the possibility that I might be killed for being an Israeli Jew. People could harm me in order to put pressure on Ahmad. Not all of his relations go smoothly, and in Bedouin life conflicts may be solved with violence. Taking justice in one's hands and retaliation through attacks on those close to a target person is something common in Bedouin society and among rural Palestinians. This almost happened with the brother of our refugee friend Abdalla (see "Stories of Friendship: The Netstick"). I learned of more than a few other stories involving Palestinian friends in which things became physical. With this in mind, I thought that those upset with Ahmad could possibly take out their anger on me. The danger of becoming the target of physical violence did bother me and I recall circumstances in which I was scared, especially when I was left alone in times of either political unrest or when I knew Ahmad was in conflict with someone.

The friendship put me in a variety of frightening positions. I recall that one of Ahmad's family members from Gaza was hospitalized in Israel, and he wanted me to visit her on his behalf, since he could not enter the country. This was an example in which I recognized and participated in the collective Bedouin way of living, as I doubt that I would have visited a Jewish acquaintance in the hospital. The hospital was an Arab hospital, minutes driving from my house, in East Jerusalem on the Mount of Olives. Realistically, there was nothing serious that could happen to me; at worst, I would be told that I am not welcome. However, because of the enormous divide between Jews and Arabs, this is a place where no Jew would come. I was scared to death. Israeli social and general media tend to relate to Gaza as if all its inhabitants are terrorists. I knew that this perception of people from Gaza was not true, but still it was on my mind as the ruling view in Israel. I searched for the sick woman in the hospital, feeling like an infiltrator, on the brink of being caught. I clung to my Dutch passport. Concurrently, I was furious that Ahmad, who had sent me there, did not answer my phone calls to comfort me. Nothing terrible happened. I found the elderly lady, who was positively surprised, gave her the family's greetings and some food, as customary in Bedouin culture, and went home. In hindsight, it is amazing to realize the effects of the Israeli–Palestinian conflict on one's psyche, as all I did was visit an old lady in the nearby hospital, which I experienced as something like a suspense movie.

I used these same situations as a way to conquer my apprehension and become more self-secure. Having trust, I took more risks in the company of Ahmad than I used to take before we were acquainted. I took these risks because not only he is my friend and expected me to do so, but also because it looked as if this was the thing one does in his culture. Gradually, I went through a process of habituation, and now these same scary conditions do not create the same fears anymore. Still, the political context requires me to question to what extent I can trust that I will be safe while wandering around in Palestinian villages. Some level of apprehension remains.

Trust was the main factor mediating my risk taking. Trust is a requisite in the development of close friendships but can be a delicate issue, especially in intercultural friendships. It seems that the larger the cultural distance, the harder it is to trust. To be able to develop trust and enhance the depth of the friendship, both Ahmad and I had to feel safe within the relationship. For me, the need for safety concerned mostly physical security, as I showed above. In contrast, he was much more concerned in our relationship with the security of his privacy and his image, fearing that I would disclose too much or act in a manner that was embarrassing for him. Although I am mostly perceived as a pleasant and trustworthy person, I needed Ahmad in order to obtain trust from those in his environment. In these surroundings it is out of the ordinary to see an Israeli Jew. Only because of Ahmad's standing, those around him would trust that I am not there to collect intelligence, draft collaborators, or incriminate them. Altogether, we needed each other's protection from those with less positive intentions toward either of us, whether Israeli or Palestinian, individuals or authorities.

Giving one's trust to someone who is difficult to understand and who does not act according to one's expectations feels risky, so with highly different personalities and socio-cultural backgrounds, mutual trust did not come easily. Our divergent lifestyles, especially in the field of uncertainty, made each of us periodically doubt the trustworthiness of the other as a friend. I must admit that in the first years of our friendship and in periods of political unrest, there were instances in which it occurred to me that eventually Ahmad would kill me, either because of socio-political pressure or for money. I even vividly recall a situation with him in an elevator, thinking that I would not come out alive. He was insulted when I told him this at the time, since it touched his honor. This thought is one of the things that he did not want me to share with others, even though it only is a thought of mine, as it has the danger of putting him in a bad light. In Bedouin life killings, but not those of friends, are acceptable in the right circumstances. Several years passed and I considered apologizing to him for sharing this fragment here anyway, making use of my superiority in finalizing this text, and in the belief that it is important to show what the Israeli–Palestinian conflict does to one's mind and relationships. However, as this book is a joint project and disclosure a delicate concern, I decided to approach him on the issue once more. Circumstances change and this time he agreed on publication.

As the result of our recurrent misunderstandings and my difficulty in predicting his actions, in later years as in the beginning I found it challenging to rely on him, doubting how good a friend he is, and sometimes wondering to what extent he will be at my side in case of need. I questioned now and then how he perceives me and whether our friendship will last, perhaps for life, or end abruptly. He felt similarly. We found trust to be like a seismograph, with each of us experiencing varying feelings of trust in the other over time.

Despite the doubts, we felt that the other cares and as a consequence, the level of mutual trust remained relatively high. This explains why Ahmad was willing to introduce me in his home and family, something which in his world is out of the ordinary, and why I was willing to be with him in places and situations that were considered by my friends as tremendously dangerous. The mutual trust also enabled us to travel abroad together. Going out of the country for vacation may seem ordinary for two Western friends, but in both our environments, the idea of an Israeli Jew and a Muslim Bedouin taking a vacation together was something unheard of.

6 Conclusion: Uncertainty Avoidance

Hofstede (2001) found Israelis to be relatively avoidant of uncertainty, and Arabs about the world average. The Dutch are below average, to say, they are *less* avoidant of or deal better with uncertainty. My observations suggest – like those by Hofstede – that as regarding uncertainty avoidance Dutch and Bedouin cultures are worlds apart. However, in contrast, the direction of the difference I found is opposite of what would be anticipated on the basis of Hofstede's findings. Many of those around me, the Israelis and more so the Dutch, as well as myself, are *more* reluctant about uncertainty, or putting it another way, tend more to certainty, than my friend and many other Bedouins I met. Hofstede refers to those cultures more avoidant of uncertainty as those planning for the future, and those less avoidant as letting things happen. From my perspective, the Dutch have a strong tendency to plan, whereas the Bedouins have a strong tendency to let things happen; Israeli being somewhere in between.

UNCERTAINTY AVOIDANCE

This is not in line with Hofstede's thinking, which places Israel as the most avoidant of uncertainty and the Netherlands as the least avoidant.

Before addressing the cultural aspects, I need to mention the uncertainty as a result of the occupation. In the Palestinian Authority, and particularly in Area C, where most of the friendship takes place, the occupation causes substantial uncertainty. The authoritative measures are taken by "them, the Israelis, the Jews, the oppressor", which challenges the feeling of safety. More than that, life among the Palestinian Bedouins is objectively much less certain than for most people in either Israel or the Netherlands. This has not changed much in the last decade when I visited, as the state of occupation continues to prevent improvement in the harsh economic situation. The difference is striking. I do not imply that there is no poverty in the Netherlands or in Israel, but I – like most of those in the developed world – never have to worry about running water or electricity. I always have more than enough to eat and petrol in my car. For many a Palestinian Bedouin, and for many rural Palestinians, this is not the case. Water that comes in tanks may run out. Electricity may fail, sometimes for the whole village, because of a broken cable. If one did not work that week, there may be no food. And cars may stand idle because one cannot afford petrol. Israeli soldiers can enter villages at any time, and halt or arrest you, or prevent entrance to or exit from a village. In addition, one can never be sure that checkpoints are open when one needs to pass. Undoubtedly, living in these circumstance forces people to cope better with uncertainty.

In Israel as well, the authorities have a profound impact over one's life. This is felt especially in the present times since grave measures are being taken in order to cope with COVID-19 and there is much uncertainty about the future. But even in better days, Israeli citizens are to some extent dependent on authorities, albeit direct interference by authorities in the lives of residents is much less than in the West Bank. Moreover, Israeli authorities are for the most part seen as "our" authorities, who operate with – at least some form of – fairness and on which we have – at least some – influence, some feeling of control, even if largely imaginary.

Back to Hofstede's theory. Hofstede (Hofstede n.d.-a) argued that countries exhibiting high uncertainty avoidance maintain rigid codes of belief and behavior and are intolerant of unorthodox behavior and ideas. This description, relating primarily to issues such as tradition and deviation from social norms, seems to depict accurately life among the Bedouins but less so among the Dutch. He also claims that in uncertainty avoidant cultures there is an emotional need for rules (even if the rules never seem to work). Time is money, people have an inner urge to be busy and work hard, precision and punctuality are the norm, innovation may be resisted, and security is an essential element in individual motivation. This need for discipline may accurately explain Dutch culture but is in striking contrast to what I encountered in Bedouin culture.

A possible explanation for this reversal could be that Hofstede used three distinctively work-related questions for the creation of the Uncertainty Avoidance Index. The questions refer to how often one feels nervous or tense at work (stress), how long one intends to continue working for the company (employment stability), and to one's attitude toward breaking the company's rules (rule orientation). It may be postulated that one can only partially infer from work-related uncertainty avoidance to uncertainty avoidance in other fields. Actually, Hofstede (2001) writes: "It is possible that other and perhaps better survey indicators of national levels of uncertainty avoidance can be developed" (p. 148).

My understanding is that my Dutch upbringing encouraged me to develop my own independent thoughts but made me highly wary of any uncertainty as regards daily life, and anxious if things do not go as planned; putting it otherwise, I am inclined toward a life of stability. I learned to speak and act in clearly defined ways with an emphasis on both directness and control. In my thinking, writing, and actions I may be creative, but I tend to go straight from one point to another heading toward a certain predetermined goal, as is customary in the Netherlands (cf. Ulijn 1995). I found myself vulnerable in situations that were ambiguous or unplanned, and looked for rules. This fits well with what others say about the Dutch. A guidebook on Dutch culture suggested that for an ostensibly liberal country, the Netherlands knows a multitude of rules, which to foreigners may be perceived as repressive (White and Boucke 2006). In contrast, Ahmad was socialized differently, leaving more space for flexibility. He would move – whether in his mind or in his actions – from one point to another in a digressive way, while accustoming throughout to changing circumstances.

Thus, the use of the term "uncertainty avoidance" as a value dimension appeared problematic. The field seems broad and ill-defined and the term is confusing both in its content and in its phrasing (a double negative). In my view, we could divide this cultural dimension in two parts, namely "tradition" and "discipline". In some cultures, these value orientations interlink, while in others they may be less related.

Uncertainty avoidance in the sense of adherence to tradition seems comparable to the basic value of tradition in the value classification proposed by Schwartz (Schwartz and Sagiv 1995) for individual value differences, which was defined as: "Respect, commitment and acceptance of the customs and ideas that traditional culture or religion provide the self" (p. 95). Among the Jahalin Bedouins there is great emphasis on tradition. As a result, there seems to be less flexibility than common in either Israel or the Netherlands when it comes to the freedom of belief, ideas, or general way of living. Among the Bedouins, the "important things in life" are dealt with according to tradition, variance is less accepted than in the West; ways of living that are different from the norm and less certain are frowned upon and avoided. For example, one is expected to believe in God, to marry, and to conceive children. The idea that someone, as is common in the Netherlands, would not believe in God is unheard of, as is the notion that a person would choose not to marry someone from the other sex or remain childless by choice. Although Dutch culture does have its traditions, overall it seems less concerned with tradition. If we relate to "uncertainty avoidance" in the sense of adherence to tradition, the direction of the differences between Bedouin and Western dominant cultures is in line with the direction proposed by Hofstede, with Dutch culture less adherent to tradition than Bedouin culture.

I need to make a comment here about religion, which is a major aspect of tradition, but was not central in the friendship. Both Ahmad's Muslim environment and my Jewish environment rely heavily on religion. However, both of us are independent thinkers and take a pragmatic stance toward religion, occasionally taking part in religious traditions. We now and then spoke about the existence or non-existence of God, and about our respective religions and their practices. When the subject arose, it was apparent that we have dissimilar views and practices. Therefore, one could anticipate that religion and/or religiousness be topics of conflict within the friendship, especially when taking into account the socio-political context. But we found these discrepancies easily bridgeable, and neither religion nor religiousness became prominent issues within the friendship. Clearly, the national conflict, being Palestinian versus being Israeli, overshadowed the conflict of being Muslim versus being Jewish.

It was our diverse valuation of discipline, and specifically self-discipline, which created most cultural tension. Discipline as a value orientation may be defined as the extent to which value is given to the ability to go without instant and immediate gratification and pleasure. The notion of uncertainty avoidance in the sense of discipline seems to be partly overlapping with the basic value of conformity as identified by Schwartz (Schwartz and Sagiv 1995). Conformity as a basic value was defined as: "Restraint of actions, inclinations, and impulses likely to upset or harm others and violate social expectations or norms" (p. 95). Conformity was found to be close but distinct from the basic value of tradition and to a large extent culturally dependent (Fischer and Schwartz 2010).

The proposed value orientation of discipline matches the classification proposed by Hall (1970; Hall and Hall 1990) as regarding monochromic and polychromic cultures. Dutch dominant culture emphasizes monochromic time: people value privacy, personal property, and doing one thing at a time. Moreover, the Dutch will value extensive planning and measures of control. They will tend to be strict in their interpretation of words and rules and be goal-oriented and committed. They will leave little room for risk or error. In contrast, Jahalin Bedouin culture emphasizes polychromic time: people value relationships, sharing of personal property, and doing many things together. The Bedouins will value staying in the moment, favor indirect communication, and be comfortable with unclear, ambiguous, or unexpected conditions, and changes of plans. Consequently, the Bedouin will flow with the stream of events, whereas the Dutch will try to direct them. In my experience, uncertainty avoidance in the sense of adherence to discipline is displayed within the realm of the friendship in ways opposite of that postulated by Hofstede. Differently said, the Dutch adhere more to discipline – or in this sense are more avoidant of uncertainty – than the Bedouins.

Other researchers too have struggled with Hofstede's dimension of uncertainty avoidance. One study proposed splitting this dimension in two separate dimensions that do not necessarily coincide: the level of national stress and the level of national rules. Moreover, they raised the point that there is a negative relationship between values and practice in this field, with societies having more rules wanting less and vice versa (Venaik and Brewer 2010). This latter notion matches the relationship between Ahmad and me. Ahmad much wants to be more organized, while I would like to learn to go more with the flow.

Having clarified the difficulties in the concept of "uncertainty avoidance", let us now turn briefly to the challenges and opportunities in this field. Of the four value dimensions discussed, undoubtedly the challenges related to uncertainty avoidance were most difficult for me in all three realms: emotional, cognitive, and behavioral. If we split this cultural orientation in two parts, as suggested above, it becomes clear that difficulties were especially in the field of discipline, where the required adjustment was massive, and much less so in the field of tradition. It was as if both of us had read the work of Hall (1970; Hall and Hall 1990) on monochronic and polychronic people and tried to stick to the book. (If I had read Hall's work in an earlier stage of the friendship, this would have saved me significant frustration and pain, because it addresses many of the cultural dissimilarities I experienced.)

Let us first look at the cognitive level. I grew up with the notion that things need to be precise, a time, a word, a fact, that belongings are either mine or yours, and that plans are agreements. This became ingrained in my mind. Life in Israel made me realize that other cultures do not necessarily have a similar worldview, but I found the Bedouin way amazingly difficult to grasp. I could neither accept that my views in this field are not naturally seen as better than theirs, nor that one would choose a less efficient manner of coping with a situation, when more efficient options are available. Adapting to the idea of the world as being in constant flux took me many years.

As for the behavioral level, because I had a tough time accepting the cultural difference on a cognitive level, I did not adjust behaviorally fast enough. Accordingly, things went wrong quite often. I would wait for Ahmad when I should not have waited. I built on plans and agreements when they never were intended to be fixed. Only after I grasped things on a cognitive level, I changed my behavior and learned to handle circumstances in a more appropriate way. However, from the start of the friendship I adapted to the idea of taking more risks and put this in practice.

On the emotional level, I found it harsh to deal with all the uncertainty. I became distraught time after time after time. Additionally, I experienced the risks in, and because of, the friendship as an emotional burden. When the uncertainty in the friendship felt like too much to tolerate, I tried to relate to it as a lesson in living differently. Understanding cognitively and coping better behaviorally improved how I felt emotionally.

The cultural contrast regarding discipline became more of a stressor when others were involved, in particular when they were Westerners. Once in a while, I would bring along non-Palestinians, friends, relatives, or others. In those situations, I would feel responsible for making both sides of the encounter content and tried my best in preparing them, especially visitors not acquainted with Middle Eastern cultures. I would relate to differences on all dimensions but primarily to those in the field of discipline, giving special attention to issues of time and planning. It was not an easy task to explain to a Dutchman, for example, who is acquainted with a predictable lifestyle and concerned with the exact hour at which we will meet Ahmad, that whatever time we plan, Ahmad may not be there at all. If this had happened without prior notice, many a Dutchman would take affront.

The encounter was extraordinarily difficult for Ahmad too on this dimension. He often felt pressured by my expectations for clarity, structure, and going according to the rules. He was aware that he could not give me the certainty I requested but often did not understand why it was so difficult for me to cope with ambiguity. He tended to see my attitude as a kind of deficit, though gradually he gained knowledge of its cultural aspects. Over the years, he accommodated my expectations to some extent. All the same, at the time most of our fights arose around issues related to certainty/uncertainty.

To conclude, I realize in hindsight that the difference between us on this value orientation is related to a disparity in the perception of locus of control. The Dutch perceive the individual as being in control of his or her life (internal locus of control), whereas the Bedouins view the individual as controlled primarily by socio-political and environmental forces (external locus of control). As long as the cultures do not mix, things will flow perfectly. But when one culture meets the other, a frustrating confrontation for both sides is inevitable, unless one makes a point of establishing the legitimacy of each coping style. Both ways of dealing with life can be highly effective, but restrictions in each culture could limit possibilities in achieving change. Bedouin culture appears fit for coping with situations that require flexibility, whereas Dutch culture is better equipped for dealing with situations that require efficiency. Learning from both cultures could create an optimal setting for change.

CHAPTER 7

Masculinity and Femininity

The cultural variance regarding "masculinity and femininity" comprises the third dimension for review.

> The masculinity side of this dimension represents a preference in society for achievement, heroism, assertiveness and material reward for success. Society at large is more competitive. Its opposite, femininity, stands for a preference for cooperation, modesty, caring for the weak and quality of life. Society at large is more consensus-oriented.
> HOFSTEDE n.d.-b

On the scale for masculinity, a higher score indicates a greater tendency to masculinity and a lower score indicates a stronger tendency to femininity, as compared to other countries. The Arab countries ranked 23 on this scale out of 53 countries and regions. This is only slightly above the world average and to those who view Arab society as an exceptionally male oriented this may come as a surprise. In almost half of the surveyed countries masculinity is valued more than is the case in the Arab world. Having said this, we may postulate that the Bedouins, who are mostly religious Muslims and conservative in their worldview, make a more significant distinction between male and female gender roles than the average person in the Arab world does. Israel ranked 29, which is slightly below the world average, showing that its population is inclined to femininity only a little more than the population in the Arab countries. The Netherlands ranked 51, and is among the countries with the lowest tendency to masculinity, that is to say the highest tendency to femininity, with only Norway and Sweden leaning more to femininity (see Figure 8).

Differences in value orientation as regarding masculinity and femininity also express themselves in friendship. Several of the previously told stories of friendship included gender issues but in this chapter the focus will be on gender. I will relate specifically to men, women, and the – lack of – relations between them, as this came about in the friendship, and then to the topic of being a man. Afterwards, I will expand on the notion of the survival of the fittest – the idea that one needs to fight to be a man.

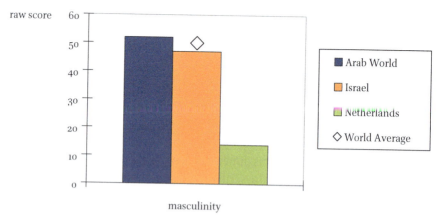

FIGURE 8   Masculinity scores
BASED ON HOFSTEDE (2001)

1   Women and Men

There is a huge discrepancy in attitudes toward gender roles and segregation between the Netherlands, Israel, and the Bedouins, which I will explain. The issue of sex segregation goes beyond Hofstede's theory about masculinity and femininity but is related in the sense that it keeps the masculine and feminine worlds apart from each other. This issue cannot be ignored as it had a direct effect on the friendship. Let us start with three incidents.

Stories of Friendship: Wives; Don't Ask, Don't Tell…

Three incidents:

Jerusalem, April 2008. Ahmad, our Palestinian friend Dahud, and I were sitting in my living room. I mentioned Ahmad's wife, and Ahmad became furious. I was very confused. What did I do wrong?

Hizma, January 2011. Ahmad and I were sitting in the garage office. I asked something about his wife, and he instantly became angry. I had not noticed that another person had entered behind my back. This time I understood. I wished I had bitten off my tongue, but the question had passed my lips before I could stop it.

Near az-Zaʿayyem, June 2011. In the car with Ahmad and the new mechanic, Mustafa, Ahmad asked me to tell Mustafa whether his wife is tough. Surprised, I asked if he is sure that he wants me to talk about his wife with

Mustafa. He replied: "Only about her toughness." So, I told Mustafa that Ahmad's wife is tough like Ahmad, and I could not resist adding that I think Ahmad married her because of that. Ahmad expressed his agreement.

1.1   Gender Roles

The Dutch, relative to other nations, have few norms pertaining to the distinctive behavioral tasks and roles of women and men. You can find masculine women and feminine men, and anything in between. In the dominant Dutch culture, this is not perceived as a problem and one is comfortable with quite some gender variance. Among Dutch minorities this may be different. Rising numbers of Muslim immigrants show a more conservative attitude toward gender. In Israel, there is substantial variance in this respect within different subcultures, and a generational difference among secular Jews, with younger generations experiencing blurring gender role boundaries. Having said that, being by now in my 50s, my experience is that overall, Israeli men are supposed to behave in a manly fashion. For the Bedouins, a man is supposed to behave like a man; this primarily means to be strong and assertive, "macho"; possibly impulsive and aggressive. Manhood requires social proof. When manhood is threatened, physically aggressive thoughts may be activated (Vandello et al. 2008) and in Bedouin life these thoughts are often also expressed, something that is universally accepted as being manly. Although there certainly are Bedouin men who are less masculine or aggressive, feminine behavior among men is unacceptable in Bedouin views. This norm is engrained in Bedouin thought and I have not encountered any deviance.

For the traditional Bedouins, life outside the family is seen as dangerous. Women, who are required to be modest and prudent, are considered as being in need of protection from external dangers, especially from men. Therefore, men watch over their families and assume a guardian stance toward women and children. In a harsh environment, this is not necessarily a negative thing, and is perhaps even something to be admired. An example can be found in the story about Suleiman, the brother of our Sudanese friend, Abdalla (see "Stories of Friendship: The Netstick"), in which his inappropriate behavior toward one of the women of a Bedouin family resulted in death threats by the men of her family. The downside of the situation lies in the fact that this protection may take the form of possessiveness, in which the women are subordinate to the men. In most cases, it is the head of the family, the man, who makes decisions for the family. I will present more on power differentials in the next chapter.

In practice, Bedouin women and men live separate lives, with a traditional role division. The women will take care of the home, while the men go out to work. Women are not tolerated even in those jobs in which in many other cultures it is common to see mainly women in positions such as cashiers, waitresses, or cleaning people. In all the years that I have frequented Palestinian villages and small towns, I have met only a handful of female shop employees. One of the women I met relatively often and who is an exception to the rule is the director of the Peace Center for Palestinian Heritage. She is a non-Bedouin Palestinian and has a university degree, contrary to most women around her. I never met a female employee of Bedouin origin. Bedouin women are kept out of the public sphere. In recent years, there have been changes in this respect, with increasingly greater public exposure of Bedouin women, such as Bedouin girls finishing secondary school and enrolling in university. Nonetheless, the attitude at home usually remains traditional (cf. Braun-Lewensohn et al. 2019). The situation is different in Palestinian cities, such as in the capital Ramallah, where one finds more women involved in professional jobs and business, but still much less than men.

The differentiation of gender roles among the Bedouins is in sharp contrast with what is common in the dominant cultures of most countries in the West. Both in the Netherlands and in Israel women are seen in any job or function. But in Israel gender roles are more accentuated than in the Netherlands, where girls and boys, as well as women and men, can appear and behave in similar ways.

Ward et al. (2001) referred to the idea that a visit of someone from a male-dominant society in a gender-equal society influences mutual perceptions, and this was certainly true for us. On our visits to the Netherlands and even in Israel, it was hard for Ahmad to grasp the freedom of women. He was not accustomed to unmarried men and women touching and kissing each other in public, which in a Bedouin environment would have put those involved in physical danger. Moreover, dancing by male–female couples in public places, such as in a discotheque or at a social event, is unheard of in Bedouin circles. In Bedouin life, there is no public intimacy, even among married couples. Differently said, in these surroundings, single Bedouins of opposite sexes could have been killed for their (public) intimacy. He was shocked when he heard that a married couple – friends of mine – considered the option of an open relationship. His response was: "How could a man let his wife sleep with someone else?"

As a consequence, I had not anticipated Ahmad's comment about his wife's toughness in the third story above, since this is not a quality that usually would be emphasized or valued among Bedouin women and does not fit well with what I knew about Bedouin gender roles. I accepted it as another exception to the rule.

Regarding the expectation of masculinity of men, this is something of which I am constantly aware. The perception of femininity itself is something culturally dependent. Although my behavior usually is not very feminine according to Western norms, it may be perceived as feminine – or at least as non-masculine – both in Israel and in the Palestinian Authority. Despite the hardships, I found there to be something attractive in all this masculinity. Therefore, I have tried at times to change myself and become more manly, and then again gave up on the idea. I believe that changing my manhood worked to a certain degree, and that life with the Bedouins did make me tougher. However, I still cannot consider myself masculine. I will return to this in the next sections.

1.2 Segregation

In Dutch society, there is no segregation between the sexes. In the secular Israeli community in which I live, there is no segregation either. In contrast, among Orthodox Jews in Israel, there is sex segregation beginning at an early age, the intensity of which depends on the particular form of Orthodoxy. In recent years, I have been teaching the ultra-Orthodox. Being acquainted with strict sex segregation among the Bedouins, which at first had felt peculiar, I could adapt relatively easily to the notion of segregation in the ultra-Orthodox community as it follows a similar pattern.

The physical separation between women and men among the Jahalin Bedouins starts in childhood and continues into adulthood. It is based on the understanding that exposing women to men is dishonorable. Hence, Bedouin women are not supposed to be seen, not even in a picture. Men may neither photograph Bedouin women, nor show pictures of female family members to others. This custom is comparable to that of ultra-Orthodox Jews, for whom I had to exclude images of women from my presentations directed at a men's class. However, among different groups of ultra-Orthodox Jews, I have encountered some variance in this respect. Many Jahalin Bedouin men, unlike ultra-Orthodox Jewish men, are reluctant to have their pictures published. An example of this is on Facebook, where quite a few men have an image other than their face as their profile picture. Therefore, I believe this phenomenon is a matter of modesty as well as protection.

When a man comes to visit a Jahalin Bedouin family, the women will disappear from the scene instantly and retreat to the inner quarters of the home. As Ahmad once explained, when he visits a Bedouin friend, he will sit down in the living room in such a way that he cannot see the women in the house because seeing them is forbidden. When serving drinks or food, it is customary for the wife to knock on the door of the living room, at which point the husband will go out to bring in whatever she had to offer, so that she remains out of sight. (Drinks could be brought in by the children, while the host remains with the guests.) In case one needs to use the bathroom, a Bedouin host will go first and check to make sure that the guest will not meet his wife or other women in the household.

This form of segregation is also customary in rural Palestinian families that are not of Bedouin origin. Not long ago, I found myself in an awkward situation after forgetting to stick to the rule, by simply going to the bathroom in a Palestinian home before my host had asked the women in the family to retreat to the back rooms. Luckily, as a foreigner, I tend to be forgiven in such situations. This is not the case with fellow Palestinians. Lately, two friends of mine clashed over the fact that one had presumably looked at the other's wife, which was perceived by the other as a misdemeanor. Note that the circumstances were not that he was "flirting with"; my understanding is that he must have simply glanced in her direction. This was enough to create upheaval. Exceptions are made for close family members who may meet one's entire family, including the women.

There was some gradual change in my relations with Ahmad's close family. At first, Ahmad did not let women in his family come before my eyes. He would either ask them to hide or would take me around in such a way that we would not meet. Only after years of friendship was I regarded as a family member. This gave me the happy opportunity to meet female members of his family, first his wife – who is Palestinian but not Bedouin, and less conservative – and then his mother. With both of these women I could sit down and converse to the extent that language difficulties allowed. Later, I was permitted to meet other female members of the close family, his sisters and his aunt, but only in the presence of a chaperone, usually Ahmad and sometimes his mother, and only to say "hello".

This situation required behavioral modification on my part. For example, in order to take Ahmad's children for a ride or bring something to the home in his absence, I had to take care not to encounter his wife so that neither she nor I would get into conflict with the extended family. When once I met her on the veranda in Ahmad's absence, she immediately received a phone call from his brother who lived nearby, requesting that I leave. This attitude was similar among other Bedouin family members. Although I have been acquainted with Ahmad's brother, Abu Omar, for over a decade and have frequently visited him at home, only twice did I accidentally see his second wife. On one occasion I saw her from the corner of my eye, when he showed me around in his newly built house. The other occasion was when I visited him in the hospital. She was fully covered in black and when I entered the sickroom, she left on the spot.

MASCULINITY AND FEMININITY

The rules are so strict that when Ahmad's nephew asked me to send a picture of him from my phone to his wife's phone, since he did not have a smartphone, he made sure that I erased her number immediately afterwards, so that there could not be any contact between us. When I came to visit the home of another Bedouin family member, and we were to leave together, including his wife, the man asked me to exit a few minutes before them, so that his wife and I would not be seen together.

One considers traveling by car as an exception, for example, when going to a celebration. There is segregation in cars too, with the women in the back and the men in the front. After arrival at such an event, men and women will have separate parties. I saw Abu Omar's first wife only once, when I took both of them by car to her family. She was just a little less covered than his second wife. Segregation between the sexes in villages is more rigorous than in towns, and among the Bedouins stricter than among non-Bedouin Palestinians. In Palestinian cities and in modern hangouts there may be some intermingling between men and women. On one occasion, Ahmad's wife asked me for a ride from Ramallah to the village. She had no problem sitting beside me in the city but moved to the back of the car when we came to the area where they lived. She asked me to drop her off before entering the village so that we wouldn't be seen together, and she continued by foot.

Bedouin men will have their own pastimes, separately from the women. One hardly sees Bedouin couples together. Not obeying the basic rule of separation between the sexes can lead to severe punishment, even if this concerns merely being seen together in a car, as will be shown later (see "Stories of Friendship: Mustafa's Wife Has a Sister"). So, when I had my birthday party with Palestinian – mostly Bedouin – friends in the desert, it was an issue whether I could invite a certain couple. The difficulty was not so much around the notion that the couple was Israeli and Jewish, but in the fact that a woman would attend. Eventually, I did invite both the man and the woman and we all had an excellent time.

There is some indication that among the Jahalin Bedouins sex segregation is becoming stricter in younger generations. This contrasts with what happens in secular societies between the sexes but coincides with knowledge from older Jewish ultra-Orthodox people, who informed me that – at least in Jerusalem – segregation was not as strict when they were younger. An interesting cultural anomaly in this respect occurs at Jahalin Bedouin weddings, to which I referred in the context of celebrations in Chapter 5, "Individualism versus Collectivism". At the large open-air wedding parties, when men are dancing, it is common to have a traditionally dressed female figure dancing in the middle of the square, making the crowd enthused. The first time I encountered this, I was flabbergasted to see a female dancer among the men. Aware that Bedouin men are not in any way allowed to be feminine, my astonishment did not change after finding out that entertainer was a man, covered from head to toe. Ahmad explained that in previous times the enticing figure would have been one of the older women in the tribe, but with segregation becoming stricter, older women were no longer allowed to join the men at weddings.

The segregation between the sexes is not only in the physical realm but extends to the conversational realm as well. As Ahmad once commented, "you don't talk with others about things at home, like family problems, and certainly not about your wife." In theory, this is simple; one does not mention in the presence of other – Bedouin or Palestinian – males any female of the family. Not obeying this rule – even by accident – is a major mistake. At some point, Ahmad clarified that another reason for being strict in not speaking with me in public about his family life stems from the fact that I am a Jewish Israeli. He imagines that those around him will frown upon the idea that a Jewish Israeli knows intimate details about his family, and about his wife specifically. Nevertheless, the practice of not mentioning women so deviates from Western norms that one is bound to fail now and then. In the illustration above, I showed the process of my learning experience. In the first instance, I was taken by surprise, but I learned the rule. In the second instance, I knew immediately that I broke the rule. In the third instance, Ahmad surprised me by breaking the rule himself. Actually, in that situation I took a risk, while both comparing Ahmad with his wife and adding information on his personal choices, things that he would not necessarily appreciate. However, he was fine with it.

All this is not to say that Bedouin men do not talk about women. The men may refer to women they would like to marry, joke about women in general, or mention women who are not part of the family. Still, my experience is that among Bedouin men women are mentioned in conversation much less than among Israeli or Dutch men.

2 Being a Man

It is not self-evident how to be a man, but among the Bedouins manhood has rules. I will focus on two aspects of manhood: emotional expression among men as it became relevant within the realm of the friendship and physical appearance. I will relate in the chapter on power distance the relevance of "honor", which for the Palestinian Bedouins is intrinsically related to "being a man". First, two little stories concerning my manhood; one among Palestinians and one among Israeli Jews.

Stories of Friendship: Be a Man!

az-Zaʿayyem, September 2010. I had been looking forward to a day trip to a well in the desert with Ahmad and Dahud. It would be the first time in months that we would do something nice, out of the ordinary, and have some leisure time together. Things turned out differently. Our departure was delayed and delayed. It took hours before we left. Instead of the original plan, we went to the woods on a hill close by. Ahmad and Dahud arranged a barbecue. Men – many unknown to me – were coming and going. The scenery was fantastic, and I love barbecuing, but all were talking in Arabic and I did not understand a word. I became increasingly disappointed and angry but felt helpless about the situation. At some point, I left the group, sat down on the slope of the hill, and started to cry. After a few minutes, Ahmad came to check on me and made me return. Back with the others, and seeing my upset face, he raised his voice and commanded: "Be a man! You can do it!" I was perplexed. My initial reaction was of hurt, and I wanted to get up and leave. But, after Dahud explained that Ahmad – in his way – tried to assist me in getting over my anguish, I calmed down and stayed some more.

Jerusalem, Saturday morning, June 2009. It was on my weekly walk in the woods with an Israeli Jewish friend. I told her that Ahmad had returned from a trip to Yemen, where he had studied the origins of the Bedouins, and had brought me a ring as a present. It was a large ring with a stone. I showed her a picture of it in my smartphone. Her immediate reaction was "I hope you do not intend to wear it." I felt disappointed and hurt.

2.1 Emotional Expression

The communication of emotions is another cultural issue in which we differ. I tend to express my feelings when I feel sad or hurt and do so in a direct way, verbally or nonverbally. If I am very angry, I will tell Ahmad on the same day, usually face-to-face, and will not let a night pass. In such states, Ahmad is almost always able to calm me down. My emotional states are relatively stable. This is not to say that my mood does not change, but this happens gradually. In contrast, when Ahmad is hurt, he will rarely express this directly. He regards the sharing of most "negative" emotions as a thing for women, and he is not alone in this. When he does opt for communicating his bad feelings, he tends to do so by expressing anger. At least for the outsider, his anger may rise suddenly, but also end abruptly. He switches easily between emotional states (see "Stories of Friendship: At the Garage"). Over the years, I have noticed substantial changes in Ahmad regarding the expression of his feelings and emotions within the realm of our friendship. Although he still rarely shares how he experiences things Between us, he does tell me how he feels in general or as regarding certain developments in his life.

My character is not as rough or tough as many of the men I met around Ahmad. I tend to smile a lot and speak softly, and this is not considered manly in these surroundings. I found myself more easily hurt than them, by jokes or comments that were not intended negatively. Moreover, situations of uncertainty, and these were many, raised my apprehension. For Ahmad, being a man means being masculine and this idea is central in his identity. He had a challenging time coming to terms with my unique way of relating to my gender. Much of his trouble had to do with my emotional reactivity, which concerned both the way I take things emotionally and the way in which I display emotions. Once I asked Ahmad what he found the most difficult about me, and he answered, "your sensitivity". When asked what he liked most about me, he replied, "your sensitivity as well". It is obvious that he meant two sides of being sensitive. The difficulties he referred to stemmed from his perception of me as unmanly, vulnerable, and fearful, whereas what he enjoyed in me was my awareness of the feelings and attitudes of others.

In Ahmad's view, it is not appropriate for men to cry and one needs to be ashamed of crying, unless it is about something major such as the loss of someone close. When a man cries, he loses face. He told me that there is a Bedouin saying referring to the gravity of a situation when a man cries. The saying is "When men cry, know that worries have exceeded mountain peaks."

Ahmad did not consider the incident above, in which I started to cry, of a dramatic nature; this is something with which I could agree. He therefore perceived my crying as out of place; this is something with which I would disagree, or at least disagreed at the time. I felt disappointed regarding our plans, out of my comfort zone in this unfamiliar place, bewildered concerning what was going on with men coming and going, helpless as I did not understand a word, and left out since I did not receive much attention. That is what made me cry. In my life, I do not see crying as something exceptional. I cry when I feel like crying, and only rarely try to stop myself from doing so. This can be when I am upset about something, but also when watching a sad movie, or even an emotional YouTube clip. I guess that makes me cry more than many Bedouin or Israeli men. (I do not know how this compares with Dutch men.) For Ahmad, crying is something highly exceptional.

I thus may be perceived as emotionally vulnerable. When one struggles for survival, as in Bedouin life and to some extent in Israeli life as well, there is no place for vulnerability. In contrast, vulnerability – if not exaggerated – may be perceived as a virtue in other cultures, as well as in my profession as a psychologist. Regarding my fearfulness, this is also a question of perspective.

Though Ahmad perceived me as fearful, Israeli friends questioned my ostensible lack of fear in reference to Palestinians and considered me not cautious enough in my actions. Over the years, there was a change in me in this respect. My self-confidence increased and my fears lessened the more I became involved with Palestinians and acquainted with various Palestinian localities and conditions.

2.2   *Physical Appearance*

In the Netherlands, men and women dress in a modern way, which in daily life tends to be unisex. Men may wear all colors and their hairstyle is usually short but longer hair is acceptable as well. At the same time, there are strict dress codes for all kinds of events. I was used to this. As a teenager, my father would comment if I left more than the upper button of my shirt open or appeared unshaven for breakfast. Dress codes in secular Israel are less formal than in the Netherlands, but colors for men's clothing are usually more sober than is common in the Netherlands. In Orthodox Jewish surroundings, in Jerusalem for example, the dress code is stringent, whereas in ultra-Orthodox surroundings men are dressed very similarly, virtually only in black and white. The dress code for ultra-Orthodox women is somewhat more lenient than for the men, but no trousers are allowed. Orthodox men and married women have their heads covered; ultra-Orthodox married women wear a wig. It took me time to become accustomed to the differences in dress codes. I remember that in my first years in Israel, I more than once bought clothes during vacations in the Netherlands. Only when I returned to Israel did I realize that I would not be able to wear these comfortably because of their colorfulness.

In general, Jahalin Bedouin men take care to appear modest. Bedouin men of senior age tend to dress in traditional clothing with a white or grey *jalabiya* (long robe) and possibly a *keffiyeh* (a white, white and black, or red shawl that covers the head). This outfit was the rule in previous generations but seems to be disappearing slowly. I got a *jalabiya* and every now and then wear it at home, but I never wear it in public. The idea of wearing the *jalabiya* in public, even among Bedouins, felt uncomfortable. Although my friends would possibly have enjoyed seeing me in their traditional outfit, to me it felt as cultural appropriation, which I seem to feel less when I am at home. Younger Bedouin men dress in modern clothes. They go mostly in blue jeans or sometimes in dark trousers, and a T-shirt or polo shirt. They tend to refrain from wearing bright or "girly" colors. I have perceived changes in the appearance of Palestinian men throughout the years. Thus, some younger Palestinians who are not of Bedouin origin may nowadays wear, for example, shorts or a pink shirt, but this is more the exception than the rule and uncommon among Bedouins.

Regarding hair styles, all Bedouin men have short black hair, though in recent years I have seen one Jahalin Bedouin man with longer hair. As he is of high standing, he can afford this, image-wise.

The Bedouins I met do not want to be seen in an undershirt or shorts, and do not undress in public. Nudity is out of the question, even partial nudity, unless it is at water's edge. They take care that their body is covered. This also affected me. Once I came to help Ahmad with work in the house. It was hot, and I had remained in my undershirt. When another man appeared to help as well, Ahmad asked me to put on a shirt. This now reminds me of a situation from more than 30 years ago, when I still was a student. A Jewish Orthodox male friend at whose place I had slept over had asked me to put on a shirt, so that his wife could enter the room. At the time, this felt strange to me; now at least I understand the reasoning.

In almost two decades, I have seen only a few Bedouin women, apart from those instances mentioned above within Ahmad's family. When I did, this was either on the street or at the Al-Quds University. Older Bedouin women wear traditional garments, often beautifully embroidered *thobes*, long dresses. Younger women may wear modern clothing, including trousers. Still, all adult women in public will be fully dressed and have their head covered with a shawl, a *hijab*, or *niqab*, the latter showing only their eyes.

Westerners may easily recognize the masculine appearance of Bedouins, but there may be points of confusion. Among Bedouins, a necklace is uncommon, and no earrings or piercings are allowed. In contrast, Bedouin men may wear a ring – a wedding ring or another kind of ring – often large by Western measures. This would be less common in the dominant male populations in either Israel or the Netherlands. In both countries that kind of jewelry would be associated with the gay community or in Israel possibly with Jews of Eastern origin. In the illustration above, Ahmad gave me the ring out of plain friendship, while my Israeli friend's negative remark about the ring was related to her finding it inappropriate that I would associate ostensibly with either gays or Jews of Eastern origin.

I usually do not care so much about appearance, but before meeting Ahmad and his friends I would always check to make certain that I am dressed "manly" enough and rarely err. I did not realize that he was aware of my lesser need for looking manly until a day at his place, when I asked to borrow a shirt and he gave me a canary yellow one, something I doubt he would wear himself.

Related to both the issue of emotional expression and physical appearance is the practicality of physical closeness. There is cultural variance in what is considered appropriate and manly also when it comes to physical closeness. I have touched on the issue of kissing between men before, when discussing greeting behavior, but the issue of physical closeness among men is much broader. For instance, Bedouin men, like men in many other Arab cultures, may go arm in arm in the street, touch, hold hands, or hug. This kind of behavior would be common in many Western cultures among women, but it would usually be considered inappropriate or interpreted as "gay" among men. In this respect my position was extraordinary. Although I am more physical with Bedouin and rural Palestinian friends than with Israeli and Dutch friends, I keep more physical distance than common among Bedouins men. The reason for doing so is that I believe that as an outsider it would be deemed less appropriate for me to express physical contact with Bedouin men. Writing this, I realize that I do not know if I am right in this interpretation of others' reaction toward physical contact from my side.

3 Survival of the Fittest

It appears that the mode of living for most Palestinian Bedouins is based on survival. This could also be true to some extent for many rural Palestinians and some Israelis as well, though this has rather divergent backgrounds and comes in rather dissimilar forms. Survival requires strength, stamina, and sometimes violence. These topics are foreign in Dutch culture, but central in the life of the Bedouins; I will discuss them after another story of friendship. This section could easily be put in the next chapter on power distance, but since it is so much related to "being a man", it appears here.

Stories of Friendship: Hit Me!

Jerusalem, my home, February 2009. It was in the period that Ahmad was still able to cross the border and visit me relatively freely. While I was taking something out of the refrigerator, he suddenly turned to me and asked me to hit him. Though quite astonished, I gave him a soft punch on the chest. We then sat down, and he explained that he believes I need to learn to beat up people. When he found out that I never physically attacked anyone in my whole life, he was surprised. He said that I would not necessarily have to use force but that I must know how to use it in case of need. Although I was initially appalled by the idea, I had a strong feeling that he was right. He had touched a sensitive spot concerning my lack of self-protection, which is not that obvious because of my usually pretty self-confident appearance.

3.1 *Strength*

On several occasions in my life, I had paid a price for the tendency to withdraw when attacked. In fact, 40 years before the incident above, when I was five, my father had instructed me to hit him in a similar way as Ahmad did. He also did it to teach me, after other children had bullied me. However, since then, during my youth in the Netherlands, and as an adult in Israel, I never attached much importance to physical strength. It was not something I felt I needed in life (apart from those occasions in which I had to change a car tire). In contrast, strength is important for Palestinian Bedouins, and required not only in everyday life but also as part of one's manliness. The Dutch proverb says: "If you're not strong, you need to be clever." Among the Bedouins, you better be strong. As in this story, Ahmad demanded that I become stronger and less fearful. He explained: "In the desert, if you're not tough, you won't have a chance. You simply won't survive." His claim, based on the lack of security in his environment, made sense to me. It coincides with the literature that found that those who fear crime tend to have a preference for ideal friends who are aggressive and formidable (Meskelyte and Lyons 2020). I am less muscular than Ahmad and many of those around him, and although I do some sports and there were years in which I frequented a gym, I found it hard to change my physique.

I will give an example of how this plays out in the friendship. Once I was waiting to have my hair cut by my Bedouin friend Fouad, the hairdresser, when one of the muscled men present looked at me and said: "You don't have a biceps." I responded with "it seems you have four of them," after which he replied, "and Fouad eight." It was not said in a negative way, but still it was an indication of me being not only different but also inferior, at least in this respect. My experience was that now and then I was looked down upon for not being stern enough. Luckily for me, this mostly coincided with being esteemed for other qualities. In contrast, Ahmad is known for his force. His physical strength came in handy and at times astonished me. If needed, he would lift me with one hand, as in the incident in which we climbed a mountain, and I jumped off a cliff. On another occasion, after the car got stuck up a wall in a narrow alley, he simply lifted and moved it bare-handed – seriously. I looked up to Ahmad for his physical strength, but in the first years of our friendship I feared that time would come, and he would use it against me.

It is not only the strength of the individual that counts but also the strength of the family. Ahmad explained that this is one of the reasons why Bedouin families tend to have many children; six or more children – possibly from different wives – are common. It is not the state, but the family that gives security; therefore, more children provide more security. Ahmad recalled an incident from his childhood in which his second-oldest brother Abu Ya'akub (named after his oldest son) hit his brothers. Their father then told Abu Yaʻakub not to use his physical strength on his brothers, but – according to the lines of a Bedouin saying – "show his strength by keeping the family together and bringing water." The saying refers to the idea that in previous generations water was scarcer than now and is an asset. Families turning up at the well in larger numbers and with more strength returned with more water. Even at the present time there is fierce competitiveness over resources among the Bedouins.

Ahmad clarified that one could figure the Bedouin family as an army. Its members are trained to be tough and they will always assist one another. In Bedouin life, if there is disagreement among men, one brings along one's family and friends to strengthen one's position, as he did when bringing in Dahud when he conducted a *sulha* (see "Stories of Friendship: Settling a Theft"). Under such circumstances people may also bring along firearms, or basically anything that can function as a club. (They usually remain unused.) I was involved in two of these events in which a group of family and friends came to strengthen someone's position. On the first occasion, a small group of people with clubs came to put pressure on someone who had done wrong to one of Ahmad's brothers. On the second occasion, a group of about 10 unarmed people came to put pressure on a garage owner who had delivered less than optimal work and had charged a high price. Both incidents were solved without actual violence. In this sort of event, there is often an issue of honor involved and things may end with a peace-restoring *sulha*.

3.2   *Violence*

Before, I shared thoughts about expression of emotions and strength, but the issue of violence receives a special place in the environment of the friendship. Dutch dominant culture is avoidant of overt aggression, whether physical or verbal. Whereas assertiveness is usually appreciated, not disturbing others is the norm in almost any situation. Children learn that one may protect oneself against violence, but one does not initiate aggressive actions or even raise one's voice. It would be common for children to be told to lower their voice and be quiet. According to the Dutch dominant culture, physical aggression is perceived as unacceptable. There is a Dutch saying, with negative connotation, for someone who tends to become physically aggressive: "He has loose hands." Israeli culture is more open to violence, which is mainly verbal. Raising your voice in Israel and calling people names are acceptable in many situations and coercion is not a rare phenomenon.

The Bedouins are mostly welcoming and tend to embrace other people heartily. Nevertheless, bullying and other forms of violence are an overt part of Palestinian Bedouin life. As Ahmad expected me to integrate into Palestinian life, he believed I needed to learn to be physically aggressive, and that is what he tried to achieve in the event described above. Palestinian Bedouin men may verbally express their superiority, shout at each other or physically assault someone – usually, but not always, in a playful way. Many times I was in violent situations. For example, I was once in the garage, sitting with a friend. Suddenly there were screams. I saw Ahmad physically attacking one of the clients (possibly an acquaintance). They wrestled for a few moments, and then Ahmad released him. A few minutes later, I saw them laughing together. I often found it complicated to interpret whether some violent incident was playful or not. The existence of violence as a common form of communication, even if sometimes used in a playful way, was a huge change from the calm and protected surroundings I had lived in. Furthermore, I found it at times stressful not to know whether there is something serious at stake.

Once in a while there may also be violence within the family. Wife (or wives) and children are expected to obey the husband, or father, and disobedience may result in aggressive reactions. When Ahmad is angry, he raises his voice substantially; he does so with anyone, including his wife and children. The casual aggression in daily living among the Palestinian Bedouins is in sharp contrast with what I was accustomed to in the Netherlands. I found it both disturbing and intriguing. When I once asked Ahmad about his shouting, he replied that "one needs to know how to shout with respect; when you shout in order to show another person his mistake, he has to understand that you love him." In other circumstances, he told me about a Bedouin saying that if you hit your wife, you need to do so as if you hold a book under your armpit. The saying thus refers to the need to reduce force in using one's power within the family.

I will give one more example of a violent incident that I still find hard to believe I was involved in. Ahmad and I were calmly driving through his village, az-Za'ayyem, when he received a phone call. He suddenly asked me to stop, left the car, grabbed one of several young men hanging out in the street, pushed him against the car, and talked to him in a tough way. The person had a knife in one hand and a pistol in the other. All youngsters disappeared from the scene immediately and Ahmad got back into the car a few moments later as if nothing had happened. There obviously had been something he had to deal with, but it was unclear to me what the issue was. I asked Ahmad why he was not scared, to which he replied that they would not dare harm him, because that could "put on fire the whole village". He meant to say that if someone harmed him, this would create a fight between the families; something that I will explain in the next chapter. Remember, there are no police around here, and the families provide security and insurance.

The harsh and occasionally violent environment was both adventurous and threatening; it provided a thrill but frightened me as well. Physical aggression was never used against me, but in a few incidents I was bullied by Palestinian strangers who stopped when Ahmad appeared at the scene. Interestingly, I forgot the details of these events, but I know they occurred. (That is the way my psyche seems to handle this sort of incident.) Violence played a role in our relationship as well. His bursts of anger toward others at times alarmed me and therefore I tried not to aggravate him. Ahmad would try not to shout at me, because he knew that instead of shouting back at him, as those around him would, I would take offense. In a few incidents in which he expressed his anger toward me, I begged him to reduce the force, and – well aware of the different context – reminded him of the Bedouin saying about keeping a book under your armpit. In those few situations in which I became the subject of Ahmad's verbal aggression, I found it difficult to take it easy and set things aside like my Palestinian friends for whom aggression is something casual. Instead, I sulked for days about what happened. In fact, Ahmad claimed to be calmer in my company than with most others.

Within the realm of the friendship, I had to learn anew how to cope with anger, which was quite a struggle. In the culture I was acquainted with, I was angry much less often and if I was, I would be upfront about it. However, Ahmad would react badly in those circumstances in which I accused him of not being okay with me. So I tried alternative ways of expression. On a few occasions I shared my anguish with mutual Palestinian friends, in the hope that the discontent with Ahmad's actions would somehow reach him. I once brought along a water pistol to demonstrate my anger and truly it was me who once attacked him physically, and not the other way around. Although I assaulted him in a playful manner, Ahmad did not like it at all. He had encouraged me in becoming more aggressive, but this was not meant to be toward him. Sometimes, I managed to share frustration in a calm manner, and we would be able to examine things, but often I would "swallow" it, so as not to create an escalation of conflict.

4   Conclusion: Masculinity and Femininity

On the dimension of masculinity/femininity, the differences between us were large, and more pronounced than expected from Hofstede's findings. Hofstede found that in the Netherlands, the tendency toward masculinity, which is so common in many other countries, is among the lowest in the world. The preference for masculinity in Israel and in the Arab world is about world average, with Arabs tending just a little more to masculinity than Israelis. My experience through Ahmad is that among the Palestinian Bedouins, the division in gender roles is immense and the tendency to masculinity enormous. Among the Bedouins, any resemblance of femininity in a man is frowned upon, perceived as blame, and regarded as lowering a man's status. Possibly, the importance of manhood is more important among the Palestinian Bedouins than in the Arab world at large.

Various socio-cultural factors influence the field of masculinity versus femininity. Among these is the Israeli–Palestinian conflict, and the occupation specifically. The conflict confronts many a Palestinian repeatedly with situations of feeling helpless, rising from difficulties in mobilization, blockades, violent arrests, and more. More than once I was perplexed as to how my friends were able to emotionally contain setbacks one after the other. It is not that they were void of frustration, it just looked that with years of frustration for them it was "more of the same". The blatant oppression encourages being manly, rough, and tough, primarily on the Palestinian side, but to some extent on the Israeli side, the side of the oppressor, as well. As it continues for decade after decade, the younger generations do not even know otherwise. This is not to say that the tendency for Bedouins to be rough is because of the occupation; it seems that the occupation accentuates their anyway rough existence, which emphasizes manliness.

As with the other dimensions, this dimension required cognitive, emotional, and behavioral aspects of adaptation. The cultural differences were not particularly hard to pick up, but its cognitive aspects were challenging. The difficult part was the question of what I think about all this: the strict gender-based behavioral norms and the segregation between the sexes. I remained ambivalent. Coming from a human rights background, I found it hard to accept that men and women are supposed to behave according to certain gender-based rules. I do believe that these rules should be more flexible but accept it as it would be out of place for me as an individual to create perceptual changes among Bedouin men; the women I hardly met. Moreover, there are three things that I found problematic: first, men perceive their gender as superior; second, women are oppressed; and third, women are kept out of sight. However, the situation is complex. The task of the women in running the household is incredibly important in Bedouin life. Apart from this, it is not that the men have it all and the women are helpless. Bedouin men have a tough life and do not have a choice other than fighting for survival (cf. Inglehart 2006), and Bedouin women actually lead a more protected life. Bedouin women may have less freedom and they are excluded from men's activities, but likewise, Bedouin men are not free to participate in women's activities.

The emotional hardships related to the intercultural differences on this dimension were delicate. The differences in the perception of gender obliged me to accustom myself in this sphere. Seeing myself through the eyes of my Bedouin friends, I at times found myself not being considered a man. I was too vulnerable, not loud enough, not aggressive enough, and perhaps not seen as fit to survive. The intensive contact with Palestinian and Bedouin men had an impact on my own perception of myself, in the sense that at some points it made me too doubt my manhood, something that created internal turmoil. Paradoxically, I found that also Bedouin men are vulnerable in some sense, since they cannot afford to appear unmanly.

The behavioral aspects of adjustment were relatively simple to cope with. I used to have many female friends and colleagues, and probably even the majority of the people around me were women. The invisibility of women was something I had heard of, but meeting the Bedouins also gave me firsthand experience of it. The first thing to learn was simply being among men only. This initially felt strange, but over the years, I started to enjoy the more masculine or instrumental attitude of being together among Palestinian Bedouin men. It was more about being and doing, and less about talking or sharing of emotions, which I had done most of my life. Having said that, even today I must be cautious of accidentally approaching Bedouin women (the few that are seen), for whatever reason, because this is not done.

I found it cumbersome that among the rural Palestinians, and Bedouins specifically, aggression and coercion are integrated and accepted in daily living to such an extent. Part of this has to do with the lack of law enforcing authorities in Area C of the West Bank. In Western dominant cultures, we are so much accustomed to the idea that police and justice are part of the protective processes in our nation, that it is hard to believe that life can be lived differently. It took me years to adjust to aggressive behavior as a way of life. When I did encounter aggressive situations, I found that there was not much that I could do, apart from once in a while comment on the – in my eyes inappropriate – situation. So, I mostly accepted the aggressive state as is and remained a passive observer, even if someone was hurt physically. Writing this causes cognitive dissonance, but I calm myself by convincing that there would not have been much that I could do, at least not without putting myself and/or my reputation in danger.

As regarding my own masculinity, the contrast between me and Bedouin and Palestinian men is sharp. I experienced both massive social pressure – though usually in an indirect and subtle way – and limited freedom. I felt I had to live up to "being a man", which was demanding, and now and then created internal conflict, since I was unsure whether to go along with the expectation or resist it. More precisely, Ahmad would monitor my actions, making it clear immediately when my behavior was not tough enough in his view. I did not always succumb to his wishes but mostly adapted to them. Eventually, my participation in Bedouin life truly resulted in me becoming sterner in character and more daring in my behavior. Still, unlike many of the Bedouin men, I continued to refrain from violence, whether physically or verbally. More on aggression as related to honor and authority will follow in the next chapter, in which I will address issues of power distance.

Back to theory. For the most part, my experiential findings fitted Hofstede's understanding of masculine versus feminine cultures, but not fully. As outlined at the onset of this chapter, Hofstede referred to the more feminine-oriented cultures as those putting more emphasis on cooperation and modesty, among others. Though in Bedouin culture there may not be much cooperation on a daily basis, in threatening situations Bedouins will stick together, as I portrayed in Chapter 5, "Individualism versus Collectivism". Therefore, one cannot say that there is lack of cooperation. Cooperation, though, may be less organized, as organization requires planning, which is not a strong component of the culture. Regarding modesty, in contrast to what the theory claims regarding highly masculine cultures, among the Bedouins this is perceived as a most valued quality. It is unlikely to hear a Palestinian Bedouin boast about his wealth or achievements, and even if more affluent, this would not be clear from one's appearance. Moreover, most Bedouins will prefer living in simple conditions.

To end, I would like to point out that this chapter was most difficult to write. Ahmad did not leave much room for negotiation about what I could or could not publish. I decided to accept his stance and culturally censored the writings in this chapter, considering that for him, much that is related to gender, sexuality, and the family has to be kept in the private realm and that bringing these things in the open would not be respectful.

CHAPTER 8

Power Distance

"Power distance" is the last dimension I will explore.

> This dimension expresses the degree to which the less powerful members of a society accept and expect that power is distributed unequally. The fundamental issue here is how a society handles inequalities among people. People in societies exhibiting a large degree of power distance accept a hierarchical order in which everybody has a place, and which needs no further justification. In societies with low power distance, people strive to equalize the distribution of power and demand justification for inequalities of power.
> HOFSTEDE n.d.-b

On the scale for power distance a higher score indicates greater power distance; that is to say, people expect power to be distributed unequally. The Arab countries ranked 7 on the Power Distance Index out of 53 countries and regions, thus being among those countries with the largest power distance. Only Malaysia, the Philippines, Guatemala, Venezuela, Panama, and Mexico ranked higher. This means that in Arab countries those with less power tend to more willingly accept it that others have the power. It is possible that the Bedouins, who stick to a traditional and hierarchical family structure, have even higher power distance than the average person in tNe Arab world. The Netherlands ranked 40, which is far below the world average, with the Dutch expecting a more equal division of power. Israel ranked 52, with only Austria ranking lower. This means that in Israel, those with less power tend *not* to accept their lack of power (Hofstede 2001). Note that on this scale the dissimilarity between the Arab countries and Israel is enormous (see Figure 9).

I will build on the concept of "power distance" to exemplify how issues of power and inequality affected the friendship. Relating to the notion of power distance in a broad sense, I will focus on two of its aspects, namely honor and authority. This will be followed by a section on how the Israeli occupation, the ongoing power struggle that is part of the Israeli–Palestinian conflict, affected the friendship. I explained issues of gender inequality, which are closely related to the concept of power distance, in the previous chapter.

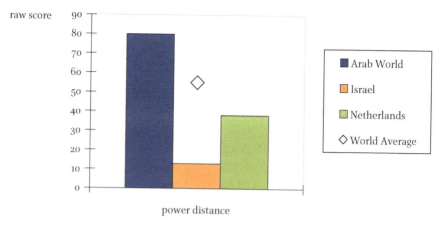

FIGURE 9   Power distance scores
BASED ON HOFSTEDE (2001)

1   Honor and Dignity

In the first part of this book, I described in detail issues of honor and dignity. Honor does not seem an essential part in Dutch life, while dignity is self-evident. For the Bedouins honor is central, and for men often considered as crucial. Honor is part of all relationships, and if honor is at stake, beware.

Stories of Friendship: No "No" for an Answer

The Palestinian town of Abu Dis, March 2011. One day I took my uncle from the Netherlands and his Chinese girlfriend to Al-Quds University, where we intended to visit the Prisoners Movement Museum, a museum dedicated to the stories of Palestinians detained by Israeli authorities, including their lives and their art. When we arrived at the gate, we found the museum closed. I called Ahmad, who at the time was finishing his studies and happened to be at the campus, and he invited us to come in and have a drink at the university. However, the guard did not let us through. Confronted with a closed gate, my uncle and I suggested having a drink somewhere else. Nevertheless, for Ahmad the idea that we could not respond to his invitation became an issue of honor. He made a lot of effort to have us enter the university. He contacted influential people in the university and tried to get us through any possible entrance. My relatives were more bothered by the time taken up by this incident and did not care where to have coffee. I felt caught in the middle and – recognizing both cultural perspectives – I tried to accommodate both parties.

1.1 *Honor and the Family*

The story above is one of many stories I could share about honor. The honoring of guests is valued highly in Bedouin culture. In this case, the fact that someone prevented Ahmad from getting what he wanted was an issue of honor. The affront was worse because it involved the invitation of his guests. Interestingly, my uncle's girlfriend – raised in a Chinese environment – instantly grasped that Ahmad's "face" was at stake, thus providing an indication about the similarity between the Asian idea of "face" and the Arab idea of "honor".

Honor is central in Palestinian Bedouin culture, with status and respect being highly related to the concept of honor; the more honor, the more status, and the more respect. Among the Jahalin Bedouins honor is perceived primarily as an attribute of one's family. When one's family is honored, this will give honor to the individuals in the family. However, honor is also affected by one's individual merits and especially one's masculinity as expressed in one's power over others, physically, financially, mentally, or otherwise. Honor-related disputes are based on a thought process like "How dare you? I am a man and you will not offend me or my family. You are going to pay a price for this." The threat that honor may be jeopardized is something to be constantly aware of.

For Ahmad – and many Palestinian Bedouins – if honor is at stake, it is as if the world stops. He will use all his power to resolve the situation. He will abruptly end a conversation, a meeting, his work, or get out of his car in the middle of a street, to regain honor for himself or for his family. To family and friends this is self-evident. If needed, they will leave whatever they are doing and come to assist him. Even if the honor-related incident occurred between two individuals initially, soon the individual loses importance and it becomes an issue between families. Accordingly, a conflict between two individuals can easily escalate and something comparably minor can turn into a big feud between clans. As Ahmad explained, "the family is holy." And, if women are somehow involved, the situation may become especially volatile.

Honor is a matter of trade-offs and honor disputes can be settled when the two sides of the conflict are even. Individuals and clans will therefore take revenge in response to perceived insults to their honor. They may do so through destroying property or by physical assaults, possibly on family members who were not directly involved in the conflict. In grave situations it may reach the stage of killings, which they will feel obliged to carry out. Reactions are often immediate, but it is not uncommon to wait for years until the time is ripe. In Palestinian Bedouin society, regulating misbehavior by individuals and settling issues of honor through the use of family, friends, and power is not only accepted but expected and – at least in this context – rather efficient. One of the things making the issue of honor complex has to do with retaliation and the possibility that there will be an ongoing spiral of mutual destruction between the sides in the conflict.

I will provide two more friendship stories that evolved around honor. Both stories concerned not just Bedouins but are of the same type that could happen in the Bedouin community. In one incident, someone stole a jerry can of liquid soap from an Israeli petrol station. My friend Dahud, a Palestinian but not a Bedouin, worked at the station on the night this happened. He told me the story the day after and asked to use my cellular phone to make some calls to his family about the incident. Later, he informed me that on the following day hundreds of men came to the station and from there to the family of the thief to settle the issue. (Probably, the "hundreds of men" was a figure of speech and his way of saying that many people had come to his help.) Eventually, things were dealt with without violence.

The perception of this situation and the way it was handled were highly dissimilar from the expected interpretation and response in the West. In Palestinian life, the issues of collectivism and power converge. The theft concerned a member of one family taking something that a member of another family was in charge of. Thus, the honor of the extended families of both Dahud and the thief became the focal point of conflict, whereas the individuals involved and the soap lost their importance. In contrast, a Westerner in an analogous situation would likely be concerned primarily with the soap, either giving up on it or filing a complaint with the police. One would certainly not get the extended families involved.

Incidents in which the honor of either of us, Ahmad's family and friends, or the entire Jahalin tribe was at stake, were frequent topics of our conversations in the period of the stories of friendship in this book. Another honor-related story that I followed closely, via Ahmad and his friends, started around the matter of giving right of way. Although I had been present in situations in which two drivers fought over their right of way, this event took things a few steps further. In the town of al-Eizariya, a driver from a Bedouin clan from outside town did not give right of way to a driver from a local clan. In revenge, the second man drove his car into the first man's car. They got into a verbal fight, at which point families were called in. It turned into a physical fight in which several body parts were broken, and one person was stabbed. A few days later this was followed by a car chase, succeeded by a gunfight between the clans. The issue was then brought to a solution through a *sulha* between representatives of both families.

Sulhas, though, can be revoked and in this case the reconciliation did not hold. The tensions between the clans continued to simmer and about half a year after the initial incident, the situation escalated to another fight in which many were involved, and three men were killed. While the original event occurred in an area controlled by Palestinian authorities, the killings were in an area controlled by Israel. This last development, which was unusual even for Bedouins, reached the news in Israel. From then on, justice was being sought on two levels. The families looked for justice on the grounds of the pre-modern practice of blood vengeance, while both the Palestinian and the Israeli police tried to enforce modern legal practices. It took another few months until a close relative of Ahmad was killed by one of the families involved, and Ahmad was threatened at gunpoint. The story that began as a minor and distant event now became frighteningly near and encouraged us to be more careful.

Issues of honor have complex dynamics, are emotionally laden, and relevant to the friendship in many ways. For instance, I needed to be particularly aware not to damage Ahmad's honor by putting him on the spot or potentially shaming him. I had to take care not to embarrass him more than I do with friends of European or Israeli background; for example, no jokes about possible weaknesses. I also had to be careful not to harm the honor of Ahmad's family. For example, when I once got into conflict with someone from another family, Ahmad advised me not to take measures that were more drastic, since this could bring his whole extended family into a fight with the other family.

My own honor became relevant as well. I had to ascertain that my behavior is honorable and in no sense harms my public image or, indirectly, Ahmad's image. My position as foreigner, without the protection of my own family, made me especially vulnerable to dishonor (cf. Kamir 2002). Nevertheless, this is a situation that can be solved, since in Bedouin life more powerful families can assume responsibility over those lower in hierarchy. Hence, my known friendship with Ahmad and his family – who are of high standing – to some extent covered for my lack of family protection and honor. In Ahmad's habitat, people generally behaved kindly to me, and it was clear that this was not only for who I am but also because of our relationship. In other words, as honor is transferable, I am honored because of the honor he and his family receive. Since he is well respected, they will respect me too, as indicated in the story of friendship described in the next section. There were rare situations in which Palestinians with whom I had little prior acquaintance would act in a rude or degrading way toward me. In those cases that someone did not honor me, Ahmad would take care of it, not just to protect *me* but also since dishonoring me would be an indirect attack on his own honor.

Over the years, things changed somewhat in this respect. If at first, I received honor solely on the basis of friendship with Ahmad, with the passing of time I began receiving honor for who I am. Actually, in the presence of others – from whatever cultural origin – each of us would make a point of complimenting the other in attempt to enhance the other's honor, something I would not do with friends from different cultural background. When we meet people who do not know me, Ahmad will speak about me in many superlatives, and often I will add positive things about him.

If I wanted to be a good friend, I had to be there in support of my friend's honor. Thus, like in the incident at the university, I needed to find an elegant solution out of circumstances in which Ahmad was not able to deliver what he intended. In those circumstances in which honor needed to be restored, often in some form of violence or threat, Ahmad mostly let me off the hook and probably would not have been insulted if I had not joined him. When he did take me along, I was intrigued about this way of dealing with conflict and I experienced it as a kind of test of my friendship. So I participated in two incidents of minor gravity in which a group of family and friends assembled to put pressure on someone who allegedly had misbehaved vis-à-vis Ahmad's family and restore their honor.

The notion of honor was new to me and it took time and effort to fully understand it. Eventually, I grasped the idea and managed to cope with the pitfalls around honor, while erring only infrequently. Restoring honor is for Ahmad routine and he moves in and out of confrontational situations without much effort. By contrast, I experience confrontations as unpleasant and emotionally exhausting. Confrontations in my friendships are exceptional since I mostly prefer the circumvention of conflicts or their solution in calmer ways.

It must be noted that the stress I experienced around incidents such as those mentioned above resulted not so much from what happened in the events themselves, as from grappling with my own value system, in which one neither threatens people nor takes the law into one's own hands. I recall that once it came to my mind that people enjoy this kind of thing in a movie but that I am not watching a movie but playing a realistic part.

1.2 *Dignity and Respect*

In honor cultures one is entitled to a certain attitude based on social or personal merits, whereas in dignity cultures one has innate rights to respectful and ethical treatment. Western cultures tend to be oriented toward dignity (or respect) (cf. Kamir 2002; Weisstub 2002). I was raised in the Netherlands with the idea that one relates to others with dignity, whatever their socio-economic status or personal characteristics. I was brought up expecting to be treated fairly, and in a way respecting my time, money, possessions, and wants. For me dignity was a truism, for which I fought as a human rights activist; not something to be questioned. Through the discussion with Ahmad of my writings on honor, I became aware that not just honor plays an important part in our friendship, but the related concept of dignity plays a part as well. Dignity is to some extent in conflict with honor, since honor refers to some people rightfully being regarded more favorably than others, whereas dignity assumes equality. We may regard the example above at the university as a conflict between dignity and honor. While Ahmad tried to honor his guests any way he could, the guests were more concerned about his (dis)respect of their schedule, as the whole incident took a substantial amount of time, and they wanted to move on.

In all cultures, there are distinctions between individuals or groups of different social status, but in Palestinian Bedouin day-to-day life social hierarchy is more evident than in many Western countries. Among the Palestinian Bedouins, people are honored but not regarded as equal, and even if they pay tribute to dignity, honor is considered key. It is considered proper and appropriate that those with more power be taken into account more, and those who are weaker receive less attention. This can be seen in all parts of life. In many incidents within the friendship I experienced the unpleasant feeling of not being taken into account and/or being disrespected. This happened in widely different situations: plans were changed without my consent, my investment of substantial amounts of time was considered self-evident, or my ideas were overruled without discussion. Ahmad experienced me as a guest in his environment, and therefore regarded it as obvious that he could decide for me. Making me feel disrespected was never the intention of Ahmad (or the others involved), as he made clear on those occasions when I confronted him. He expected that I would oppose him in those cases in which I did not want to go along, as he would have done. In other situations, people would go out of their way to make my life comfortable, since I was a guest; the best available chair, the best part of the food, and more.

Both Ahmad and I were acutely aware of circumstances in which people were victimized – though in diverse circumstances. I found that in various power-related situations in Bedouin culture conduct will be guided by the inclination to avoid shame. A situation revealing lack of power, ability, or other weakness would be perceived by many a Bedouin as shameful and in need of concealment. By contrast, in dominant Western cultures conduct tends to be motivated more by the inclination to avoid guilt than by concern over the disclosure of weaknesses. In a situation in which there is use of force to subordinate another, many a Westerner is prone to feel uncomfortable or guilty, as opposed to the Bedouin who regards inequality and the use of power as inherent in the social hierarchy, as long as it is acted out in a fair and appropriate manner.

I will give you an example. At the garage there once was a junior worker who had beaten another. Although the former was a family member, and as such of higher standing, Ahmad had decided to send him home. At dinner with the workers, I made the mistake of making a remark about the wounded face of the one who had been beaten. The young man left the meal and returned only after being reminded by others that I am a foreigner and that my words were not intended badly. Concurrently, Ahmad became angry with me for embarrassing his protégé in public. Although my intent was empathetic, I learned from the reaction that I had done something wrong; mentioning the wound was perceived as pointing out the man's weakness, which is perceived as inappropriate. My emotional reaction was a feeling of guilt, which was intensified by Ahmad's response. However, when the latter saw me brooding over the situation, he said that the whole thing would be forgotten the next day. This event can be seen also as an example of how situations in Bedouin life can easily escalate and just as easily cool down.

2 Authority

Expectations concerning authority and leadership among Bedouins are quite distinct from those common in Western societies. Here I will review the themes of rules and leadership within the realm of the friendship, and the place of the oldest son.

Stories of Friendship: Who Is the Boss?

Hizma, June 2011. One night at the garage Montasser came in. Montasser is a member of Ahmad's extended family; he is heavily built and not the gentlest person. Ahmad and Montasser sat down with Fawaz, one of the mechanics. There had been trouble with Fawaz all along. He has a good name in his profession but is highly unorganized and somehow costs more than he brings in. There had already been several talks with Fawaz about his problematic way of handling things. This time the discussion took about three hours, during which there was a lot of shouting and one instance in which Montasser hit Fawaz on the head with a telephone.

The burst of aggression toward the mechanic appalled me, but Fawaz did not seem bothered. From the few words I understood, it seemed that despite the hardships, they were going to make Fawaz responsible over the other workers. At some point they called in all the workers and explained the new situation. *Although I thought it was a mistake to make a person responsible over others if he had not proven much responsibility in his own work, I was more upset about the sudden involvement of Montasser in the garage. In fact, it was not clear to me how Montasser became involved. A major event was occurring and I as friend and partner in the business was uninformed. I asked Ahmad, who responded that he would tell me about this another day.*

The next day I confronted Ahmad. He then informed me that a few days before there had been an incident in which a notorious man, rich from drug dealing, had refused to pay his debts to the garage. Moreover, the guy had offered Fawaz a job. The incident had escalated almost to the point of gunfire since Ahmad did not want Fawaz to leave because of his qualities as a mechanic. At that point, Montasser had interfered in the incident and things had cooled down. Since Fawaz feared Montasser, Ahmad had decided to involve Montasser in the garage and put things in order.

When asked, Ahmad said he had not seen it as important to inform me, although I am his partner in the business. I realized that actually no one knows I am a partner. I asked Ahmad why this is the case. Ahmad replied that he does not see the need for people to know that I am involved. That would weaken his position and give the impression that he is not able to cope financially on his own. He made it clear that he wants to keep it like that. He added that if this does not suit me, he would give me back the money I invested.

Then, Ahmad tried to understand the source of my concern. He wondered whether I was concerned that I am honored less because of the workers' unawareness of my status as part-owner and asked if I felt that people do not give me enough honor. He said that he had spoken with the workers about the fact that I am a good friend of his, and that as such they will have to honor me. I replied that I do feel honored, after which he added that if I have any concern in this regard, I need to inform him, so that he can take care of it.

2.1 Rules and Leadership

In the dominant cultures in Western Europe and North America, there are official rules for almost anything; they are an integral part of life. Order is taken care of by the police and trespassers are brought to court. In contrast, life among the Palestinian Bedouins looks unorganized, without anyone in charge of order. For example, the Bedouins do not seem to care about such things as traffic rules (see "Stories of Friendship: The Traffic Jam"). Moreover, if a Bedouin is angry, he may physically threaten or assault the person who is the object of his anger. But rules exist; they are simply different and as in the story above, it is not the official authorities but the strongest who rules and restores harmony by using his power.

Bedouin law, as described previously, is central in Ahmad's life and in his academic studies too, having written his master's thesis on this subject. Here I will briefly relate to the matter since it affects the friendship as well. Our divergent perceptions on law and order are blatant both in situations that occur between us, as well as in our dealings with others. Hence, an incident as in the story above is highly unlikely to happen in a Western setting. I was raised with the belief that the authorities are on your side and with the understanding that one does not break the rules. As a result, I would feel highly uncomfortable about breaking the national law (of whatever country). Ahmad would commit himself to Bedouin law more than to national law. He was raised with the knowledge that the national authorities – whether Israeli or Palestinian – are not on his side. In his view, the authorities are not there to protect you; they are out to get you. His – and my – Palestinian friends had similar views. For example, they were surprised when while driving I put a seatbelt, although in this area there is neither Palestinian nor Israeli police. I would be concerned with safety and doing what one is supposed to do in a car, whereas my friends did not see a need to put on a seatbelt without risk of a fine or arrest. Grown-ups would realize my different point of view, but more than once I had to explain to young adolescents why I wear a seatbelt.

In practice, it was the two of us together who created the rules of what is acceptable (or not) in our relationship as well as in our interactions with the world around us, as often happens in the realm of friendship (cf. McCall 1970) and as I have shown in several of our stories. In many circumstances Ahmad would act according to the rule of what he considered fair. For instance, on our visit to Rome we had bought tickets for an archeological park but did not realize that they were valid only on the day of issuance, which was the day before. After unsuccessfully trying to convince the cashier and the door attendant to let us in anyway, he jumped the three-meter-tall wall. With my Dutch upbringing, in which one learns to respect rules, written or not, I did not even contemplate joining him and bought a new ticket for myself. On other occasions, I did break rules with him but often with a heavy heart. For example, on the same trip, he could not fathom the idea of waiting for hours to enter St. Peter's Basilica at the Vatican. So we simply bypassed the people waiting and entered in an instant. The idea of queuing felt weird to him; he had the power to enter, so he used it, as one does among Bedouins.

Although not every Bedouin leader will be like Montasser or Ahmad, the event described does provide an indication of what is acceptable in a Bedouin environment. In the workplace there is relatively little planning, high power distance, and use of aggression. People are not regarded as equal and do not get equal chances. These ideas seem to be generally accepted in Bedouin society. The boss decides. As regarding men on the job, family members are of higher status, and often preferred over others, since they are supposed to be more loyal, and employing family is a way of keeping resources in the family. Seniority provides status as well. Workers do not have written contracts, fixed salaries, or social benefits. A worker can and will be fired on the spot in case there is disagreement between him and the boss, as I have seen in the garage more than once. Unlike the situation in many other cultures, this same person may receive a second or a third chance a few weeks later. Many Bedouins, including friends, would justify aggression and violence as part of good leadership, and consequently even admire people like Saddam Hussein and Muammar Gaddafi, who were regarded as tyrants in the West. For me this was shocking.

Aware that this is a generalization, my personal experience is that Israeli leaders – somewhat like the Bedouins – tend to be relatively authoritarian and that they have a way of making quick decisions. In comparison with the Bedouin leader, the Israeli leader does not receive much respect and his or her authority is contested continuously. People will tell him or her to their face what they think, and everyone wants to have a say. Aggression and coercion are common among Israeli leaders but not as much as in Bedouin society, where their use is an inherent part of leadership and perceived as appropriate management by both leaders and subordinates.

For the Dutch, the person in charge is the one elected or appointed, which typically is not for reasons of descendance (apart from the king). He or she is accepted to be the boss and is supposed to behave in a polite manner without using overt aggression. Generalizing, my experience is that the Dutch will tend to agree placidly and submit to the person in charge. For example, it was on our visit to Amsterdam that Ahmad and I came back from a party by bus around 3 AM. It was surprisingly clear that the bus driver – the one in charge – did not know his way, but no one gave him any directions, although there must have been people in the bus who knew the route. (We did not know the right way.) At a certain moment, the bus got stuck in a dead-end alley, and could not turn. While the driver called for assistance from the bus company, the passengers remained in their seats. They kept silent for at least half an hour, although there were a few whispers. This time, Ahmad could hardly believe what he saw. A comparable situation was unlikely to happen in either Israel or the Palestinian Authority. First, someone would have interfered the moment the driver made a wrong turn with some kind of exclamation about him making the wrong turn. Then, when stuck in the alley, it would have taken less than a minute until many people would be involved. They probably would shout angrily at the driver for his "stupidity" and give him directions or simply take the steering wheel.

Ahmad and I are relatively independent persons as compared to other people in our respective environments. We strongly prefer to make our decisions alone, do not easily rely on friends, and are relatively resistant to social pressures. We both have a clear sense of direction and a strong feeling of justice but may have divergent views on what is the right direction or on what constitutes justice. We tend to fulfill leadership roles but have different perceptions of how a leader should behave. For both of us, the perception of leadership corresponds with what is acceptable from leaders in our social surroundings. I tend to take a democratic stance in my leadership roles, with more input from those less powerful, which is common in Western cultures.

Ahmad opts for "paternalistic authority" (Sennett 1980), which is more common in the Arab world. Ahmad, in general and more specifically in his function of sheikh, is both police officer and judge and he may use his personal charms, superior intelligence, higher education, and good human insight as well as his physical strength, in order to have things done his way. He feels entitled to decide for others and for his actions to be received favorably. He acts like a father toward those who are not his children in order to promote their well-being or protect them from harm, whether this is in the garage or elsewhere. The risk in this form of leadership is in the possible abuse of power, which needs to be prevented by checks and balances (Kets de Vries 2003). Ahmad's self-insight and openness to criticism, as well as family scrutiny, are ways to keep the balance. He stressed that not all Bedouins are like him and explained his attitude and behavior by the fact that he was raised in a family of sheikhs, and therefore he is expected to tell people what to do.

Ahmad's paternalistic attitude was also clearly present in our relationship. In many circumstances he was inclined to tell me what to do, expecting me to adapt to his way. When this involved an instrumental matter, his way often concerned more force. I mean this in a most practical way; when I could not open the door, he would suggest giving it a kick. Interestingly, when this involved social relations, he would often be more considerate than I, taking a very balanced view; for example, when I was angry at someone, he would try to show me the other side. He felt that I try to impose my Western ideas of rules and leadership on him, with too much talking and planning and too little flexibility.

2.2 *The Oldest Son*

The oldest, in the tribe as well as in the family, hold a special place. This does not appear from the story but is still worthwhile mentioning. The elders of the tribe are highly respected, they will be part of any important event, and they will be consulted when questions are raised. They live by themselves, supported by family members, or come to live with their children. This is quite different from the Netherlands or Israel, where mostly elderly people live in homes for the elderly or are supported by caretakers (in Israel often foreign) who are not family members. Although this is not universal, many older people lose their status, and some are left rather alone. Among the Bedouins, one keeps one's status until death and remains part of the tribe and the family. Homes for the elderly exist but are rare in the Palestinian Authority, and homes for the elderly do not exist in Bedouin life.

There is respect for the oldest son within the nuclear Bedouin family as well. The oldest boy is of such an importance, that – as I mentioned previously – the parents are named after him, Abu (father of) and Um (mother of). But when Ahmad's father died, it was the one but oldest, Abu Yaʿakub, the most responsible and who most resembled their father, that took over the responsibility for the family. Abu Yaʿakub fulfills this role even today, although all the children are married and Ahmad, the youngest, is in his 40s. Once at the garage I happened to meet Abu Yaʿakub, who at that time had heard about our friendship but only vaguely. (Later we became friendlier.) During this meeting he told me that the family's honor is something especially important. In this respect, he takes care not only of his own 10 children but also of his brothers. Previously Ahmad had told me that his brother is tough and later he told me that only in recent years have they come to have a good relationship. I wondered how this coincides with the two of them putting so much emphasis on the notion of family. Ahmad did not see any contradiction and explained that even when they did not get along, they would be there for each other in case of need. Abu Yaʿakub is aware of his own toughness and added that he knows that his brothers will not tell him things about their lives that could make him angry. Concerning Ahmad, Abu Yaʿakub worried mostly that Ahmad might go with other women or start drinking alcohol. I assured him that Ahmad is "on the right path". Scrutiny is one of his tools to monitor the behavior of family members and before leaving, he asked me to watch over Ahmad.

Ahmad's firstborn, Nimer, is an adorable boy; both he and I much enjoyed each other's company until eight years ago, when his mother took him and his brothers to the U.S. and did not return. Nimer and Ahmad were much attached. They did a lot of rough-and-tumble play and it was obvious that Nimer tried to imitate his father's behavior. I had noticed on several occasions that Nimer – who was four years old at the time – often behaved unkindly with his younger brothers and sometimes hit them. I suggested to

Ahmad that perhaps he should do something about that. Ahmad replied that also his wife had told him about this behavior of Nimer, but he does not see a need to make Nimer change it; he actually is quite happy about it. He explained that Nimer does not beat his brothers when he is around; only when he is absent. Some days later, when I confronted Ahmad with this to me striking response of satisfaction with his son's aggressive conduct, he gave a slightly different view. He then stated that he does not think that Nimer should hit his brothers but in his absence, he does want Nimer to be respected as the oldest man at home (even at age four!). Ahmad expects Nimer to behave like him, assert his authority and be responsible for the family. According to Ahmad, a Bedouin father will teach his children to respect the oldest son, so that the eldest will be able to take over his place when he leaves this world.

Ahmad noted that in my family the oldest son (me) does not receive respect for being the oldest, which is true. As adolescent, I did have the responsibility of looking after my brothers when my parents were away, and I did experience somewhat higher expectations from me as the oldest. Nevertheless, I experienced neither the responsibility nor a protected and more respectful position as the oldest. One may argue that this is related to the fact that I left the Netherlands for Israel at age 17. Still, I doubt that after reaching adulthood my brothers would have seen me in any way responsible either for them or for the honor of the family, in case I had stayed in the Netherlands. I think that in the dominant culture in the Netherlands the eldest does not receive the prominent place that the oldest Bedouin child gets.

In Israel, the place of the firstborn depends on the specific subculture, with more honor for the firstborn male in Jewish families originating in Arab countries.

3   The Occupation

Previously, I discussed the impact of the Israeli–Palestinian conflict on the friendship through the perspective of individualism/collectivism. I will now do so from the perspective of power distance. We can find many forms of inequality in power in the story below, based on language, knowledge, nationality, socio-economic status and more. I will relate here primarily to the issues of wealth and freedom of movement in the realm of the Israeli–Palestinian conflict, as far as they became relevant for the friendship.

Stories of Friendship: Dancing with the Drug Dealer

Palestinian Authority, after midnight, June 2011. Some of the garage workers, as well as Ahmad and I were on our way, with two cars, to have a barbecue. After quite some driving around and not being content with two earlier picnic places, we finally settled down at the petrol station near Almog. There were several reasons already for me not being in a good mood. Among others, Akram – the same person from the story of the netstick and for whom my dislike had grown since – had joined. I had made a fuss out of this. Ahmad had reacted angrily to my behavior, to which in turn I had responded badly. In addition, the Israeli police stopped both our cars. They wanted to search the car for drugs, but eventually I convinced them not to do so. With three young Palestinians inside, I had been frightened, not knowing what they would find or how the police would treat us.

At the petrol station, we encountered Hamuda. Ahmad and Hamuda had not seen each other for about 14 years. They told me that Hamuda had been a good friend of Ahmad's cousin who was killed by the police in his teens. I received a detailed description of the qualities of the youngster – specifically about his many girlfriends and his manliness – and about the four gunshot wounds in his shoulder and head. Ahmad told a story in which his cousin had been seen with a girl. This had enraged 15 to 20 men, who then came after him. Ahmad had fought the men to protect his cousin.

Hamuda said that he used to spend about NIS 30.000 (about €8.600) a day. I could not believe the sum but accepted that he was rich. When I asked how he became so rich, Hamuda replied that it is better not to ask. From the conversation between Ahmad and Hamuda – in Arabic – I caught the word "cocaine". Ahmad and Hamuda continued to enjoy themselves at the barbecue and Hamuda became the center of the happening, while making jokes and dancing. In the meantime, I became increasingly disturbed. It went through my head that this friend of Ahmad became rich through ruining others' lives with drugs. Ahmad encouraged me to join Hamuda in dancing. With the others standing around and clapping, I experienced severe group pressure. Although in other situations I would have enjoyed dancing to Arabic music, this was different when it was with a drug dealer. I made a few dancing steps, and then withdrew.

The party came to a close. Although Ahmad had said earlier that we would have time to sit together and talk through some issues that we needed to discuss, this did not happen. After doing the cleaning up, he told me to "take the kids home", referring to bringing the young workers back to the garage and added that he would remain with Hamuda. I was angry and told Ahmad that I consider leaving me alone as inappropriate. My thinking was that the whole evening I had hardly understood a word, because all had spoken Arabic, and I had had an enervating time. Now he wanted to use me as a taxi driver and run off with a drug dealer. Ahmad did not appreciate my reaction at all, and I did not want to make too big of a scene in front of the others, so eventually I agreed. I took the workers back to the garage and arrived home at about 3.30 AM. I had to get up at 8 AM but was not able to fall asleep. I was too upset.

The next day I confronted Ahmad. He was astonished. How did I arrive at the understanding that Hamuda is a drug dealer? This was not the case. Yes, in his younger years he had made good money in stolen cars, but he was never into drugs. Now he is working as an electrician. I grappled with the size of my error of interpretation. Later that day Ahmad provided some additional information on Hamuda and their acquaintance. They got to know each other when they were youngsters in the early 1990s during the first intifada, At that time, the Palestinian political organizations encouraged stealing from Israelis, since that was a way of returning what was taken from them.

Filling in the gaps of information according to what made sense for me and then believing my own creation was a recurring process in those times in the friendship, in which my comprehension of the situation was limited. This time, being aware of my previous misinterpretations, I was prepared for the possibility that Ahmad's version of what had happened the night before would be rather different from mine; and it was.

3.1   *Wealth and Poverty*

My financial situation is relatively fine. I own a 79-square-meter (850 square feet) apartment, in which I live and work. The apartment is in a comparably inexpensive neighborhood on the outskirts of Israel's capital, Jerusalem. I also own a small secondhand car. I try to limit unnecessary expenses but can afford spending money to have a good time. I have a bank account, a series of credit cards, and bank cheques, and I hardly worry about money. Most of my Israeli friends live in a similar socio-economic environment, but several of them are considerably worse off, despite their academic education, and struggle to manage financially. Most of my European and American friends and family are in a better financial state.

Virtually all my Palestinian friends live in much worse conditions. Many rural Palestinians around Jerusalem are out of work, live in poverty, and struggle to earn a living. Some do not have the money to pay for outgoing phone calls, local travel, or even basic food. Their housing, though similar in size, is often less stable as regarding electricity, water supply, and sewage. Many Bedouins I met live hand-to-mouth and do not have the opportunity to accumulate financial reserves. They may not have a bank account at all, and if they have, they do not use credit cards, and only a few use bank cheques. Those who do manage to make money invest it in their house or in land.

The asymmetry in finances occasionally causes tensions. I was not fond of the idea of someone being a thief, like the person we met in the event described above, but this was not something out of the ordinary. With the present harsh financial climate, one must find alternative ways to accumulate resources, and in these surroundings stealing from Israelis is hardly considered a crime. Besides, according to Ahmad, until now political organizations such as Hamas and Islamic Jihad promote stealing from Israelis, albeit less so than in the past. In contrast, Ahmad believes that stealing between Bedouins is rare, because of the power of the families and their strong adherence to Bedouin law.

Mostly, one did not dare stealing from me. However, on one occasion, my phone was stolen from my car in the garage, as I mentioned before. This was by a non-Bedouin Palestinian, in the middle of the day and in front of the workers. Ahmad went through great pains to get it back. We first visited the family of the thief, who lived in Hizma, not far from the garage, but soon it became clear that they themselves did not have control over him. In the meantime, many neighboring shop owners became involved and supported the idea that we go to the Palestinian police. This is not something usually done, but this was not the first time that things were stolen from customers, possibly by the same person, and they wanted to stop it. So we went to the Palestinian police, who – against the odds and to my great surprise – managed to return the phone within a couple of weeks. I believe that in Israel the police would not go after a stolen phone.

On another occasion, driving Ahmad's family to their home in Ramallah, and passing the refugee camp Qalandia, a boy of perhaps 10 years old stopped us in a traffic jam and tried to make me buy water from him. In Jerusalem, where I live near the border with the Palestinian Authority, and even more frequently in the Palestinian Authority, one encounters small Palestinian boys and sometimes men or women trying to sell water, gum, or other merchandise at traffic squares. Some may aggressively insist when one refuses to buy. This time, I did not want to buy anything, but the boy insisted and eventually I agreed to buy a small bottle. Then, he threw two more bottles through the window and wanted me to pay for them. Angrily, I threw them back and the boy started to shout. His terrible screams gave the impression that I had taken his bottles without paying and he attracted the attention of others on the road. I was afraid that people would come after me and could not imagine much good would happen when they realized that I am Israeli. Eventually, we moved out of the traffic jam and left him behind. This highly unpleasant experience made me feel both angry at and sorry for the boy. It also taught me about the desperate financial situation these people live in, which is in striking contrast with the relative wealth of the Israelis – including me – living nearby.

We can look at the issue of wealth also from the perspective of the blatant divergence in living conditions between the Bedouin villages and the neighboring settlements. Part of Ahmad's clan live in Khan al-Ahmar, the village that has been in the midst of a legal battle, as I explained in Chapter 3, "The Worlds We Live In". This was one of the villages to which Ahmad and I took visitors so that they can get a sense of Bedouin life with all its hardships. The inhabitants of Khan al-Ahmar, who do not have legal ownership of the land, live in wooden and tin huts, and conditions are abominable. The Israeli authorities have plans to evacuate the Jahalin Bedouins from this and many other villages in order to make room for Israeli housing and industry (see Figure 4). They now and then destroy buildings belonging to the tribe, based on the notion that these buildings are illegal. Although I realize the importance of adhering to national law, in the present circumstances I identify with Ahmad and the Jahalin Bedouins regarding these unjust events. Amnesty International, the organization in which I volunteer, and several other human rights organizations campaign to protect the Jahalin Bedouins from being evacuated.

Khan al-Ahmar is in conflict with the neighboring Israeli settlement Kfar Adumim over the use of land. The conflict is mostly in the legal field, but through the years there have been several incidents of violence. Kfar Adumim was established in 1979, decades after the Bedouins were moved to these surroundings. It is a beautifully built place, fully serviced, with lots of greenery and a swimming pool with an amazing view over the desert. It is a different world from Khal al-Ahmar, and has a much higher standard of living. People choose to live in a settlement for distinct reasons. Although some live there based on the ideology that it is important to get hold of the land as "this land is ours," others move there because of better and cheaper living conditions. Some of the settlers are right wing, possibly extremists, while others are not.

Despite the conflict between Kfar Adumim and Khan al-Ahmar, there is a small group of activists in Kfar Adumim, called "Friends of the Jahalin", who have been supporting their Bedouin neighbors (Ziv 2018). I have good friends in Kfar Adumim, whom I enjoy visiting. Ahmad, who is well acquainted with these same friends, would have liked to visit there too, but without an Israeli entrance permit he, like most of the Jahalin Bedouins, is not allowed to pass the gate of the settlement. This puts me in a very awkward position. To complicate things further, I have friends who tell me that by visiting Kfar Adumim I support the occupation and hold me accountable for going there. This paradoxical situation raises many delicate questions about my position vis-à-vis the various friends involved.

3.2   *Freedom*

My physical freedom used to be something so self-evident that I never considered it before I became acquainted with Palestinians. I was always allowed to go wherever I wanted, could leave my home, had the opportunity to go to another town or country, and I was never arrested.

This contrasts sharply with Ahmad's experience. As a consequence of the vast Israeli security measures meant to prevent terrorism, he is highly restricted in his freedom and mobility, by Israeli police, soldiers, and border police. I will relate here to the three bodies as a whole since the distinction is virtually irrelevant for the friendship. Ahmad and most rural Palestinians are limited because of the checkpoints all-over the West Bank and since soldiers may stop them anywhere for any reason, and possibly detain them. This may be a bit exaggerated, but the sentiment is exactly like that. The ongoing presence of Israeli forces in some localities and their sudden appearance in other places causes overwhelming feelings of uncertainty and powerlessness. The possibility of transportation is limited anyway, since many do not have cars, or if they have a car, it may not have a license, or they may not have money for petrol. Public transport has improved in recent years but is not reliable. This is the main reason that I am frequently asked to assist with my car.

Leaving the West Bank is even more complicated. Ahmad – like many Palestinians – cannot go freely to Jerusalem, the town that is only minutes driving from his home and which, until the construction of the separation wall, was the place where he worked, socialized, and spent most of his time. In addition, and although Ahmad and I managed to travel abroad, it is exceedingly difficult for him or for other Palestinians to obtain an entry permit to Western countries. (Visiting an Arab, African, or an Asian country is somewhat easier.)

More than once, Palestinians approached me in the erroneous belief that with my freedom, I can also achieve more freedom for them and get them an entrance permit to Israel or a visa to another country. These people often find it difficult to realize that I cannot. A visa to either Europe (the Schengen countries) or the United States requires sponsorship, including a letter of invitation among other things. Coming from a culture inspired by collectivism, my Palestinian friends were certain that friends of mine in the Netherlands or in the United States would readily invite them. However, no Dutch or American friend I have would sign an invitation to a Palestinian person unknown to them. This simply does not correspond with their culture. In the view of my Western friends and family, a friend of a friend is not necessarily a friend. From their perspective, the responsibility behind an invitation is too high and there is too much risk involved, especially considering the reputation Palestinians have.

I once asked Ahmad why he is so eager to go to the United States. He replied: "Because of the freedom there; you can go wherever you want and relate to whomever you want." I responded that I am not at all sure that he would like it in the United States, since in the United States, as in Europe, there might be other kinds of limitations, which he is not used to. Freedom in Western Europe and Northern America is controlled through enforcement of national laws and institutional rules, much more than in the Palestinian Authority. He answered that I may be right, but the idea that in Palestine he is not free to move is too bothersome for him.

As could be seen from the incident in which we were detained (see "Stories of Friendship: Crossing the Border"), there is a large difference between Palestinian and Jewish friends in their attitude toward the institutes enforcing the Israeli law. Israelis tend to justify both discrimination and harsh or degrading attitudes by the authorities toward Palestinians and the limitation of their freedom as well, on grounds of the danger of terrorism. Palestinians see the Israeli police and soldiers mainly as the arm of the "Jewish" occupation force. In fact, it is common for Palestinians to refer to the Israeli forces, or even to Israelis in general, as "the Jews", notwithstanding the fact that Israelis, and also the armed forces, include people from other religious and ethnic groups as well, like Druze and Bedouins, albeit in small numbers.

From a Palestinian perspective, we were treated unfairly when we were detained, as well as in the story above in which we were stopped. In my friends' eyes, halting our car was another unacceptable deed by Israeli authorities, interfering in their freedom. Israelis, in a dominant social position, and identifying with the need for protection against terrorists, would have perceived the attitude by the police as legitimate and justified. I am rather certain that if there had been only Palestinian youngsters in the car, it would have been searched, and if there had been only Jews, the police would have let us through more easily. Our mixed group of both Palestinians and an Israeli was in that time and place an extraordinary combination. In the end things went well and we could move on to settle down for the picnic at the petrol station near Almog. One needs to understand that this location is in the middle of the desert, with the ancient city of Jerusalem (Israel) to the west, the ancient city of Jericho (Palestinian) to the north, Jordan to the east, and the Israeli kibbutz settlement Almog and the Dead Sea, both to the south. Though this is not the reality, the place feels like no one's land. Not surprisingly, it was more than once the location where my Palestinian friends and I went to relax (see also "Stories of Friendship: 'Garage of Peace'").

The disparity in attitude between my Palestinian and Israeli friends toward limitations on freedom could also be explained by a different attitude to the police and to authorities in general. Legitimacy has a strong influence on the public's reactions to the police, and furthermore, the key antecedent of legitimacy is the fairness of the procedures used by the police (Sunshine and Tyler 2003). The development of national institutes and national law enforcement started later in the Palestinian Authority than in Israel and is in rural areas still in a stage of acquiring recognition. As a result, many Palestinians, and Bedouins specifically, not only disregard Israeli authorities, but question the authority of Palestinian law enforcement as well.

An incident illustrating the complex interaction between the aspects of freedom, wealth, and friendship within the realm of the occupation, concerned my hairdresser Fouad. Fouad is from a different Bedouin tribe than Ahmad, through whom we became acquainted. Fouad has a salon in the refugee camp Shu'afat, just behind one of the checkpoints, which I can pass, but he cannot. Once I came to his place to have my hair done and found him distraught. He told me that Israeli soldiers had arrested him in the Palestinian town of al-Ram, and had kept him in prison for 10 days. According to his story, the reason for the detention was that they found a small barber's knife on him. This was during the period of the Arab holiday of Eid al-Adha, a time at which he could have made more money than usual, something he desperately needed. Just after Fouad told me his tale, one of his clients asked whether I am Jewish, to which I responded that I am Dutch but live in al-Ram. Fouad added that I have a Dutch mother and a Bedouin father. In response to the unbelieving face of the client, I informed him that I am from the Abu Sahra (Ahmad's) family.

I usually do not have difficulty saying that I am Jewish when among Palestinian acquaintances and later tried to understand why I felt the need to lie and disguise my religious and Israeli background. I believe that our practical joke was born out of my difficulty in coping emotionally with various identities. After Fouad told his story about the unfair treatment by Israelis and his lack of freedom and money because of the occupation, I found it too unpleasant to admit being a comparably wealthy Israeli Jew who is free to go – almost – wherever he wants and take part in the oppression of Palestinians. I presume that Fouad, who considers me like a brother, felt similar dissonance about my identity and made up part of the story to prevent embarrassment to either of us.

I found myself in a peculiar and confusing socio-political situation. I grew up in reform Jewish Zionist tradition, and I was educated about the oppression of Jews all through the ages. I subscribe to the right of existence of Israel and to the right of its population to live in safety. Furthermore, I was for many years an officer in the Israeli army and as such took part in Israel's defense, which is for a large part directed against possible Palestinian terrorist attacks. I can understand the background and justification of the actions of the Israel Defense Forces. Having said that, I oppose the occupation, and had recurrent feelings of guilt throughout the friendship about what "we" are doing to the Bedouins and the Palestinians; injustices such as economic deprivation, travel restrictions, and other human rights issues. The feeling of guilt intensified the more I became painfully aware of the variety of hardships my Palestinian friends endure and of my privileged position as free, well-to-do, and with an abundance of opportunities. Guilt made me more accepting of behaviors by Ahmad and other Palestinians that did not coincide with Israeli laws or were unfriendly toward me.

It must be noted though that I am not an Israeli citizen but a permanent resident. With this in mind, I much preferred to look at myself as Dutch in nationality and as a peace activist. As such, I felt bad about what "they" (the Israelis) are doing to the Bedouins and the Palestinians in general. I wanted to share life on the Israeli side of the fence with my Palestinian friends; life that has much to offer. I found it highly annoying that these friends could not visit me – as I could visit them – and regard the lack of possibility for mutual hosting as complicating friendships. This perspective, although it saved me from feeling overly guilty, generated anger and frustration in me. Moreover, my objection to the occupation may be acceptable within the international human rights community but is far from mainstream thought in Israeli society, in which the human rights scene is tiny. Consequently, my familiarity with Palestinians mostly made me feel like an outsider in Israeli society – one looked down upon.

I cannot finish this part without some comments concerning COVID-19, which temporarily turned things upside down: at the time of this writing, there were many more people ill in Israel than in the Palestinian Authority. When visiting Palestinian villages around the time of the pandemic, I was looked at in a way that I interpreted as they being afraid I may spread the virus. Then Israeli authorities confined me and all Israelis to home for several weeks, whereas in the Palestinian Authority, there were restrictions but not as severe as those in Israel.

When the lockdown was lifted, my Bedouin friends were eager to see me, but in a Palestinian supermarket I was told that as a Jew I am not welcome. In the end, a couple of employees came to my assistance, telling the person in charge that I am "one of them", after which I was allowed to continue my shopping. I believe that there was more behind it than simply the virus, since among Palestinians, distrust of Jews is often simmering. On several occasions I heard Palestinians and Bedouins making guesses about who planned COVID-19, as the idea that the pandemic was unplanned does not seem feasible. Once, a Palestinian well-educated man with whom I am friendly even told me that he is sure the coronavirus is either a Jewish or an Israeli conspiracy. Returning to the incident in the supermarket, it took place on Holocaust Remembrance Day, something of which those involved were probably not aware. However, being told that I am not welcome as a Jew, especially on this day was an eye-opening experience. Although for many Palestinians and Bedouins the notion of not being wanted because of one's identity is a common experience, I was rarely rejected for being a Jew.

The occupation has vast impact on freedom and in the realm of the coronavirus even more. I already referred to this aspect, when I shared with you in Part 1 the story of my friend Mahmood in the Dheisheh refugee camp who ran out of money for necessities. Fouad, my hairdresser, told me the other day that on his way between two Palestinian villages in Area C he was halted by the Israeli police, and fined NIS 500 (€125) for being too far from his home during the COVID-19 pandemic. Fouad was upset and viewed the incident as racist. It is not so clear to me why Israeli police had the right to fine him, as this was in the Palestinian Authority, where limitations because of the virus were less strict, but I clarified that in Israel people were fined a similar sum. However, for many Palestinians like Fouad, this sum of money is a substantial part of his income, whereas for most Israelis it is not. This comes on top of the fact that as a hairdresser he was not allowed to work for a substantial period because of the virus. But life in the Palestinian Authority went back to normal soon. All shops are open again and I am among the few who keeps going around with a mask, which in Israel is still mandatory.

4 Conclusion: Power Distance

Differences in the friendship on the dimension of power distance were exceptionally large and along a similar pattern as Hofstede's findings on Dutch, Israeli, and Arab cultures. According to Hofstede, the Arabs are accustomed to high power distance, i.e., expect power to be distributed unequally, while Israelis are among those with lowest power distance and the Dutch somewhere in between. My experience was that the acceptance of large power differentials is a dominant factor within Palestinian Bedouin society, possibly even more than in the Arab world as a whole. We could compare this cultural discrepancy with the distinction postulated by Schwartz (2006), regarding cultures favoring hierarchy versus those favoring egalitarianism.

Although Palestinian Bedouins tend to accept the power differential among themselves, they do not accept the power differential vis-à-vis Israel, or more specifically the many burdens and limitations put on them in the realm of the Israeli occupation that complicate their lives so much.

Cognitive adjustment as regarding power distance and the use of power in general was primarily to the extent of learning that in Bedouin culture things function differently from what I am accustomed to. In the field of individualism versus collectivism, Ahmad and I have diverse value orientations, but I often experienced them as complementary more than as conflicting. In both the fields of uncertainty avoidance and masculinity versus femininity, the contrast in value orientations created more dissonance. In the field of power distance, Ahmad's value orientation did at times collide with some of my basic values.

In my mind there were alternating thoughts and feelings. There was something attractive in the idea of being entitled to decide for others, and there were moments in which I felt jealous over the – for me – extraordinary respect that the oldest son receives in a Bedouin family. I also found it at times astonishing how effectively things are handled in a manner that is so dissimilar from the one I was used to, by means of using power. However, raised in an egalitarian society and adhering to the notion that humans are equal in their fundamental worth, I had strong feelings of unfairness as the result of power differentials, including but not limited to those between Ahmad and myself. I found the less egalitarian attitude toward authority difficult to accept; especially when I was the person affected but also when others were concerned. I was well aware that individualistic cultures tend to be more concerned with human rights than collectivistic cultures (Hofstede 2001) and that human rights possibly conflict with culture and religion (cf. Antonius 1997; Vera 2009). At the same time, in this dimension more than on the others I found it hard not to be judgmental of the Palestinian Bedouin attitudes and actions. Specifically, it was hard to digest the understanding that a good leader is tough. Thus, throughout the friendship I observed other forms of authority, while retaining my own interpretation that authority is to be practiced in a democratic way.

On the behavioral level, I needed to adapt enormously. I learned to act according to a new set of assumptions that applied to a wide variety of circumstances and participated in new ways of decision making. Moreover, I had to accept that issues of honor can interfere with any activity and allow for challenge of – for me – basic behavioral rules. I continually had to remind myself of these different rules. I found acting accordingly difficult and erred repeatedly. The discrepancies between the expectations from me, my experiences, and my thoughts created substantial internal conflict and stress for me on this dimension. I am in "his" world, so do I go along with his values? Do I interfere when I encounter injustice? A passive stance on my behalf made our dealings easier. Sometimes, I would do it my way and paid a price for it as when I spoke up, Ahmad was likely to draw back or become angry. Neither solution was satisfying, but eventually we would work things out.

Dealing emotionally with the power differential between the two of us was most complicated. I am highly privileged in many ways and have superior power in several realms. I have a steady income that is several times higher than that of many of the Palestinians I interacted with. I always have money in my pocket, while some of the friends I made are occasionally without and struggle to make money to buy necessities. I have a licensed car, with which I can drive from place to place without fear of being stopped by police or the army, unless in parts of the Palestinian Authority where Israelis are not allowed. Most striking though is my ability to move between Israel and the Palestinian Authority without much hindrance. In addition, I am superior in my knowledge, especially in respect to the use of internet in general and locating information specifically. I am happy to be in this position and simultaneously this creates feelings of guilt. Using my resources to help Bedouin and other Palestinian friends provides me with a sense of significance and reduces the guilt. Still, in former years I regularly found myself troubled over the question of sharing too much or too little of what I have. This still concerns me today but much less so than in the past

In the present socio-political context, with me living a relatively free and comfortable life, one could anticipate that I as Israeli would feel powerful, while Ahmad would feel powerless. Nonetheless, the occupation created a power differential between us, which made me feel uncomfortable and sometimes lonely. I felt unable to change much in those situations of Palestinians versus Israeli authorities. Though I more than once assisted Bedouin friends in legal matters, in most cases I was not able to help. Moreover, the situation was paradoxical, with Ahmad often expressing force, while showing lack of fear, and me feeling powerless and fearful for a variety of reasons. I felt that it is me who is in the inferior position, because of my lack of command of the Arab language, my trouble in grasping the context and my occasional clumsiness in actions. I feared being objectified as an easy prey for those wanting to (ab)use me because I am an Israeli, and because of my freedom and resources, which I would be expected to share with those less privileged (cf. Gruenfeld, Inesi, Magee and Galinsky 2008).

Since both our societies are not that accepting, I worried that somehow either Ahmad or I would get into difficulties with the authorities, either Palestinian or Israeli, because of the friendship. So, despite my objective situation of being on the more powerful side, I felt at times all those characteristics associated with reduced power: negative moods and emotions, awareness of threat, heightened attentiveness to the needs of others and tendency to act contingently to expectations by others, and inhibition of my own free behavior (Keltner, Gruenfeld and Anderson 2003).

In the chapter on masculinity and femininity, I had to censor my writings so they would be more or less in line with what is culturally acceptable. In this chapter I had to censor texts from a political perspective as well. I had to bear in mind that neither his environment nor mine is very tolerating of crossing social, cultural, or political lines. I did not want to complicate either his or my life more than necessary by disclosure of information. Still, people told me that the openness that I (we) demonstrate on this dimension could endanger us both.

CHAPTER 9

Challenges and Opportunities

In the previous chapters, I have addressed the scope of the research, the professional literature on interculturality and friendship, and the findings as concerning the friendship with a Palestinian Bedouin on four cultural dimensions. In this chapter I will provide a summary of the findings, a peek into the complexity of doing a study with a Bedouin Palestinian, and thoughts about personal growth. The last section includes implications from the study of the friendship and recommendations.

1 Hofstede's Cultural Dimensions

In summarizing a case study, one loses its richness and complexity. Moreover, generalization may often be highly difficult, if not impossible (Flyvbjerg 2004). In addition, using Hofstede's theory as the basis of this study had limitations. I will start this section with some thoughts about the use of Hofstede's theory. This will be followed by a recap of the main challenges and opportunities in this friendship for each of the four dimensions: individualism versus collectivism, uncertainty avoidance, masculinity and femininity, and power distance. However, before the more theoretically oriented summary, I will provide an experiential summary in the form of a detailed story that includes a mixture of the themes addressed earlier. The story, which was extreme for both of us, depicts the cultural differences as they became apparent in the friendship. We encounter several of the characters and places we met before. I believe the themes are self-evident, and – not as previously – will leave their interpretation fully up to the reader.

Stories of Friendship: Mustafa's Wife Has a Sister

Israel and the Palestinian Authority, November 2011
8.00 AM *I am at home, not yet dressed. Ahmad calls me; something highly unusual at this time of the day, and even more so since he calls from an unknown number. He asks me to immediately contact the cellular phone company and shut down his phone since it was stolen. He adds that he will explain later what had happened.*

I am apprehensive. Shortly after, I receive a call from his wife, Um Nimer, who tells me that Ahmad has killed someone. She asks me to come and pick her up in the Palestinian town of al-Eizariya. Killings are not rare in this environment, but I had not expected Ahmad to kill someone. Never did I need to ask myself whether I was willing to remain friends with a killer. Moreover, would I be regarded as an accomplice if I go along with Um Nimer's intention to bring Ahmad his passport so that he will be able to escape to Jordan?

9.15 AM   *Despite some earlier misdirection, I find Um Nimer and their youngest, Yasser (by now 10 months old). She asks me to drive them first to their new home in the Palestinian town of Ramallah to fetch her own passport, so that she can come with me to Jerusalem. On the way she explains that Ahmad had sex with the sister of the wife of Mustafa, the mechanic. She is furious and uses my phone to call all over and find out more. I hear her on the phone suggesting to Ahmad that he will take this other woman as a second wife. Clearly, she is less concerned about the killing than I am.*

10.00 AM   *There is a lot of traffic on the way to Ramallah. In the meantime, no one provided me with any clear explanation, and I am trying to figure out what happened. The best I can make of it is that Ahmad had sex with another woman, and that when her husband detected them, they got into a fight, in which Ahmad killed him.*

11.00 AM   *We drive to Um Nimer's mother and take the passport, continue to fetch Um Nimer's daughter from her school, so that the daughter can take care of the kids while Um Nimer is away, and then take the oldest son, Nimer, from kindergarten. Surprisingly, despite being only four years old Nimer knows to direct me in the car to their home. Um Nimer changes Yasser's diapers, and then the three of us drive back to Jerusalem, where Ahmad is supposed to be. (It is unclear to me how Ahmad got by the wall and where exactly he is.)*

12.00 PM   *In order to enter Jerusalem, one must pass a checkpoint. At the checkpoint near Hizma we are stopped by soldiers and I fail to get them through. I had expected that with their U.S. passports it would not be such a problem, but I was mistaken. They do not have an entry permit to Israel. Um Nimer does not give up easily. She asks me to try again at the checkpoint near Az-Za'ayyem, the* village where they lived before. I refuse; assuming that there is communication between the checkpoints, I am afraid that another trial will get us into serious trouble. I suggest that I drop them off in the village near the checkpoint and continue into Jerusalem alone.

12.30 PM Without my Palestinian friends, it is easy to pass the checkpoint. At the other side, I suddenly notice Um Nimer with Yasser on her arm. I had imagined that they will wait in the village, but instead they crawled through the barbed wire. I realize that they could be arrested any moment for what they did. I feel that I cannot leave them standing there, and take them in the car, acutely aware that this would be considered a legal transgression for all of us. There are soldiers only tens of meters away, and if they looked in our direction and understood what is going on, I would have to spend time in jail, as collaboration is considered a serious crime. But we arrived in Jerusalem without hindrance.

1.00 PM Um Nimer, who had kept contact with Ahmad, tells me that he is supposed to come to my place. We wait for him there. This is the first occasion in which Um Nimer visits my home, and I would have preferred better circumstances for this occasion. Both Um Nimer and I are anxious.

2.00 PM Ahmad has not appeared, and his phone is turned off. I try to find out through friends where he could be but without success. On her request, I take Um Nimer to the Old City of Jerusalem.

3.20 PM Ahmad calls to tell that he is on his way to me. This looks to me as one of the worst possible scenarios. Um Nimer had already gone into town (with the passport). Furthermore, I freed up the whole morning, but my clinic is at home, and in ten minutes I have a client and three more clients afterwards. Ahmad asks how I am doing, and I reply that I am going crazy. He killed someone and he does not even explain what happened. He answers: "I what? What are you talking about?" I explain what I heard about the killing, and he replied that there was no killing at all and that I should not listen to stories. I tell him that I will talk to him after I finish with the client.

4.20 PM My client left, and I try to call Ahmad but again his phone is off.

5.00 PM I am sitting with the next client, a 12-year-old, when suddenly there is a ring at the door, and someone enters the house. My client is surprised by the noise and tries to figure out what is going

	on. I had imagined that this could happen, and I had therefore left the door open but feel ill at ease. I somehow manage to convince the boy that things are ok.
5.20 PM	After the boy leaves, I do not have time to tell Ahmad that I am upset with the way he entered, because he proceeds to tell me that Um Nimer and Yasser are on their way back to my place. Having in my mind that the next client tends to paranoia and may react gravely to any unexpected people, I reply with a "not possible". We agree that they will be waiting in the car.
6.20 PM	Client number three leaves and I go down to the parking lot to say hello and see if things are all right. They are sitting in the car. I have one more client to go.
7.18 PM	Another ring at the door; my client is still inside. There they all are! I shuffle Ahmad and family into the kitchen, beg them to stay quiet for another few minutes, and get the client out. We then have dinner and Ahmad finally tells me the story. Last night, the sister of Mustafa's wife needed to go somewhere and, since transportation between and within Palestinian villages is scarce, she had asked him for a ride. Ahmad took her on his way, but then he was surrounded by cars with men from her village who tried to stop him. He somehow escaped with the car, after bumping slightly into a car that crossed his way. No killings and no sex, but yes, giving an unaccompanied woman a ride at night was seen as a breach of honor.

Information kept coming to me in pieces. Later that night I asked how the story was blown that much out of proportion – at least from my perspective. It turned out that Um Nimer had heard about the girl and that there was an issue of "blood". She had interpreted this as that a person was killed. (As in English, the Arabic word for "blood" has several meanings, referring among others to "the taking of life".) I also learned that at some point in the race Ahmad had escaped by foot, crossing several valleys, while leaving behind his car, phone, and netstick.

Many people had become involved and in the following days a "sulha" was arranged between Ahmad, the family of the woman, and the villagers. Ahmad's main argument was that according to Bedouin law he did not do anything wrong. Although it may be questionable whether the woman would be allowed to address an unknown male in the circumstances, Ahmad had not approached her in any way and his sole intention was to offer help.

Nonetheless, Ahmad's brothers were furious about his behavior that allegedly put blame on their family. Their discontent could possibly lead to a physical attack on him or even to his expulsion from the family, which is considered an extreme punishment. Thus, Ahmad sat down with several of his brothers to explain the situation. Initially, he thought that things were settled, but he had not spoken with the two oldest, who were still annoyed with him. For reasons of honor, he did not want to talk with Abu Ya'akub, the head of the family. Instead, he turned to Abu Youssouf, who is his uncle and a more senior member of the extended family. Ahmad expected that Abu Youssouf could and would arrange things with Abu Ya'akub. We went to visit and have tea with Abu Youssouf in his tent in the desert. Although Abu Youssouf was favorably disposed to Ahmad in this matter, things did not work out as planned and the tension between Ahmad and his brothers remained.

I decided to interfere, in the hope that as a good friend of Ahmad I may be in the position to mediate between him and his brothers, but I was wary that this could be a critically wrong decision. I arranged a meeting with his brother Abu Ya'akub. I did not inform Ahmad in advance about this initiative, in order to prevent any uncomfortable position for him vis-à-vis his brother. Abu Ya'akub invited me to his second villa on the Mount of Olives (Jerusalem), and honored me with the traditional sheep dish, "mansaf". I was delighted, since this was an indication that my visit was appreciated. Abu Ya'akub spoke during our meeting about the family honor, claiming that even if Ahmad is more modern than he is, he should have known that his actions do not correspond with Bedouin tradition. I tried as much as I could to explain Ahmad's situation, in the hope that this would temper Abu Ya'akub's anger. In the weeks after, there were some more talks between the brothers and slowly things calmed down within the family.

This was not the end. The day after the incident, Israeli police towed away Ahmad's car. Later, we discovered that it was severely damaged – unclear by whom. My car, which had been heavily used by both Ahmad and me throughout these last days, broke down as well. As a result, we remained without private transportation for over a month, which was most inconvenient. With significant efforts by both of us, and by others, we first got his car back and then had the two cars repaired, which cost a great deal of money. In the meantime, the woman – with whom the event began – went to the Palestinian police and filed a complaint – probably to protect her honor – in which she stated that Ahmad had kidnapped her. In addition, the owner of the car hit by Ahmad at the beginning of the story complained to the Palestinian police. As a result, Ahmad was arrested while on his way to meet me. While *arrested, he was not allowed to make any calls and therefore neither his friends nor his family knew about this latest development. Um Nimer and I – both overly concerned – searched for him everywhere until he reappeared a day and a half later as if nothing had happened.*

The saga depicted above ended after about a month and a half, when a marriage was arranged for the sister of Mustafa's wife with a well-to-do Palestinian. It had been nerve-wracking for all involved, but for me it was a learning experience as well. The events confronted me with the understanding that I am not any longer a curious outsider, or a passive bystander, as I had perceived myself previously. Through the friendship I became an active participant in Palestinian – and particularly, in Bedouin – life and culture, assisting where I could. In fact, I now felt acquainted enough with this culture to make independent decisions and intervene in and influence social processes, albeit on a micro-scale.

One afternoon a few weeks after this incident, Ahmad and I were driving in Ahmad's village, when we were stopped by two women with two infants who asked for a ride. We took them to their home. With the previous incident still fresh in my mind, I asked Ahmad why he had agreed to take them. He replied that he had believed the older woman to be the mother of the younger one, and therefore deemed it safe to take them in the car.

1.1 The Use of Hofstede's Theory

In this autoethnographic study, I looked at the differences between cultures as found by Hofstede (2001) through the perspective of intercultural friendship. Though I have brought in tales about others, the focus was on one specific friendship, between me, a Jewish Israeli man of Western European (Dutch) origin, and my Muslim Palestinian friend of Bedouin descent. I analyzed a series of "stories of friendship" according to four cultural dimensions, or value orientations: individualism/collectivism, uncertainty avoidance, masculinity/femininity, and power distance. In the friendship, dissimilarities on all four cultural dimensions were large and easily discernible. The large cultural distance between our respective cultures, based on divergent value systems, and the lack of social support from those surrounding me, greatly increased the difficulties in the cognitive, emotional, and behavioral realms. This finding is in line with a series of quantitative studies in this field (cf. Ward et al. 2001).

Hofstede's findings are being used extensively in a range of academic fields but primarily in quantitative studies. This study strongly supports the use of Hofstede's value dimensions as the basis for qualitative – and more specifically, autoethnographic – research. The use of Hofstede's framework with its four cultural dimensions facilitated categorization of the cultural differences between the two friends in this study, and of the challenges and opportunities stemming from the friendship. The framework thus provided a more coherent view of the various fields of intercultural variance than would have been possible without categorization. While doing so it shed light on findings in the field of uncertainty avoidance that did not fit well with the theory, as will be described later.

Undoubtedly, the use of Hofstede's theory came with certain costs. Looking at events through an a priori selected prism puts the emphasis on certain aspects and ignores others. It organizes our perception of situations in a certain manner, which is counter to staying on the impressionist level and being open to whatever comes to mind. However, the latter option too would create for a certain selection of material, which would have been less conscious, since it is impossible to share everything that comes to one's mind.

There are other relevant theories of culture, as I showed in Chapter 2, "When Cultures Meet". Thus, I could have used as my lens the value orientations postulated by Kluckhohn and Strodtbeck (Samovar et al. 2009). I then would have put more emphasis on dissimilarity in the dimension of activity orientation. On this dimension, Ahmad and many other Bedouins I met primarily alternate between the position of "being" (in which the self is defined by its relationships) to that of "being-in-becoming" (in which the self is defined by self-development), whereas I and many of those around me, raised in the West, primarily alternate between "being-in-becoming" to "doing" (in which the self is defined by action). I also would have investigated the differences between us regarding the dimension of attitude to nature. I probably would have used different stories, like those about the slaughtering of animals, the attitude toward dogs, my becoming vegetarian (like Ahmad's father), the use of plastic cups, and the disposal of garbage; stories that do not appear in this book. I then would have made presumptions about Bedouins from the perspective of the relationship with nature.

There were alternative kinds of organizing this book, not necessarily based on a predetermined value theory. For example, I could have organized stories chronologically or worked according to recurring themes in the friendship, in which case certainly the occupation would receive a chapter by itself. The question of how findings would diverge if I had taken another theoretical stance remains open.

It needs to be noted that Hofstede (2001) himself suggested that his IBM-based instrument may not be the most appropriate for any cultural comparison, that his theory is not finished, and that his findings are a step in an ongoing exploration. In addition, it is important to remember that he referred to national cultures. He was aware that this does injustice to subcultures. Thus, Israeli society, being a mixture of immigrants from many countries, knows a variety of subcultures. Hofstede also realized that cultures are not necessarily restricted by national boundaries, as is the case for Bedouin culture. At the time, the comparison of nations was more feasible than other ways of comparison. Moreover, with the loss of specific findings from several Arab countries, he related to the Arab world as one entity, ignoring national differences within this socio-geographical cluster. On top of this, we need to keep in mind that Hofstede never intended to describe the culture of individuals, as this is much more complex than comparing national cultures. Ahmad identifies with both Bedouin and Palestinian cultures that are close but still have their own specifics, whereas I identify with dominant cultures in both Israel and the Netherlands, cultures that are far apart. For all the aforementioned reasons, one needs to be very careful about cultural generalization based on the attitudes and behaviors of individuals.

Despite the limitations, I found it helpful to map the commonalities and discrepancies as I encountered these in the realm of the friendship along the cultural dimensions proposed by Hofstede. The cultural dimensions assisted immensely in highlighting and organizing the various aspects of cultural difference.

1.2 *Four Dimensions*

It is obvious that no situation stands alone and often in the friendship there were challenges and opportunities simultaneously on more than one cultural dimension. The reason for providing the forthcoming outline separately for each dimension is an attempt to clarity.

Individualism/collectivism: "Individualism can be defined as a preference for a loosely knit social framework in which individuals are considered to take care of themselves and their immediate families only. Its opposite, collectivism, represents a preference for a tightly knit framework in society in which individuals can expect their relatives or members of a particular in-group to look after them in exchange for unquestioning loyalty" (Hofstede n.d.-b). Differences between my friend and me on the dimension of individualism/collectivism displayed a similar pattern to findings by Hofstede (2001). Bedouin life is highly collectivistic, oriented toward the family, the clan, the tribe. In most situations, my friend tended to a collective stance. Possibly, the decades-long presence of threats by Israeli authorities heightened the sense of collectiveness. I tended to an individualistic stance, as is common in the Netherlands. It took me time to understand and appreciate, but eventually I became accustomed to and valued the collectivistic attitude to life. I started to enjoy collective ways of doing things and often prefer this to a more individualistic approach. In a variety of settings, I now attempt to integrate both individualistic and collectivistic perspectives. In contrast, my friend remained ambivalent about individualism. We both experienced social pressure from our respective environments. Within the political context, at times I felt "caught" in between two collectives, Jewish Israeli and Palestinian friends, and I felt pressured – both by my friends and intra-psychic – to choose between these groups.

Uncertainty avoidance: "The uncertainty avoidance dimension expresses the degree to which the members of a society feel uncomfortable with uncertainty and ambiguity. [...] Countries exhibiting strong UAI [Uncertainty Avoidance Index] maintain rigid codes of belief and behavior and are intolerant of unorthodox behavior and ideas. Weak UAI societies maintain a more relaxed attitude in which practice counts more than principles" (Hofstede n.d.-b). Hofstede found Israelis to be relatively avoidant of uncertainty, the Dutch relatively non-avoidant, and Arabs around the world average. Findings from the friendship did not fit well with the theory. The discrepancy between the findings from this study and those from Hofstede's studies may be related to the fact that I referred to uncertainty avoidance in daily life, whereas Hofstede based the Uncertainty Avoidance Index on three questions only, which were distinctly work related. The index may be highly relevant in some fields but may not necessarily explain uncertainty avoidance at large. Daily life for the Jahalin Bedouins is extremely uncertain. In the present political context, they not only cope with the burdens and restrictions of the Israeli occupation, as do many Palestinians, but also many of the Bedouin villages are under threat of demolition. Possibly, living under arduous socio-political and economic conditions forced them to cope better with uncertainty.

I have pointed out the difficulty in using the concept "uncertainty avoidance" and suggested dividing this field into two separate cultural dimensions, namely "tradition" and "discipline". The dimension "tradition" is comparable to the basic value of tradition suggested by Schwartz and Sagiv (1995). The dimension "discipline" is partly overlapping with the basic value of conformity suggested by Schwartz and Sagiv (1995), and also matches the dimension of polychronic versus monochronic time suggested by Hall and Hall (1990). If we relate to uncertainty avoidance in the sense of "adherence to tradition", impressions from the friendship are in line with Hofstede's theory, with Bedouins valuing tradition more than Western cultures. Differences in adherence to tradition, though, were not essential to the friendship. If we relate to uncertainty avoidance in the sense of "adherence to discipline", impressions from the friendship display the reverse of what Hofstede proposed, with Bedouins less disciplined and less likely to be obedient to authority outside the family. My explanation is that my Dutch, organized upbringing made me value discipline highly, while emphasizing verbal communication, rules, and planning. In this sense I am wary of any uncertainty. In contrast, my friend did not grow up on discipline. He feels comfortable with high levels of ambiguity, indirect communication, and lack of rules or plans. The friendship taught me to live with much less discipline/more uncertainty than I had been used to and I instructed my friend about the advantages of planning. However, even though both of us invested substantial efforts to make things work in this field too, the dimension of discipline created ongoing hardship and tensions between the two of us. More research is required to verify the existence of tradition and discipline as separate dimensions.

Masculinity/femininity: "The masculinity side of this dimension represents a preference in society for achievement, heroism, assertiveness and material reward for success. [...] Its opposite, femininity, stands for a preference for cooperation, modesty, caring for the weak and quality of life" (Hofstede n.d.-b). As concerning the dimension of masculinity/femininity, the contrast between us was huge; larger than would be expected from Hofstede's findings. Hofstede found that among the Dutch differences between men and women are among the lowest in the world, whereas these differences for Israelis and in the Arab world are about world average, with Arabs tending just a little more to masculinity than Israelis. My experience through my friend is that among the Palestinian Bedouins gender role differences are immense and any resemblance to femininity in a man is frowned upon, perceived as blame, and considered as lowering his status. Possibly, the importance of manhood is more important among the Palestinian Bedouins than in the Arab world at large. This could be partially explained by the fact that their existence is under continuing threat, a factor enhancing masculinity. Within the friendship, both my friend and I had to adjust to the other's perception of being a man. Although I insisted on occasionally revealing vulnerabilities, I felt substantial social pressure in this respect. If I wanted to fit into his circle of friends, I had to take care that my public image is masculine enough. The friendship was an opportunity to learn to become more masculine, which at the same time was quite a challenge.

Two points of reservation need to be made. Hofstede related to those cultures on the more feminine site as putting more emphasis on modesty and cooperation. Despite the tendency to masculinity, the Bedouins value modesty highly. Though there is competition between the families and cooperation is not noticed so much in daily life, under threat of the Israeli occupation and otherwise, Palestinian Bedouins stick together.

Power distance: "People in societies exhibiting a large degree of power distance accept a hierarchical order in which everybody has a place, and which needs no further justification. In societies with low power distance, people strive to equalize the distribution of power and demand justification for inequalities of power" (Hofstede n.d.-b). Disparity in the friendship on the dimension of power distance was substantial, and along a similar pattern as found by Hofstede. According to Hofstede, the Arabs are accustomed to high power distance, whereas Israelis are among those with lowest power distance and the Dutch somewhere in between. My impression was that power is a dominant factor in Palestinian Bedouin life, perhaps even more than in the Arab world as a whole. Differences between us in the perception of the intertwined values of power, honor, and authority, created delicate and sometimes explosive situations within the friendship. In many instances, my friend was inclined to tell me (and others) what to do, expecting me to obey. In contrast, I would have chosen a more democratic approach. A passive stance on my behalf made our dealings easier, but this occasionally made Israeli friends believe that I am being exploited.

Power issues on the political level, in the realm of the Israeli–Palestinian conflict and the occupation specifically, influenced the friendship as well. The situation for Israelis is much more favorable than for the Palestinians as far as it concerns socio-economic resources and freedom, and in practice my life is much more comfortable and freer than that of my friend. Paradoxically, it was often I, and not my friend, who felt in an inferior position, as an outsider among Palestinians and as an outcast in Israeli society, which increasingly turns against those with more liberal views.

2   Studying My Friendship with Ahmad

The study of my friendship with Ahmad was a challenge by itself, as well as an excellent opportunity to learn more about the cultural diversity between us. The following story of friendship will exemplify how this study fits into Bedouin life, and how its creation was influenced by the same four cultural dimensions on which we differ so much. Afterwards, I will expand on the interaction between us around the study, which will be followed by a discussion of some of the challenges I encountered in using the friendship itself as a research tool. This section will end with dilemmas around representativeness of this study that were of major concern to me throughout the process of writing.

Stories of Friendship: Getting Ahmad's View

Palestinian Authority, April 2011. The other day Ahmad had heard some strange noises from my car and suggested that I bring it to the garage. At half past ten in the morning, I called him to let him know that I am coming. Since some of the workers were still sleeping – they pass the nights at the garage – he suggested coming an hour later. At half past eleven his phone was turned off, but I decided to go anyway. I took my laptop with me. Who knows? Perhaps, today I will manage to discuss with him some of what I wrote. On the way, I visited Abu Omar's petrol station in az-Za'ayyem. This morning Omar (his son) was working. Omar asked about his uncle, Ahmad, and begged me to stay, but I wanted to move on.

At the garage in Hizma, one of the workers looked at the car. Subsequently, Ahmad took the driver's seat, told me to get in the car and drove out of the garage. Surprised, I asked where we were heading. He told me that we would need to check the car's electricity. I assumed that this would be in a local garage, where he had done this before, but Ahmad continued in the direction of the Palestinian town of Ramallah. Luckily, I had my European passport with me, since without that I cannot enter; Israelis are not allowed. I told Ahmad that I really wanted us to go over things I had written for this study, and Ahmad replied that we can do that later. We had the car checked and did some other errands. We spoke in English when strangers were around with the purpose of disguising my identity and as a measure of reducing security risks. On our way back, we gave a ride to the former owner of the garage. (Only later I discovered that this had been planned.) Back in the garage, the workers took care of my car.

In the meantime, I made coffee and tea for all present, something usually done by one of the junior men in the garage. At some point, when Ahmad was away, one of the workers, Aziz, came up to me and said: "Now you're the boss." He clarified that this means that I will need to give them money to buy food. I called Ahmad and asked him what to do. Ahmad responded that the workers receive enough money from him, which is also for food. At about 4 PM we had lunch prepared by the workers, eggs with tuna, hummus, white cheese, and pita bread. Everyone was invited. Since it was Passover, I had brought some matzo bread. The lunch break took less than half an hour, but during lunch, two Israeli clients, who had not wanted to join the meal, walked out. Ahmad got angry with the workers for losing these clients. He shouted at them, but they did not look bothered by his behavior.

After lunch, I finally had the opportunity to share with Ahmad one of the stories of friendship I had put in writing. It was one that included a comment on being satisfied with myself for not crying. Ahmad was astonished. To him this comment was highly inappropriate because one could infer from it that I cry. He would never have written such a thing and he suggested that I skip this part (an objection that he eventually withdrew). We discussed the incident, in which he had become angry at me for raising a certain topic for discussion. He explained that I am not sensitive enough to circumstances. I tend to ask straightforwardly whether we can talk about something (which I regarded an "improvement" as compared to the Israeli style of simply raising the issue). However, according to him, I need to understand from the situation, and – if needed – from indirect questions, whether it is appropriate to raise a certain subject. Ahmad then walked out of the garage office.

I was not in the mood for waiting, so after a quarter of an hour, I called him. He informed me that he had left the garage to take care of some urgent things and that he will not return soon. It was 7 PM and I went home, quite content with my day.

2.1 Studying Our Friendship

This book is about "friendship as research method" (cf. Ellis 2007; Owton and Allen-Collinson 2014; Tillmann-Healy 2001, 2003), since the main tool of this study was the friendship itself. This kind of research is a collaborative effort, offering an intense and intimate look at a friendship, which is in many ways closer than what would have been possible if an outsider investigated the friendship. It provides the opportunity to use firsthand tales about the friendship as data for the study. Making the friend an active partner in the research – as I did – can be enlightening in many ways. The friend may point out issues that otherwise could be overlooked, and his or her perspective will add more context and possibly put events and processes in a different light.

However, the friend's way of relating may not necessarily be in line with common standards of research. Some more general complications common in friendship research I mentioned in the first chapter. Here I will refer to a couple of aspects influencing the research, relating specifically to our friendship. I need to say that Ahmad was well acquainted with the discussion of broad ideas and metaphors, at times taking pains to make me acknowledge his ideas. He was less experienced with the academic discourse needed for a research study and the importance of getting the facts right. Consequently, one of the difficulties in friendship as method is related to making one's friend an active partner in the research while remaining focused on the intent and goals of the study. Ahmad had clear ideas about what is essential for the study and told me tales that he wanted me to include in the text. Although these stories were often highly interesting, I did not always agree with him about their importance for this study. For example, he gave me a detailed and painful account of the arduous lives of his parents and grandparents, who – apart from his mother – had passed away many years ago. Although I put his ancestors' stories in writing, with the risk of insulting Ahmad, I decided not to incorporate this – by itself highly interesting – knowledge, since I found it too distant from the topic of this study, which is the friendship itself.

Collaboration with a Bedouin on a text is not like authoring a paper with a colleague from your university. In Western cultures, it could have been possible to either communicate about a text by email or fix a date and time to discuss it. In these surroundings, collaboration worked in a vastly different manner. Ahmad's input in this study was crucial but often circumstantial. Written communication was out of the question and we could never make definite plans to meet. Even when he intended to go over the writings with me, it was hard for him to get to the job. As a result, it habitually took hours to get his undivided attention. When finally he was attentive, I read the texts from my laptop, in bits and pieces, while translating them into Hebrew to help him understand. Typically, there were other people around, and noise from the garage or a television, and in these circumstances, I was mostly unable to get into nuances of the text. Workers, clients, friends, suppliers, and others would walk in or call for advice. Repeatedly, such an interruption would be the end of our conversation. Thus, it became usual to travel around together half a day or more, while eventually speaking about part of the texts and in the meantime collecting more stories, like the one above. I regularly came to visit him in the hope that we could talk about my work but to no avail.

When reviewing texts, we usually agreed on the general terms, but Ahmad would often provide additional information or an enriching viewpoint that I had not considered. Discussing texts was therefore highly interesting but sometimes created tension and required "negotiated consent". For instance, I told Ahmad that I had written that it looks as if "planning" for the Bedouins is something unheard of. This made him upset and he replied that the Dutch are like machines, which made me upset in turn. We got into a small quarrel, after which he explained that what I wrote damages his honor, and that things are not as I had portrayed them. He added that, as I should have known, he does have plans, but they are long-term and much more general. I need to admit that he was right. I was aware of his plans, but from my perspective they were awfully vague. Ignoring his plans was a form of stereotyping from my side. He stereotyped as well. I reflected on his comments describing me – and the Dutch – as "cold" and "like a machine" and tried to make it clear to him that his words were painful to me. Eventually, we agreed that we both have plans but that mine are firmer than his, and that I may be cold and inflexible as compared to Bedouins but not as compared to other Dutch people. He then suggested including this particular conversation in the book.

Some of the events described were enervating, and observing the relationship in action was stressful, especially for the dimensions of masculinity/femininity and power distance. The dissimilarities on these dimensions are sensitive and my thinking conflicting, so that pondering over the various incidents and turning these into comprehensible stories caused anxiety. Another source of anxiety and an additional burden was the need to be careful about what I could or could not write, because things might not be accurate or too delicate to disclose. Writing my experiences was a form of catharsis, a way to relieve my stress and vent possible frustration with Ahmad's actions (or non-actions). Accordingly, discussing the stories of friendship with him was a recap of our experiences; a way of integrating both our views on what had happened and a way of psychologically working through the often complicated and heavily loaded events. Thus, many of our serious conversations (and some of our arguments) originated from the study, while examining with him its ideas, its texts, or the comments I received from others.

The study came to play a significant part in the friendship, and it is hard to imagine the friendship without it, because during its process I came to know him, his lifestyle, and Bedouin culture much better than before. I would not have asked him for so many clarifications if it were not for this research. There were periods in which I almost gave up on Ahmad's input, since it seemed he had lost interest. Nevertheless, the more the study developed, the more encouraging were his attitude and active involvement. The friendship also received attention from other directions, such as the Dutch media (Amnesty International 2011; Laparlière 2011; Thooft 2011). As a consequence, interviews of Ahmad and me became part of our shared experience. These interviews provided the opportunity to look at our friendship through foreign eyes and strengthened the idea that it may be significant for others. Eventually, it was Ahmad who pushed me to publish our story in book form.

2.2   *Representativeness*

A major question in doing autoethnographic research concerns the issue of representativeness. Though one may claim that case studies do not necessarily have to be representative, throughout the process of writing I found myself repeatedly concerned with the representativeness of the friendship, and of my stories in particular, similar to Wall (2008) when she wrote about her experience as an adoptive mother. Clearly, one cannot directly deduce from the dynamics created by the interaction of two friends and their social environment at a certain time and geographical place. Still, I wondered to what extent it would be possible to generalize from the findings and specifically mulled over two concerns that obviously affected these findings. One concern involved the degree of my adaptation within the friendship and my value adjustment specifically; the other involved the difficulty in separating the cultural from the individual. It is not that easy to look back seventeen years, evaluate in retrospect my values at the start of this friendship, and compare these with my present value appraisal. It also is quite a challenge to separate the personal from the cultural. In this section, I will attempt to provide a more general response to these concerns, and in the next section on personal growth I will add a few examples of specific changes that I perceive to have occurred.

Repeatedly, other Jews – friends, family, and teachers – questioned my way of dealing with the value conflict in the relationship with Ahmad. They raised the possibility or decided that I accommodate him too much, and they warned that I should not have given up so much of my own values. They regarded my extent of adaptation as extraordinary and therefore some of them disputed my inferences from the findings. It is true that If I had coped in another manner during numerous situations of conflict, many of the stories and the friendship as a whole would have taken a different turn. Also, it remains unclear what would have happened if I had a different personality. I can understand their apprehension, but my perception of the situation is otherwise.

People considered me to have overly adapted. They thus assumed that it is my original values that constitute "me" and that I betrayed myself, my values, and them. However, culture is an ever-changing process. My perspective is that adhering less to certain values and more to others that previously were less important to me was a positive development. My new persona feels as much "me" as the one that existed before, and I experience myself as expanding, while being able to manage within a – for me, newly acquired – value system. In the friendship I discarded some values I used to adhere to, and it is very well possible that I did so to a greater extent than others would have been willing to do in similar circumstances. My understanding was that I either take the relationship as it is or leave it. There would have been no way that I could become so much involved while sticking to my Dutch Israeli value orientation. Furthermore, I participated in this friendship out of choice and could have ended it if I had wanted to. If I had continued to insist on Ahmad's respect for my – especially "Dutch" – values, we would have remained distant friends or – more likely – the friendship would have dissolved long before. From a theoretical point of view, I used the approximation strategy of integration, accommodating to certain aspects of the other culture while retaining aspects of my original culture. This intercultural strategy is considered to be eventually the most psychologically healthy and adaptive (Pessate-Schubert 2003).

The second concern in the course of writing is related to the complexity in grasping what aspects in the friendship are culturally determined. This division is needed in order to generalize from this friendship, and thus is relevant to the significance of this study. When analyzing individuals, it is an unfeasible venture to disentangle personal from cultural variables, since there is a complex relationship between personal narratives of identity and the master narratives of our societies (Hammack 2008). We can see the importance of individual variety by looking at our brothers. Ahmad once remarked on the difference between him and one of his brothers: "He is Dutch; for him, everything needs to be exact." Another brother of his, Abu Omar, whom I met frequently and described before, obviously has a gentler character than Ahmad has. Likewise, some of my brothers are more sociable than I am, while others take fewer risks in life than I do. When examining personal and cultural characteristics, we need to take into account the interactive effects between the individual and the culture. However, not only do some cultures enhance certain personal characteristics, but characteristics could be viewed differently depending on the cultural context. Hence, it is doubtful whether Ahmad's "Dutch" brother, who in his culture is viewed as pedantic, would be perceived likewise in Dutch culture, and I know that, for example, my risk taking is perceived differently from a Dutch, Israeli, or Palestinian perspective.

Thus, conflictual situations in our friendship made me wonder to what extent they are caused by the personal characteristics of Ahmad and me and to what extent they have a cultural base. Clearly, we both have our unique personalities that affect the friendship, but as much as possible I wanted to dwell in the study on attitudes and behaviors that were culturally representative. Now and then, I received cues about the degree of representativeness of Ahmad's conduct through communications with other Bedouins. This was the case for Ahmad's recklessness, which others – also in his environment – regarded as extreme. At the same time, it needs to be noted that his behavior was not necessarily perceived as culturally inappropriate, only more radical. Hence, also Abu Omar would at times become annoyed with Ahmad for his behavior, mentioning that he takes things to the edge. I tried to make use of this extremity, considering that in qualitative research extreme cases are good to get a point across (cf. Flyvbjerg 2004).

The idea that in an encounter any moment could be the last is another issue about which I was unsure whether or not it is determined culturally. I found it hard to believe that someone can simply "walk out" on one's friend without any verbal comment on a pending separation, as Ahmad did once in a while with me. This felt extraordinarily strange and inappropriate to me. I was certain that other Dutch or Israeli people – had they been in such an incident – would have similar reactions to mine. I wondered whether these "disappearances" (from my viewpoint) and "other immediate things to do" (from his point of view) were some individual characteristic of Ahmad. Eventually, I realized that even if there may be some personal factors, the phenomenon has a cultural base. During the incident addressed before, Abu Omar, who otherwise has a relatively considerate personality, came in and left in exactly the same way as Ahmad did, before I even had a chance to talk with him. (Therefore, his name is not even mentioned in the story.) At the time, the workers in the garage were all Palestinian, but except for Ahmad only one – Fawaz, whom I mentioned before – was Bedouin. He too would arrive and go without prior notice, like other Bedouins I met. No one seemed to be concerned about this conduct. This shows that Ahmad is not alone in this kind of behavior, which appears to be an accepted form of action.

3 Personal Growth

I will expand here more on the notion of transformative learning as a result of this friendship, personal efficacy and the stress involved in changing. This will be followed by some thoughts on the topic of value change, with reference to indications of change in Ahmad.

Stories of Friendship: Where Is Christine?

Hizma, at the garage, June 2011. Ahmad and I had taken my human rights friend and colleague Christine on a tour of Bedouin life circumstances. Both Ahmad and I had enjoyed Christine's company. Afterwards, I posted a picture of Christine with a camel on Facebook. When Ahmad saw the picture, he was enthusiastic and exclaimed: "What a wonderful picture of the sunset with a camel!"

3.1 *Transformative Learning*

It was suggested that the cross-cultural encounter could be both stressful and an opportunity for growth (Montuori and Fahim 2004; Tesoriero 2006; Ward et al. 2001). In addition, growth may result from close encounters and connectedness with others (Jordan 2001; Kern et al. 2001). Accordingly, cross-cultural friendships that enable close encounters and connectedness are excellent ways to generate personal growth. This is especially so when there is an attempt to understand the experiences, which can take the form of constructing narratives (Armengol-Carrera 2009). Creating narratives (stories) is precisely what I did here. Reading the extensive literature, writing down and making sense of the stories of friendship, all contributed highly to my personal development. I never would have asked myself so many questions about my own outlook on life without this friendship and I never would have posed that many questions about our friendship and my position in it without this study.

Mezirow (1997, 2000) referred to the concept of "transformative learning", the process of affecting change within a frame of reference, as key to adult education. "Transformations in frames of reference take place through critical reflection and transformation of a habit of mind, or they may result from an accretion of transformations in points of view" (Mezirow 1997: 7). He exemplified transformative learning through the idea of ethnocentrism, and he claimed that when meeting people from other cultures, we learn by taking various points of view and reflecting critically on our own misconceptions. If we do so with people from diverse cultural groups, it is likely to transform our ethnocentric habit of mind and make us more tolerant. Others have looked at transformative learning as a developmental process, while noting the irreversibility of grasping new perspectives, and referring to the prominent place of feelings and relationships in it (Taylor 2017). Several studies referred to the idea of transformative learning as part of intercultural programs for students, but noted diverse effects between individuals, dependent partly on intent and willingness to engage in critical dialogue (Hart, Lantz and Montague 2020; Onosu 2020).

My experience shows that intercultural friendship can be an exceptional way to achieve transformative learning. I learned many things about the life, language, and customs of the Palestinian Bedouins, as well as about their socio-political situation. I escaped the "psychic prison" in which I had been living (cf. Lowe 2002; Morgan 2007), and doing so I encountered aspects of my own cultures – both the Israeli and the Dutch – of which I had been unaware. I learned more about my Jewish friends and family, and about the tremendous reluctance of many of them to see the good things in the friendship with Ahmad. The friendship opened a new world for me, or – more accurately – it shook my worldview. At times, it felt as if the elements of life were taken like a pack of cards and reshuffled. It repeatedly happened that Ahmad and I looked at the same thing or situation and saw something different, as in the story above. He gave me the opportunity to enter situations that taught me new ways of looking at and interpreting the world and "forced" me to cope in ways that had been foreign to me.

We could look at this also in terms of hybridity, a concept used by Bhabha "to describe the construction of cultural authority within conditions of political antagonism or inequity [...] the hybrid strategy or discourse opens up a space of negotiation where power is unequal but its articulation may be equivocal" (Bhabha 1998: 34). While moving from a position of cultural supremacy toward hybridity, matters that were self-evident to me lost their obviousness. Life did not become easier, but my horizons widened and consequently I became humbler as regarding the standing of my culture. The acquired knowledge about Bedouin life and culture helped me taking new perspectives and broadened my outlook on life beyond Bedouin culture. It stirred the belief that my cultural way was the "right" way and taught me that numerous situations in life can be dealt with in other ways than those familiar to me. Nowadays, I can accept more readily that my way of looking at the world is one out of many. This made me less dependent on the common knowledge in my environment, and more flexible in taking various points of view and/or ways of action. My experience is comparable with the findings from an extensive review that general cross-cultural competencies contribute more to intercultural effectiveness than do more specific skills and knowledge regarding a particular culture (Abbe, Gulick and Herman 2007).

The story depicted above is an acute example of transformative learning. It reminded me of one of these optical illusions in which one can see different things, depending on what is considered foreground, and what is perceived as background. It had not occurred to me that one could see something other than what I saw: a woman. Ahmad was well aware of Christine's presence in the picture, but he was more attuned to the environment. In contrast, for me the person is central (in most circumstances), and I had not even noticed the sunset. One could see here the different relationship we have with nature (cf. Samovar et al. 2009). Ahmad was about to leave a comment on Facebook of what he saw: a wonderful picture of the sunset with a camel. However, taking into account that Christine is European, I felt uncomfortable about him leaving her out. Therefore, I suggested that he mention her as well, which he did. On hindsight, I realized that it was my interference that was inappropriate. I tried to show a Bedouin how he was supposed to see the world, while Christine is not the person who would be offended had he written what he intended.

Through my connection with the Bedouins, life changed in more ways. Until the first years of the friendship with Ahmad most of my friends had been Israeli Jewish women. When the bond with him grew stronger, much of my free time was spent with him and other Palestinian men on the West Bank.

I enjoyed simply being together and doing, on the Palestinian side, more than social gatherings on the Israeli side. I had enjoyed the social gatherings with Jewish friends for two decades, but I came to experience them as either too calm or too demanding, with too much talking. In addition, and this may seem paradoxical, but despite the momentous adaptations I had to make among Palestinians in order to fit in, with them I didn't feel as much that I needed to live up to something, or to prove myself as I did in the Israeli Jewish world. As it was virtually impossible to meet with both groups together, contacts with several of my Jewish friends diluted or dissolved completely. Over time, my attitudes and pastimes changed. To give a practical example, until I met Ahmad I would regularly go to the movies with Jewish friends. After we became involved, I stopped doing so. The explanation is that with the Bedouins, I have enough drama and thought-provoking stimuli in my life, and I do not need more.

I would agree with the understanding that the true impact of friendship is found "not only by harmonic friendships but also, or even more, by friends who fight their way through all the complications and contradictions that characterize different kinds of friendships in real peer life" (Krappmann 1998: 36). Certainly, we fought through complications and contradictions and tried – sometimes forcefully – to make the other adapt to our respective cultural orientations. At times this felt like a boxing match over diverging outlooks on life. There was no winner, though often I felt he had the cultural upper hand, and that is what he thought about me as well.

One of the most striking examples of the culture fight between us was around situations in which Ahmad had intended to visit me in Jerusalem, which he still tried until the early years of this century. Occasionally, he would arrive some point after the time he had mentioned, but regularly something interfered in his way and he would change his direction. This could be someone else he encountered, some work to do, the presence of soldiers near the wall or anything else. He would not care to tell me, and I would usually find out why he had not arrived only the next day. These situations made me angry and frustrated because I had adapted my plans and had waited for him. I also would be highly worried, since on his way to meet me more than once he was arrested by Israeli soldiers and detained for hours. In such incidents, I often felt that he tied me down by not informing me about his change of direction. This was something that I found unacceptable. Similarly, he felt that my expectation that he would tell me was a type of interference in his manner of living in flux and a – to him unacceptable – way of tying him down. Fights about this kind of situation, in which both of us felt disrespected in our respective cultures, commonly left both of us hurt. Paradoxically, and as unpleasant as these fights were for both of us, they made our friendship more intense.

I needed to learn a new cultural language that was dissimilar to anything I had learned until then. Had I read the literature for this study beforehand, I would have felt more prepared. However, I did not. I believe that many – if not most – people who become involved in intercultural friendships do not invest ahead of time in preparation for such a friendship. Like me, they are apt to be caught by surprise again and again, through smaller or bigger events in which the other reacts or behaves in a – to us – incomprehensible way. The conviction that eventually one will manage to conquer the hardships is crucial for maintaining the friendship.

Let us look at this from the perspective of self-efficacy. Perceived personal efficacy (or self-efficacy) is the belief that one has the power to effect changes by one's actions. Self-efficacy is enhanced, among others, through mastering experiences, while "resilient efficacy requires experience in overcoming obstacles through perseverant effort" (Bandura 2008: 169). Clearly, the friendship provided many opportunities to enhance self-efficacy through its numerous challenging experiences. My experience is in line with the self-expansion model, which portrays the individual as looking for self-expansion to increase his self-efficacy potential. According to this model, self-efficacy is enhanced through the incorporation of material and social resources, perspectives, and identities that will facilitate the achievement of goals (Wright et al. 2005).

One major change that occurred through the friendship, and which I felt as a leap in self-efficacy, concerns the issue of expectations. The friendship taught me that people will not necessarily behave as I expect them to behave and that therefore, I should lower my expectations. The consequences of this change went far beyond the friendship itself and became part of my day-to-day life and my relationships with family, friends, colleagues, clients, and even strangers. I am now always aware that people may not act like I had expected and may not even be interested in acting in what I see as a reasonable manner. This may be self-evident now, but for me it was not previously. From interactions with others, I learned that many have this same erroneous assumption that people will behave as expected or at least in a reasonable manner for them. They may not, since both expectations and reason are culturally bound, and people have different perspectives, culturally and otherwise.

It is not just through mastery of events and lowering expectations that I increased self-efficacy but also through incorporation of some of my friend's attributes. Incorporating the other in the self, by ways of personal relations, like friendships, is one of the ways to create self-expansion. Accordingly, interpersonal closeness is to some extent motivated by the wish to include attributes of the other. People usually tend to choose their friends from within their in-groups. Nonetheless, intergroup friendships provide better opportunities for self-expansion, because of the many different attributes the out-group member possesses. Consequently, intergroup friendships are regarded attractive to some people (Davies, Wright et al. 2011; Wright et al. 2005). At the same time, intergroup contact may create feelings of disintegration and self-loss, and this too is what I experienced. "Self-expansion can be stressful, as a large number of new self-aspects are incorporated into the existing self-structure and periods of rapid self-expansion may need to be followed by periods of self-integration" (Wright et al. 2005: 136). Moreover, acquiring self-efficacy concerns achieving control over potentially threatening circumstances. Since these circumstances are not always under one"s personal control, they are anxiety provoking (Bandura 1988).

I realize that on many occasions in this friendship I have felt anxious, confused, helpless, lonely, scared, bewildered, angry, disappointed, or sad. No doubt that I suffered immensely from acculturation stress. Every now and then, I found it hard to contain my own emotions and, once in a while, situations were disturbing to such an extent that I developed minor psychosomatic symptoms. Only a few years ago, I was totally upset by many of the incidents in which I took part, and had sleepless nights, while unsuccessfully trying to make sense of situations. Thus, the process of growth was certainly frustrating and painful. I experienced the change as so massive and intense, that I was afraid to remain with stretch marks in my psyche.

I wondered why I need a relationship that creates so much stress in my life. The answer remained the same: the friendship is also highly rewarding. This is not simply because I appreciate Ahmad's company but also because he gave me the opportunity to look into a new world. The same stressful situations were eye opening and broadened my personal boundaries tremendously. Moreover, the friendship provides a strong feeling that I matter, a perception that enhances well-being (cf. Matera, Bosco and Meringolo 2019). The friendship makes me feel significant not only for Ahmad and his close ones, but for our respective communities as well, while using the friendship as a statement of peace and providing a living example of an alternative form of relating across the Israeli–Palestinian divide.

3.2 Value Change

The main challenge in bridging cultural differences stems from our diverse value orientations. We discussed before these differences in value orientations and my behavioral, cognitive, and emotional adjustments, which varied between the cultural dimensions. Bardi and Goodwin (2011) identified five facilitators of value change, which are priming, adaptation, identification, consistency maintenance, and direct persuasion. As I will illustrate subsequently, all factors played a role for me. It would be challenging to separate value changes that occurred because of the friendship from those resulting from other processes in my life. Throughout the last years, this friendship comprised a growing part of my life, but my life also involved other pastimes and events that were influential. Still, I believe most changes in me can be attributed to the friendship. To better understand what happened to my values, let us look at a couple of specific values and the ways in which they changed.

Bardi and Goodwin (2011) described the dual way to value change, with one automatic route and one route that required effort, which may be combined. I walked both routes. For most of the values, the process of change was automatic and unconscious. It happened gradually through the years, without me being much aware of it. Some values, such as "cleanliness", I relinquished easily. There is an enormous difference between the Dutch and Bedouin perceptions of cleanliness, but this was so little an issue in the friendship that I did not care to address it until this point. In contrast, the related value of orderliness was an issue in the friendship. I am much more orderly than Ahmad. Though the two of us are still far apart on this value, it did lose some of its importance to me, and I am less troubled than in the past by both my own lack of order and that of others. To make this more explicit, in the past, I was not able to work if my table was not organized, now I am able to concentrate when there are heaps of papers, books, and other things around me.

Maintaining consistency between my values and my actions was tricky, especially when the friendship called for actions that were not in line with these values. I was ambivalent in my willingness to change certain values. For example, I took a middle path for the value of "toughness", agreeing that at times one needs to exhibit one's vigor but rejecting that one always needs to be tough and insisting on the right to also expose vulnerability. Some values with which I had not been so concerned before took on more meaning. Thus, I reluctantly increased the importance of "preserving public image", which is so important in Bedouin life. In addition, there were values for which I adjusted only on a behavioral level, an example of which is "honesty". Within the context of the friendship, I had to give evasive answers or lie sporadically to other people involved in order not to create major problems for either Ahmad or me. For instance, in response to questions about my family situation, I more than once replied that I have four wives. Still, I did not substantially change my perception of honesty as highly important. In these situations, the gap between my behavior and my thinking created a certain degree of unpleasant dissonance within me.

Value change can be a cognitive process based on choice (Roccas et al. 2002). Some values, such as "hospitality", I internalized readily since I found it easy to see their quality and came to identify with them. For other values, the change took a lot of effort. I was acutely aware of my own process of change concerning "security" and "daringness". I exposed myself to increasingly adventurous situations while making cognitive decisions in that direction and habituating myself to mounting levels of discomfort. This happened partly because of environmental stimuli and partly because of an internal desire to change. This change was not just in the realm of the friendship and can be noticed in many aspects of my life. I now take more risks than before, also outside the friendship – time-wise, financially, and physically.

I realized that there was no way that I could make Ahmad or other Bedouins adapt to my interpretation of time as inflexible. Therefore, feeling more or less "culturally forced" to do so, I consciously gave up on the importance of "punctuality". This is an example of a value for which Ahmad used his willpower and direct persuasion to make it clear that I am supposed to adapt, since I am in his cultural habitat. This situation caused me to create a double standard, heightening or lowering the importance of certain values, such as "punctuality", depending on the cultural context. I became more lenient as regarding time in my interactions with Bedouins than with Jewish Israeli or Western friends. For example, I would anticipate Israelis and Westerners to be – at least more or less – on time but would not require the same from Bedouins and other Palestinians. This differentiation seems based on the notion of priming (cf. Bardi and Goodwin 2011). One culture primes a certain value orientation, whereas the other culture primes another orientation. Although I did lower the importance I gave to this value in my life a bit, the change was mostly in the realm of the friendship.

Bardi and Goodwin (2011) also differentiated between initial and temporary versus long-term and stable value change. The friendship has existed for close to two decades, in which I changed my values and corresponding outlook toward a wide scale of situations. Although I do not know what would happen to these values if the friendship dissolved, I believe much of the value change will remain. In the meantime, the continuing confrontation with the hardships of Bedouin and other rural Palestinian friends strengthened my human rights perspective and made me change my political stance. Although I always held a socialist view, in line with my new values the friendship made me move politically more to the left. Had I had the right to vote in the national elections – remember, I am an Israeli resident, but not an Israeli citizen – and now more aware of Arab concerns, I believe I would have voted for the Arab party. In the realm of the Israeli–Palestinian conflict and being a Jew, we could consider this as some form of crossover.

This book looked at the friendship primarily from my point of view. While reading things that were written through my eyes, it may seem to a Westerner that I am enormously flexible, whereas Ahmad hardly accommodated me. Neither Ahmad nor I see it that way. One needs to bear in mind that he lives in an environment that is culturally more homogenic than my surroundings. Consequently, I am more experienced than he is in meeting other cultures. So, Ahmad too experienced accommodation and personal growth. Some of Ahmad's adjustments I pointed out before and I will mention here a few more. He learned to be more considerate with me than he is used to in his dealings with Palestinian men. In addition, he introduced me into his circle of friends, home, and family; the latter being especially uncommon even with Bedouin or Palestinian friends. This is still more exceptional when it is taken into account that I am a foreigner – and besides that a Jewish Israeli. He would share with me his personal thoughts, something that for him is out of the ordinary, and generally became more open toward others about his life, because of our friendship.

Ahmad's adjustment was partly driven by instrumental needs. Thus, he acknowledges that he learned about "modern life" from me and in particular about the advantages of planning. For him I became a catalyst of change in the field of communications. With my assistance he started using a smartphone and the Internet for e-mail, Facebook, Skype, and WhatsApp. He would enjoy these methods of communication, but with less availability of these facilities, he initially could remain days without a phone, or weeks without Internet access, without experiencing much concern. Although this lack of need to communicate changed with the years, he remained less dependent on modern communication methods than many academic Westerners or me. In general, Ahmad finds it terribly difficult "to be both Bedouin and 'modern'", as he puts it, and he succeeds only partially in combining both outlooks on life. He often has a challenging time with me, feeling that I demand too much adjustment from him but – unlike me – only infrequently complains. He once said, "neither he nor other Bedouins can live up to Western expectations." Nevertheless, he hopes that his children will fare better, and would like to see them grow up while being able to be more flexible than him and manage well in both Bedouin and modern Western cultures. Meanwhile, the cultural differences are barely bridgeable. This he sees as one more reason for Bedouins to keep distant from both Israelis and from Westerners.

Many organizations for human rights and/or social justice are active in the Palestinian Authority, and some of them are involved with the Bedouins. Through these organizations there are social contacts between Bedouins, Israeli Jews, and foreigners, but they do not reach our level of closeness. Close intercultural friendships are scarce among the Jahalin Bedouins; so much so that throughout the many years of friendship and involvement in Palestinian

Bedouin life, I have met only two other Israeli Jews – both social activists and tour guides – who reached a similar level of personal involvement. We therefore can consider our friendship as both unique and paradigmatic.

4 Implications and Recommendations

The study of this friendship bears implications for the field of cultural psychology, for the notion of multicultural personality and for the combat against prejudice and social injustice. I will briefly discuss these three issues, which all have to do with being aware of cultural difference and our own tendency to be judgmental of other cultures.

Stories of Friendship: Raising Awareness

The following story is a portrayal of one of our attempts in using the friendship as a means to create more awareness outside our respective communities to social injustice involving the Jahalin Bedouins. The Bedouin Life Tour, one of the projects Ahmad and I did together, illustrates both the hardships and the complexity of Palestinian Bedouin life but also tries to counter some cultural stereotypes (such as "all Bedouins live in tents").

Jerusalem and Palestinian Authority, Saturday, February 2011. I brought Miriam back to the bus. Miriam is a volunteer at an international human rights organization. Ahmad and I had visited her last year in the Netherlands and today took her on a tour to the Bedouins. We visited the village of Arab al-Jahalin, built from the compensation the Bedouins received after they were evacuated from the Ma'ale Adumim settlement. The village, with its many villas, is located near Jerusalem's garbage dump. We also visited the Prisoners Movement Museum at the Al-Quds University, the same one we could not enter with my uncle (see "Stories of Friendship: No "No" for an Answer"), which displays both the horrific stories of Palestinian detainees and the beautiful works of art made in prison. On our way to the Jahalin primary school at Khan al-Ahmar, the village that is still pending demolition, we drove down the road where we were in the traffic jam with my teacher (see "Stories of Friendship: The Traffic Jam"). The school, built of car tires and cement, is planned to be demolished, and Miriam would like to do a human rights activity, with Dutch and Bedouin children exchanging drawings.

4.1 Cultural Psychology

For those in the helping professions, learning to cope with cultural diversity is of utmost importance. Still, for many psychologists, and clinical psychologists specifically, the influence of cultural issues on the lives and development of their clients is something that goes almost unnoticed. Competent engagement in intercultural encounters was suggested as a way to attain personal as well as professional growth (cf. Tesoriero 2006). My immersion in Bedouin culture made me more aware of cultural variations in general. I found this not only helpful in my personal life but also in the work with clients of many cultural backgrounds. As a psychotherapist and consultant, I try to empower people, make them more aware of themselves and their environment, and enhance their personal growth. More than before, I see how my own cultural background may bias the way I perceive clients. I was taught extensively about how one's personal and family background affects one's emotions, cognitions, and actions. Now, I am more able to reflect on how a person's cultural background affects one's dealings with variant social environments and one's perception of others' attitudes and behaviors.

Three examples from my practice with male Israeli clients show how a cultural perspective is relevant in psychotherapy: (1) An older client of Dutch origin complained that people in Israel will not call you back despite promising to do so, and – as a consequence of this behavior – referred to most Israelis as dishonest and liars. He therefore found it hard to trust Israelis. (2) A young Jewish client of Yemenite origin complained that at his place of work, one of the female Jewish employees became friendly with a male Arab employee. This upset him to such a degree that he contemplated quitting his job. (3) A client in his 20s went on vacation to Thailand with two friends. When at some point they decided to separate, he became so anxious about being alone in the strange environment that he took the first possible flight home.

The first example demonstrates a misinterpretation of another culture. I could help this client see that his difficulty may be based on distinct cultural perspectives regarding uncertainty, or more specifically the use of language and the fluidity of life, and that the people he encounters are not necessarily "bad" people. The second example reveals a conflict between individualism and collectivism. Although I did try to show this client other perspectives, realizing his collectivistic view in light of the Israeli–Palestinian conflict, I could appreciate how he took the interfaith friendship of his co-worker as a betrayal of the Jewish people. The third example is one of culture shock. The client called me from Thailand, and I tried to comfort him while he was having a panic attack. But as he at the time was not able to adjust, he felt he must return immediately to a familiar environment, home. I encountered a comparable situation a couple of years later with another client in another part of the world.

I also changed in my work with groups and organizations. Through my involvement with cultural challenges, I was inspired to create a workshop on the encounter with another culture. In this workshop, participants looked at the growth-enhancing aspects in their own cultures and in those cultures they encountered. As an organizational consultant, I try to highlight more than before the organization's cultural setting and underlying assumptions, which go often unnoticed and as a result cause counterproductive tension.

The changes I went through are all signs of the culture blindness I suffered from in my profession. I suspect that many psychologists like me have experienced similar deficits in their professional education. With increasing cultural intermingling, the understanding of the socio-cultural surroundings of a client – or an organization and its members – becomes of utmost importance. Therefore, in the training of psychologists, especially clinical psychologists, more emphasis on cultural aspects is required.

In addition, and though the bulk of research on intercultural friendship is growing, there is a tendency for research to focus on Western cultures. Friendship-related research on non-Western cultures remains limited and more research is requested.

4.2   *Multicultural Personality*

Being born in the Netherlands to Jewish parents and migrating to Israel had a major impact on my cultural identity. Dutch culture is ingrained in my personality, and Jewish customs are an integral part of my personal history. Migration and life in Israel forced me to adapt to new cultural ways of looking at things. I experienced many more cultural influences on my life and personality because of the interaction with various social and professional groups in which I participated throughout the years. In this friendship, I also experienced gradually adding Bedouin or Palestinian Arab elements to my life and identity. This happened in a variety of ways. For example, my experience is that acquiring a new language comes with the development of a new part in my identity. It is as if I am a little different when I think in different languages, experiencing distinct mind-sets. This is comparable to findings on multilingual adolescents who experience life differently and create various subjectivities based on their use of different languages (Kramsch 2006). It is obviously not just the language making the difference. I found that my behavior and thoughts automatically adapted to the values in the environment. Thus, in the car I listen to a radio station with classical music when in a Jewish neighborhood, and I turn to Arab music when driving to Ahmad. My personal experience coincides with the finding that people of dual nationality were found to keep distinct value systems, each of which may be primed in distinct situations (Stelzl and Seligman 2009). In addition, talking and writing about my friendship with Ahmad were instrumental in constructing my present identity (cf. Anthony and McCabe 2015).

I think of myself as having a "multicultural personality". A multicultural personality was defined in diverse ways. Adler (1977) identified the individual with a multicultural personality as embodying three postulates: (1) Every culture or system has its own internal coherence, integrity, and logic; (2) No one culture is inherently better or worse than another; (3) All persons are, to some extent, culturally bound. In contrast, van der Zee and van Oudenhoven (2000) defined multicultural personality as a combination of the following traits: openness, emotional stability, social initiative, and flexibility. A series of publications related to the notion of the multicultural personality, defined as having certain personality traits, and to its relevance for acculturation processes (Bakker, van der Zee and van Oudenhoven 2006; Dana 2000; Dewaelea and van Oudenhoven 2009; van der Zee and van Oudenhoven 2000). In most studies, biculturalism was found to be related to positive psychological indicators (Chae and Foley 2010; Chen, Benet-Martinez and Bond 2008; Ward et al. 2001) as were multicultural personality traits (Brumett, Wade, Ponterotto, Thombs and Lewis 2007; Dewaelea and van Oudenhoven 2009; Downie, Koestner, ElGeledi and Cree 2004). Ponterotto (Ponterotto 2010; Ponterotto et al. 2007; Ponterotto, Mendelowitz and Collabolletta 2008) even recommended actively promoting the development of multicultural personalities in order to enhance optimal psychological functioning in culturally heterogeneous societies. Recent studies found that multicultural personality traits play an important role in the relationship between cross-group friendship and positive outgroup attitudes, as those with these traits tend to spend more time with friends from other cultures, which, in turn, promotes more positive outgroup attitudes (Korol 2017, 2019).

The notion of "multicultural personality" is partly overlapping with the concept from the field of social psychology of "global identity" (e.g., Arrow and Sundberg 2004; Barth, Jugert, Wutzler and Fritsche 2015; Harush, Lisak and Glikson 2018; Shokef and Erez 2006), which in turn overlaps partly with another idea, from the field of education, namely "global citizenship" (e.g., Karlberg 2008; Lindner 2006; Pani 1999; Pike and Sillem 2018; Sklad, Friedman, Park and Oomen 2016). I can identify with all three concepts – multicultural personality, global identity, and global citizenship – which deal with breaking societal boundaries, feeling social responsibility, and creating some form of social oneness.

With more and more people moving around the globe, there is a growing need for people to become multicultural, and there is no doubt that intercultural friendship assists in this need. There is still much to do regarding research in this field, as the research on multicultural identity, personalities and/or traits leaves room for study in many directions, among others in relation to dealing with interpersonal, social, and political conflict.

4.3   *Prejudice and Social Injustice*

I have been a social activist for many years and in a variety of settings. In line with other mental health professionals (cf. Burkard, Knox, Groen, Perez and Hess 2006; Chen, Chan, Bond and Stewart 2006; Chirkov, Ryan and Willness 2005; Cushman 2000; Tesoriero 2006; Watts 2004), I see the acknowledgment of and combat against racism, prejudice, and injustice as part of my profession. Ahmad, whose fight for the rights of Palestinians has taken him to jail, may be considered a social activist as well. In fact, I regard the friendship between us as a form of social activism (cf. Joubran and Schwartz 2007). As suggested by Chen (2002), I believe that presentation of a friendship in public not just enhances commitment to the relationship but also counters social stigma. This friendship takes place in the midst of a longstanding socio-political controversy. The Arab–Israeli conflict is intense, and characterized by racism and oppression of Israeli Jews versus Palestinians (Herzog, Sharon and Leykin 2008; Mizrachi and Herzog 2012; Shalhoub-Kevorkian 2004). Both our social habitats are relatively ethnocentric, with those around me reluctant to accept Muslims and Arabs, and those around Ahmad reluctant to accept Israelis and Jews. This is to the point that people not necessarily let someone of the other group into ones' house, even if a friend of a friend. One could argue that friendships have little impact on this situation, but we prefer Bandura's emphasis on optimism in social relations in order to overcome rejection, and produce change (Bandura 1988). Therefore – and though this may seem naïve – we believe that friendships across Israeli–Arab boundaries could slightly counter the blatant antagonism between Jews and Muslims, and between Israelis and Palestinians.

The effect of the friendship goes much broader than between the two of us. Ahmad and I created a multitude of intercultural encounters in our surroundings. I joined him in an endless number of Bedouin or Palestinian gatherings, he from time to time joined me at social events in Israel, and three times we traveled to Europe. In addition, I shared the stories about my friendship with many people, both orally and in writing, both in person and through the media. I learned from the responses that I often astounded people not only with the cultural differences but also with the hardships with which Ahmad, many Bedouins, and other rural Palestinians must cope.

With the support of Ahmad, I initiated a range of small projects to raise awareness regarding the Jahalin Bedouins. I have mentioned "Jahalin Tours", through which we have taken around those interested in Bedouin life and the Peace Center for Heritage with the online shop. In addition, I created the Jahalin Facebook page, providing automatic news items on Bedouins (Weishut n.d.-a, n.d.-b, n.d.-c). None of this I could have done without the friendship. Obviously, the intensity of my involvement in this friendship and my attempts to make a change on a broader scale are outstanding. However, my expectation is that most close cross-cultural friendships enhance intergroup understanding between the partners in friendship. Better understanding is a step on the road to a change in attitudes, which eventually could lead to change in behavior.

Since friendships develop in a social context, other people are likely to become acquainted with the intergroup friendship and might get involved. Many studies found that actual encounters between people from other cultures reduce prejudice (e.g., Ari and Laron 2014; Gareis and Jalayer 2018; Laar, Levin, Sinclair and Sidanius 2005; Velasco Gonzalez et al. 2008; Wright et al. 2005). Intergroup friendships were suggested as unique in their ability to promote positive attitudes between groups, by means of strong psychological mechanisms underlying friendship and group interactions. There are indications that the mere knowledge of a close intergroup relationship by a group member and other interactions across group boundaries are sufficient to improve intergroup attitudes (Davies and Aron 2016; Davies, Tropp, Aron, Pettigrew and Wright, 2011). In my situation, Israeli and other friends and family conquered their fears, joined me on my trips to the Palestinian Territories, either as part of the above-mentioned projects, or as part of a visit to Ahmad, and changed their views. For several of them, this was a behavioral change, since in recent decades they had considered visits to the Palestinian Authority as inconceivable.

Friendships like ours thus could produce social change, even though this would be on a tiny scale. This study therefore supports the notion that intercultural friendships can improve interracial or intercultural attitudes and may play a fundamental role in promoting greater social equality (cf. Aberson et al. 2004; Christopher 1999). This is another reason to support the creation of intercultural friendships.

Epilogue

Looking back at some of the male friendships throughout my life, I can discern a clear pattern. In my best friendships my role was that of a nerd, a person always behaving according to the norms: kind, gentle, balanced, restrained, and okay with those around me, sometimes to the point of disregarding my own needs. In contrast, my best friends were tough and independent; they would not necessarily go along with what is socially acceptable and would every now and then go to the extreme. Thus, for example, my best friend in primary school was the one who physically attacked our (female) schoolteacher, and my best friend in grammar school was so critical of our fellow classmates and our teachers that he made himself highly unpopular. I could expand here on my psychological needs and on the benefits of being perceived as the "nice guy", while having in my friend a "tough guy" alter ego but will leave that for another occasion.

Although I made quite a few changes in my personal life, in my late 30s I viewed myself as dull. In an attempt to change this, I decided on a life motto, a guide for decisions in my life, which was "living, loving, and leading". The motto made me strive for both inner and outer changes in these directions. It encouraged me in decisions – among others – about becoming more curious and outgoing, expanding my circle of friends, and taking on several leadership functions. My new acquaintance with Ahmad was part of the realization of this motto. After achieving what I had sought, I opted for another motto, which was "flowing, knowing, and growing". Whenever I needed to make a decision, I considered whether or not it is something that heightened my flexibility, enhanced my knowledge, and/or gave me a feeling of personal growth. Both the friendship and my doctoral studies were part of the realization of this same motto. Ahmad asked me where I want to be in another five years, pushed me to start my doctoral studies, and remained a principal encouraging and motivating force throughout.

At the time, neither of us knew that our friendship would become central in my writing. In the process of choosing a subject for my doctoral dissertation in psychology, it was self-evident that I wanted to invest my time and energy in something related to those fields that were close to my heart, like social activism and personal growth. I also was interested in the "large group". While investing more in the subject, I became conscious of the fact that my own encounters with other cultures, and in particular my friendship with Ahmad, were worthwhile studying. It was not an easy step to start writing about myself and I wondered how others would accept this. The first colleagues to whom I told my plans – outside my own cohort of students – reacted negatively. They regarded my ideas as stemming from narcissistic needs. Despite the objections, my plans crystallized, the study expanded, and I am happy to conclude that eventually even the skeptics among my friends became supportive.

The situation was different as far as it concerned support for the friendship. My friendship with Ahmad follows to some extent the same pattern as that of previous friendships in which I am the "nice guy" and he is the "tough guy", which can be observed in many of the stories described. Nevertheless, in this friendship it is apparent how – through my self-imposed life motto – I slowly incorporated aspects of his character and lifestyle. I became more daring, more challenging, and – as a result – deviated more from my original social environment. In the beginning of our friendship, I was inclined to focus on how we can compensate each other and combine our strengths to achieve something bigger (see Figure 1). As the bond between Ahmad and me became stronger, I became attuned to the need to defend Ahmad and our friendship. Increasingly, I felt under attack and tried to protect us from enemies and friends with good intentions; so, two and a half years after creating the first image (see Figure 1), I sent Ahmad another one, reflecting this (see Figure 10).

I was sad that quite a few friends did not appreciate my choices. Some expressed difficulty in looking beyond the group (cultural) level of Palestinian/Arab/Muslim/Bedouin, which to many Jewish Israelis is all the same, and seeing Ahmad for the individual he is. Others saw him but had a hard time respecting his embeddedness in a culture so unlike mine/ours. These friends were concerned because they considered my conduct inappropriate, which explains part of their anger at and pressure on me to choose a more acceptable social environment. Still others continued to show interest and support of the friendship. With years gone by, the friendship became less of an issue. Both his

FIGURE 10 Ahmad and Daniel – The world against us (November 2011)

EPILOGUE

and my family and friends got used to and accepted the fact that we are important aspects in each other's lives, and they relate to us accordingly. It must be said though that in recent years, I experienced fewer frightening events with him. I believe this is primarily because both of us are older and calmer. Today, the friendship is stronger than ever and enriches my life with a mental freedom that had been previously unknown to me. My present motto is "reach, teach, and touch", in the realm of which I published this study.

Before concluding, I would like to refer to the commentary on the ancient Hindu text *Bhagavad Gita* (Easwaran 1979). Easwaran, a Hindu man, writes about his close friendship with a Muslim man in a period in which relations between Hindus and Muslims throughout India were particularly strained. Everyone knew that they were the best of friends, and they were being watched closely. People were overly critical and kept telling them that this is an exceptionally dangerous situation and that both of them will be hurt. At first, they found themselves isolated, but despite their difference, the friendship remained strong and slowly people around them became closer. He explained that it is not differences of opinion that disrupt relationships but lack of faith. He referred to the concept of "jnana" as it appears in the *Bhagavad Gita,* a form of spiritual knowledge, with which one maintains complete trust in a relationship. This was a revelation for "how just two little people trying to practice the unity of life can change the direction of a whole community" (Easwaran 1979: 33). This is what the *Bhagavad Gita* calls "vijnana, the skillful capacity to apply this awareness of unity to heal the deep divisions of people's hearts and minds and to bring them together in trust and harmony" (Easwaran 1979: 30). Like Easwaran and his friend, I find that many people around me gradually habituated themselves to our friendship and that the people in Ahmad's surroundings are even more accepting. As Ahmad's brother Abu Omar once remarked: "When I see the two of you together, it makes me feel good." Both Ahmad and I hope that our friendship, and this book in particular, will be of some significance in bringing closer to each other Palestinians and Israelis, Jews and Muslims, Arabs and "Westerners", and encourage all in making friends with those from other cultures.

Stories of Friendship: The Other Color

Throughout this book, Ahmad's perspective was presented through the filter of my experience. His voice was inserted in the text in bits and pieces, while molding these for a Western reader in readily digestible form, apart from his full statements both in the prologue and in "Stories of friendship: 'Garage of Peace'". Here I will once more cite him and share *his* language, while adhering to his spoken words, which I wholeheartedly support. They demonstrate our persistent optimism, despite the often-discouraging hardships. Although the transcription from Hebrew lost some of its original flavor, I believe you will still be able to grasp the idea.

Almog, September 2011. One night, at an Israeli petrol station café on the way between the ancient towns of Jerusalem and Jericho, the same place where I danced with the "drug dealer", Ahmad reacted to a draft version of this epilogue: "There are two colors in the world – black and white – and there is what one calls "good" and "not good", Satan and angel. There are people who work on this side and those who work on that side. There are people who love to live in the day, and those who love living at night. People live in groups. Everyone thinks that his group is the best, and that is an error. One needs to know who the other is. If every person would give a chance to those he does not like, there would be less hate. If each color would think it is able to go with another color, there will be other colors. It is possible to make more colors. That is good... If we would get out of our groups – that is like leaving our homes – we could come back with food. If we would think about peace and friendship more than about hate and war, we could break the wall and live better."

Bibliography

Abbe, A., Gulick, L.M., and Herman, J.L. (2007). *Cross-cultural competence in army leaders: A conceptual and empirical foundation.* Arlington, VA: Army Research Institute for the Behavioral and Social Sciences.

Aberson, C.L., Shoemaker, C., and Tomolillo, C. (2004). 'Implicit bias and contact: The role of interethnic friendships.' *The Journal of Social Psychology* 144(3): 335–347.

Abu Aleon, T., Weinstock, M., Manago, A.M., and Greenfield, P.M. (2019). 'Social change and intergenerational value differences in a Bedouin community in Israel.' *Journal of Cross-Cultural Psychology* 50(5): 708–727. https://doi.org/10.1177/0022022119839148.

Abu Rabia, R. (2017). 'Trapped between national boundaries and patriarchal structures: Palestinian Bedouin women and polygamous marriage in Israel.' *Journal of Comparative Family Studies* 48(3): 339–349.

Abu-Lughod, L. (1985). 'Honor and the sentiments of loss in a Bedouin society.' *American Ethnologist* 12(2): 245–261.

Abu-Rabia, A. (1994). 'The Bedouin refugees in the Negev.' *Refuge* 14: 15–17.

Abu-Rabia-Queder, S. (2007). 'Coping with "forbidden love" and loveless marriage: Educated Bedouin women from the Negev.' *Ethnography* 8: 297–323.

Adair, W.L., and Brett, J.M. (2005). 'The negotiation dance: Time, culture, and behavioral sequences in negotiation.' *Organization Science* 16(1): 33–51.

Adams, G., and Plaut, V.C. (2003). 'The cultural grounding of personal relationship: Friendship in North American and West African worlds.' *Personal Relationships* 10(3): 333–347.

Adams, G., Anderson, S.L., and Adonu, J.K. (2004). 'The cultural grounding of closeness and intimacy.' In D.J. Mashek and A.P. Aron (Eds.), *Handbook of Closeness and Intimacy*, pp. 321–329. Mahwah, NJ, US: Lawrence Erlbaum Associates Publishers.

Adams, R.G., and Allan, G.A. (1998). *Placing friendship in context. Structural analysis in the Social Sciences.* New York, NY: Cambridge University Press.

Adams, R.G., and Blieszner, R. (1994). 'An integrative conceptual framework for friendship research.' *Journal of Social and Personal Relationships* 11(2): 163–184.

Adler, P.S. (1977). 'Beyond cultural identity: Reflections on multiculturalism.' In R.W. Brislin (Ed.), *Culture Learning: Concepts, Applications, and Research*, pp. 24–41. Hawaii: East-West Center, University Press of Hawaii.

Adwan, S., Bar-Tal, D., and Wexler, B.E. (2016). 'Portrayal of the other in Palestinian and Israeli schoolbooks: A comparative study.' *Political Psychology* 37(2): 201–217. http://doi.org/10.1111/pops.12227.

'Ahmad.' (n.d.). Retrieved March 24, 2018, from http://quranicnames.com/ahmad/.

Akhtar, S. (2009). 'Friendship, socialization, and the immigrant experience.' *Psychoanalysis, Culture & Society* 14(3): 253–272.

Akiba, D., and Klug, W. (1999). 'The different and the same: Reexamining east and west in a cross-cultural analysis of values.' *Social Behavior and Personality* 27(5): 467–474.

Akkuş, B. (2019). 'The Israeli-Palestinian conflict from the perspective of identity perception: An analysis in the framework of institutions.' *The Journal of International Social Research* 12(65). https://doi.org/10.17719/jisr.2019.3434.

Albzour, M., Penic, S., Nasser, R., and Green, E.G.T. (2019). 'Support for "normalization" of relations between Palestinians and Israelis, and how it relates to contact and resistance in the West Bank.' *Journal of Social and Political Psychology* 7(2): 978–996. https://doi.org/10.5964/jspp.v7i2.877.

Al-Krenawi, A. (1996). 'Group work with Bedouin widows of the Negev in a medical clinic.' *Affilia* 11(3): 303–318. http://doi.org/10.1177/088610999601100303.

Al-Krenawi, A. (1999). 'Explanations of mental health symptoms by the Bedouin-Arabs of the Negev.' *International Journal of Social Psychiatry* 45(1): 56–64. http://doi.org/10.1177/002076409904500107.

Al-Krenawi, A., and Graham, J.R. (1997). 'Social work and blood vengeance: The Bedouin-Arab case.' *British Journal of Social Work* 27(4): 515–528.

Al-Krenawi, A., and Graham, J.R. (2000). 'Culturally sensitive social work practice with Arab clients in mental health settings.' *Health & Social Work* 25(1): 9–22. http://doi.org/10.1093/hsw/25.1.9.

Al-Krenawi, A., and Slonim-Nevo, V. (2008). 'Psychosocial and familial functioning of children from polygynous and monogamous families.' *The Journal of Social Psychology* 148(6): 745–764.

Allan, G. (1998). 'Friendship, sociology and social structure.' *Journal of Social and Personal Relationships* 15(5): 685–702.

Allan, G. (2008). 'Flexibility, friendship, and family.' *Personal Relationships* 15(1): 1–16. http://doi.org/10.1111/j.1475-6811.2007.00181.x.

Allen, L. (2008). 'Getting by the occupation: how violence became normal during the Second Palestinian Intifada.' *Cultural Anthropology* 23(3): 453–487.

Al-Makhamreh, S.S., and Lewando-Hundt, G. (2008). 'Researching "at home" as an insider/outsider.' *Qualitative Social Work* 7(1): 9–23. http://doi.org/10.1177/1473325007086413.

Alon, I., and Brett, J.M. (2007). 'Perceptions of time and their impact on negotiations in the Arabic-speaking Islamic world.' *Negotiation Journal* 23(1): 55–73.

Altenburger, K.M., and Ugander, J. (2018). 'Monophily in social networks introduces similarity among friends-of-friends.' *Nature Human Behaviour 2018*: 1. http://doi.org/10.1038/s41562-018-0321-8.

Altman, N. (2000). 'Black and white thinking: A psychoanalyst reconsiders race.' *Psychoanalytic Dialogues* 10(4): 589–605.

Amara, M. (2007). 'Teaching Hebrew to Palestinian pupils in Israel.' *Current Issues in Language Planning* 8(2): 243–254.

BIBLIOGRAPHY

Amnesty International. (2010a). *As safe as houses? Israel's demolition of Palestinian homes.* Amnesty International.

Amnesty International. (2010b). *Israel: Demolition of Bedouin village imminent.*

Amnesty International. (2011, March 18). 'De week van Daniel Weishut.' Retrieved from www.amnesty.nl.

Amnesty International. (2012). *Israel: Cancel plan to forcibly displace Jahalin Bedouin communities.*

Amnesty International. (2018). *Amnesty International Report 2017/18: The State of the World's Human Rights.* London, United Kingdom: Amnesty International.

Anderson, C.A., and Bushman, B.J. (2002). 'Human aggression.' *Annual Review of Psychology* 53: 27–52. http://doi.org/10.1146/annurev.psych.53.100901.135231.

Anderson, R.E., McKenny, M., Mitchell, A., Koku, L., and Stevenson, H.C. (2017). 'EMBRacing racial stress and trauma: Preliminary feasibility and coping responses of a racial socialization intervention.' *Journal of Black Psychology*, 9579841773293. http://doi.org/10.1177/0095798417732930.

Anderson, W., and Hiltz, S. (2001). 'Culturally heterogeneous vs. culturally homogeneous groups in distributed group support systems: Effects on group process and consensus.' In *HICSS*, p. 1030. Hawaii.

Ang, S., Ng, K.Y., and Rockstuhl, T. (2020). 'Cultural competence.' In *Oxford Research Encyclopedia of Psychology.* https://doi.org/10.1093/ACREFORE/9780190236557.013.567.

Antal, A.B., and Friedman, V.J. (2008). 'Learning to negotiate reality: A strategy for teaching intercultural competencies.' *Journal of Management Education* 32: 363–386.

Anthony, A.K., and McCabe, J. (2015). 'Friendship talk as identity work: Defining the self through friend relationships.' *Symbolic Interaction* 38(1): 64–82. http://doi.org/10.1002/symb.138.

Antonius, R. (1997). 'Human rights and cultural specificity: Some reflections.' In N.S. Hopkins and S.E. Ibrahim (Eds.), *Arab society: Class, gender, power and development*, pp. 469–477. Cairo: American University in Cairo Press.

Ari, L.L., and Laron, D. (2014). 'Intercultural learning in graduate studies at an Israeli college of education: Attitudes toward multiculturalism among Jewish and Arab students.' *Higher Education* 68(2): 243–262. http://doi.org/10.1007/s10734-013-9706-9.

Aristotle. (350BC). 'Nicomachean Ethics.' Retrieved January 30, 2018, from http://classics.mit.edu/Aristotle/nicomachaen.html.

Armengol-Carrera, J.M. (2009). 'Of friendship: Revisiting friendships between men in American literature.' *The Journal of Men's Studies* 17(3): 193–209.

Arnold, L.B. (1995). 'Through the narrow pass: Experiencing same-sex friendship in heterosexual (ist) settings.' *Communication Studies* 46(3): 234–244.

Arrow, H., and Sundberg, N. (2004). 'International identity: Definitions, development and some implications for global conflict and peace.' In A. Supratiknya, B. Setiadi,

W.J. Lonner, and Y.H. Poortinga (Eds.), *Ongoing themes in psychology and culture.* Melbourne, FL: International Association for Cross-Cultural Psychology.

Avila Tapies, R. (2008). 'Building friendship networks and intercultural spaces: The case of Japanese women in Spain.' *Migracijske i Etničke Teme* 24(4): 341–352.

Avissar, N. (2007a). 'Author's response: Who's afraid of politics? Or, psychotherapists as political entities.' *Israel Journal of Psychiatry and Related Sciences* 44: 17–18.

Avissar, N. (2007b). 'Politics and Israeli psychologists: Is it time to take a stand?' *Israel Journal of Psychiatry and Related Sciences* 44(1): 1.

Avissar, N. (2009). 'Clinical psychologists do politics: Attitudes and reactions of Israeli psychologists toward the political.' *Psychotherapy and Politics International* 7(3): 174–189. http://doi.org/10.1002/ppi.196.

Avissar, N. (2017). 'Israeli psychotherapy, politics and activism: Is there a way out of the trap?' *Journal of Contemporary Psychotherapy* 47(2): 125–134. http://doi.org/10.1007/s10879-016-9346-3.

Awad, H. (2018). 'Letter from Jerusalem Khan al-Ahmar: The onslaught against Jerusalem Bedouins.' *Jerusalem Quarterly* (76): 14–23.

Awawda, O. (2018). 'Palestinian workers in Israeli settlements: Their status and rights.' *IUP Journal of International Relations* 12(2).

Ayer, L., Venkatesh, B., Stewart, R., Mandel, D., Stein, B., and Schoenbaum, M. (2017). 'Psychological aspects of the Israeli–Palestinian conflict: A systematic review.' *Trauma, Violence, & Abuse* 18(3): 322–338. http://doi.org/10.1177/1524838015613774.

B'Tselem – The Israeli Information Center for Human Rights in the Occupied Territories. (2015, April 14). 'Military punishes Hizma's 7,000 residents by closure on village for alleged stone- throwing on nearby road.' Retrieved March 29, 2020, from https://www.btselem.org/freedom_of_movement/20150414_siege_on_hizma.

Bachika, R., and Schulz, M.S. (2011). 'Values and culture in the social shaping of the future.' *Current Sociology* 59(2): 107–118. http://doi.org/10.1177/0011392110391128.

Bagci, S.C., and Çelebi, E. (2017). 'Cross-group friendships and outgroup attitudes among Turkish-Kurdish ethnic groups: Does perceived interethnic conflict moderate the friendship-attitude link?' *Journal of Applied Social Psychology* 47(2): 59–73. http://doi.org/10.1111/jasp.12413.

Bagci, S.C., Piyale, Z.E., and Ebcim, E. (2018). 'Imagined contact in high conflict settings: The role of ethnic group identification and the perspective of minority group members.' *Journal of Applied Social Psychology* 48(1): 3–14. http://doi.org/10.1111/jasp.12485.

Bahns, A.J. (2017). 'Preference, opportunity, and choice: A multilevel analysis of diverse friendship formation.' *Group Processes & Intergroup Relations* 136843021772539. http://doi.org/10.1177/1368430217725390.

Bakker, W., van der Zee, K., and van Oudenhoven, J.P. (2006). 'Personality and Dutch emigrants' reactions to acculturation strategies.' *Journal of Applied Social Psychology* 36(12): 2864–2891.

Bandura, A. (1988). 'Self-efficacy conception of anxiety.' *Anxiety Research* 1(2): 77–98.

Bandura, A. (2008). 'An agentic perspective on positive psychology.' In S.J. Lopez (Ed.), *Positive psychology: Exploring the best in people*, pp. 167–196. Westport, CT: Praeger Publishers.

Bank, B.J., and Hansford, S.L. (2000). 'Gender and friendship: Why are men's best same-sex friendships less intimate and supportive?' *Personal Relationships* 7(1): 63–78.

Barber, B.K. (1999). 'Political violence, family relations, and Palestinian youth functioning.' *Journal of Adolescent Research* 14(2): 206–230. http://doi.org/10.1177/0743558499142004.

Bardi, A., and Goodwin, R. (2011). 'The dual route to value change: Individual processes and cultural moderators.' *Journal of Cross-Cultural Psychology* 42(2): 271–287. http://doi.org/10.1177/0022022110396916.

Barnes, C.D., Brown, R., and Tamborski, M. (2012). 'Living dangerously: Culture of honor, risk-taking, and the nonrandomness of "accidental" deaths.' *Social Psychological and Personality Science* 3: 100–107.

Bar-Tal, D. (2017). 'Self-censorship as a socio-political-psychological phenomenon: Conception and research.' *Political Psychology* 38: 37–65. https://doi.org/10.1111/pops.12391.

Bar-Tal, D., Halperin, E., and Oren, N. (2010). 'Socio-psychological barriers to peace making: The case of the Israeli Jewish society.' *Social Issues and Policy Review* 4(1): 63–109.

Barth, M., Jugert, P., Wutzler, M., and Fritsche, I. (2015). 'Absolute moral standards and global identity as independent predictors of collective action against global injustice.' *European Journal of Social Psychology* 45(7): 918–930. http://doi.org/10.1002/ejsp.2160.

Baum, N. (2007a). 'It's not only cultural differences: Comparison of Jewish Israeli social work students' thoughts and feelings about treating Jewish Ultra-Orthodox and Palestinian Israeli clients.' *International Journal of Intercultural Relations* 31(5): 575–589.

Baum, N. (2007b). 'Social work practice in conflict-ridden areas: Cultural sensitivity is not enough.' *British Journal of Social Work* 37(5): 873–891.

Baum, N. (2010). 'After a terror attack: Israeli–Arab professionals' feelings and experiences.' *Journal of Social and Personal Relationships* 27: 685–704.

Baum, N. (2011). 'Issues in psychotherapy with clients affiliated with the opposing side in a violent political conflict.' *Clinical Social Work Journal* 39(1): 91–100. http://doi.org/10.1007/s10615-010-0291-4.

Baumeister, R.F., and Newman, L.S. (1994). 'How stories make sense of personal experiences: Motives that shape autobiographical narratives.' *Personality and Social Psychology Bulletin* 20(6): 676–690.

Baxter, D. (2007). 'Honor thy sister: Selfhood, gender, and agency in Palestinian culture.' *Anthropological Quarterly* 80(3): 737–775.

Belge, C. (2009). 'From expert rule to bureaucratic authority: Governing the Bedouin.' *Israel Studies Forum* 24(1): 82–108.

Bello, R.S., Brandau-Brown, F.E., Zhang, S., and Ragsdale, J.D. (2010). 'Verbal and nonverbal methods for expressing appreciation in friendships and romantic relationships: A cross-cultural comparison.' *International Journal of Intercultural Relations* 34(3): 294–302.

Ben-Ari, A. (2004). 'Sources of social support and attachment styles among Israeli Arab students.' *International Social Work* 47(2): 187–201.

Bender, S.T. (1999). *Attachment style and friendship characteristics in college students*. ETD Collection for University of Connecticut. University of Connecticut.

Benish-Weisman, M., and Horenczyk, G. (2010). 'Cultural identity and perceived success among Israeli immigrants: An emic approach.' *International Journal of Intercultural Relations* 34: 516–526.

Bennett, M.J. (1986). 'A developmental approach to training for intercultural sensitivity.' *International Journal of Intercultural Relations* 10(2): 179–196.

Bennett, M.J. (2017). 'Developmental model of intercultural censitivity.' In Y.Y. Kim (Ed.), *The International Encyclopedia of Intercultural Communication*, pp. 1–10. Hoboken, NJ, US: John Wiley & Sons, Inc. http://doi.org/10.1002/9781118783665.ieicc0182.

Bergamaschi, A., and Santagati, M. (2019). 'When friendship is stronger than prejudice. Role of intergroup friendships among adolescents in two distinct socio-cultural contexts of immigration.' *International Review of Sociology* 29(1): 36–57. https://doi.org/10.1080/03906701.2019.1609750.

Berman, A., Berger, M., and Gutmann, D. (2000). 'The division into Us and Them as a universal social structure.' *Mind and Human Interaction* 11(1): 53–72.

Berman, E. (2002). 'Beyond analytic anonymity: On the political involvement of psychoanalysts and psychotherapists in Israel.' In J. Bunzl and B. Beit-Hallahmi (Eds.), *Psychoanalysis, Identity, and Ideology: Critical essays on the Israel/Palestine case*, pp. 177–200. Boston, MA: Springer US. http://doi.org/10.1007/978-1-4757-6324-9_8.

Berman, E. (2007). 'Commentary: How can we facilitate change?' *Israel Journal of Psychiatry and Related Sciences* 44(1): 9–12.

Beugelsdijk, S., Maseland, R., and van Hoorn, A. (2015). 'Are scores on Hofstede's dimensions of national culture stable over time? A cohort analysis.' *Global Strategy Journal* 5(3): 223–240. http://doi.org/10.1002/gsj.1098.

Bhabha, H.K. (1994). 'DisseminNation: time, narrative, and the margins of the modern nation.' In H.K. Bhabha (Ed.), *Nation and Narration*, pp. 291–322. New York: Routledge.

Bhabha, H.K. (1998). 'Culture's in between.' In D. Bennett (Ed.), *Multicultural States: Rethinking Difference and Identity*, pp. 31–36. London: Routledge.

Bilsky, W., and Schwartz, S.H. (1994). 'Values and personality.' *European Journal of Personality* 8(3): 163–181.

Bishara, A. (2015). 'Driving while Palestinian in Israel and the West Bank: The politics of disorientation and the routes of a subaltern knowledge.' *American Ethnologist* 42(1): 33–54. https://doi.org/10.1111/amet.12114.

Blake, M.K. (2007). 'Formality and friendship: Research ethics review and participatory action research.' *ACME: An International E-Journal for Critical Geographies* 6(3): 411–421.

Bochner, A.P. (2017). 'Heart of the matter.' *International Review of Qualitative Research* 10(1): 67–80. http://doi.org/10.1525/irqr.2017.10.1.67.

Bond, M.H. (2004). 'Culture and aggression: From context to coercion.' *Personality and Social Psychology Review* 8(1): 62–78.

Boomkens, R. (2010). 'Cultural citizenship and real politics: the Dutch case. *Citizenship Studies* 14(3)': 307–316.

Bowman, J.M. (2008). 'Gender role orientation and relational closeness: Self-disclosive behavior in same-sex male friendships.' *The Journal of Men's Studies* 16(3): 316–330.

Braun-Lewensohn, O., Abu-Kaf, S., Al-Said, K., Huss, E., Braun-Lewensohn, O., Abu-Kaf, S., ... Huss, E. (2019). 'Analysis of the differential relationship between the perception of one's life and coping resources among three generations of Bedouin women.' *International Journal of Environmental Research and Public Health* 16(5): 804. http://doi.org/10.3390/ijerph16050804.

Breen, L.J. (2007). 'The researcher "in the middle": Negotiating the insider/outsider dichotomy.' *The Australian Community Psychologist* 19: 163–174.

Brenner, I. (2009). 'The Palestinian/Israeli conflict: a geopolitical identity disorder.' *The American Journal of Psychoanalysis* 69(1): 62–71.

Brigg, M., and Bleiker, R. (2010). 'Autoethnographic international relations: Exploring the self as a source of knowledge.' *Review of International Studies* 36(3): 779–798.

Brislin, R.W., and Kim, E.S. (2003). 'Cultural diversity in people's understanding and uses of time.' *Applied Psychology* 52(3): 363–382.

Brockhill, A., and Cordell, K. (2019). 'The violence of culture: The legitimation of the Israeli occupation of Palestine.' *Third World Quarterly* 40(5): 981–998. https://doi.org/10.1080/01436597.2019.1581057.

Brumett, B.R., Wade, J.C., Ponterotto, J.G., Thombs, B., and Lewis, C. (2007). 'Psychosocial well-being and a multicultural personality disposition.' *Journal of Counseling and Development: JCD* 85(1): 73.

Buda, R., and Elsayed-Elkhouly, S.M. (1998). 'Cultural differences between Arabs and Americans.' *Journal of Cross-Cultural Psychology* 29(3): 487–492. http://doi.org/10.1177/0022022198293006.

Budgeon, S. (2006). 'Friendship and formations of sociality in late modernity: The challenge of "post traditional intimacy".' *Sociological Research Online* 11(3): 1–11. http://doi.org/10.5153/sro.1248.

Bullough, R.V., and Pinnegar, S. (2001). 'Guidelines for quality in autobiographical forms of self-study research.' *Educational Researcher* 30(3): 13–21.

Burkard, A.W., Knox, S., Groen, M., Perez, M., and Hess, S.A. (2006). 'European American therapist self-disclosure in cross-cultural counseling.' *Journal of Counseling Psychology* 53(1): 15.

Busbridge, R. (2017). 'The wall has feet but so do we: Palestinian workers in Israel and the 'separation' wall.' *British Journal of Middle Eastern Studies* 44(3): 373–390. https://doi.org/10.1080/13530194.2016.1194187.

Bushman, B.B., and Holt-Lunstad, J. (2009). 'Understanding social relationship maintenance among friends: Why we don't end those frustrating friendships.' *Journal of Social and Clinical Psychology* 28(6): 749–778.

Caldwell, M.A., and Peplau, L.A. (1982). 'Sex differences in same-sex friendship.' *Sex Roles* 8(7): 721–732.

Canetti, D., Elad-Strenger, J., Lavi, I., Guy, D., and Bar-Tal, D. (2017). 'Exposure to violence, ethos of conflict, and support for compromise.' *Journal of Conflict Resolution* 61(1): 84–113. http://doi.org/10.1177/0022002715569771.

Carey, R.M., and Markus, H.R. (2017). 'Social class shapes the form and function of relationships and selves.' *Current Opinion in Psychology* 18: 123–130. https://doi.org/10.1016/j.copsyc.2017.08.031.

Chae, M.H., and Foley, P.F. (2010). 'Relationship of ethnic identity, acculturation, and psychological well-being among Chinese, Japanese, and Korean Americans.' *Journal of Counseling & Development* 88(4): 466–476.

Chen, L. (2002). 'Communication in intercultural relationships.' In W.B. Gudykunst and B. Mody (Eds.), *Handbook of international and intercultural communication*, vol. 2, pp. 241–257. Thousand Oaks, CA: Sage Publications, Inc.

Chen, S.X., Benet-Martinez, V., and Bond, M.H. (2008). 'Bicultural identity, bilingualism, and psychological adjustment in multicultural societies: Immigration-based and globalization-based acculturation.' *Journal of Personality* 76(4): 803–838.

Chen, S.X., Chan, W., Bond, M.H., and Stewart, S.M. (2006). 'The effects of self-efficacy and relationship harmony on depression across cultures: applying level-oriented and structure-oriented analyses.' *Journal of Cross – Cultural Psychology*: 37(6): 643–658.

Chen, Y.-W., and Nakazawa, M. (2012). 'Measuring patterns of self-disclosure in intercultural friendship: Adjusting differential item functioning using multiple-indicators, multiple-causes models.' *Journal of Intercultural Communication Research* 41(2): 131–151. http://doi.org/10.1080/17475759.2012.670862.

Cheney, R.S. (2001). 'Intercultural business communication, international students, and experiential learning.' *Business Communication Quarterly* 64(4): 90–104.

Cheng, S.T., and Kwan, K.W.K. (2008). 'Attachment dimensions and contingencies of self-worth: The moderating role of culture.' *Personality and Individual Differences* 45(6): 509–514.

Chirkov, V.I., Ryan, R.M., and Willness, C. (2005). 'Cultural context and psychological needs in Canada and Brazil.' *Journal of Cross-Cultural Psychology* 36(4): 423–443. http://doi.org/10.1177/0022022105275960.

Choi, S.C., and Kim, U. (2004). 'Emotional attachment as the basis of trust and interpersonal relationships: Psychological, indigenous and cultural analysis.' In B.N. Setiadi, A. Supratiknya, W.J. Lonner, and Y.H. Poortinga (Eds.), *Ongoing themes in psychology and culture*. Melbourne, FL: International Association for Cross-Cultural Psychology.

Christopher, J.C. (1999). 'Situating psychological well-being: Exploring the cultural roots of its theory and research.' *Journal of Counseling and Development* 77: 141–152.

Chung, R.C.Y., Bemak, F., Ortiz, D.P., and Sandoval-Perez, P.A. (2008). 'Promoting the mental health of immigrants: A multicultural/social justice perspective.' *Journal of Counseling & Development* 86(3): 310–317.

Church, K. (Ed.). (1995). *Forbidden narratives: Critical autobiography as Social Science*. Luxembourg: Gordon and Breach Publishers.

Church, T.A. (2010). 'Current perspectives in the study of personality across cultures.' *Perspectives on Psychological Science* 5(4): 441–449. http://doi.org/10.1177/1745691610375559.

Cockburn, C. (2014). 'The dialogue that died.' *International Feminist Journal of Politics* 16(3): 430–447. http://doi.org/10.1080/14616742.2013.849964.

Cohen, D., and Leung, A.K. (2010). 'A CuPS (Culture X Person X Situation) perspective on violence and character.' In M. Mikulincer and P.R. Shaver (Eds.), *Understanding and reducing aggression, violence, and their consequences*, pp. 187–200. Washington, DC: American Psychological Association.

Cohen, D., Nisbett, R.E., Bowdle, B.F., and Schwarz, N. (1996). 'Insult, aggression, and the southern culture of honor: An "experimental ethnography".' *Journal of Personality and Social Psychology* 70(5): 945–960.

Cohen, D., Vandello, J., and Rantilla, A.K. (1998). 'The sacred and the social: Cultures of honor and violence.' In P. Gilbert and B. Andrews (Eds.), *Shame: Interpersonal behavior, psychopathology, and culture; Series in affective science*, pp. 261–282. New York: Oxford University Press.

Cole, D.P. (2003). 'Where have the Bedouin gone?' *Anthropological Quarterly* 76(2): 235–267.

'Comfort zone.' (n.d.). Retrieved March 28, 2020, from https://en.wikipedia.org/wiki/Comfort_zone.

Cottam, M., Dietz-Uhler, B., Mastors, E.M., and Preston, T. (2004). *Introduction to political psychology*. New Jersey: Lawrence Erlbaum Associates, Inc., Publishers.

Council of Europe. (2019). 'Interculturality.' Retrieved March 15, 2019, from https://definedterm.com/interculturality.

Curtin, M.L. (2010). 'Coculturation: Toward a critical theoretical framework of cultural adjustment.' In T.K. Nakayama and R.T. Halualani (Eds.), *The Handbook of Critical Intercultural Communication*, pp. 270–285. Oxford, UK: Wiley-Blackwell. http://doi.org/10.1002/9781444390681.ch16.

Cushman, P. (2000). 'White guilt, political activity, and the analyst: Commentary on paper by Neil Altman.' *Psychoanalytic Dialogues* 10(4): 607–618.

Dalal, F. (2008). 'Thought paralysis: Tolerance, and the fear of Islam.' *Psychodynamic Practice* 14(1): 77–95.

Dana, R.H. (2000). *Handbook of cross-cultural and multicultural personality assessment*. Mahwah, NK: Lawrence Erlbaum.

'Daniel.' (n.d.). Retrieved April 6, 2018, from https://en.wikipedia.org/wiki/Daniel_(biblical_figure).

Daoud, N., Shoham-Vardi, I., Urquia, M.L., and O'Campo, P. (2014). 'Polygamy and poor mental health among Arab Bedouin women: Do socioeconomic position and social support matter?' *Ethnicity & Health* 19(4): 385–405. http://doi.org/10.1080/13557858.2013.801403.

Darweish, M. (2010). 'Human rights and the imbalance of power: The Palestinian-Israeli conflict.' In V. Dudouet and B. Schmelzle (Eds.), *Human rights and conflict transformation: The challenges of just peace*. Berlin: Berghof Conflict Research.

David, A. (2015). *An improbable friendship: The remarkable lives of Israeli Ruth Dayan and Palestinian Raymonda Tawil and their forty-year peace mission*. Skyhorse Publishing.

David, S.R. (2020). 'Coping with an existential threat.' In R.O. Freedman (Ed.), *Israel under Netanyahu*, pp. 197–215. Routledge. https://doi.org/10.4324/9780429342349-11.

Davidov, E., Schmidt, P., and Schwartz, S.H. (2008). 'Bringing values back in: The adequacy of the European Social Survey to measure values in 20 countries.' *Public Opinion Quarterly* 72(3): 420–445. http://doi.org/10.1093/poq/nfn035.

Davies, K., and Aron, A. (2016). 'Friendship development and intergroup attitudes: The role of interpersonal and intergroup friendship processes.' *Journal of Social Issues* 72(3): 489–510. http://doi.org/10.1111/josi.12178.

Davies, K., Heaphy, B., Mason, J., and Smart, C. (2011). 'Interactions that matter: researching critical associations.' *Methodological Innovations Online* 6(3): 5–16.

Davies, K., Tropp, L.R., Aron, A., Pettigrew, T.F., and Wright, S.C. (2011). 'Cross-group friendships and intergroup attitudes.' *Personality and Social Psychology Review* 15(4): 332–351. http://doi.org/10.1177/1088868311411103.

Davies, K., Wright, S.C., and Aron, A. (2011). 'Cross-group friendships: How interpersonal connections encourage positive intergroup attitudes.' In L.R. Tropp and R.K. Mallett (Eds.), *Moving beyond prejudice reduction: Pathways to positive intergroup relations*, pp. 119–138. Washington, DC: American Psychological Association.

De Bony, J. (2005). 'Dutch decision as rooted in Dutch culture: An ethnologic study of the Dutch decision process.' In *Decision making in organizations: Unlocking the potential*, pp. 1–18. Berlin: EGOS.

Deane, B.R. (1991). 'A model for personal change: Developing intercultural sensitivity.' *Cultural Diversity at Work Journal* 3: 1–2.

Dekker, R., Belabas, W., and Scholten, P. (2015). 'Interethnic contact online: Contextualising the implications of social media use by second-generation migrant youth.' *Journal of Intercultural Studies* 36(4): 450–467. http://doi.org/10.1080/07256868.201 5.1049981.

Demir, M., Doğan, A., and Procsal, A.D. (2013). 'I am so happy 'cause my friend is happy for me: Capitalization, friendship, and happiness among U.S. and Turkish college students.' *The Journal of Social Psychology* 153(2): 250–255. http://doi.org/10.1080/0 0224545.2012.714814.

Demir, M., Ozdemir, M., and Weitekamp, L.A. (2007). 'Looking to happy tomorrows with friends: Best and close friendships as they predict happiness.' *Journal of Happiness Studies* 8(2): 243–271.

Demir, M., Tyra, A., and Özen-Çıplak, A. (2018). 'Be there for me and I will be there for you: Friendship maintenance mediates the relationship between capitalization and happiness.' *Journal of Happiness Studies*: 1–21. http://doi.org/10.1007/s10902-017-9957-8.

Denson, T.F., O'Dean, S.M., Blake, K.R., and Beames, J.R. (2018). 'Aggression in women: Behavior, brain and hormones.' *Frontiers in Behavioral Neuroscience* 12: 1–20. https://doi.org/10.3389/fnbeh.2018.00081.

Desai, A., and Killick, E. (2013). *The ways of friendship: Anthropological perspectives*. New York/Oxford: Berghahn Books.

Dessel, A.B., and Ali, N.B. (2012). 'Arab/Jewish intergroup dialogue courses: Building communication skills, relationships, and social justice.' *Small Group Research* 43(5): 559–586. https://doi.org/10.1177/1046496412453773.

Deutsch, A.W. (1985). 'Social contacts and social relationships between Jews and Arabs living in a mixed neighborhood in an Israeli town.' *International Journal of Comparative Sociology* 26(3–4): 220–225. http://doi.org/10.1177/002071528502600307.

Devere, H. (2010). 'Cross-cultural understandings in the language and politics of friendship.' *Canadian Social Science* 3(6): 14–29.

Devere, H. (2014). 'The many meanings of friendship.' *AMITY: The Journal of Friendship Studies* 2(1): 1–3. http://doi.org/10.5518/AMITY/7.

Devos, T., Spini, D., and Schwartz, S.H. (2002). 'Conflicts among human values and trust in institutions.' *The British Journal of Social Psychology* 41: 481–494.

Dewaelea, J.M., and van Oudenhoven, J.P. (2009). 'The effect of multilingualism/multiculturalism on personality: no gain without pain for Third Culture Kids?' *International Journal of Multilingualism* 6(1): 1–17.

Diab, K., and Mi'ari, M. (2007). 'Collective identity and readiness for social relations with Jews among Palestinian Arab students at the David Yellin Teacher Training College in Israel.' *Intercultural Education* 18. 427–444.

Dibiasi, C.M. (2015). 'Changing trends in Palestinian political activism: The second intifada, the wall protests, and the human rights turn.' *Geopolitics* 20(3): 669–695. https://doi.org/10.1080/14650045.2015.1028028.

Dinero, S. (2004). 'New identity/identities formulation in a post-nomadic community: The case of the Bedouin of the Negev.' *National Identities* 6(3), 261–275.

Dodd, P.C. (1973). 'Family honor and the forces of change in Arab society.' *International Journal of Middle East Studies* 4(1): 40–54.

Downie, M., Koestner, R., ElGeledi, S., and Cree, K. (2004). 'The impact of cultural internalization and integration on well-being among tricultural individuals.' *Personality and Social Psychology Bulletin* 30(3): 305–314. http://doi.org/10.1177/0146167203261298.

Duek, R. (2009). 'Dialogue in impossible situations.' *Organisational and Social Dynamics: An International Journal of Psychoanalytic, Systemic and Group Relations Perspectives* 9(2): 206–224.

Dufty, R. (2010). 'Reflecting on power relationships in the "doing" of rural cultural research.' *Cultural Studies Review* 16(1): 131–142.

Dunbar, R.I.M. (2018). 'The anatomy of friendship.' *Trends in Cognitive Sciences* 22(1): 32–51. http://doi.org/10.1016/j.tics.2017.10.004.

'Dutch uncle.' (n.d.). Retrieved April 6, 2018, from https://en.wikipedia.org/wiki/Dutch_uncle.

Earley, P.C. (1993). 'East meets West meets Mideast: Further explorations of collectivistic and individualistic work groups.' *Academy of Management Journal* 36(2): 319–348.

Earley, P.C., and Ang, S. (2003). *Cultural intelligence: Individual interactions across cultures.* Stanford, CA: Stanford Business Books.

Easwaran, E. (1979). *Like a thousand suns: The Bhagavad Gita for daily living, Volume 2.* Berkeley, CA: Nilgiri Press.

El Kurd, D. (2019). 'Who protests in Palestine? Mobilization across class under the Palestinian Authority.' In A. Tartir and T. Seidel (Eds.), *Palestine and Rule of Power*, pp. 105–128. Springer International Publishing. https://doi.org/10.1007/978-3-030-05949-1_5.

Elbedour, S., Shulman, S., and Kedem, P. (1997). 'Adolescent intimacy: A cross-cultural study.' *Journal of Cross-Cultural Psychology* 28(1): 5–22.

Elias, N., and Kemp, A. (2010). 'The new second generation: Non-Jewish olim, black Jews and children of migrant workers in Israel.' *Israel Studies* 15(1): 73–94.

Ellis, C. (2007). 'Telling secrets, revealing lives.' *Qualitative Inquiry* 13(1): 3–29.
Ellis, C., and Bochner, A.P. (2000). 'Autoethnography, personal narrative, reflexivity: Researcher as subject.' In N.K. Denzin and Y.S. Lincoln (Eds.), *Handbook of Qualitative Research*, 2nd ed., pp. 733–768. Thousand Oaks Calif.: Sage Publications. http://doi.org/10.1111/j.1365-2648.2001.0472a.x.
Eringa, K., Caudron, L.N., Rieck, K., Xie, F., and Gerhardt, T. (2015). 'How relevant are Hofstede's dimensions for inter-cultural studies? A replication of Hofstede's research among current international business students.' *Research in Hospitality Management* 5(2): 187–198. http://doi.org/10.1080/22243534.2015.11828344.
Eskelinen, V., and Verkuyten, M. (2018). 'Support for democracy and liberal sexual mores among Muslims in Western Europe.' *Journal of Ethnic and Migration Studies*. https://doi.org/10.1080/1369183X.2018.1521715.
Falah, G. (1985). 'How Israel controls the Bedouin in Israel.' *Journal of Palestine Studies* 14: 35–51.
Falk, R., and Tilley, V. (2017). 'Israeli practices towards the Palestinian people and the question of apartheid.' *Palestine – Israel Journal of Politics, Economics, and Culture* 22(2/3): 191–196.
Fares, S., Milhem, F., and Khalidi, D. (2006). 'The sulha system in Palestine: Between justice and social order.' *Practicing Anthropology* 28(1): 21–27.
Festinger, L. (1950). 'Informal social communication.' *Psychological Review* 57(5): 271.
Festinger, L. (1957). *A theory of cognitive dissonance*. Stanford, CA: Stanford University Press.
Fischer, A.H., and Mosquera, P.M.R. (2002). 'What concerns men? Women or other men?: A critical appraisal of the evolutionary theory of sex differences in aggression.' *Sexualities, Evolution & Gender* 3(1): 5–25.
Fischer, R., and Schwartz, S.H. (2010). 'Whence differences in value priorities? Individual, cultural, or artifactual sources.' *Journal of Cross-Cultural Psychology* 41: 135–151. http://doi.org/10.1177/0022022110381429.
Fischer, R., Vauclair, C.M., Fontaine, J.R.J., and Schwartz, S.H. (2010). 'Are individual-level and country-level value structures different? Testing Hofstede's legacy with the Schwartz Value Survey.' *Journal of Cross-Cultural Psychology* 41(2): 135–151. http://doi.org/10.1177/0022022109354377.
Fishman, L. (2019). 'Pushing for a political breakthrough: Kurds in Turkey and Palestinians in Israel.' *Current History*: 355–360.
Fitzsimmons, S.R. (2013). 'Multicultural employees: A framework for understanding how they contribute to organizations.' *Academy of Management Review* 38(4): 525–549. http://doi.org/10.5465/amr.2011.0234.
Flache, A., and Macy, M.W. (2011). 'Small worlds and cultural polarization.' *The Journal of Mathematical Sociology* 35(1): 146–176.

Florack, A., Rohmann, A., Palcu, J., and Mazziotta, A. (2014). 'How initial cross-group friendships prepare for intercultural communication: The importance of anxiety reduction and self-confidence in communication.' *International Journal of Intercultural Relations* 43: 278–288. https://doi.org/10.1016/J.IJINTREL.2014.09.004.

Flynn, H.K. (2007). *Friendship: A longitudinal study of friendship characteristics, life transitions, and social factors that influence friendship quality.* University of California, Davis.

Flyvbjerg, B. (2004). 'Five misunderstandings about case-study research.' *Qualitative Research Practice*: 420–434.

Franke, W. (2018). 'Empathy as political action: Can empathic engagement disrupt narratives of conflict.' *Journal of Social Science Research* 13: 2860–2870.

Freidson, Y. (2019, June 11). 'Despite pledge, Netanyahu again seeks to delay removal of West Bank village.' *Ynet*.

'French Hill attacks.' (n.d.). Retrieved March 28, 2020, from https://en.wikipedia.org/wiki/French_Hill_attacks.

Frisch, H., and Hofnung, M. (2007). 'Power or justice? Rule and law in the Palestinian Authority.' *Journal of Peace Research* 44(3): 331–348. http://doi.org/10.1177/0022343307076639.

Fronk, C., Huntington, R.L., and Chadwick, B.A. (1999). 'Expectations for traditional family roles: Palestinian adolescents in the West Bank and Gaza.' *Sex Roles* 41(9): 705–735.

Fujimoto, Y., Bahfen, N., Fermelis, J., and Hartel, C.E.J. (2007). 'The global village: Online cross-cultural communication and HRM.' *Cross Cultural Management: An International Journal* 14(1): 7–22.

Furman, R., Collins, K., Garner, M.D., Montanaro, K.L., and Weber, G. (2009). 'Using Social Work theory for the facilitation of friendships.' *Smith College Studies in Social Work* 79(1): 17–33.

Galin, A., and Avraham, S. (2009). 'A cross-cultural perspective on aggressiveness in the workplace: A comparison between Jews and Arabs in Israel.' *Cross-Cultural Research* 43(1): 30–45.

Garcia Yeste, C., Joanpere, M., Rios-Gonzalez, O., and Morlà-Folch, T. (2020). 'Creative friendship and political diversity in Catalonia.' *Journal of Social and Personal Relationships*. https://doi.org/10.1177/0265407520916827.

Garcia, A., Pereira, F.N., and Corrêa de Macedo, M.D. (2015). 'Friendship and happiness in Latin America: A review.' In M. Demir (Ed.), *Friendship and Happiness*, pp. 225–234. Dordrecht: Springer Netherlands. http://doi.org/10.1007/978-94-017-9603-3_13.

Gareis, E. (2000). 'Intercultural friendship: Five case studies of German students in the USA.' *Journal of Intercultural Studies* 21(1): 67–91.

Gareis, E., and Jalayer, A. (2018). 'Contact effects on intercultural friendship between East Asian students and American domestic students.' In Y. Ma and

M. Garic-Murillo (Eds.), *Understanding International Students from Asia in American Universities*, pp. 83–106. Cham: Springer International Publishing. http://doi.org/10.1007/978-3-319-60394-0_5.

Gareis, E., Goldman, J., and Merkin, R. (2019). 'Promoting intercultural friendship among college students.' *Journal of International and Intercultural Communication* 12(1): 1–22. https://doi.org/10.1080/17513057.2018.1502339.

Gellman, M., and Vuinovich, M. (2008). 'From Sulha to Salaam: Connecting local knowledge with international negotiations for lasting peace in Palestine/Israel.' *Conflict Resolution Quarterly* 26(2): 127–148.

Gelobter, E.M. (2018). 'Illegal Israeli settlements in the Occupied Territories: Is annexation the answer?' *SSRN Electronic Journal*. https://doi.org/10.2139/ssrn.3132053.

George, A.L., and Bennett, A. (2005). *Case studies and theory development in the social sciences*. Cambridge, MA: The MIT Press.

Gibson, C.B., and Manuel, J.A. (2003). 'Building trust: Effective multicultural communication processes in virtual teams.' In S.G. Cohen and C.B. Gibson (Eds.), *Virtual teams that work: Creating conditions for virtual team effectiveness*, pp. 59–86. San Francisco, CA: Jossey Bass.

Gilin, B., and Young, T. (2009). 'Educational benefits of international experiential learning in an MSW program.' *International Social Work* 52(1): 36–47. http://doi.org/10.1177/0020872808093347.

Gillespie, N., De Jong, B., Williamson, I.O., and Gill, C. (2017). 'Trust congruence in teams: The influence of cultural diversity, shared leadership, and virtual communication.' *Academy of Management Proceedings* 2017(1): 15580. http://doi.org/10.5465/AMBPP.2017.15580abstract.

Giovannetti, M. (2019, February 2). 'Israel opens "apartheid road" in occupied West Bank.' *AlJazeera*.

Goffman, E. (1955). 'On face-work: An analysis of ritual elements in social interaction.' *Psychiatry: Journal for the Study of Interpersonal Processes* 18: 213–231.

Gordijn, A. (2010). 'What about the influence of Dutch culture on integration?' *European Journal of Social Work* 13(2): 217–229.

Grabill, C.M., and Kerns, K.A. (2000). 'Attachment style and intimacy in friendship.' *Personal Relationships* 7(4): 363–378.

Greenberg, A. (2010, August 16). 'New hope for the Jahalin Bedouin, who "fell between the cracks".' *Haaretz*.

Gruenfeld, D.H., Inesi, M.E., Magee, J.C., and Galinsky, A.D. (2008). 'Power and the objectification of social targets.' *Journal of Personality and Social Psychology* 95(1): 111–127.

Guroglu, B., Haselager, G.J.T., van Lieshout, C.F.M., Takashima, A., Rijpkema, M., and Fernandez, G. (2008). 'Why are friends special? Implementing a social interaction simulation task to probe the neural correlates of friendship.' *Neuroimage* 39(2): 903–910.

Haaretz. (2020, February 26). 'Lieberman says government to be formed without Netanyahu: No chance for unity.' *Haaretz*.

Hager, T., Saba, T., and Shay, N. (2011). 'Jewish Arab activism through dialogical encounters: changing an Israeli campus.' *Journal of Peace Education* 8(2): 193–211.

Haj-Yahia, M.M. (2002). 'Attitudes of Arab women toward different patterns of coping with wife abuse.' *Journal of Interpersonal Violence* 17(7): 721–745. http://doi.org/10.11 77/0886260502017007002.

Hall, E.T. (1970). 'The paradox of culture.' In B. Landis and E.S. Tauber (Eds.), *In the name of life. Essays in honor of Erich Fromm*, pp. 218–235. New York: Holt, Rinehart and Winston.

Hall, E.T., and Hall, M.R. (1990). *Understanding cultural differences*. Yarmouth, Maine: Intercultural Press.

Hammack, P.L. (2008). 'Narrative and the cultural psychology of identity.' *Personality and Social Psychology Review* 12(3): 222–247.

Hammack, P.L. (2009). 'Exploring the reproduction of conflict through narrative: Israeli youth motivated to participate in a coexistence program.' *Peace and Conflict: Journal of Peace Psychology* 15(1): 49–74.

Hammack, P.L. (2010). 'The cultural psychology of Palestinian youth: A narrative approach.' *Culture & Psychology* 16(4): 507–537.

Hammack, P.L. (2011). *Narrative and the politics of identity: The cultural psychology of Israeli and Palestinian youth*. Oxford: Oxford University Press.

Hammack, P.L., and Pilecki, A. (2015). 'Power in history: Contrasting theoretical approaches to intergroup dialogue.' *Journal of Social Issues* 71(2): 371–385. http://doi.org/10.1111/josi.12116.

Hammer, M.R. (2005). 'The intercultural conflict style inventory: A conceptual framework and measure of intercultural conflict resolution approaches.' *International Journal of Intercultural Relations* 29(6): 675–695.

Hardin, A.M., Fuller, M.A., and Davison, R.M. (2007). 'I know I can, but can we? Culture and efficacy beliefs in global virtual teams.' *Small Group Research* 38(1): 130–155.

Hart, A., Lantz, C., and Montague, J. (2020). 'Identity, power, and discomfort: Developing intercultural competence through transformative learning.' In *Multicultural instructional design: Concepts, methodologies, tools, and applications*, pp. 1020–1040. USA: Information Resources Management Association. https://doi.org/10.4018/978-1-5225-9279-2.ch048.

Hartung, P.J., Fouad, N.A., Leong, F.T.L., and Hardin, E.E. (2010). 'Individualism-Collectivism.' *Journal of Career Assessment* 18(1): 34–45. http://doi.org/10.1177/106 9072709340526.

Harush, R., Lisak, A., and Glikson, E. (2018). 'The bright side of social categorization: The role of global identity in reducing relational conflict in multicultural distributed teams.' *Cross Cultural & Strategic Management* 25(1): 134–156. http://doi.org/10.1108/CCSM-11-2016-0202.

Hass, A. (2012, February 6). 'Bedouin community wins reprieve from forcible relocation to Jerusalem garbage dump.' *Haaretz*.

Hasson, N. (2019, January 10). 'New Jerusalem 'apartheid road' opens, separating Palestinians and Jewish settlers.' *Haaretz*.

Hays, R.B. (1988). 'Friendship.' In S. Duck (Ed.), *Handbook of personal relationship: Theory, research, and interventions*, pp. 391–408. New York: Wiley.

Heaphy, B., and Davies, K. (2012). 'Critical friendships.' *Families, Relationships and Societies* 1(3): 311–326. http://doi.org/10.1332/204674312X656257.

Heider, F. (1958). *The psychology of interpersonal relations*. Hillsdale, New Jersey London: Lawrence Erlbaum Associates.

Helms, J.E., Nicolas, G., and Green, C.E. (2012). 'Racism and ethnoviolence as trauma: Enhancing professional and research training.' *Traumatology* 18(1): 65–74. http://doi.org/10.1177/1534765610396728.

Heneiti, A. (2016). 'Bedouin communities in greater Jerusalem: Planning or forced displacement?' *Jerusalem Quarterly* (65): 51–68.

'Henna.' (n.d.). Retrieved March 25, 2020, from https://en.wikipedia.org/wiki/Henna#Israel.

Hertz-Lazarowitz, R., and Zelniker, T. (2004). 'Arab-Jewish coexistence programs.' In *Journal of Social Issues*, vol. 60, p. 2. Wiley-Blackwell.

Herzog, H., Sharon, S., and Leykin, I. (2008). 'Racism and the politics of signification: Israeli public discourse on racism towards Palestinian citizens.' *Ethnic and Racial Studies* 31(6): 1091–1109.

Herzog, S. (2004). 'Differential perceptions of the seriousness of male violence against female intimate partners among Jews and Arabs in Israel.' *Journal of Interpersonal Violence* 19(8): 891–900. http://doi.org/10.1177/0886260504266885.

Hindriks, P., Verkuyten, M., and Coenders, M. (2017). 'Evaluating political acculturation strategies: The perspective of the majority and other minority groups.' *Political Psychology* 38(5): 741–756. https://doi.org/10.1111/pops.12356.

Hirsch-Hoefler, S., Canetti, D., Rapaport, C., and Hobfoll, S.E. (2016). 'Conflict will harden your heart: Exposure to violence, psychological distress, and peace barriers in Israel and Palestine.' *British Journal of Political Science* 46(04): 845–859. https://doi.org/10.1017/S0007123414000374.

Ho, D.Y. (1976). 'On the concept of face.' *American Journal of Sociology* 81(4): 867–884.

Hofstede, G. (2001). *Culture's consequences: Comparing values, behaviors, institutions, and organizations across nations*. Thousand Oaks, Ca.: SAGE Publications, Inc.

Hofstede, G. (n.d.-a). 'Geert Hofstede™ Cultural Dimensions.' Retrieved January 26, 2018, from http://www.geert-hofstede.com/hofstede_dimensions.php.

Hofstede, G. (n.d.-b). 'Insights on Hofstede's research into national and organizational culture.' Retrieved January 26, 2018, from http://geert-hofstede.com.

Holt, N.L. (2008). 'Representation, legitimation, and autoethnography: An autoethnographic writing story.' *International Journal of Qualitative Methods* 2(1): 18–20.

Hopper, E. (2003). 'Aspects of aggression in large groups characterised by (ba) I:A/M.' In S. Schneider and H. Weinberg (Eds.), *The large group revisited: The herd, primal horde, crowds and masses*, pp. 58–72. London: Jessica Kingsley Pub.

Houjeir, R., and Brennan, R. (2016). 'Trust in cross-cultural b2b financial service relationships: The role of shared values.' *Journal of Financial Services Marketing* 21(2): 90–102. http://doi.org/10.1057/fsm.2016.4.

Howard, A., and Tappan, M. (2009). 'Complicating the social and cultural aspects of social class.' In E. Malewski (Ed.), *Curriculum studies handbook: The next moment*, pp. 322–324. New York: Taylor & Francis.

Howarth, C., Wagner, W., Magnusson, N., and Sammut, G. (2014). '"It's only other people who make me feel black": Acculturation, identity, and agency in a multicultural community.' *Political Psychology* 35(1): 81–95. http://doi.org/10.1111/pops.12020.

Howarth, W.L. (1974). 'Some principles of autobiography.' *New Literary History* 5(2): 363–381.

Hsu, S.-Y., Woodside, A.G., and Marshall, R. (2013). 'Critical tests of multiple theories of cultures' consequences.' *Journal of Travel Research* 52(6): 679–704. http://doi.org/10.1177/0047287512475218.

Hughes, P.C., and Heuman, A.N. (2006). 'The communication of solidarity in friendships among African American women.' *Qualitative Research Reports in Communication* 7(1): 33–41. http://doi.org/10.1080/17459430600964869.

Hui, B.P.H., Chen, S.X., Leung, C.M., and Berry, J.W. (2015). 'Facilitating adaptation and intercultural contact: The role of integration and multicultural ideology in dominant and non-dominant groups.' *International Journal of Intercultural Relations* 45: 70–84. http://doi.org/10.1016/J.IJINTREL.2015.01.002.

Humphreys, M. (2005). 'Getting personal: Reflexivity and autoethnographic vignettes.' *Qualitative Inquiry* 11(6): 840–860.

IJzerman, H., van Dijk, W.W., and Gallucci, M. (2007). 'A bumpy train ride: A field experiment on insult, honor, and emotional reactions.' *Emotion* 7(4): 869–875.

Imahori, T.T., and Cupach, W.R. (2005). 'Identity management theory: Facework in intercultural relationships.' In W.B. Gudykunst (Ed.), *Theorizing about intercultural communication*, pp. 195–210. Thousand Oaks, CA: SAGE Publications, Inc.

Inglehart, R. (2006). 'Mapping global values.' *Comparative Sociology* 5(2–3): 115–136.

Inglehart, R. (n.d.). 'World Values Survey.' Retrieved April 6, 2018, from http://www.worldvaluessurvey.org.

Ingram, P., and Roberts, P.W. (2000). 'Friendships among competitors in the Sydney hotel industry.' *The American Journal of Sociology* 106(2): 387–423.

International Labour Organization. (1973). *ILO Convention No. 138*. Geneva.

Ir Amim. (2019). Greater Jerusalem [map].

Israel Central Bureau of Statistics. (2020). 'Population of Israel.' Retrieved April 23, 2020, from https://www.cbs.gov.il/.

Israel Central Bureau of Statistics. (2017). 'Selected data on the occasion of "Tu BeAv".' Retrieved March 24, 2018, from http://www.cbs.gov.il.

Jackson, D. (1990). 'Patriarchy, class and language: A critical autobiography.' *English in Education* 24(2): 8–19.

Jaffe-Hoffman, M., Ahronheim, A., Sharon, J., and Halon, E. (2020, April 3). '10 Israelis die in one day, near 7,000 infected, Bnei Brak in lockdown.' *Jerusalem Post*.

Jakubowska, L. (2000). 'Finding ways to make a living: Employment among the Negev Bedouin.' *Nomadic Peoples* 4: 94–106.

Jamal, A. (2007). 'When is social trust a desirable outcome?' *Comparative Political Studies* 40(11): 1328–1349. http://doi.org/10.1177/0010414006291833.

Jamieson, L., Morgan, D., Crow, G., and Allan, G. (2006). 'Friends, neighbours and distant partners: Extending or decentring family relationships?' *Sociological Research Online* 11(3): 1–9. http://doi.org/10.5153/sro.1421.

Jang, M. (2018). 'Aristotle's Political Friendship (politike philia) as Solidarity.' In L. Huppes-Cluysenaer and N. Coelho (Eds.), *Aristotle on Emotions in Law and Politics*, pp. 417–433. Springer, Cham. http://doi.org/10.1007/978-3-319-66703-4_20.

Jerusalem Post Staff. (2020, March 5). 'Naftali Bennett closes Bethlehem, Abbas declares state of emergency.' *Jerusalem Post*.

Jones, J.M. (2010). 'I'm white and you're not: The value of unraveling ethnocentric science.' *Perspectives on Psychological Science* 5(6): 700–707. http://doi.org/10.1177/1745691610388771.

Jordan, J.V. (2001). 'A relational-cultural model: Healing through mutual empathy.' *Bulletin of the Menninger Clinic* 65(1): 92–103.

Josselson, R.E., and Lieblich, A. (2003). 'A framework for narrative research proposals in psychology.' In D.P. McAdams, R.H. Josselson and A. Lieblich (Eds.), *Up close and personal: The teaching and learning of narrative research*, pp. 259–274. Washington, DC: American Psychological Association.

Josselson, R.E., Lieblich, A.E., and McAdams, D.P. (2007). *The meaning of others: Narrative studies of relationships*. Washington, DC: American Psychological Association.

Joubran, N., and Schwartz, S.H. (2007). 'From enemies to friends: Personal conflict resolution at Imagine.' *Journal of Humanistic Psychology* 47(3): 340–350.

Kabuiku, J. (2017). 'Immigrating to Northeast America: The Kenyan immigrant's experience.' *Journal of Social, Behavioral, and Health Sciences* 11(1).

Kamir, O. (2002). 'Honor and dignity cultures: The case of Kavod and Kvod Ha-Adam in Israeli society and law.' In D. Kretzmer and E. Klein (Eds.), *The concept of human dignity in human rights discourse*, pp. 231–262. The Hague, The Netherlands: Kluwer Law International.

Kaplan, D. (2006). *The men we loved: Male friendship and nationalism in Israeli culture.* New York: Berghahn Books.

Kaplan, D. (2007). 'Folk models of dyadic male bonds in Israeli culture.' *Sociological Quarterly* 48(1): 47–72.

Karlberg, M. (2008). 'Discourse, identity, and global citizenship.' *Peace Review: A Journal of Social Justice* 20(3): 310–320.

Kasser, T. (2011). 'Cultural values and the well-being of future generations: A cross-national study.' *Journal of Cross-Cultural Psychology* 42(2): 206–215. http://doi.org/10.1177/0022022110396865.

Kaufman, R. (2018). 'Peace as opportunity for social justice: Establishment of new social change organizations in Israel in the wake of the Oslo Peace Accords.' *International Social Work* 61(3): 368–382. https://doi.org/10.1177/0020872816639369.

Keller, M. (2004). 'A cross-cultural perspective on friendship research.' *ISBBD Newsletter* 46: 10–14.

Kelly, T. (2005). 'Law, culture and access to justice under the Palestinian National Authority.' *Development and Change* 36(5): 865–886.

Keltner, D., Gruenfeld, D.H., and Anderson, C. (2003). 'Power, approach, and inhibition.' *Psychological Review* 110(2): 265–284. http://doi.org/10.1037/0033-295X.110.2.265.

Kern, D.E., Wright, S.M., Carrese, J.A., Lipkin Jr, M., Simmons, J.M., Novack, D.H., ... Frankel, R. (2001). 'Personal growth in medical faculty: A qualitative study.' *Western Journal of Medicine* 175(2): 92.

Kernes, J., and Kinnier, R. (2008). 'Meaning in psychologist's personal and professional lives.' *The Journal of Humanistic Psychology* 48(2): 196.

Kets de Vries, M.F.R. (2003). *Leaders, fools and impostors: Essays on the psychology of leadership.* Lincoln, NE: iUniverse Inc.

Khatimah, K., and Kusuma, R.S. (2019). 'Intercultural friendship as strategy to reduce anxiety and uncertainty of Zimbabwe students in Muhammadiyah Surakarta university.' *Komuniti: Jurnal Komunikasi Dan Teknologi Informasi* 11(1): 45–57. https://doi.org/10.23917/komuniti.v10i3.5900.

Khuri, M.L. (2004). 'Facilitating Arab-Jewish intergroup dialogue in the college setting.' *Race Ethnicity and Education* 7(3): 229–250.

Klasios, J. (2019). 'Aggression among men: An integrated evolutionary explanation.' *Aggression and Violent Behavior* 47: 29–45. https://doi.org/10.1016/j.avb.2019.02.015.

Knafo, A., Roccas, S., and Sagiv, L. (2011). 'The value of values in cross-cultural research: A special issue in honor of Shalom Schwartz.' *Journal of Cross-Cultural Psychology* 42(2): 178–185. http://doi.org/10.1177/0022022110396863.

Kokkonen, A., Esaiasson, P., and Gilljam, M. (2015). 'Diverse workplaces and interethnic friendship formation – A multilevel comparison across 21 OECD Countries.' *Journal of Ethnic and Migration Studies* 41(2): 284–305. http://doi.org/10.1080/1369 183X.2014.902300.

Korol, L.D. (2017). 'Is the association between multicultural personality and ethnic tolerance explained by cross-group friendship?' *Journal of General Psychology* 144(4): 264–282. https://doi.org/10.1080/00221309.2017.1374118.

Korol, L.D. (2019). 'Does multicultural personality moderate the relationship between cross-group friendship and allophilia?' *Journal of Social Psychology* 159(6): 649–663. https://doi.org/10.1080/00224545.2018.1549012.

Kouvo, A., and Lockmer, C. (2013). 'Imagine all the neighbours: Perceived neighbourhood ethnicity, interethnic friendship ties and perceived ethnic threat in four Nordic countries.' *Urban Studies* 50(16): 3305–3322. http://doi.org/10.1177/0042098013484538.

Kramsch, C. (2006). 'The multilingual subject.' *International Journal of Applied Linguistics* 16(1): 97–110.

Krappmann, L. (1998). 'Amicitia, drujba, shin-yu, philia, freundschaft, friendship: On the cultural diversity of a human relationship.' In A.F. Newcomb, W.W. Hartup and W.M. Bukowski (Eds.), *The company they keep: Friendship in childhood and adolescence*, pp. 19–40. Cambridge: Cambridge University Press.

Kudo, K., and Simkin, K.A. (2003). 'Intercultural friendship formation: The case of Japanese students at an Australian university.' *Journal of Intercultural Studies* 24(2): 91–114.

Kuriansky, J. (2007). *Beyond bullets and bombs: Grassroots peacebuilding between Israelis and Palestinians*. Westport, CT: Praeger Publishers.

Laar, C.V., Levin, S., Sinclair, S., and Sidanius, J. (2005). 'The effect of university roommate contact on ethnic attitudes and behavior.' *Journal of Experimental Social Psychology* 41(4): 329–345.

Lakoff, G., and Johnson, M. (2003). *Metaphors we live by*. Chicago: University of Chicago Press.

Lang, S. (2002). 'Sulha peacemaking and the politics of persuasion.' *Journal of Palestine Studies* 31(3): 52–66.

Laparlière, M. (2011, September 28). 'Unieke vriendschap Nederlander en woestijnsjeik.' *Radio Nederland Wereldomroep*.

Laungani, P. (2002). 'Understanding mental illness across cultures.' In S. Palmer (Ed.), *Multicultural counselling: a reader*, pp. 129–156. London/Thousand Oaks/New Delhi: SAGE Publications.

Lazaroff, T. (2020, March 12). 'Erekat: West Bank E1 road start of annexation and apartheid.' *Jerusalem Post*.

Lazaroff, T. (2020, March 12). 'Khan al-Ahmar to ICC: this is our only chance to halt Israeli war crimes.' *Jerusalem Post*.

Leder, S. (2005). 'Nomadic and sedentary peoples – A misleading dichotomy? The Bedouin and Bedouinism in the Arab past.' In S. Leder (Ed.), *Shifts and drifts in nomad-sedentary relations*, pp. 401–419. Wiesbaden: L. Reichert.

Ledwith, M., and Springett, J. (2010). *Participatory practice: Community-based action for transformative change*. Bristol, UK: Policy Press.

Lee, P.W. (2006). 'Bridging cultures: Understanding the construction of relational identity in intercultural friendship.' *Journal of Intercultural Communication Research* 35(1): 3–22.

Lee, P.W. (2008). 'Stages and transitions of relational identity formation in intercultural friendship: Implications for identity management theory.' *Journal of International and Intercultural Communication* 1(1): 51–69.

Leszczensky, L., and Pink, S. (2019). 'What drives ethnic homophily? A relational approach on how ethnic identification moderates preferences for same-ethnic friends.' *American Sociological Review* 84(3): 394–419. https://doi.org/10.1177/0003122419846849.

Leung, A.K.Y., and Cohen, D. (2011). 'Within-and between-culture variation: Individual differences and the cultural logics of honor, face, and dignity cultures.' *Journal of Personality and Social Psychology* 100: 507–526.

Lewin-Epstein, N., and Cohen, Y. (2019). 'Ethnic origin and identity in the Jewish population of Israel.' *Journal of Ethnic and Migration Studies* 45(11): 2118–2137. https://doi.org/10.1080/1369183X.2018.1492370.

Li, N. (2019). 'Exploring the Israeli-Palestinian conflict from religious perspectives.' *The Journal of Living Together* 6(1): 65–74.

Lichtenberg, P., Vass, A., and Heresco-Levy, U. (2003). 'Politics and psychopathology in an Arab-Israeli Patient.' *Psychiatry* 66(4): 360.

Lieblich, A., Tuval-Mashiach, R., and Zilber, T. (1998). *Narrative research: Reading, analysis and interpretation*, vol. 47. Thousand Oaks, CA: SAGE Publications, Inc.

Lin, X., and Shen, G.Q.P. (2019). 'How formal and informal intercultural contacts in universities influence students' cultural intelligence?' *Asia Pacific Education Review*: 1–15. https://doi.org/10.1007/s12564-019-09615-y.

Lindner, E.G. (2006). 'How becoming a global citizen can have a healing effect.' In *ICU-COE Northeast Asian Dialogue: Sharing Narratives, Weaving/Mapping History*. International Christian University (ICU), Tokyo, Japan.

Linley, P.A., and Joseph, S. (2004). 'Positive change following trauma and adversity: A review.' *Journal of Traumatic Stress* 17(1): 11–21.

Lowe, S. (2002). 'The cultural shadows of cross cultural research: images of culture.' *Culture and Organization* 8(1): 21–34.

Lu, J.G., Hafenbrack, A.C., Eastwick, P.W., Wang, D.J., Maddux, W.W., and Galinsky, A.D. (2017). '"Going out" of the box: Close intercultural friendships and romantic relationships spark creativity, workplace innovation, and entrepreneurship.' *Journal of Applied Psychology* 102(7): 1091–1108. http://doi.org/10.1037/apl0000212.

Lubel, S., Wolf, Y., and Cohen-Raz, L. (2001). 'Perception of aggression as a function of ethnic affiliation: Moral judgment of violence among Jews and Arabs in Israel.' *International Journal of Group Tensions* 30(4): 385–392.

Lyons, J.L. (2010). 'Autonomous Cross-Cultural Hardship Travel (ACHT) as a medium for growth, learning, and a deepened sense of self.' *World Futures* 66(3): 286–302.

Macduff, I. (2006). 'Your pace or mine? Culture, time, and negotiation.' *Negotiation Journal* 22(1): 31–45.

Mackay, J., Levin, J., De Carvalho, G., Cavoukian, K., and Cuthbert, R. (2014). 'Before and after borders: The nomadic challenge to sovereign territoriality.' *International Politics* 51(1): 101–123. https://doi.org/10.1057/ip.2013.24.

Mahfud, Y., Badea, C., Verkuyten, M., and Reynolds, K. (2018). 'Multiculturalism and attitudes toward immigrants: The impact of perceived cultural distance.' *Journal of Cross-Cultural Psychology* 49(6): 945–958. https://doi.org/10.1177/0022022117730828.

Malacarne, T. (2017). 'Rich friends, poor friends: Inter–socioeconomic status friendships in secondary school.' *Socius: Sociological Research for a Dynamic World.* https://doi.org/10.1177/2378023117736994.

Maliepaard, M., and Verkuyten, M. (2018). 'National disidentification and minority identity: A study among Muslims in Western Europe.' *Self and Identity* 17(1): 75–91. https://doi.org/10.1080/15298868.2017.1323792.

Malik, N.M., and Lindahl, K.M. (1998). 'Aggression and dominance: The roles of power and culture in domestic violence.' *Clinical Psychology: Science and Practice* 5(4): 409–423.

Mallory, P. (2017). 'Political friendship and the social bond.' In *Interrogating the Social*, pp. 37–60. Cham: Springer International Publishing. http://doi.org/10.1007/978-3-319-59948-9_2.

Mallory, P., and Carlson, J. (2014). 'Rethinking personal and political friendship with Durkheim.' *Distinktion: Journal of Social Theory* 15(3): 327–342. http://doi.org/10.1080/1600910X.2014.918045.

Manago, A.M., and Vaughn, L. (2015). 'Social media, friendship, and happiness in the millennial generation.' In *Friendship and happiness*, pp. 187–206. Dordrecht: Springer Netherlands. http://doi.org/10.1007/978-94-017-9603-3_11.

Manrai, L.A., and Manrai, A.K. (1995). 'Effects of cultural-context, gender, and acculturation on perceptions of work versus social/leisure time usage.' *Journal of Business Research* 32(2): 115–128.

'Mansaf.' (n.d.). Retrieved April 6, 2018, from https://en.wikipedia.org/wiki/Mansaf.

Manstead, A.S.R. (2018). 'The psychology of social class: How socioeconomic status impacts thought, feelings, and behaviour.' *British Journal of Social Psychology* 57(2): 267–291. https://doi.org/10.1111/bjso.12251.

Maoz, I. (2000a). 'An experiment in peace: Reconciliation-aimed workshops of Jewish-Israeli and Palestinian youth.' *Journal of Peace Research* 37(6): 721–736. http://doi.org/10.1177/0022343300037006004.

Maoz, I. (2000b). 'Power relations in intergroup encounters: A case study of Jewish-Arab encounters in Israel.' *International Journal of Intercultural Relations* 24(2): 259–277.

Maoz, I., and Ron, Y. (2016). 'The road to peace: The potential of structured encounters between Israeli Jews and Palestinians in promoting peace.' In K. Sharvit and E. Halperin (Eds.), *A Social Psychology perspective on the Israeli-Palestinian conflict. Peace Psychology Book Series*, pp. 243–252. Springer, Cham. http://doi.org/10.1007/978-3-319-24841-7_16.

'Maqluba.' (n.d.). Retrieved April 6, 2018, from https://en.wikipedia.org/wiki/Maqluba.

Mares, R. (2017). 'The language of the Bedouins: A social-ethnic Arab structure.' *Contemporary Readings in Law and Social Justice* 9(2): 440–445.

Margalit, A. (2017). 'The Israeli Supreme Court and Bedouin land claims in the Negev: A missed opportunity to uphold human and indigenous rights.' *International Journal on Minority and Group Rights* 24(1): 57–69. http://doi.org/10.1163/15718115-02401002.

Matera, C., Bosco, N., and Meringolo, P. (2019). 'Perceived mattering to family and friends, self-esteem, and well-being.' *Psychology, Health and Medicine.* https://doi.org/10.1080/13548506.2019.1626454.

Matsumoto, D. (2006). 'Culture and cultural worldviews: Do verbal descriptions about culture reflect anything other than verbal descriptions of culture?' *Culture & Psychology* 12(1): 33–62.

Matsumoto, D., and Hwang, H.S.C. (2019). 'Culture, Emotion, and Expression.' In K.D. Keith (Ed.), *Cross-Cultural Psychology*, pp. 501–515. Chichester, UK: John Wiley & Sons, Ltd. https://doi.org/10.1002/9781119519348.ch24.

Matsumoto, D., Yoo, S.H., Fontaine, J., Anguas-Wong, A.M., Arriola, M., Ataca, B., ... Boratav, H.B. (2008). 'Mapping expressive differences around the world: The relationship between emotional display rules and individualism versus collectivism.' *Journal of Cross-Cultural Psychology* 39(1): 55–74. http://doi.org/http://dx.doi.org/10.1177/0022022107311854.

Maydell, E. (2010). 'Methodological and analytical dilemmas in autoethnographic research.' *Journal of Research Practice* 6(1): Article M5.

McAdams, D.P., Healy, S., and Krause, S. (1984). 'Social motives and patterns of friendship.' *Journal of Personality and Social Psychology* 47: 828–838.

McCall, M. (1970). *Friendship as a social institution*. Routledge. http://doi.org/10.4324/9780203791493.

Meir, A. (1988). 'Nomads and the state: The spatial dynamics of centrifugal and centripetal forces among the Israeli Negev Bedouin.' *Political Geography Quarterly* 7(3): 251–270.

Merkin, R., and Ramadan, R. (2010). 'Facework in Syria and the United States: A cross-cultural comparison.' *International Journal of Intercultural Relations* 34(6): 661–669.

BIBLIOGRAPHY

Meskelyte, J., and Lyons, M. (2020). 'Fear of crime and preference for aggressive-formidable same-sex and opposite-sex friends.' *Current Psychology*: 1–6. https://doi.org/10.1007/s12144-020-00679-3.

Mesquita, B. (2001). 'Emotions in collectivist and individualist contexts.' *Journal of Personality and Social Psychology* 80(1): 68–74.

Mezirow, J. (1997). 'Transformative learning: Theory to practice.' *New Directions for Adult and Continuing Education* 74(74): 5–12.

Mezirow, J. (2000). 'Learning to think like an adult: Core concepts of transformation theory.' In J. al Mezirow (Ed.), *Learning as transformation: Critical perspectives on a theory in progress*, pp. 3–33. San Francisco: Jossey-Bass.

Mi'ari, M. (1999). 'Attitudes of Palestinians toward normalization with Israel.' *Journal of Peace Research* 36(3): 339–348. http://doi.org/10.1177/0022343399036003006.

Migliaccio, T. (2009). 'Men's friendships: Performances of masculinity.' *The Journal of Men's Studies* 17(3): 226–241.

Minkov, M., and Hofstede, G. (2011). 'Hofstede's fifth dimension: New evidence from the World Values Survey.' *Journal of Cross-Cultural Psychology* 42. http://doi.org/10.1177/0022022110388567.

Minkov, M., and Hofstede, G. (2014a). 'A replication of Hofstede's uncertainty avoidance dimension across nationally representative samples from Europe.' *International Journal of Cross Cultural Management* 14(2): 161–171. http://doi.org/10.1177/1470595814521600.

Minkov, M., and Hofstede, G. (2014b). 'Clustering of 316 European Regions on Measures of Values.' *Cross-Cultural Research* 48(2): 144–176. http://doi.org/10.1177/1069397113510866.

Minkov, M., Dutt, P., Schachner, M., Jandosova, J., Khassenbekov, Y., Morales, O., and Blagoev, V. (2019). 'What would people do with their money if they were rich? A search for Hofstede dimensions across 52 countries.' *Cross Cultural and Strategic Management* 26(1): 93–116. https://doi.org/10.1108/CCSM-11-2018-0193.

Mitra, R. (2010). 'Doing ethnography, being an ethnographer: The autoethnographic research process and I.' *Journal of Research Practice* 6(1): Article M4.

Mizrachi, N., and Herzog, H. (2012). 'Participatory destigmatization strategies among Palestinian citizens, Ethiopian Jews and Mizrahi Jews in Israel.' *Ethnic and Racial Studies* 35(3): 418–435. https://doi.org/10.1080/01419870.2011.589530.

Mizrachi, N., and Weiss, E. (2020). ' "We do not want to assimilate!": Rethinking the role of group boundaries in peace initiatives between Muslims and Jews in Israel and in the West Bank.' *European Journal of Cultural and Political Sociology*. https://doi.org/10.1080/23254823.2020.1727350.

Mjdoob, T., and Shoshana, A. (2017). 'Palatable Arabs: Palestinian professionals in work organizations in Israel.' *Sociological Quarterly* 58(2): 163–181. https://doi.org/10.1080/00380253.2017.1296337.

Montuori, A., and Fahim, U. (2004). 'Cross-cultural encounter as an opportunity for personal growth.' *Journal of Humanistic Psychology* 44(2): 243–265.

Moon, D.G. (1996). 'Concepts of "culture": Implications for intercultural communication research.' *Communication Quarterly* 44(1): 70–84. http://doi.org/10.1080/01463379609370001.

Moon, D.G. (2010). 'Critical reflections on culture and critical intercultural communication.' In T.T. Nakayama and R.T. Halualani (Eds.), *The Handbook of Critical Intercultural Communication*, pp. 34–52. Oxford, UK: Wiley-Blackwell. http://doi.org/10.1002/9781444390681.ch3.

Morgan, G. (2007). *Images of Organization*. Thousand Oaks, CA: SAGE Publications, Inc.

Morray, E.B., and Liang, B. (2005). 'Peace talk: A relational approach to group negotiation among Arab and Israeli youths.' *International Journal of Group Psychotherapy* 55(4): 481–506.

Mosquera, P.M.R., Manstead, A.S.R., and Fischer, A.H. (2000). 'The role of honor-related values in the elicitation, experience, and communication of pride, shame, and anger: Spain and the Netherlands compared.' *Personality and Social Psychology Bulletin* 26(7): 833–844.

Mosquera, P.M.R., Manstead, A.S.R., and Fischer, A.H. (2002a). 'Honor in the Mediterranean and Northern Europe.' *Journal of Cross-Cultural Psychology* 33(1): 16–36.

Mosquera, P.M.R., Manstead, A.S.R., and Fischer, A.H. (2002b). 'The role of honour concerns in emotional reactions to offences.' *Cognition & Emotion* 16(1): 143–163.

Musil, B., Rus, V., and Musek, J. (2009). 'The Rokeach value survey in comparative study of Japanese and Slovenian students: towards the underlying structure.' *Studia Psychologica* 51(1): 53–68.

Musso, P., Inguglia, C., Lo Coco, A., Albiero, P., and Berry, J.W. (2017). 'Mediating and moderating processes in the relationship between multicultural ideology and attitudes towards immigrants in emerging adults.' *International Journal of Psychology* 52(S1): 72–77. http://doi.org/10.1002/ijop.12290.

Muttarak, R. (2014). 'Generation, ethnic and religious diversity in friendship choice: Exploring interethnic close ties in Britain.' *Ethnic and Racial Studies* 37(1): 71–98. http://doi.org/10.1080/01419870.2014.844844.

Myers-JDC-Brookdale Institute. (2018). *The Arab population in Israel: Facts & figures 2018*.

Mykhalovskiy, E. (1996). 'Reconsidering table talk: Critical thoughts on the relationship between sociology, autobiography and self-indulgence.' *Qualitative Sociology* 19(1): 131–151.

Najm, N.A. (2015). 'Arab culture dimensions in the international and Arab models.' *Open Science* 3(6): 423–431. http://doi.org/7090270.

Navon, E., and Diskin, A. (2019). 'Israel: Political development and data for 2018.' *European Journal of Political Research Political Data Yearbook* 58: 143–148. https://doi.org/10.1111/2047-8852.12266.

Nederlands Centraal Bureau voor de Statistiek. (2020). 'Nederland in cijfers.' Retrieved April 1, 2020, from https://opendata.cbs.nl/statline/#/CBS/nl/.

Nisbett, R.E., and Cohen, D. (1996). *Culture of honor: The psychology of violence in the South*. Boulder, CO: Westview Press.

Obeidat, B., Shannak, R.O., Masa'deh, R., and Jarrah, I. (2012). 'Toward better understanding for Arabian culture: Implications based on Hofstede's cultural model.' *European Journal of Social Sciences* 28(4): 512–522.

Oberg, K. (1954). 'Culture Shock.' Presentation at Women's Club of Rio de Janeiro.

Oetzel, J., Garcia, A.J., and Ting-Toomey, S. (2008). 'An analysis of the relationships among face concerns and facework behaviors in perceived conflict situations: A four-culture investigation.' *International Journal of Conflict Management* 19(4): 382–403.

Oetzel, J., Ting-Toomey, S., Masumoto, T., Yokochi, Y., Pan, X., Takai, J., and Wilcox, R. (2001). 'Face and facework in conflict: A cross-cultural comparison of China, Germany, Japan, and the United States.' *Communication Monographs* 68(3): 235–258.

Ohaeri, J.U., and Awadalla, A.W. (2009). 'The reliability and validity of the short version of the WHO Quality of Life Instrument in an Arab general population.' *Annals of Saudi Medicine* 29: 98–104.

Onosu, O.G. (2020). 'Cultural immersion: A trigger for transformative learning.' *Social Sciences* 9(2): 20. https://doi.org/10.3390/socsci9020020.

Orr, Z., and Ajzenstadt, M. (2020). 'Beyond control: The criminalization of African asylum seekers in Israel.' *International Review of Sociology* 30(1): 142–165. https://doi.org/10.1080/03906701.2020.1724369.

Oswald, D.L., Clark, E.M., and Kelly, C.M. (2004). 'Friendship maintenance: An analysis of individual and dyad behaviors.' *Journal of Social and Clinical Psychology* 23(3): 413–441.

Owton, H., and Allen-Collinson, J. (2014). 'Close but not too close.' *Journal of Contemporary Ethnography* 43(3): 283–305. http://doi.org/10.1177/0891241613495410.

Oyserman, D. (1993). 'The lens of personhood: Viewing the self and others in a multicultural society.' *Journal of Personality and Social Psychology* 65(5): 993–1009.

Page-Gould, E., Mendoza-Denton, R., and Tropp, L.R. (2008). 'With a little help from my cross-group friend: Reducing anxiety in intergroup contexts through cross-group friendship.' *Journal of Personality and Social Psychology* 95(5): 1080–1094.

Pahl, R., and Spencer, L. (2010). 'Family, friends, and personal communities: Changing models-in-the-mind.' *Journal of Family Theory & Review* 2(3): 197–210. http://doi.org/10.1111/j.1756-2589.2010.00053.x.

Paine, R. (1970). 'Anthropological approaches to friendship.' *Humanitas* 6(2): 139–159.

Palestinian Central Bureau of Statistics. (2015). 'Number of documented cases using alternative judiciary systems.' Retrieved March 18, 2018, from http://www.pcbs.gov.ps.

Palestinian Central Bureau of Statistics. (2017). 'Median age at first marriage.' Retrieved March 18, 2018, from http://www.pcbs.gov.ps.

Palestinian Central Bureau of Statistics. (2018, February). 'Prelimanary results of the population, housing and establishments, Census 2017.' Retrieved April 17, 2020, from http://www.pcbs.gov.ps/portals/_pcbs/PressRelease/Press_En_Preliminary_Results_Report-en.pdf.

Panepinto, A.M. (2017). 'Jurisdiction as sovereignty over occupied Palestine.' *Social & Legal Studies* 26(3): 311–332. http://doi.org/10.1177/0964663916668002.

Pani, R. (1999). 'The pangs of global citizen participation.' *Peace Review* 11(1): 161–164.

Paolini, S., Wright, S.C., Dys-Steenbergen, O., and Favara, I. (2016). 'Self-expansion and intergroup contact: Expectancies and motives to self-expand lead to greater interest in outgroup contact and more positive intergroup relations.' *Journal of Social Issues* 72(3): 450–471. http://doi.org/10.1111/josi.12176.

Park, P. (1993). 'What is participatory research? A theoretical and methodological perspective.' In P. Park, M. Brydon-Miller, B. Hall and T. Jackson (Eds.), *Voices of change: Participatory research in the United States and Canada*, pp. 1–20. Westport, CT: Bergin & Garvey.

Parkinson, C., Kleinbaum, A.M., and Wheatley, T. (2018). 'Similar neural responses predict friendship.' *Nature Communications* 9(1): 332. http://doi.org/10.1038/s41467-017-02722-7.

Pedersen, P. (Ed.). (1995). *The five stages of culture shock: Critical incidents around the world*. Westport, CT: Greenwood Pub Group.

Pely, D. (2009). 'Resolving clan-based disputes using the Sulha, the traditional dispute resolution process of the Middle East.' *Dispute Resolution Journal* 63: 80–88.

Pely, D. (2010). 'Honor: The Sulha's main dispute resolution tool.' *Conflict Resolution Quarterly* 28(1): 67–81.

Pely, D. (2011). 'Women in Sulha – excluded yet influential: Examining women's formal and informal role in traditional dispute resolution, within the patriarchal culture of Northern Israel's Arab community.' *International Journal of Conflict Management* 22(1): 89–104.

Penbek, S., Yurdakul, D., and Cerit, A.G. (2009). 'Intercultural communication competence: a study about the intercultural sensitivity of university students based on their education and international experiences.' In *European and Mediterranean Conference on Information Systems*. Izmir, Turkey.

Pérez-Huertas, J.L., and Barquín-Rotchford, G. (2020). 'Doing business in the Islamic world: A cultural approach from the Hofstede Model.' *Journal of the Sociology and Theory of Religion* 9: 1–15. https://doi.org/10.24197/jstr.0.2020.1-15.

Persky, I., and Birman, D. (2005). 'Ethnic identity in acculturation research: A study of multiple identities of Jewish refugees from the former Soviet Union.' *Journal of Cross-Cultural Psychology* 36(5): 557–572.

Pessate-Schubert, A. (2003). 'Changing from the margins: Bedouin women and higher education in Israel.' *Women's Studies International Forum* 26(4): 285–298.

Peterson, T.J. (2007). 'Another level: Friendships transcending geography and race.' *The Journal of Men's Studies* 15(1): 71–82.

Pike, G., and Sillem, M. (2018). 'Study abroad and global citizenship: Paradoxes and possibilities.' In I. Davies, et al. (Eds.), *The Palgrave Handbook of Global Citizenship and Education*, pp. 573–587. London, UK: Palgrave Macmillan. http://doi.org/10.1057/978-1-137-59733-5_36.

Plonski, S. (2018). 'Material footprints: The struggle for borders by Bedouin-Palestinians in Israel.' *Antipode*. http://doi.org/10.1111/anti.12388.

Ponterotto, J.G. (2010). 'Multicultural personality: An evolving theory of optimal functioning in culturally heterogeneous societies.' *The Counseling Psychologist* 38: 714–758.

Ponterotto, J.G., Costa-Wofford, C.I., Brobst, K.E., Spelliscy, D., Kacanski, J.M., Scheinholtz, J., and Martines, D. (2007). 'Multicultural personality dispositions and psychological well-being.' *The Journal of Social Psychology* 147(2): 119–135.

Ponterotto, J.G., Mendelowitz, D., and Collabolletta, E. (2008). 'Promoting multicultural personality development: A strengths-based, positive psychology worldview for schools.' *Professional School Counseling* 12(2): 93.

Pratsinakis, M., Hatziprokopiou, P., Labrianidis, L., and Vogiatzis, N. (2017). 'Living together in multi-ethnic cities: People of migrant background, their interethnic friendships and the neighbourhood.' *Urban Studies* 54(1): 102–118. http://doi.org/10.1177/0042098015615756.

Pratt, G., and Rosner, V. (2012). *The global and the intimate: Feminism in our time.* Columbia University Press.

Presbitero, A., and Attar, H. (2018). 'Intercultural communication effectiveness, cultural intelligence and knowledge sharing: Extending anxiety-uncertainty management theory.' *International Journal of Intercultural Relations* 67: 35–43. https://doi.org/10.1016/j.ijintrel.2018.08.004.

Qouta, S., Punamaki, R.L., Miller, T., and El-Sarraj, E. (2008). 'Does war beget child aggression? Military violence, gender, age and aggressive behavior in two Palestinian samples.' *Aggressive Behavior* 34(3): 231–244.

Rabinowitz, D. (1992). 'Trust and the attribution of rationality: Inverted roles amongst Palestinian Arabs and Jews in Israel.' *Man* 27(3): 517–537.

Rahman, T. (2001). 'Language-learning and power: A theoretical approach.' *International Journal of the Sociology of Language* 2001(152): 53–74.

Ramírez-i-Ollé, M. (2019). 'Friendship as a scientific method.' *The Sociological Review* 67(2): 299–317. http://doi.org/10.1177/0038026119829760.

Rawlins, W.K. (1989). 'Cultural double agency and the pursuit of friendship.' *Cultural Dynamics* 2(1): 28.

Ray, T.N., and Parkhill, M.R. (2019). 'Examining disgust and emotion regulation difficulties as components of aggression toward perceived gay men.' *Psychology of Violence*, Advance on. https://doi.org/10.1037/vio0000265.

Reebye, P.N., Ross, S.E., and Jamieson, K. (n.d.). 'A literature review of child-parent/caregiver attachment theory and cross-cultural practices influencing attachment.' Retrieved January 28, 2018, from http://www.attachmentacrosscultures.org/research.

Remennick, L., and Prashizky, A. (2019). 'Generation 1.5 of Russian Israelis: Integrated but distinct.' *Journal of Modern Jewish Studies* 18(3): 263–281. https://doi.org/10.1080/14725886.2018.1537212.

Rijke, A. (2020). 'Checkpoint knowledge: Navigating the tunnels and Al Walaja checkpoints in the Occupied Palestinian Territories.' *Geopolitics*. https://doi.org/10.1080/14650045.2020.1737020.

Robinson, G.E. (2008). 'Palestinian tribes, clans, and notable families.' *Strategic Insights (on-Line Journal of the Center for Contemporary Conflict)* VII(4).

Roccas, S., Horenczyk, G., and Schwartz, S.H. (2000). 'Acculturation discrepancies and well-being: The moderating role of conformity.' *European Journal of Social Psychology* 30(3): 323–334.

Roccas, S., Sagiv, L., Schwartz, S.H., and Knafo, A. (2002). 'The big five personality factors and personal values.' *Personality and Social Psychology Bulletin* 28(6): 789–801.

Rogoff, B. (2003). *The cultural nature of human development*. New York: Oxford University Press.

Roseneil, S. (2004). 'Why we should care about friends: An argument for queering the care imaginary in social policy.' *Social Policy and Society* 3(4): 409–419. http://doi.org/10.1017/S1474746404002039.

Roseneil, S., and Budgeon, S. (2004). 'Cultures of intimacy and care beyond "the family": Personal life and social change in the early 21st century.' *Current Sociology* 52(2): 135–159.

Rosenthal, L., and Levy, S.R. (2016). 'Endorsement of polyculturalism predicts increased positive intergroup contact and friendship across the beginning of college.' *Journal of Social Issues* 72(3): 472–488. http://doi.org/10.1111/josi.12177.

Rotter, J.B. (1975). 'Some problems and misconceptions related to the construct of internal versus external control of reinforcement.' *Journal of Consulting and Clinical Psychology* 43(1): 56.

Rybak, A., and McAndrew, F.T. (2006). 'How do we decide whom our friends are? Defining levels of friendship in Poland and the United States.' *The Journal of Social Psychology* 146(2): 147–163.

Rydgren, J., Sofi, D., and Hällsten, M. (2013). 'Interethnic friendship, trust, and tolerance: Findings from two North Iraqi cities.' *American Journal of Sociology* 118(6): 1650–1694. http://doi.org/10.1086/669854.

Ryff, C.D., Keyes, C.L.M., and Hughes, D.L. (2003). 'Status inequalities, perceived discrimination, and eudaimonic well-being: Do the challenges of minority life hone purpose and growth?' *Journal of Health and Social Behavior* 44(3): 275–291.

Sagi, A. (1990). 'Attachment theory and research from a cross-cultural perspective.' *Human Development* 33(1): 10–22.

Sagie, A., Kantor, J., Elizur, D., and Barhoum, M.I. (2005). 'A cross-cultural investigation of personal values: The Israeli-Palestinian case.' *Problems and Perspectives in Management* 2: 148–157.

Sagy, S., Orr, E., Bar-On, D., and Awwad, E. (2001). 'Individualism and collectivism in two conflicted societies.' *Youth & Society* 33(1): 3–30. http://doi.org/10.1177/0044118X01033001001.

Sahgal, N., and Cooperman, A. (2016). *Israel's religiously divided society*. Washington.

Said, E.W. (1985). 'Orientalism reconsidered.' *Cultural Critique* 1(1): 89–107.

Samovar, L.A., Porter, R.E., and McDaniel, E.R. (2009). *Communication between cultures* (7th Ed.). Boston, MA: Wadsworth Pub Co.

Sampson, R.J. (1988). 'Local friendship ties and community attachment in mass society: A multilevel systemic model.' *American Sociological Review* 53(5): 766–779.

Sanchez-Burks, J., Nisbett, R.E., and Ybarra, O. (2000). 'Cultural styles, relationship schemas, and prejudice against out-groups.' *Journal of Personality and Social Psychology* 79(2): 174–189.

Sasson-Levy, O. (2013). 'Ethnic generations: Evolving ethnic perceptions among dominant groups.' *Sociological Quarterly* 54(3): 399–423. https://doi.org/10.1111/tsq.12035.

Savelkoul, M., Tolsma, J., and Scheepers, P. (2015). 'Explaining natives' interethnic friendship and contact with colleagues in European regions.' *Journal of Ethnic and Migration Studies* 41(5): 683–709. http://doi.org/10.1080/1369183X.2014.931802.

Sawyerr, O.O., Strauss, J., and Yan, J. (2005). 'Individual value structure and diversity attitudes: The moderating effects of age, gender, race, and religiosity.' *Journal of Managerial Psychology* 20(5/6): 498–521.

Schaefer, J.A., and Moos, R.H. (1992). 'Life crises and personal growth.' In B.N. Carpenter (Ed.), *Personal coping: Theory, research, and application*, pp. 149–170. Westport, CT: Praeger Pub.

Schalk-Soekar, S.R.G., van de Vijver, F.J.R., et al. (2008). 'The concept of multiculturalism: A study among Dutch majority members.' *Journal of Applied Social Psychology* 38(8): 2152–2178.

Schmitt, D.P. (2003). 'Are men universally more dismissing than women? Gender differences in romantic attachment across 62 cultural regions.' *Personal Relationships* 10(3): 307–331.

Schroeder, J., and Risen, J.L. (2016). 'Befriending the enemy: Outgroup friendship longitudinally predicts intergroup attitudes in a coexistence program for Israelis and Palestinians.' *Group Processes & Intergroup Relations* 19(1): 72–93. http://doi.org/10.1177/1368430214542257.

Schwartz, A.L., Galliher, R.V., and Domenech Rodríguez, M.M. (2011). 'Self-disclosure in Latinos' intercultural and intracultural friendships and acquaintanceships: Links with collectivism, ethnic identity, and acculturation.' *Cultural Diversity and Ethnic Minority Psychology* 17(1): 116–121. http://doi.org/10.1037/a0021824.

Schwartz, S.H. (1992). 'Universals in the content and structure of values: Theoretical advances and empirical tests in 20 countries.' In M.P. Zanna (Ed.), *Advances in experimental social psychology*, vol. 25, pp. 1–65. San Diego, CA: Academic Press.

Schwartz, S.H. (1994). 'Are there universal aspects in the structure and contents of human values?' *Journal of Social Issues* 50(4): 19–45.

Schwartz, S.H. (2006). 'A theory of cultural value orientations: Explication and applications.' *Comparative Sociology* 5(2–3): 137–182.

Schwartz, S.H. (2011). 'Studying values: Personal adventure, future directions.' *Journal of Cross-Cultural Psychology* 42(2): 307–319. http://doi.org/10.1177/0022022110396925.

Schwartz, S.H. (2014). 'Rethinking the concept and measurement of societal culture in light of empirical findings.' *Journal of Cross-Cultural Psychology* 45(1): 5–13. http://doi.org/10.1177/0022022113490830.

Schwartz, S.H. (2017). 'The refined theory of basic values.' In *Values and Behavior*, pp. 51–72. Cham: Springer International Publishing. http://doi.org/10.1007/978-3-319-56352-7_3.

Schwartz, S.H. (n.d.). 'Basic human values: An overview.'

Schwartz, S.H., and Bardi, A. (2001). 'Value hierarchies across cultures: Taking a similarities perspective.' *Journal of Cross-Cultural Psychology* 32(3): 268–290.

Schwartz, S.H., and Boehnke, K. (2004). 'Evaluating the structure of human values with confirmatory factor analysis.' *Journal of Research in Personality* 38(3): 230–255.

Schwartz, S.H., and Rubel, T. (2005). 'Sex differences in value priorities: cross-cultural and multimethod studies.' *Journal of Personality and Social Psychology* 89(6): 1010–1028.

Schwartz, S.H., and Sagie, G. (2000). 'Value consensus and importance: A cross-national study.' *Journal of Cross-Cultural Psychology* 31(4): 465–497.

Schwartz, S.H., and Sagiv, L. (1995). 'Identifying culture-specifics in the content and structure of values.' *Journal of Cross-Cultural Psychology* 26(1): 92–116.

Schwartz, S.H., and Sortheix, F. (2018). 'Values and subjective well-being.' In E. Diener, S. Oishi, and L. Tay (Eds.), *Handbook of well-being*, pp. 1–25. Salt Lake City, UT: DEF Publishers. http://doi.org/nobascholar.com.

Seder, J.P., and Oishi, S. (2009). 'Ethnic/racial homogeneity in college students' Facebook friendship networks and subjective well-being.' *Journal of Research in Personality* 43(3): 438–443.

Selvanathan, H.P., and Leidner, B. (2020). 'Modes of ingroup identification and notions of justice provide distinct pathways to normative and nonnormative collective action in the Israeli–Palestinian conflict.' *Journal of Conflict Resolution.* https://doi.org/10.1177/0022002720907660.

Sennett, R. (1980). *Authority.* New York: Secker & Warburg.

Shalev, N. (2009). 'The hidden agenda: The establishment and expansion plans of Ma'ale Adummim and their human rights ramifications [report].' Jerusalem: B'Tselem & Bimkom.

Shalhoub-Kevorkian, N. (2004). 'Racism, militarisation and policing: police reactions to violence against Palestinian women in Israel.' *Social Identities* 10(2): 171–193.

Shalit, E. (1994). 'The relationship between aggression and fear of annihilation in Israel.' *Political Psychology* 15(3): 415–434.

Shamoa-Nir, L. (2017). 'A dialogue with the "self": Identity exploration processes in intergroup dialogue for Jewish students in Israel.' *Learning, Culture and Social Interaction* 13: 1–10. http://doi.org/10.1016/J.LCSI.2017.01.001.

Shanes, J. (2019). 'Netanyahu, Orbán, and the resurgence of antisemitism: lessons of the last century.' *Shofar* 37(1): 108–120. https://doi.org/10.5703/shofar.37.1.0108.

Shani, M., and Boehnke, K. (2017). 'The effect of Jewish–Palestinian mixed-model encounters on readiness for contact and policy support.' *Peace and Conflict: Journal of Peace Psychology* 23(3): 219–227. http://doi.org/10.1037/pac0000220.

Sharabany, R., Eshel, Y., and Hakim, C. (2008). 'Boyfriend, girlfriend in a traditional society: Parenting styles and development of intimate friendships among Arabs in school.' *International Journal of Behavioral Development* 32(1): 66–75. http://doi.org/10.1177/0165025407084053.

Shelton, J.N., Trail, T.E., West, T. V, and Bergsieker, H.B. (2010). 'From strangers to friends: The interpersonal process model of intimacy in developing interracial friendships.' *Journal of Social and Personal Relationships* 27(1): 71–90.

Sherer, M., and Karnieli-Miller, O. (2004). 'Aggression and violence among Jewish and Arab youth in Israel.' *International Journal of Intercultural Relations* 28(2): 93–109.

Shiau, H.-C. (2016). 'Easily connected but difficult to become intimate? Intercultural friendships on social media among Taiwanese ESL students in the US.' *Cogent Social Sciences* 2(1): 1264152. http://doi.org/10.1080/23311886.2016.1264152.

Shimoni, M.T.K., and Schwarzwald, J. (2003). 'Perceived threat and prejudice in three domains of inter-group tension in israeli society [In Hebrew].' *Megamot* 42(4): 549–584.

Shokef, E., and Erez, M. (2006). 'Global work culture and global identity, as a platform for a shared understanding in multicultural teams.' *National Culture and Groups* 9: 325–352.

Shoshana, A. (2016). 'The language of everyday racism and microaggression in the workplace: Palestinian professionals in Israel.' *Ethnic and Racial Studies* 39(6): 1052–1069. https://doi.org/10.1080/01419870.2015.1081965.

Shtern, M. (2017). *Polarized labor integration: East Jerusalem Palestinians in the city's employment market.* Jerusalem: Jerusalem Institute for Policy Research.

Shtern, M., and Yacobi, H. (2019). 'The urban geopolitics of neighboring: Conflict, encounter and class in Jerusalem's settlement/neighborhood.' *Urban Geography* 40(4): 467–487. https://doi.org/10.1080/02723638.2018.1500251.

Shupe, E.I. (2007). 'Clashing cultures: A model of international student conflict.' *Journal of Cross-Cultural Psychology* 38(6): 750–771.

Sias, P.M., and Bartoo, H. (2007). 'Friendship, social support, and health.' In L. L'Abate (Ed.), *Low-cost approaches to promote physical and mental health*, pp. 455–472. New York: Springer.

Sias, P.M., Drzewiecka, J.A., Meares, M., Bent, R., Konomi, Y., Ortega, M., and White, C. (2008). Intercultural friendship development. *Communication Reports* 21(1): 1–13.

'Significant other.' (n.d.). Retrieved March 28, 2020, from https://en.wikipedia.org/wiki/Significant_other.

Sklad, M., Friedman, J., Park, E., and Oomen, B. (2016). '"Going Glocal": A qualitative and quantitative analysis of global citizenship education at a Dutch liberal arts and sciences college.' *Higher Education* 72(3): 323–340. http://doi.org/10.1007/s10734-015-9959-6.

Sloan, C.A., Berke, D.S., and Zeichner, A. (2015). 'Bias-motivated aggression against men: Gender expression and sexual orientation as risk factors for victimization.' *Sex Roles* 72(3–4): 140–149. https://doi.org/10.1007/s11199-014-0443-z.

Slonim-Nevo, V., and Al-Krenawi, A. (2006). 'Success and failure among polygamous families: The experience of wives, husbands, and children.' *Family Process* 45(3): 311–330.

Smart, C., Davies, K., Heaphy, B., and Mason, J. (2012). 'Difficult friendships and ontological insecurity.' *The Sociological Review* 60(1): 91–109. http://doi.org/10.1111/j.1467-954X.2011.02048.x.

Smith, P.B. (2011). 'Communication styles as dimensions of national culture.' *Journal of Cross-Cultural Psychology* 42(2): 216–233.

Smooha, S. (2011). 'Arab-Jewish relations in Israel: Alienation and rapprochement.' Washington, DC: United States Institute of Peace.

Sonnenschein, N., Bekerman, Z., and Horenczyk, G. (2010). 'Threat and the majority identity.' *Group Dynamics* 14(1): 47–65.

Soy, S.K. (1997). 'The case study as a research method.' Austin.

BIBLIOGRAPHY

Spajić-Vrkaš, V. (2009). 'Learning for intercultural dialogue: concepts and strategies.' In *Intercultural Dialogue and Education*. Croatia.

Sparkman, D.J., Eidelman, S., and Blanchar, J.C. (2016). 'Multicultural experiences reduce prejudice through personality shifts in openness to experience.' *European Journal of Social Psychology* 46(7): 840–853. http://doi.org/10.1002/ejsp.2189.

Spence, L.J. (2004). 'Forever Friends?: Friendship, dynamic relationships and small firm social responsibility.' In *Business Ethics*, vol. 1, p. 3. Ljubljana, Slovenia. http://doi.org/English.

Srour, R. (2015). 'Transference and countertransference issues during times of violent political conflict: The Arab therapist–Jewish patient dyad.' *Clinical Social Work Journal* 43(4): 407–418. http://doi.org/10.1007/s10615-015-0525-6.

Staples, D.S., and Zhao, L. (2006). 'The effects of cultural diversity in virtual teams versus face-to-face teams.' *Group Decision and Negotiation* 15(4): 389–406.

State of Israel and Palestinian Liberation Organization. (1995, September 28). 'Israeli-Palestinian Interim Agreement on the West Bank and the Gaza Strip.' Washington, DC.

Stavi, I., Kressel, G., Gutterman, Y., and Degen, A.A. (2007). 'Labor division and family cohesion among Bedouin flock raiser households in scattered rural settlements in the Negev desert, Southern Israel.' *Journal of Comparative Family Studies* 38(2): 307–319.

Stelzl, M., and Seligman, C. (2009). 'Multiplicity across cultures: Multiple national identities and multiple value systems.' *Organization Studies* 30(9): 959–973. http://doi.org/10.1177/0170840609338984.

Strous, R. (2007). 'Commentary: Political activism: Should psychologists and psychiatrists try to make a difference?' *Israel Journal of Psychiatry and Related Sciences* 44(1): 12–17.

Struch, N., Schwartz, S.H., and van Der Kloot, W.A. (2002). 'Meanings of basic values for women and men: A cross-cultural analysis.' *Personality and Social Psychology Bulletin* 28(1): 16–28.

Suleiman, R., and Agat-Galili, Y. (2015). 'Sleeping on the enemy's couch: Psychotherapy across ethnic boundaries in Israel.' *Peace and Conflict: Journal of Peace Psychology* 21(2): 187–196. http://doi.org/10.1037/pac0000072.

Sulha Research Center. (n.d.). 'What is Sulha?' Retrieved April 4, 2018, from http://www.sulha.org.

Sunshine, J., and Tyler, T.R. (2003). 'The role of procedural justice and legitimacy in shaping public support for policing.' *Law & Society Review* 37(3): 513–548.

Tartakovsky, E., and Walsh, S.D. (2019). 'Are some immigrants more equal than others? Applying a Threat-Benefit Model to understanding the appraisal of different immigrant groups by the local population.' *Journal of Ethnic and Migration Studies*. https://doi.org/10.1080/1369183X.2019.1565402.

Taylor, E.W. (2017). 'Transformative learning theory.' In A. Laros, T. Fuhr, and E.W. Taylor (Eds.), *Transformative learning meets Bildung*, pp. 17–29. Leiden: Brill.

Taylor, J. (2008). 'An autoethnographic exploration of an occupation: Doing a PhD.' *The British Journal of Occupational Therapy* 71(5): 176–184.

Tesoriero, F. (2006). 'Personal growth towards intercultural competence through an international field education programme.' *Australian Social Work* 59(2): 126–140.

The Applied Research Institute. (2012). 'Hizma village profile.' Retrieved March 29, 2020, from http://vprofile.arij.org.'

Thomas, D.C., Elron, E., Stahl, G., Ekelund, B.Z., Ravlin, E.C., Cerdin, J.L., ... others. (2008). 'Cultural intelligence.' *International Journal of Cross Cultural Management* 8(2): 1–123.

Thooft, L. (2011). 'Oases van vrede in Israel.' *Happinez, Mindstyle Magazine* 8: 52–60.

Thurlow, C. (2010). 'Speaking of difference: Language, inequality and interculturality.' In T.T. Nakayama and R.T. Halualani (Eds.), *The Handbook of Critical Intercultural Communication* (pp. 227–247). Oxford, UK: Wiley-Blackwell. http://doi.org/10.1002/9781444390681.ch14.

Tillmann-Healy, L.M. (2001). *Between gay and straight: Understanding friendship across sexual orientation*. Walnut Creek, CA: Altamira Press.

Tillmann-Healy, L.M. (2003). 'Friendship as method.' *Qualitative Inquiry* 9(5): 729–749.

'Timeline of the Israeli-Palestinian conflict.' (n.d.). Retrieved March 22, 2020, from https://en.wikipedia.org/wiki/Timeline_of_the_Israeli–Palestinian_conflict.

Ting-Toomey, S., and Kurogi, A. (1998). 'Facework competence in intercultural conflict: An updated face-negotiation theory.' *International Journal of Intercultural Relations* 22(2): 187–225.

Torres, L., and Taknint, J.T. (2015). 'Ethnic microaggressions, traumatic stress symptoms, and Latino depression: A moderated mediational model.' *Journal of Counseling Psychology* 62(3): 393–401. http://doi.org/10.1037/cou0000077.

Triandis, H.C., and Suh, E.M. (2002). 'Cultural influences on personality.' *Annual Review of Psychology* 53: 133–160.

Tsafrir, N. (2006). 'Arab customary law in Israel: Sulha agreements and Israeli Courts.' *Islamic Law & Society* 13: 76–98.

Ulijn, J.M. (1995). 'The Anglo Germanic and Latin concept of politeness and time in cross-Atlantic business communication: From cultural misunderstanding to management success.' *Hermes* 15: 1–28.

United Nations OCHA. (2014, February). 'Bedouin communities at risk of forcible transfer.' Retrieved April 24, 2020, from https://www.ochaopt.org/content/bedouin-communities-risk-forcible-transfer-september-2014.

United Nations OCHA. (2017). '46 Bedouin Communities at risk of forcible transfer in the central West Bank: A vulnerability profile.' Retrieved March 22, 2020, from https://www.ochaopt.org/page/46-bedouin-communities-risk-forcible-transfer-central-west-bank-vulnerability-profile.

United Nations OCHA. (2019, August). 'Daily police raids and clashes result in casualties and disruption of daily life in East Jerusalem neighbourhood.' Retrieved March 28, 2020, from https://www.ochaopt.org/content/daily-police-raids-and-clashes-result-casualties-and-disruption-daily-life-east-jerusalem.

United Nations OCHA. (2019, September). 'Overview | September 2019.' *The Monthly Humanitarian Bulletin*.

United Nations OCHA. (2020). 'Humanitarian atlas.' Retrieved March 22, 2020, from https://www.ochaopt.org.

United Nations OHCHR. (1989). 'Convention on the Rights of the Child.' Retrieved April 6, 2018, from http://www.ohchr.org/EN/ProfessionalInterest/Pages/CRC.aspx.

United Nations OHCHR. (2011). International Day of Solidarity with the Palestinian People, 29 November 2011: UN rights expert calls for solidarity with Palestinians.

Urbiola, A., Willis, G.B., Ruiz-Romero, J., Moya, M., and Esses, V. (2017). 'Valuing diversity in Spain and Canada: The role of multicultural ideology in intergroup attitudes and intentions to reduce inequalities.' *International Journal of Intercultural Relations* 56: 25–38. http://doi.org/10.1016/J.IJINTREL.2016.10.006.

van de Vijver, F.J.R. (2017). 'Nonverbal communication across cultures.' In *The International Encyclopedia of Intercultural Communication*, pp. 1–10. Wiley. https://doi.org/10.1002/9781118783665.ieicc0252.

van de Vijver, F.J.R., Breugelmans, S.M., and Schalk-Soekar, S.R.G. (2008). 'Multiculturalism: Construct validity and stability.' *International Journal of Intercultural Relations* 32(2): 93–104.

van der Zee, K.I., and van Oudenhoven, J.P. (2000). 'The Multicultural Personality Questionnaire: A multidimensional instrument of multicultural effectiveness.' *European Journal of Personality* 14(4): 291–309.

van Tilburg, M.A.L., and Vingerhoets, A. (Eds.). (2006). *Psychological aspects of geographical moves: Homesickness and accultuation stress*. Amsterdam, Netherlands: Amsterdam University Press.

Vandello, J.A., and Cohen, D. (1999). 'Patterns of individualism and collectivism across the United States.' *Journal of Personality and Social Psychology* 77(2): 279–292.

Vandello, J.A., and Cohen, D. (2003). 'Male honor and female fidelity: Implicit cultural scripts that perpetuate domestic violence.' *Journal of Personality and Social Psychology* 84(5): 997–1010.

Vandello, J.A., Bosson, J.K., Cohen, D., Burnaford, R.M., and Weaver, J.R. (2008). 'Precarious manhood.' *Journal of Personality and Social Psychology* 95(6): 1325–1339.

'Varieties of Arabic.' (n.d.). Retrieved March 28, 2020, from https://en.wikipedia.org/wiki/Varieties_of_Arabic.

Varisco, D.M. (2007). *Reading Orientalism: Said and the unsaid.* Seattle: University of Washington Press.

Vauclair, C.-M., Hanke, K., Fischer, R., and Fontaine, J. (2011). 'The structure of human values at the culture level: A meta-analytical replication of Schwartz's Value Orientations using the Rokeach Value Survey.' *Journal of Cross-Cultural Psychology* 42(2): 186–205. http://doi.org/10.1177/0022022110396864.

Velasco Gonzalez, K., Weesie, J., and Poppe, E. (2008). 'Prejudice towards Muslims in The Netherlands: Testing integrated threat theory.' *British Journal of Social Psychology* 47(4): 667–685.

Venaik, S., and Brewer, P. (2010). 'Avoiding uncertainty in Hofstede and GLOBE.' *Journal of International Business Studies* 41(8): 1294–1315. http://doi.org/10.1057/jibs.2009.96.

Venkateswaran, R.T., and Ojha, A.K. (2019). 'Abandon Hofstede-based research? Not yet! A perspective from the philosophy of the social sciences.' *Asia Pacific Business Review* 25(3): 413–434. https://doi.org/10.1080/13602381.2019.1584487.

Vera, E.M. (2009). 'When human rights and cultural values collide.' *The Counseling Psychologist*, 37(5): 744–751. http://doi.org/10.1177/0011000009333985.

Verbond van Verzekeraars. (2017). 'Nederland meest verzekerde land in Europa.' Retrieved February 17, 2018, from https://www.verzekering.nl/n/2017/02/15/nederland-meest-verzekerde-land-in-europa/.

Verkuyten, M., and Martinovic, B. (2006). 'Understanding multicultural attitudes: The role of group status, identification, friendships, and justifying ideologies.' *International Journal of Intercultural Relations* 30(1): 1–18.

Verkuyten, M., and Thijs, J. (2002). 'Multiculturalism among minority and majority adolescents in the Netherlands.' *International Journal of Intercultural Relations* 26(1): 91–108.

Verkuyten, M., Wiley, S., Deaux, K., and Fleischmann, F. (2019). 'To be both (and more): Immigration and identity multiplicity.' *Journal of Social Issues* 75(2): josi.12324. https://doi.org/10.1111/josi.12324.

Verkuyten, M., Yogeeswaran, K., Mepham, K., and Sprong, S. (2020). 'Interculturalism: A new diversity ideology with interrelated components of dialogue, unity, and identity flexibility.' *European Journal of Social Psychology* 50(3): 505–519. https://doi.org/10.1002/ejsp.2628.

Volkan, V.D., and Fowler, J.C. (2009). 'Large-Group narcissism and political leaders with narcissistic personality organization.' *Psychiatric Annals* 39(4): 214–223. http://doi.org/10.3928/00485713-20090401-09.

Wall, S. (2006). 'An autoethnography on learning about autoethnography.' *International Journal of Qualitative Methods* 5(2): 146–160. http://doi.org/https://doi.org/10.1177/160940690600500205.

Wall, S. (2008). 'Easier said than done: Writing an autoethnography.' *International Journal of Qualitative Methods* 7(1): 38–53. http://doi.org/10.1177/160940690800700103.

Wang, C., Horby, P.W., Hayden, F.G., and Gao, G.F. (2020). 'A novel coronavirus outbreak of global health concern.' *The Lancet* 395(10223): 470–473. https://doi.org/10.1016/S0140-6736(20)30185-9.

Ward, C.A., Bochner, S., and Furnham, A. (2001). *The psychology of culture shock* (2nd ed.). New York: Routledge.

Watts, R.J. (2004). 'Integrating social justice and psychology.' *The Counseling Psychologist* 32(6): 855–865.

Weare, S. (2018). 'From coercion to physical force: Aggressive strategies used by women against men in "Forced-to-Penetrate" cases in the UK.' *Archives of Sexual Behavior* 47(8): 2191–2205. https://doi.org/10.1007/s10508-018-1232-5.

Weinberg, H. (2003). 'The culture of the group and groups from different cultures.' *Group Analysis* 36(2): 253–268. http://doi.org/10.1177/0533316403036002011.

Weinberg, H., and Weishut, D.J.N. (2011). 'The large group: Dynamics, social implications & therapeutic value.' In J. Kleinberg (Ed.), *The Wiley-Blackwell handbook of group psychotherapy*, pp. 457–478. Chichester, UK: Wiley Blackwell.

Weinstock, M., Ganayiem, M., Igbaryia, R., Manago, A.M., and Greenfield, P.M. (2015). 'Societal change and values in Arab communities in Israel.' *Journal of Cross-Cultural Psychology* 46(1): 19–38. http://doi.org/10.1177/0022022114551792.

Weishut, D.J.N. (1989). *The meaningfulness of the distinction between instrumental and terminal values*. Hebrew University of Jerusalem.

Weishut, D.J.N. (n.d.-a). 'Jahalin Tours.' Retrieved April 2, 2018, from http://sites.google.com/site/jahalintours/.

Weishut, D.J.N. (n.d.-b). 'Palestinian Bedouin Clothing & Crafts.' Retrieved February 24, 2018, from https://sites.google.com/site/bedouinart/home.

Weishut, D.J.N. (n.d.-c). 'Jahalin Bedouins.' Retrieved April 2, 2018, from https://www.facebook.com/jahalinbedouins.

Weisstub, D.N. (2002). 'Honor, dignity, and the framing of multiculturalist values.' In D. Kretzmer and E. Klein (Eds.), *The Concept of Human Dignity in Human Rights Discourse*, pp. 263–294. The Hague, The Netherlands: Kluwer Law International.

Welch, R.D., and Houser, M.E. (2010). 'Extending the four-category model of adult attachment: An interpersonal model of friendship attachment.' *Journal of Social and Personal Relationships* 27(3): 351–366.

Welchman, L. (2009). 'The Bedouin judge, the mufti, and the chief Islamic justice: Competing legal regimes in the Occupied Palestinian Territories.' *Journal of Palestine Studies* 38(2): 6–23.

Werbner, P. (2018). 'Commentary: Urban friendship: Towards an alternative anthropological genealogy.' *Urban Studies* 55(3): 662–674.

White, C., and Boucke, L. (2006). *The UnDutchables: An observation of the Netherlands, its culture and its inhabitants* (5th. ed.). Lafayette, Colorado: White-Boucke Publishing.

White. (2009). *From Comfort Zone to Performance Management.* Baisy-Thy, Belgium: White & MacLean Publishing.

Wiggins, J.A., Dill, F., and Schwartz, R.D. (1965). 'On "Status-Liability".' *Sociometry* 28(2): 197–209.

Wilcox, D.A., and McCray, J.Y. (2005). 'Mulicultural organization competence through deliberatice dialogue.' *Organization Development Journal* 23(4): 77–85.

Wilkinson, J. (2019). 'Introduction: The public life of friendship.' In *The public life of friendship*, pp. 1–21. Cham: Palgrave Macmillan. http://doi.org/10.1007/978-3-030-03161-9_1.

Williams, D.G. (1985). 'Gender, masculinity-femininity, and emotional intimacy in same-sex friendship.' *Sex Roles* 12(5): 587–600.

Wimmer, A., and Lewis, K. (2010). 'Beyond and below racial homophily. ERG models of a friendship network documented on Facebook.' *The American Journal of Sociology* 116: 583.

Wolf, E.R. (2004). 'Kinship, friendship, and patron-client relations in complex societies.' In M. Banton (Ed.), *The Social anthropology of complex societies*, pp. 1–22. London: Routledge.

Wong, S., Bond, M.H., and Rodriguez Mosquera, P.M. (2008). 'The influence of cultural value orientations on self-reported emotional expression across cultures.' *Journal of Cross-Cultural Psychology* 39(2): 224–229. http://doi.org/10.1177/0022022107313866.

World Economic Forum. (2020). 'The Global Gender Gap Report 2020.' Retrieved March 23, 2020, from http://www3.weforum.org/docs/WEF_GGGR_2020.pdf.

Wright, S.C., Brody, S.M., and Aron, A. (2005). 'Intergroup contact: Still our best hope for improving intergroup relations.' In C.S.M. Crandall (Ed.), *Social psychology of prejudice: Historical and contemporary issues*, pp. 119–146. Lawrence, Kanzas: Lewinian Press.

Wrzus, C., and Neyer, F.J. (2016). 'Co-development of personality and friendships across the lifespan.' *European Psychologist* 21(4): 254–273. http://doi.org/10.1027/1016-9040/a000277.

Yagil, D., and Rattner, A. (2005). 'Attitudes toward the legal system among members of law and high status groups in Israel.' In *IACM 18th Annual Conference.* Seville, Spain.

Yahel, H., Kark, R., and Frantzman, S. (2017). 'Negev Bedouin and indigenous people: A comparative review.' In R. Chand, E. Nel, and S. Pelc (Eds.), *Societies, social inequalities and marginalization. Perspectives on geographical marginality*, pp. 121–144. Cham: Springer. http://doi.org/10.1007/978-3-319-50998-3_9.

Yearwood, M.H., Cuddy, A., Lamba, N., Youyou, W., van der Lowe, I., Piff, P.K., ... Spectre, A. (2015). 'On wealth and the diversity of friendships: High social class people around the world have fewer international friends.' *Personality and Individual Differences* 87: 224–229. https://doi.org/10.1016/j.paid.2015.07.040.

Yonah, Y. (1994). 'Cultural pluralism and education: the Israeli case.' *Interchange* 25(4): 349–365.

Yuchtman-Yaar, E. (2005). 'Continuity and change in Israeli society: The test of the melting pot.' *Israel Studies* 10(2): 91–128.

Zaharna, R.S. (1995). 'Understanding cultural preferences of Arab communication patterns.' *Public Relations Review* 21(3): 241–255.

Zaidi, S.N. (2020). 'Friendship between Muslims, Christians, and Jews: A Qurʿanic view.' In L. Duhan-Kaplan and H.O. Maier (Eds.), *Encountering the other: Christian and multifaith perspectives*, pp. 27–38. Eugene, OR: Wipf and Stock Publishers.

Zainuddin, M., Yasin, I., Arif, I., and Abdul Hamid, A.B. (2018, December). 'Alternative cross-cultural theories: Why still Hofstede?' *International Conference on Economics, Management and Social Study*, pp. 4–6. https://doi.org/10.1016/j.ibusrev.2018.05.008.

Zhang, S., and Merolla, A.J. (2007). 'A group project on communication and intercultural friendship.' *Communication Teacher* 21(1): 16–20.

Zigenlaub, E., and Sagy, S. (2020). 'Encountering the narrative of the "other": Comparing two types of dialogue groups of Jews and Arabs in Israel.' *Peace and Conflict: Journal of Peace Psychology* 26(1): 88–91. https://doi.org/10.1037/pac0000439.

Zilber, T.B., Tuval-Mashiach, R., and Lieblich, A. (2008). 'The embedded narrative: Navigating through multiple contexts.' *Qualitative Inquiry* 14(6): 1047–1069.

Ziv, O. (2018, July 3). '"We aren't going anywhere": This Palestinian village is preparing for the worst.' *+972 Magazine*.

Zupnik, Y.-J. (2000). 'Conversational interruptions in Israeli Palestinian "dialogue" events.' *Discourse Studies* 2(1): 85–110.

Index

acculturation   8, 41, 51, 83, 233, 240
acquaintance   9, 25, 103–107, 123, 189
administrative areas A, B, C   57, 60, 87–88, 152, 159, 183, 207
　See also West Bank
adolescents   45, 50, 57, 77–78, 194, 239
Africa   34–35, 55, 59, 93, 112, 143
aggression   42, 44–47, 52, 65, 167, 179–181, 183–184, 192, 195, 198, 201
al-Eizariya   60, 68, 89, 116, 120, 152, 153, 188, 212
Almog   28, 199, 205, 246
Amsterdam   94, 207, 142, 195
animals   15–16, 30, 56, 98, 217
anthropology   19, 23, 28, 34, 36
Arabic. *See* language: Arabic
Arabs. *See* Bedouins, Palestinians
Arab world   42, 46, 53, 54–58, 70, 218
　See also Bedouins, Palestinians
　individualism/collectivism   93, 117, 123
　masculinity/femininity   165, 181, 220
　power distance   185, 196, 208, 221
　uncertainty avoidance   128–129, 143
area E-1   64, 67, 90
army. *See* security forces
Asia   34–35, 42, 83, 93, 112
attachment   35, 40, 75, 77, 85
az-Za'ayyem   11, 48, 89–90, 104, 113, 120, 130, 147, 155, 166, 173, 180, 212, 222

Bedouins   10–11, 15, 20–21, 26, 67, 69, 216, *passim*.
　Bedouin law. *See* law & order, sulha
　hardships   15, 202, 206, 241
　history   58–63
　lifestyle   20–21, 59, 70, 149, 157, 225
　relocation   11, 59–60, 67, 149
Beer Sheba   11
Bethlehem   87, 156
birthday   100, 107, 110–111, 137
border   8–9, 65, 92, 120, 121, 124, 147, 150, 177, 201
　See also Israeli–Palestinian conflict
border police. *See* security forces
Brazil   46

business administration   14, 116

celebration   107–114, 171
　See also specific celebrations
censorship
　freedom of expression   25, 66, 184
　self-censorship   24, 84, 98, 210
children   11, 13, 29, 44, 52, 64, 104–105, 111, 147, 161, 170, 178–180, 196–198, 236, 237
　child labor   11, 27, 104, 118–120, 222
　Christians   20, 26, 48, 49, 51, 56–57, 66, 68, 104, 112
　clients   86, 116, 118, 121, 137, 139, 180, 205, 213, 222, 238
clothing   116, 142, 175–177
coffee & tea   7, 15, 49, 97, 103, 106–107, 132, 136, 215, 222
collectivism   10, 36, 38, 43, 46, 53, 55, 58, 77, 82, 93–127, 131, 218–219, 238
comfort zone   152, 174
communication   28, 55, 96, 130–134, 236
　See also language
　intercultural   28, 37–39, 43, 82, 129–137
　Jewish–Arab dialogue   39, 84–87
　nonverbal   38–39, 43, 77, 130–134, 173
　spoken   17, 24, 38–39, 77, 130–134, 173, 179–181, 184, 220, 227
　written   3, 22, 24, 50, 71, 117, 126, 130–134, 148, 223, 224
conflict   9, *passim*.
　conflict resolution   36, 38, 70, 75, 156, 190
　See also sulha
　family   170, 188–189
　See also sulha
　intercultural   30, 32, 39–42, 50, 81, 232
　internal   25, 53, 120, 183, 209
　interpersonal   42, 45, 68, 75, 181, 227
　Israeli–Palestinian. *See* Israeli–Palestinian conflict
　personal   169, 183
　political   87, 241
　religious   9, 28–30, 53, 65, 161, 205, 208
COVID-19   54, 87, 126, 139, 159, 206
crime   13, 43, 68, 71, 121, 201
　See also killing, law & order

INDEX

cultural dimensions. *See* values: value orientation
cultural relativism   26–27
culture. *See more specific entries*

dancing   112–114, 168, 171, 199
Dead Sea   57, 111, 205
death. *See* Israeli–Palestinian conflict, killing
demonstrations   122, 155
desert   3, 15, 29, 148, 171, 173, 178, 215
    Judean   11, 28, 60, 111, 204
    Negev   59–60, 149
dignity   43, 186–192
driving. *See* traffic
Druze   51, 204
Dutch. *See* language: Dutch

education   13–14, 19, 28, 41, 50, 59, 84–86, 196, 200, 229, 239–240
    See also school
electricity   60, 159, 200, 201, 222
English. *See* language: English
Europe   14, 16, 21, 26, 32, 35, 41, 53, 55, 72, 74, 105, 107, 109–110, 114, 115, 117, 121, 130, 138, 143, 145, 150, 154, 193, 203–204, 241
    See also Western world

face. *See* honor, public image
faith   58, 149
family. *See more specific entries*
farming   60
favors   102, 138–140
femininity. *See* gender, women
food   2, 100, 107, 135–136, 138, 142, 148, 159, 169, 191, 201, 222, 246
    mansaf   111, 113, 215
    maqluba   108
freedom   16, 56, 66, 89, 95, 115, 118, 124, 147, 161, 168, 182–183, 203–207
    See also censorship, Israeli–Palestinian conflict: occupation
friendship   11, 14–16, 27, 93, 128, 165, 185, *passim.*
    challenges   9, 17, 21, 81, 126, 162, 211–246
    context of conflict   83–90
    intercultural   9, 21, 78–83
    opportunities   7, 16, 81–83, 206, 211–246
    patterns   73–78
    perceptions   94–103

    stories   2, 7, 28, 48, 72, 94, 104, 107, 114, 120, 130, 137, 142, 147, 152, 166, 173, 177, 186, 192, 199, 211, 222, 228, 237, 245

Galilee   59
garage   13, 15, 28–30, 41, 73, 88–89, 99, 109, 114–115, 131, 139, 148, 154, 166, 180, 192–193, 195–197, 201, 205, 222–223
garments. *See* clothing
Gaza   57, 64, 68, 98, 121, 156
gender   10, 33, 36–37, 41, 46, 55, 59, 76–78, 94, 112, 165–184, 220, 225
    See also men, women
    Global Gender Gap   49, 52, 55
Germany   13, 29, 32, 78, 83, 104
Ghana   78
government   32, 50, 59, 69–70, 89

Hall, E.   34, 162, 219
Hamas   155, 201
happiness   8, 33, 76, 81, 119, 143, 146, 198, 209
health   59, 66, 75, 88, 98, 154
    mental   14, 81, 86, 227, 233, 241
Hebrew. *See* language: Hebrew
henna   112
herding   11, 60
Hizma   73, 88–90, 114, 116, 166, 192, 201, 212, 222, 228
Hofstede, G.   10, 33–37, 49, 52, 54, 93, 128, 165, 185, 211, 216–221
Holocaust   13, 53, 124
honor   11, 20, 24–25, 28–30, 42–44, 44–47, 57–58, 59–63, 69–70, 97, 105–106, 186–192
hospital   52, 156, 170
hospitality   49, 108, 110, 112–113, 138, 145, 147, 187, 234
housing   11–12, 67, 100, 142, 146, 149, 169–170, 201, 241
    house demolition   64, 67, 219, 237
    housing plans   64, 67, 90, 202
    tents   11, 60, 149, 215, 237

identity   2, 21, 26, 31–32, 40–41, 58, 63, 66, 81, 133, 137, 174, 205–206, 222, 227, 239–241
    See also specific groups
individualism   10, 36, 39, 43, 46, 55, 77, 93–127, 136, 218–219, 238
Indonesia   83

Inglehart. R.   34–35, 58
intercultural encounters   7, 9, 27, 32–33, 37–42, 78, 124, 238, 241
   See also communication
Islam. See Muslims
Islamic Jihad   201
Israel   9, 10, 13, 21, 51–54, 59–60
   See also Israeli–Palestinian conflict, Jews, Palestinians
   individualism/collectivism   93, 95, 100–101, 104, 110–114, 121, 123–125, 125, 219
   masculinity/femininity   165, 167, 169, 172, 173, 175
   power distance   185, 198, 204–205
   uncertainty avoidance   128, 138, 145, 155, 159, 161
Israel Defense Forces. *See* security forces
Israeli–Palestinian conflict   9, 40, 53, 63–67, 86, 121, 123, 198, 202, 241
   checkpoints   65, 88, 120, 122, 124, 133, 143, 159, 203, 205, 212
   occupation   28, 29, 65, 87–90, 127, 159, 182, 198–207, 208–209, 219–221
   separation wall   13, 15, 64, 87–90, 95, 113, 121, 124, 134, 153, 203, 212, 231, 246

Jahalin. *See* Bedouins
Jericho   28, 204, 246
Jerusalem   7, 11, 14, 48, 64–65, 88–89, 94, 106, 121, 137, 147, 166, 173, 175, 177, 203, 212–216, 231, 237, 246
   East Jerusalem   56, 60, 67–69, 88, 113, 121, 134, 201
   French Hill   14, 121–122, 200
   Issawiya   122
   Mount of Olives   113, 156, 215
Jews   2, 7, 9, 13, 20, 27, 29–30, 45–46, 51–54, 57, 60, 63, 78, 85–86, 216, 236, *passim.*
   See also communication: Jewish–Arab dialogue, Israel
   Ashkenazim   10, 52
   Mizrahim   52, 176, 198
   orthodox   112, 122, 125, 169, 171, 175–176
Jordan   13, 35, 55, 60, 68, 70, 102, 107, 111, 134, 147–148, 204, 212
   Jordan Valley   57
Judaism. *See* Jews

Kfar Adumim   202–203
Khan al-Ahmar   67–68, 202, 237
killing   29, 46, 97, 121–122, 156–157, 167–168, 187, 189, 199, 211–216
kissing   27, 105–107, 168, 177
Kluckhohn, F.   34, 217

language   129ff, 134ff
   See also communication
   Arabic   2, 10, 15, 39, 54, 58, 70, 84, 96, 105–106, 134–137, 149, 173, 200, 214
   Dutch   15, 134–137, 178
   English   2, 15, 24, 29, 34–35, 70, 130, 134–137, 222
   Hebrew   2, 15, 24, 29, 56, 70, 84, 134–137, 246
Latin America   34–35, 38, 81, 83, 93, 143
law & order   54, 67–70, 152, 192–207, 208, 220–221, 230
   family council   48, 69–70
leadership. *See* law & order, sheikh
learning   8, 13, 15, 20, 33, 36, 41, 71, 84, 98, 104, 108, 110, 112, 119, 126, 132, 134, 140–141, 146, 160, 162, 172, 177, 179, 181, 183, 192, 194, 208, 216, 238
   transformative   99, 164, 220, 228–233, 233–237
Lebanon   55, 70
leisure   27, 37, 102, 115–118, 173, 230, 240
Lod   95–97

marriage   8, 13, 50, 55, 58, 60, 62, 106, 112–114, 116, 147, 161, 167, 168, 216
   polygyny   11, 59, 62, 113
masculinity. *See* gender, men
Maʻale Adumim   64, 67, 237
media   13, 53, 126, 155, 225, 241
mediation   13, 48, 69–70, 215
men   9–10, 43, 46–47, 62, 69, 71, 103, 105–106, 112, 133, 165, 173, 186, 188, 199, 214, 216, 220
   See also gender
Middle East   27, 34–35, 42, 55, 70, 112, 143, 153
migration   8, 31–32, 37, 49–54, 80–83, 124, 167, 218, 239
minority status   8, 31–32, 42, 51, 58, 85, 167
mobility. *See* freedom, Israeli-Palestinian conflict, traffic

INDEX

money   11–12, 29–30, 49, 70, 102, 114, 132, 137–140, 144, 154, 190, 200–203, 209, 215, 222
music   199, 239
Muslims   10–11, 20, 26, 29, 32, 49–52, 54, 56, 59–60, 63, 69–70, 86, 104, 109, 112, 161, 165, 167, 216, 241

names   3, 97, 104–105, 146
nature   102, 149, 217, 230
Netherlands   7, 10, 13, 20, 26, 32, 38, 44, 49–51, 52, 224–225, 226, 227–228, 239
  individualism/collectivism   93, 99, 104–105, 107–110, 118–119, 125, 218
  masculinity/femininity   165–166, 168, 175–177, 179–181, 220
  power distance   185, 190, 195, 198, 206–207, 221
  uncertainty avoidance   128, 132, 136, 138–140, 142, 151, 160, 219
nomads. *See* Bedouins
North America   46, 48, 54, 72, 74, 103, 109, 114, 116–117, 121, 130, 143, 145, 148, 150, 193, 204
  See also Western world

Palestinian Authority   11–13, 55–56, 60, 62, 68–69, 84, 211, 222, 236, 237, 242, *passim*.
  See also Israeli–Palestinian conflict, Palestinians
Palestinians   7, 10, 20–22, 25–26, 54–58, 60, 69, 216, *passim*.
  See also communication: Jewish–Arab dialogue, Palestinian Authority
  Israeli Arabs   51–52, 56–57, 59, 63, 95
  Palestinian workers in Israel   56, 65, 87, 134, 203
personal growth   7, 9–10, 20, 42, 228–237, 238
personality   31, 33, 41, 76, 79, 226, 228
  multicultural   239–241
planning   7, 13, 15, 28, 34, 99–100, 112, 116, 118, 145ff, 147–152, 158, 162–163, 173, 191, 195, 220, 224, 236
  See also time
police   49, 69, 115, 121, 142, 152, 183, 188–189, 209, 215
  See also law & order

politics   15, 21, 26, 30, 35, 50, 60, 65, 70, 120–125, 157, 164, 198
possessions   137–142, 190
poverty   110, 140–141, 159
power distance   10, 20, 94, 177, 185–210, 221, 225
prejudice   9, 32, 50–51, 79, 85, 207, 237, 241–242
Prisoners Movement Museum   186, 237
privacy   7, 49, 78, 94, 97–101, 103, 106, 124, 126, 133, 157, 162, 184
psychology   14, 19, 28, 41
  cultural   16, 238–239
public image   81, 124, 133, 157, 176, 189, 220, 234
punishment   40, 71, 123, 171, 215

Ramallah   2, 56, 135, 146, 168, 171, 212, 222
refugees   37, 52, 66, 94–97, 101, 128, 146
  Dheisheh refugee camp   87, 156, 207
  Qalandia refugee camp   201
  Shu'afat refugee camp   205
religion   49, 52, 62–63, 66, 80, 161
  See also conflict: religious, faith
research
  autoethnography   16ff, 21ff
  friendship   19–20, 21, 24, 223–225
  methodological concerns   23–26
  narrative   17–18
  representativeness   225–228
risk taking   23, 43, 54, 89, 94–97, 103, 124, 128, 146, 152, 163, 172, 194, 204, 222, 224, 227, 235
Roma   59

Sabbath   94, 100–101
Saudi Arabia   58, 134
school   11, 45, 55, 58, 67, 84, 87, 118–119, 168, 212, 237
  See also education
Schwartz, S. H.   33–37, 219
security   2, 26, 97, 106, 121, 153, 155, 157, 160, 178, 203, 235
security forces   2, 14, 59, 77, 87–89, 121, 122, 133, 159, 203–205, 209, 212, 213, 231
self-disclosure   2, 23, 25, 75–76, 80–81, 98, 102, 124, 225
  See also censorship
self-image   84, 93, 122

settlement   29, 56, 57, 60, 64, 67, 89, 95–96, 121, 138, 202–203, 205, 237
sexuality   8, 46, 77, 80, 184
sheikh   13, 69–70, 97, 130, 196
social class   27, 78, 82, 108
social injustice. *See* prejudice
social media   8, 80–82, 111, 113, 131, 169, 228, 230, 236, 242
social work   59, 86
socio-economic status   27, 33, 35, 56, 58, 87, 190, 198, 200, 221
sociology   19, 28
soldiers. *See* security forces
Spain   44, 83
Strodtbeck, F.   34, 217
students   9, 37, 43, 57, 66, 78–83, 85, 229
Sudan   94, 95, 97, 167
sulha   48–49, 69–71, 101, 152, 179, 188, 214
   See also law & order
support   75, 100, 154, 190, 242
   instrumental/financial   14, 15, 57, 77, 102–103
   social/emotional   15, 41, 57, 77, 79, 81, 103, 123–125, 216
Suriname   39
symbols   30, 33, 51, 65, 102, 122
Syria   43, 55, 70

Taiwan   82
Tel Arad   60
Tel Aviv   107, 147
time   15, 20, 34, 59, 65, 72, 82, 94, 96, 99, 116–118, 120, 130, 136, 137, 138–140, 142–145, 147, 159, 173, 186, 187, 191, 224, 235, 243
   See also planning
tradition   16, 34–35, 51, 57–58, 68, 70, 74, 100, 106, 111–113, 125, 159–160, 162–164, 167–168, 171, 175, 185, 206, 215, 219
traffic   7, 67, 73, 90, 95, 98, 119, 120, 121, 146, 152, 180, 188, 194–195, 199, 201, 209, 212–216, 222, 239
trust   50, 63, 81, 86, 123, 155–158, 238
Turkey   32, 39, 68, 86

uncertainty avoidance   10, 36–37, 43, 53, 55, 58, 94, 128–164, 219
unconscious processes   18, 31, 50, 53, 57, 63, 156, 181, 234
United States   13, 26, 34, 43, 46, 55, 78–79, 82–83, 93, 147, 203–204
   See also North America
university   14, 29, 134, 144, 146, 168
   Al-Quds University   13, 176, 186, 237
   Hebrew University   14, 121

values   9, *passim*.
   conflict   191, 208, 226, 238
   value change   52, 233–237
   value orientation   9–10, 21, 33–37, 39–41, 57, 72, 78, 94, 126, 136, 148, 160–164, 165, 226, 231
   World Values Survey   34
violence. *See* aggression

water   56, 60, 159, 179, 181, 201
West Bank   57, 60, 70, 122, 133, 203, 230
   See also administrative areas Areas A, B, C, Palestinian Authority, Israeli–Palestinian conflict
Western world   20, 43, 108, 148–149, 153, 191, 203
   See also Europe, North America, United States
women   46, 59, 64, 69, 71, 105, 108, 113, 143, 149, 165–166, 187, 216, 220
   See also gender, marriage
work   7, 13, 14, 20, 29, 60, 81, 89, 104, 106, 109, 114–120, 130, 148, 200, 222–223, 238–239
   See also children: child labor, clients
   cultural differences   37, 82, 86, 117, 137, 143, 160, 162, 195
   honor   176, 179, 187–188, 192, 193
   unemployment   88, 200, 207
   women   109, 168, 182
   workplace   8, 15, 45, 192

xenophobia. *See* prejudice